FASHION IN PHOTOGRAPHS 1860-1880

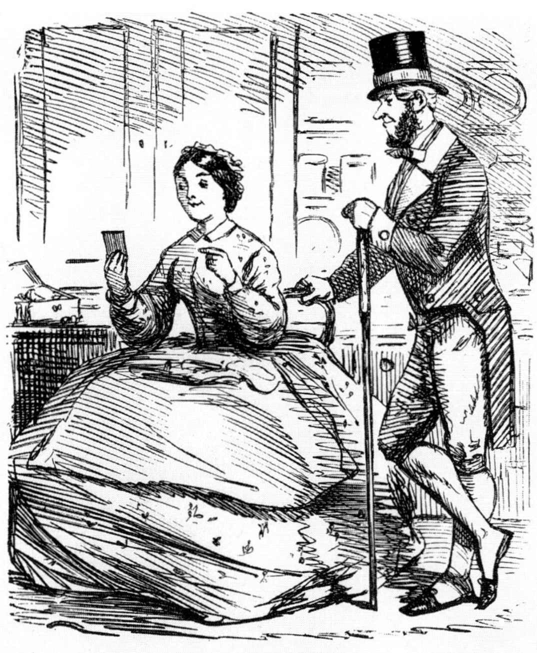

THE PHOTOGRAPH.

Mary. "Why, Tummas, it 's the very Moral of yer!"
Tummas. "Pretty thing, ain't it? Pity the Yaller of the Uniform comes so Black!"

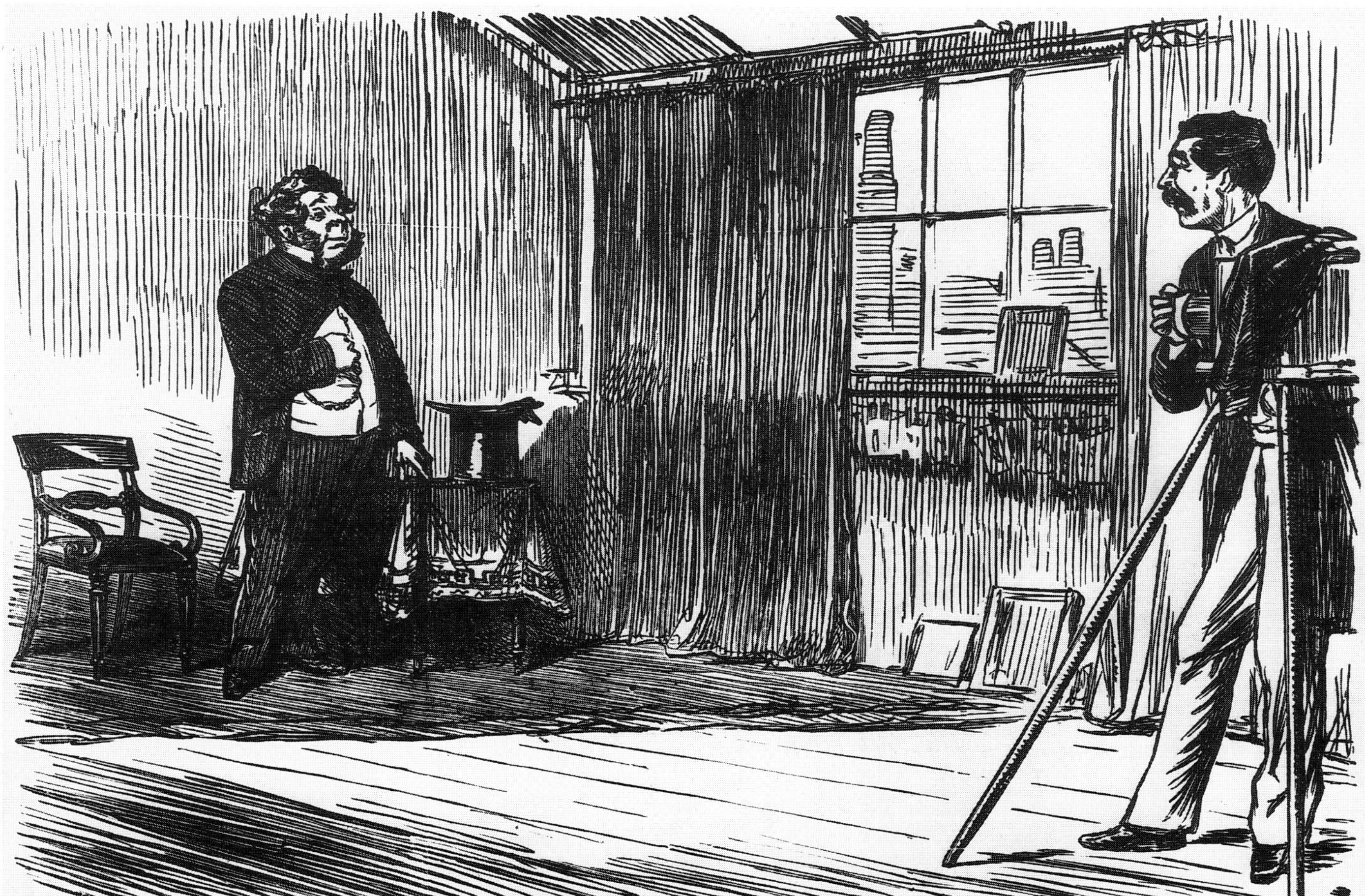

ARTFUL!

Dodge of Little Sperks, showing how Parties below the Middle Height, by the use of Miniature Background Furniture, may gain a more Imposing Stature in the Carte de Visite.

Punch

18 January 1862

FASHION IN PHOTOGRAPHS 1860-1880

Miles Lambert

IN ASSOCIATION WITH
THE NATIONAL PORTRAIT GALLERY

B.T.Batsford Ltd·London

For Anthony, Sarah and Steve

First published 1991

Typeset by Servis Filmsetting Ltd, Manchester

and printed in Great Britain by
BPCC Hazell Books, Aylesbury

Published by
B.T. Batsford Ltd
4 Fitzhardinge Street
London W1H 0AH

A catalogue record for this book is available from the British Library

ISBN 0 7134 6392 9

CONTENTS

ACKNOWLEDGEMENTS

I should like to express my gratitude to everyone who has assisted me in the preparation of this book. I am especially grateful for the help and encouragement I received from Terence Pepper and Ian Thomas at the National Portrait Gallery Archives. I should also like to thank my publishers, B.T. Batsford Ltd, and Timothy Auger, Aileen Ribeiro, and Liz Radford, for their advice and support.

Plates 40, 111, 118, 134, 141–52, 155 and 158 reproduced by kind permission of The Gallery of English Costume, Platt Hall (Manchester City Art Galleries); all other Plates reproduced by kind permission of the National Portrait Gallery Archive.

PICTURE LIST

PART 1: 1860–64

PART 2: 1865–69

PART 3: 1870–80

A NOTE ON THIS SERIES

THE AIM OF THE SERIES

This series sets out to present a photographic, and thus historically accurate, record of the clothes worn by men, women, and children during the period 1860–1940. Using unpublished photographs from the National Portrait Gallery and other archives, the authors have taken a representative selection from society (within the constraints of the collections) to demonstrate how fashion changed so enormously over these 80 years.

A general note

Some of the most notable men and women of recent history are featured here: politicians, writers, actresses and royalty. Children too are featured; some from prominent families, some virtually unknown.

For every photograph the author gives a detailed and expert description of the sitter's costume, hairstyle, footwear, jewellery and even of the studio props, as appropriate. This enables the reader to build up a picture of how fashion evolved during the period concerned. Furthermore, the authors give a glimpse of the world of past fashion through contemporary eyes, by including extracts from fashion magazines of the day, and comments from contemporary observers. They explain how designs originated, how they were made up, where they were bought and how – and by whom – they were worn and cared for.

How to use the books

In each book, approximately 150 photographs are presented in chronological order, divided into five-year periods and then further sub-divided into male, female, and group portraits. This means that even a rapid look through the photographs shows the changes in fashion that occurred over any given time.

Every caption begins with a title giving the following information (where available): name of sitter, date and location of photograph, name of photographer, and the National Portrait Gallery (or other) reference.

Beneath the title is the author's detailed description of the photograph, including biographical information on the sitter and a careful examination of the costume, as described above.

For those readers looking for a particular photograph, there is a numerical list at the front of the book or, of course, the Index, which also functions as a glossary to explain fashion terms that may no longer be current.

The sitters

Many of the people pictured in these books were prominent members of society who were considered important or interesting enough to merit a permanent record of their features. This group includes royalty, politicians, writers, artists, and industrialists. On the whole, working-class heroes, unsung campaigners, and professionals are less well represented. However, the rising prosperity of the middle-classes brought studio portraits within their reach too, and there are many surviving photographs of such families, some of which have been included here.

Photographs of men outnumber those of women in the National Portrait Gallery Archive. Men were usually more active than women in public life, and masculine hobbies, such as shooting, tended to have a higher profile than female pursuits. However, there are more photographs of women than might be expected: some wives appear, along with children, friends and servants, merely as appendages of great men. In addition, photographs of pretty women have always been sought after, and the collection is therefore comparatively rich in actresses and society beauties. Photographs of women who were considered outstanding for reasons other than their beauty, wealth, or husband are less numerous, but where these are available – such as Florence Nightingale, Frances Hodgson Burnett, Miss Buss and Miss Beale – they are included.

THE NATIONAL PORTRAIT GALLERY ARCHIVE

The National Portrait Gallery was founded in 1856 and for most of the nineteenth century the collections did not encompass photographs, since acquisition policy was directed wholly towards painted or drawn portraits of the royal family and its entourage. Moreover, for inclusion in the NPG the person depicted, unless one of the royal family, had to have been dead for at least ten years. This stipulation effectively ruled out almost all portrait photography for at least a decade. In 1895 Sir George Scharf, the first Director, bequeathed his own photographic collection to the Gallery, together with the rest of his library; and from the turn of the century other photographs were acquired. The first major acquisitions, in 1904, were the daybooks of the 1860s studio photographer Camille Silvy, which contained some 17,000 file-prints for cartes-de-visite.

In 1917 the National Photographic Record was established by the Gallery's Trustees to photograph living personalities for the collection, and this lasted until 1970. Some 7,000 portraits were taken and alongside this the reference library was active in its collection of historical photographs.

The 1960s and 1970s saw the establishment of both an outstanding collection of contemporary photographs, and also a series of much lauded exhibitions and one-man shows. The collection in the 1990s comprises over 100,000 photographs of prominent men and women, and the vast majority of illustrations in this series has come from this source. Serious students, wishing to make further research, can usually visit the archive by prior appointment.

INTRODUCTION

Of perhaps 100,000 photographs in the collection, some 20,000 date from the period 1860–80. The overwhelming majority of these, including all the albums and the Camille Silvy Daybooks, date from the years 1860–8, and this preponderance is necessarily reflected in the choice of images for this book.

Of the 158 photographs here, some three-quarters represent the decade 1860–70; the Silvy portraits alone account for some 50. The National Portrait Gallery's strength of holding in the 1860s period, and the relative lack of collection in the 1870s, can be only partly accounted for by the great wealth of carte-de-visite images produced in the first years of the earlier decade. It seems to be also purely by chance that acquisition was weighted to the first period.

PHOTOGRAPHY BEFORE THE CARTE-DE-VISITE

The first photographic images were produced in France in the late 1820s by Joseph Nicéphore Niepce and Louis Daguerre, who collaborated on a process which focused an image on to a chemically treated metal plate and fixed it there. After Niepce's death in 1833, Daguerre refined the process with improvements in the chemical techniques and with the introduction of high-speed lens design, thus managing to reduce the exposure time from a few hours (clearly inappropriate for portraiture) to a few minutes. By 1840, only two minutes were needed and the daguerreotype, as the image became known, entered the portrait-study field.

The first studio in England opened in London in March 1841. The 1840s and early 1850s saw daguerreotypes as the most widespread method of photography, although they were both expensive and fragile. Richard Beard, Antoine Claudet and William Kilburn were perhaps the most notable London practitioners, charging an average of ten to twelve shillings for a half-length portrait. The market was almost exclusively the preserve of the middle and wealthier classes, and photographers in the 1850s were often itinerant; travelling from estate to estate, plying their luxury trade. Only a major fashionable or industrial centre could support a studio of its own.

Each daguerreotype was an individual negative, presented to the sitter and viewer as a positive, and not reproducible. Daguerreotypes were mounted in cases for safety, and today present a silvered, mirror-like appearance. The cost of equipment, and the complexity and the novelty of the process conferred considerable status on these early photographers.

Contemporaneously with the development of the daguerreotype, in 1835 William Fox Talbot invented a process of 'photogenic drawing',[1] which could fix a shadow image onto paper. By 1840, he too had reduced the exposure time to several minutes, naming his photograph the 'calotype' (patented in 1841). Although not as popular as the daguerreotype, this process had two distinct advantages: it was produced on paper not glass, and it lent itself to reproduction.

There were many individual developments which advanced the photographic process through the 1850s: 1851 saw the Great Exhibition, a vast shop window for improved techniques in photography, as in all the sciences. By the middle 1850s, photography was taught at number of London institutions such as the Royal Polytechnic Institution, the London School of Photography, Newgate Street, and the University of London from 1856, with T. F. Hardwick as the first lecturer.[2]

The year 1854 saw the foundation of the Photographic Society, soon to be the Royal Photographic Society, which boasted the Queen and the Prince Consort as patrons.

The most significant introduction in the 1850s consisted in the wet-plate or wet-collodion process, first published in *The Chemist* in March 1851 by Frederick Scott Archer. Glass plates covered with silver salts fixed a negative image which produced a positive image on albumen paper. The number of professional photographers rose dramatically as a result of this new process: the official censuses of 1851 and 1861 saw a proliferation from only 51 listed, to over 2,800.[3] Photography had arrived.

'CARTOMANIA'

In November 1854, the French photographer, André Disderi patented a new multi-lensed camera which could produce eight small likenesses on a single glass negative, using the wet-collodion process. The resulting images were trimmed to a size of $3\frac{1}{2}$ in. by $2\frac{1}{4}$in. (89 mm by 57 mm) and mounted on a standard-sized card of 4 in. by $2\frac{1}{2}$ in. (102 mm by 64 mm), the usual size of a visiting card. They quickly became known as 'cartes-de-visite'. The ability to produce a number of photographs on a single plate reduced labour and material costs substantially and thus also the costs of the prints.

Cartes-de-visite were introduced into England at the end of the 1850s but only achieved dramatic popularity from 1860, after Disderi had photographed the Emperor Napoleon III, and Mayall had photographed Queen Victoria and the Prince Consort. The ensuing sudden popularity was dubbed 'cartomania' and made fortunes for fashionable studio practitioners such as Disderi, who was reported to be earning £48,000 per annum by 1861.[4]

The cost of cartes ranged from half to one guinea per dozen at reputable studios, and they were cheaper still when taken in the open by a peripatetic photographer; consequently people from most walks of life could afford a likeness and clamoured to have one. Cartes-de-visite were cheap, sturdy and reproducible, as well as convenient to handle and store. Studios multiplied to supply the burgeoning demand; in Manchester they increased from 17 in 1855 to 71 in 1865[5]; in London from 66 in 1855 to 168 in 1861 and to 284 in 1866, with 40 in Regent Street.[6] Vast numbers of cartes were printed: a fashionable photographer in Bath, Horatio King, produced 70,000 each year; and Camille Silvy in London had over 17,000 sitters between 1860 and 1867, representing perhaps 850,000 cartes.

Some commentators saw the carte-de-visite as the first substantial step along the road towards quick profits, indifferent quality and the debased 'industrialization' of the art of photography. H. P. Robinson in *The Pictorial Effect of Photography* (1869) considered that '99 out of every 100 photographic portraits are the most abominable things ever produced by any art'. Most of those 'abominable things' were produced by largely untrained, itinerant photographers, *not* the studio practitioners. Studios catered for the fashionable, well-off market; itinerant and part-time tradesmen-photographers supplied the labouring classes.

The relative cheapness of photographic equipment and the attraction of its novelty meant that parks, fairs, commons and seaside resorts became the haunt of travelling, seasonal photographers adept at working speedily and in public, and equipped with portable dark-rooms. The photographic establishment condemned these showmen as charlatans, debasing all photographic endeavour, and this complaint provided a constant theme in the letters' column of *The Photographic News*. However, cartes-de-visite were seen by most sitters as personal souvenirs, as cheap likenesses. Public opinion was unrefined and could little judge technical skill and artistic accomplishment.

After this frenetic popularity, the later 1860s and the 1870s witnessed a calmer atmosphere. Large 'cabinet'-sized photographs were introduced from 1866, measuring 4 in. by 5½ in. (102 mm by 140 mm) on a 4½ in. by 6 in. (114 mm by 152 mm) mount. These allowed greater attention to detail, especially in head-and-shoulders portraits, and they became very popular. The major technical advance of the 1870s was the invention in 1871 of the dry-plate process, by Dr Richard Maddox. Dry gelatine emulsion was used to coat the photographic plates instead of the wet collodion formerly used. Improvements in the later 1870s meant that by 1880, dry plates could be bought, stored and used when necessary, thus obviating the need for instant developing and the portable dark-room. The dry plate also reduced exposure times to a second and resulted in the first 'instantaneous' portraits.

PHOTOGRAPHIC EQUIPMENT

As *The Queen* (5 July 1862) related in its letters' page, a complete photographic apparatus 'and a certain amount of chemicals' could be purchased for between eight and ten pounds, enabling many artisans and shopkeepers to buy the wherewithal, if not the skill, to produce and sell portraits in their spare time.[7]

Studio cameras were, of course, rather more expensive than those recommended for amateurs, and also of a heavier construction. In essence, though, they were of the same type: a square-shaped bellows section connected the front-lens panel to a rear section carrying the focusing screen and plate holder. A wide focusing range allowed studio cameras to be used for a variety of work ranging from groups of perhaps a dozen to close, head-and-shoulders portraits. Exposures of up to a minute were made by removing and replacing the lens cap.

THE COMFORT OF THE SITTER

In the reputable studios, the comfort of the client was of paramount importance. A visit to the photographer's studio, particularly in the early days, was considered to be a social activity rather than a purely practical event; and the photographer was viewed as an artistic professional.

The sudden demand for cartes-de-visite from 1860 ensured that many of the existing problems with lighting, developing and backdrops were speedily ironed out. North light, illuminating the sitter from high side-windows, became the norm. Studios changed little until the end of the century, with minimal use of artificial lighting and with daylight adjusted by manual blinds.

A wide variety of backdrops was developed, each aiming to be uplifting and appropriate to the character of the sitter (and his frequently elevated impression of it): rustic scenes, castellated ramparts, stained-glass windows, nautical rigging – all were available on the painted scenery rolls. A common 24-foot (7-metre) length included six scenes: a wilderness, a lake, a garden, a staircase, a drawing room and a library. Some studios, usually in provincial settings, also possessed large grounds. For example, that of W. Savage of Winchester in 1869 included:

> surrounding grounds laid out entirely for photography: equestrian groups, cricketing groups, croquet groups, archery groups and boating groups with appropriate accessories . . . a large pool of water on which is a beautiful pair oared boat.[8]

Photographers with less room and higher rents introduced architecture into their studios: Marion & Company in London had a castellated rampart, complete with cannon, and the deck of a steamship available to their customers.

The need for complete stillness over a matter of many seconds resulted in numerous problems, particularly with very young, very old and very nervous sitters. The use of head clamps to steady the client's posture became common in studios; the photographer could not afford the poor publicity and wastage of time and materials which a blurred image would cause. At worst, this proved to be a traumatic experience for the fainthearted; at

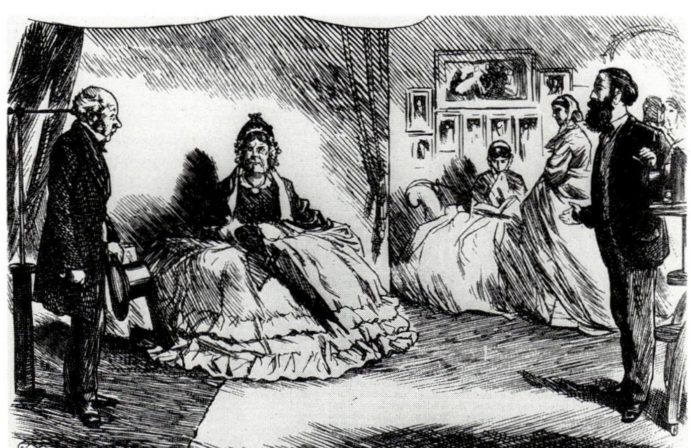

PLEASANT FOR SIMPKINS!

Photographer (*to Mr. Simpkins*). "Keep your Head Steady, please, Sir, and Look in the Direction of those Young Ladies. Steady now, Sir! Don't Wink, Sir!"

Mrs. S. (*by a look that Mr. S. quite understood*). "Just let me See him Wink!!"

Punch

2 June 1866

best, it instilled a lack of freshness and spontaneity into portraits. A smiling child or grandparent in a carte-de-visite portrait is rare indeed.

An article by Anson Hartley Turnour in *The Queen* for 12 July 1862 criticized the stultifying effect of standing motionless for a photographic session:

> The posturing is an affair of minutes. A perfect likeness of a sparkling face will not be attained until Messrs. Camille Silvy, Mayall, Watkins, or some other arrange it so that the *moment* the face is turned towards the camera, the vision is impressed permanently on the glass. The effect of standing still and not breathing and looking intently at nothing, is too awful.[9]

DRESSED FOR THE CAMERA

The vast majority of the images in the National Portrait Gallery collections dating from the 1860s and 1870s originate from photographic studios, and are imbued with their many attendant restrictions and conventions. Dress is invariably smart, formal, respectable and, presumably, often new. 'Dressing-up' for a portrait was the norm, even in the lowliest circles: Jane Carlyle in 1864 criticized precisely this on seeing a photograph of her servant, Mary:

> I don't like that photograph of Mary at all. The crinoline quite changes her character and makes her a stranger for me. I want the one that is, as I have always seen her, a sensible girl with no crinoline.[10]

Clearly, for some at least, the image on the carte presents a very different impression from reality.

Technically, photographs produced by studios are usually accomplished, providing accurate images, specific to a particular character, time and place, all of which may be documented. For the first time in history, in the mid-nineteenth century, the present could be recorded, by photography, to be shown to the future; and photographers took this 'mission' to heart.

Photographers grew artful in flattering their sitters and in producing what was desired. In costume, this often meant advising on what should and should not be worn for a sitting. The accurate reproduction of colours in the limited black-and-white range remained problematical as the photographic plates were not sensitive to all colours: yellows, oranges and reds came out deepest black; purples, pinks, mauves and light blues remained steadfastly white.

Photographers issued instructions to try to obviate their difficulties. Maull & Polyblank, West End photographers, gave some advice on the backs of their cartes in the early 1860s:

> black silks and satins are the most suitable for ladies' dresses. The colours to be avoided are white, light blue and pale pink. Black velvet and brocade dresses for women and white waistcoats for men, are likewise objectionable.[11]

This advice on the choice of dress for a sitting has had an influence on the historical records of costume as portrayed in photographs. Striking combinations and black silks are certainly very common in carte portraits. A letter in *The Queen* for 5 March 1864 advises that:

> Nothing comes out better than a black silk, made long and full and graceful. If the wearer is young, and is taken sitting, a border of black over white round the skirt is very effective. A lady not so young looks well in a black moiré antique without trimming. If the lady's figure is not good, she may wear a black lace shawl elegantly arranged, or, if of a nervous disposition, she had perhaps better be seated . . . . A light linsey woolsey takes well, and I have seen a tartan rep come out charmingly . . . blue and orange are colours always to be avoided; the former looks white, the latter black.[12]

In spite of technical advances, this advice remained current throughout the 1860s. Babies were unpopular with photographers not only because they were fidgety, but also because they were invariably dressed in white. White bridal dresses, bridesmaid dresses and presentation gowns were likewise problematic. Gentlemen in evening dress could be awkward subjects, with the extreme contrast between black and white.

Individual complexions, too, prompted advice, as in *Godey's Magazine*, the American journal, in May 1865:

> Complexion has to be much considered in connexion with the dress. Blondes can wear much lighter colours than brunettes; the latter always present better pictures in dark dresses, but neither look well in positive white . . . . lovely golden tresses lose all their transparent brilliancy, and are represented black . . . the simplest and most effective way of removing the yellow colour from the hair, is to powder it nearly white. The same rule applies to complexions. A freckle quite invisible at a short distance is, on account of its yellow colour, rendered most painfully distinct when photographed. The puff-box must be called in to the asssistance of art.[13]

'A PLEASING FACE'

Photographic portraiture looked for its conventions and psychology to its established cousin, fine-art portraiture, and

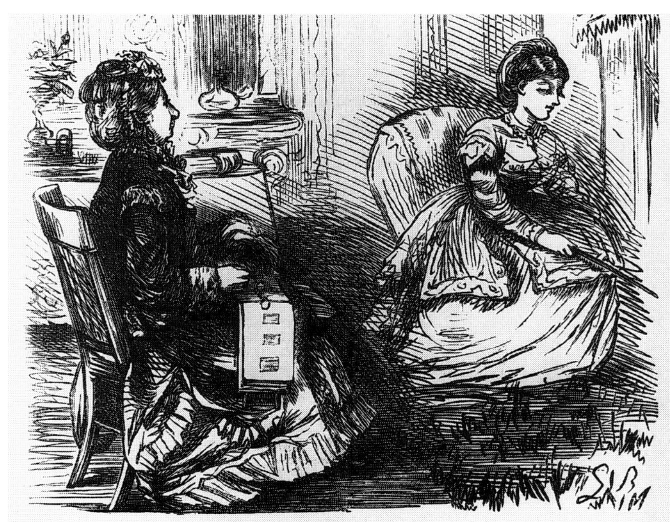

ASTONISHING FACT.

Lady (who is rather plain). "MY DEAR CECIL, WHEN YOU HAVE YOUR PHOTOGRAPH TAKEN, YOU SHOULD ALWAYS GO TO A GOOD PLACE, WHERE THE MAN IS AN ARTIST. I HAD MINE DONE THE OTHER DAY, AND IT IS *QUITE BEAUTIFUL!*"

Punch

24 December 1870

specifically to miniature portraiture. Photography, too, aimed to flatter as well as to interpret the sitter: defects were to be concealed or minimized; poses and expressions to be standardized and 'improved'; backgrounds and lighting to be sympathetic and complementary. The retouching of prints to achieve these results was a common practice, thereby 'beautifying' the sitter. This was especially common with the head-and-shoulders portraits in carte-de-visite form and with the larger cabinet-size portraits from 1866. Blemishes were removed, and figures trimmed in poses which were already conformed into staleness (*see* Plate 89).

So many photographs were retouched in the 1860s that some photographic societies took to banning coloured prints or to stipulating that negatives should be exhibited alongside.[14] A conflict is clearly apparent between those who viewed photography as a flattering and pliable art and those who saw it as a serious science of realism.

The expression of the sitter was deemed by many photographic writers to have a serious purpose in providing the best possible record of his or her character. The image, which both photographer and client aimed to project, sought to emphasize seriousness, calmness, dignity, respectability and self-control. The sitter maintained a serious pose; smiling and laughter were reserved, if used at all, for children, doting mothers and actresses. The absence of humour in the photographs of this period was thus due to both a convention and to technical inadequacy based on the necessity for long exposures. The pose of the sitter was also designed to 'improve' the final result; the attitude of the body, it was thought, should be in harmony with the sitter's expression. On the whole, poses reflected grace and ease as interpreted by the photographer, and sitters opposing their guidelines were variously described as 'difficult', or 'to be managed'.[15]

The various sizes of portraits available, and the direction in which the sitter was positioned, also expressed qualities to the contemporary viewer. The profile suggested a contemplative, calm character; the frontal view, dignity and firmness of purpose; the three-quarters view, movement and grace. Full-length portraits, usual in the early 1860s, imitated oil paintings in style and pose, and, coincidentally, implied good breeding.

Celebrated studio photographers wrote advice and essays on their approach to the 'art'. Disderi in Part Three of his *Essai Sur L'Art De La Photographie* (1863) set down scientifically his criteria for a good portrait. These included 'a pleasing face', appropriate presentation, definition of light and shadow, good proportion, details of expression and accuracy of resemblance.[16]

Critics of studio photographers complained of the forced and stylized expressions which resulted particularly when sitters were urged to pretence by solicitous photographers:

> thus the lawyer or Judge is tempted to look preter-naturally keen and knowing; the poet to assume a sublime aspect; the humorist a waggish look – all of which is very objectionable . . . . Even ladies when sitting for their portrait are not always allowed to look natural. Photographers will sometimes request their female patients to 'look pleasant', an injunction which is pretty certain to result in producing a forced expression.[17]

Certainly, when examining portraits from this period, many expressions seem 'forced', whilst the occupation of the sitter can be displayed in his or her pose to a blatant degree: actors and actresses look artful; writers assume 'artistic' and bohemian postures; priests and prelates exude serious solicitude.

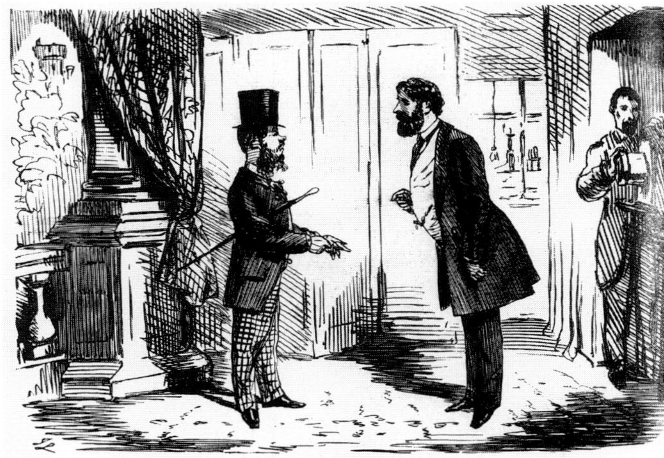

THE CARTE DE VISITE.

Gent (in Photographic Studio). "A—LOOK 'ERE, YOU KNOW, MISTER, I DON'T WANT MY CART PUBLISHED, YOU KNOW, BUT IF ANY NICE GAL, OR LADY OF RANK SHOULD WANT A COPY, WHY YOU CAN SELL IT HER, YOU KNOW!"

Punch
30 November 1861

ALBUMS AND ADVERTISEMENTS

Both cartes-de-visite and cabinet photographs lent themselves to mounting and storage. The Victorian family photograph album owed much to the universal family Bible, both in binding and appearance, and also in presenting a record of family genealogy. Details and dates of births, marriages and deaths had by tradition been inscribed in the family Bible; now a portrait could be included, and the new album created. The albums resulting in the 1860s also encouraged the multiple purchase of prints by the owner so as to facilitate the exchange of copies to friends and relatives who would have their own albums to fill.

Advertisements for albums appeared in journals and periodicals from 1860. *The Illustrated London News* for January 1862 includes advertisements for bound albums with gilt clasps from 'Asser & Sherwin, 81 The Strand', 'Frederick Hawley, 148 Regent Street', 'Parker & Gotto, 25 Oxford Street', and 'Rodrigues, 42 Piccadilly'. Prices for a 50-card album ranged from eleven to fifteen shillings. 'Dean & Son, 11 Ludgate Hill' offered the ultimate: 'a perfumed carte de visite album'.[18] 'Arranging' portraits in albums rapidly became a diverting occupation for many young women with time on their hands. *The Queen* for 21 April 1866 devotes a whole article to this theme.

Many of the album retailers also offered for sale 'portraits of the Royal Family, the Crowned Heads of Europe, and Distinguished Personalities of all Nations'.[19] Public demand seemed insatiable for these realistic pictures of celebrities formerly known only through illustrations. When the Prince Consort died on 14 December 1861, 70,000 cartes sold within a week. Photographs of British royalty in the 1860s helped to foster loyalty to the Crown and to the Establishment, particularly in the long years of the Queen's seclusion after 1861. The immensely popular and photogenic Princess of Wales and her young family proved a great boon to a monarchy paralysed by a grieving widow figurehead. W. & D. Downey's 1867 portrait of the Princess of Wales carrying Princess Louise on her back sold 300,000 copies, not counting those pirated.[20] Cartes of other celebrities were also popular, including (surprisingly perhaps for us today) those of politicians and statesmen such as Gladstone and Disraeli – both again, selling in their thousands.

The mass production and mass popularity of cartes led to the new pastime of collecting and swopping images of famous people, almost it would seem, at random. Advertisements in the press include lists of spare cartes, available for exchange either for other cartes, or for unrelated objects. *The Queen* for 16 February 1867 includes 'Photographs For Autographs: I will give two photographs carte de visite size, for a good autograph. Dr Livingstone and 'Venus rising from the sea' . . . Astarte.' For an unspecified autograph therefore, one could acquire the image of a famous explorer, and the reproduction of an equally famous work of art: desirable no doubt, for any carte-de-visite album.

A week previously, *The Queen* had printed another advertisement, offering cartes for exchange with monograms, that other collectable scrapbook memento of the mid-Victorian era:

> I have cartes de visite of HRH the Prince Consort, HM the Queen and the Prince Consort together, the Princess Frederick William of Prussia by Mayall, the Prince and Princess of Wales and Prince Victor by Hills & Saunders. . . . I should like six good clean crests or monograms or four cavalry badges for any one of these cartes. Madeleine.[21]

Naturally enough, a large assortment of portrait cartes was available for purchase, both at retail establishments and also from journals and periodicals. *Godey's Magazine*, an American journal, included regular cartes for sale from its own stock. In July 1865 it related that it had added 200 'new and choice' subjects to its catalogue, including 'distinguished military and naval officers, public men, authors, artists, etc.' It offered eight for one dollar, or twenty for two; and it concluded: 'We are mailing them by thousands, and they give the highest satisfaction. . . . If you want to fill your albums at a cheap rate, send for our catalogue.'[22]

The American, rather 'hard-sell', tone of this offer contrasts with the more restrained advertisements in English papers and journals. Even so, the underlying desire to sell was little disguised. 'Mechi & Bazin' of 112 Regent Street, offered in *The Queen* and *The Illustrated London News* from 1862 onwards: 'a large assortment always in stock to select from . . . photographs of more than two thousand celebrities.' In November 1862, they were offering them at one shilling and sixpence each. So too was 'Rodrigues' of 42 Piccadilly who offered 'distinguished persons of all Nations'. 'J. Reynolds' had 'two hundred subjects, plain and coloured, post free for 7/6 [seven shillings and sixpence], comprising engravings after Turner, Scenery of the Rhine, Views, Figures, Flowers.' Clearly, taste was eclectic, and supply correspondingly plentiful.

Shops and retail establishments seized upon photographs to help to sell their products. Peter Robinson produced a 'Book of Styles' in 1876 to launch a mail order ready-to-wear department and it issued cartes-de-visite of models wearing particular 'costumes' with fabrics, colours and prices printed on the reverse. 'Patterns of the silk, and forms for self-measurement sent by post on application.'[23] An earlier enterprising retailer, Mr Bond of Oxford Street, had used cartes to advertise false hairpieces: 'Cartes de visite of fashionable modes of hair dressing is an excellent idea which prevails at present amongst some of our most stylish coiffeurs.' A fuller explanation is given in *The Queen* of 14 April 1866: 'Mr Bond gives four medallion portraits on one card, representing two coiffures, front and back, and accompanied by explanations, which render it easy for a lady's maid in the country to arrange the hair of her mistress.' Fashions could now be transmitted easily and accurately around the country from London and the provincial centres.

The relative cheapness of cartes-de-visite also furthered the new practice of correspondence in the columns of the popular press and periodicals, either for advice on appearance, or else for discreet matchmaking. Fashion journals were often willing to give an opinion on the neatness, fashionability and beauty of any reader willing to provide a photograph; *The Young Ladies' Journal* actively solicited such correspondence:

> Mabel, Alice and Mary – You must send your photographs if you desire our opinion of your personal attractions. Enclose a stamped addressed envelope and they shall be returned.[25]

In the August issue of the same magazine, this modern-sounding correspondence continues with two very different opinions on enclosed cartes:

> Annita – you ask us our unbiased opinion of your carte. Were we to say half as much about it as we feel inclined, it might look like flattery; therefore we briefly state our opinion, which is that both face and figure are simply exquisite, and we regret it is our duty to return the carte as it would have been a pleasure to retain it.

Unfortunately, 'August' was not so blessed and there was no agonizing over the return of her carte:

> The carte is that of an intelligent, but we cannot say pretty, face.[26]

Whereas it seems to have been exclusively women who requested advice on their appearance (even if the advice given sometimes has a masculine tinge to it), both men and women wrote requesting and sending cartes-de-visite for the purpose of romance.

> Venus asks for a carte de visite from gentleman with a view to correspondence. She is twenty five, amiable, domestic and musical[27].

This type of correspondence proliferates and becomes little more than a multiple request forum, for example, *The London Journal*, 1 October 1870:

> A. C.: the following ladies wish to have this gentleman's carte de visite to open a correspondence with him:
> Golden haired Violet: a loveable little girl of seventeen who will have £2,000 on her wedding day;
> Veronica: good looking and has money;
> Mildred: sixteen, dark and pretty . . .;
> Sedate Nellie: twenty one, pretty and domestic.[28]

Doubtless 'A. C.' was spoilt for choice. Clearly, the availability of cheap, accurate portraits facilitated this type of correspondence for the first time.

PART ONE:
1860-64

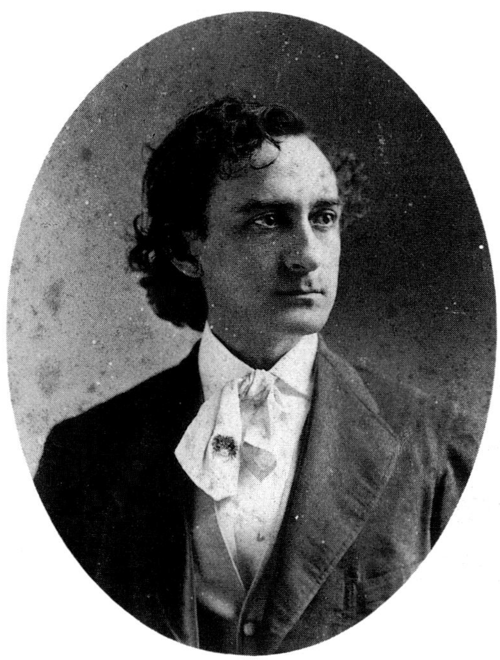

MALE

1

François Ferdinand Philippe Louis Marie d'Orléans, known as Le Prince de Joinville, was born in 1818, the son of King Louis Philippe. Entering the French navy aged 13 (his brothers the Ducs d'Orléans and d'Aumale joined the army at a similarly young age), he had a rapid career, reaching the rank of Vice Admiral at only 26. He made a suitably dynastic match in 1843, to Princess Francesca de Braganza, daughter of Pedro I of Brazil.

Abruptly reduced to the ignominious status of an *émigré* after the Revolution of 1848, Joinville lived in England until 1861, when he moved to the United States and lived there for the next ten years. Allowed back to France under the 3rd Republic, he acted for a brief spell as elected Deputy for Haute Marne, before retiring from public life in 1875.

1. Le Prince de Joinville
1860
Camille Silvy, London (Daybook 1, no. 324)

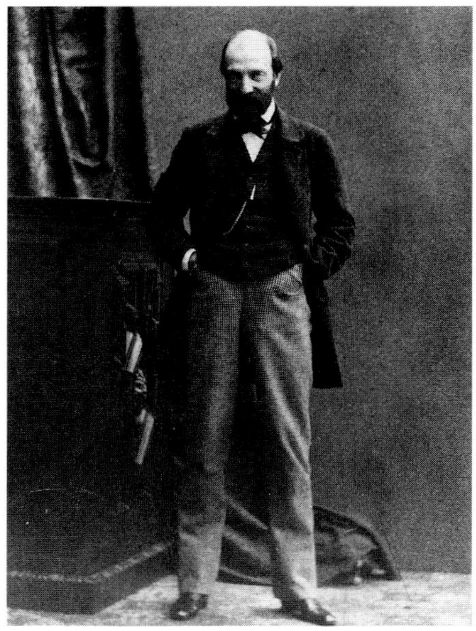

One of the first of Silvy's sitters, Joinville peers quizzically at the camera, and stands squarely and rather stiffly with his hands firmly in his pockets. He wears a dark-cloth frock coat with a single-breasted waistcoat of similar hue and narrowly checked cloth trousers. Sometimes called 'barristers' plaid', these checks were very popular throughout the mid-nineteenth century and provided some alleviation to the dark sobriety of frock and morning coat.[1]

Joinville's watch-chain or 'Albert' falls diagonally across his chest from his second waistcoat buttonhole to his right-hand waistcoat pocket. Apart from an optional wedding ring, a practical watch-chain usually provided a man's only jewellery.

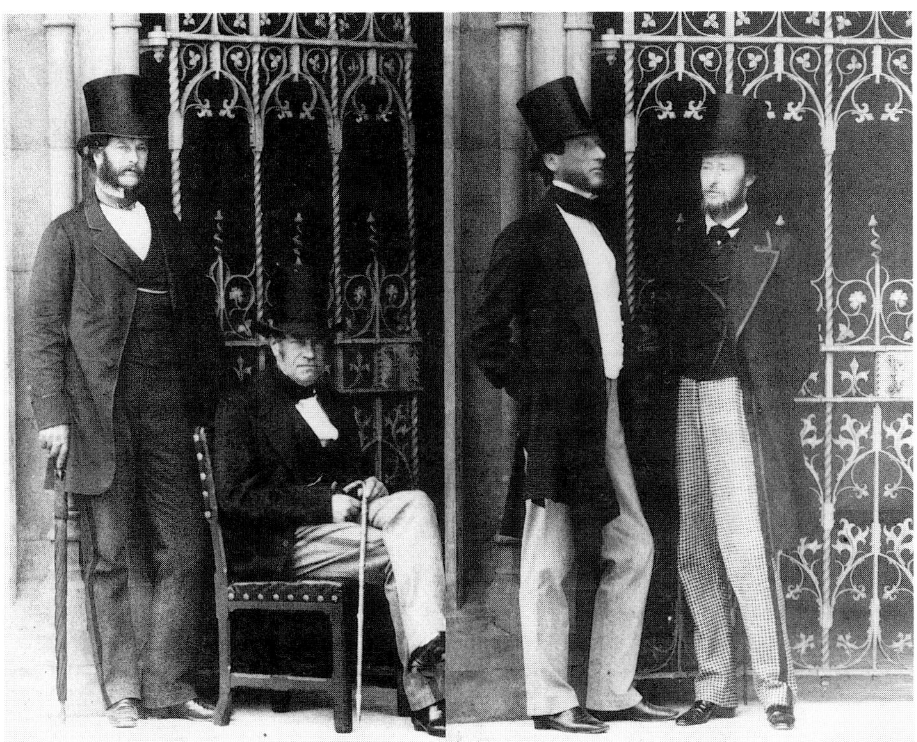

2. A group of four MPs
1860
Camille Silvy, London (Daybook 1, no. 705)

2

(From left to right:) *William Fitzroy (1819–82), Earl of Euston (6th Duke of Grafton 1863), Liberal MP for Thetford 1847–63; Henry Baring (1804–69), Liberal MP for Marlborough 1832–68; Orlando Bridgeman (1819–98), Viscount Newport (3rd Earl of Bradford, 1865), Conservative MP for South Salop 1842–65, Lord Chamberlain (1866–8) and George Weld, Colonel Forrester (1807–86), Conservative MP.*

These two pairs of portraits, posed outside a gate at the House of Commons, show a variety of coats, all accompanied by tall, black-silk top hats. Henry Baring (seated) wears a black frock coat, black waistcoat, and cravat, with contrasting lighter trousers, the respectable 'uniform' of the 1860s. Viscount Newport and Colonel Forrester (to the right) both wear frock coats also, the one with a high upstanding collar, the other with a turn-down softer collar. Lord Euston (on the extreme left), leaning rather rakishly on a furled umbrella, wears a more casual suit of 'dittos': a matching morning coat, waistcoat and trousers.

Taken out of doors, the portraits do not have the usual technical skill of Silvy's studio photographs.

3

Posing in a smart, black morning coat in the very boxy style popular around 1860, with matching double-breasted waistcoat and narrowly checked trousers, Mr Milford presents a dapper figure. His spotted silk cravat is caught with a ring near the collar, whilst his shirt has a modern, turn-down collar. He leans on a tightly furled black umbrella and has placed his pale 'summer' tall silk hat on the mock balustrade on which he leans. He sports a watch-chain with pendant attachments, apparently gold charms.

He stands before an array of Silvy's backdrops, rather incongruously juxtapositioned, comprising a rural scene, a vast damask drape, and a leaded oriel window.

Mr Milford has a centre-parted hairstyle and a small, neat moustache. Moustaches were popular with side-whiskers or full beards, but were still seen as slightly rakish by the old-fashioned and conservative element. To be clean-shaven was still associated with cleanliness and upright behaviour, and sometimes this dislike for facial hair could reach extreme proportions. As an example, *The Queen* ([illegible] April 1862) quotes the terms of the will of a certain Henry Budd who clearly spent his life earnestly preventing his two sons from indulging in moustaches. His will left them the whole of his £200,000 estate, 'on pain of forfeiture if they wear a moustache, the property in that case to be applied to the erection of a dwelling for the homeless poor of London.'[2] Perhaps the proviso should have been added that only the clean shaven should apply to this proposed 'dwelling'.

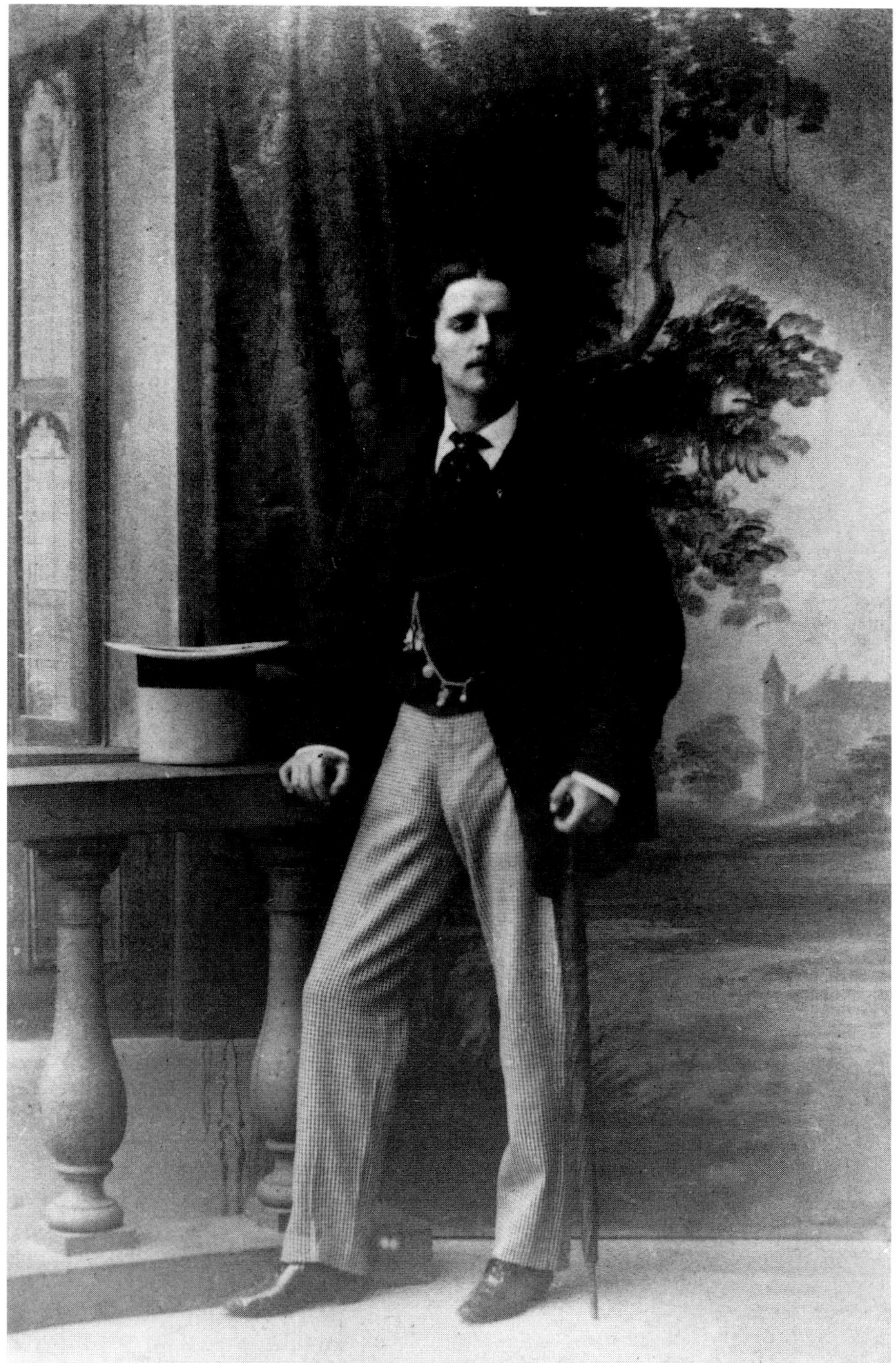

3. Mr Milford
1860
Camille Silvy, London (Daybook 2, no. 1331)

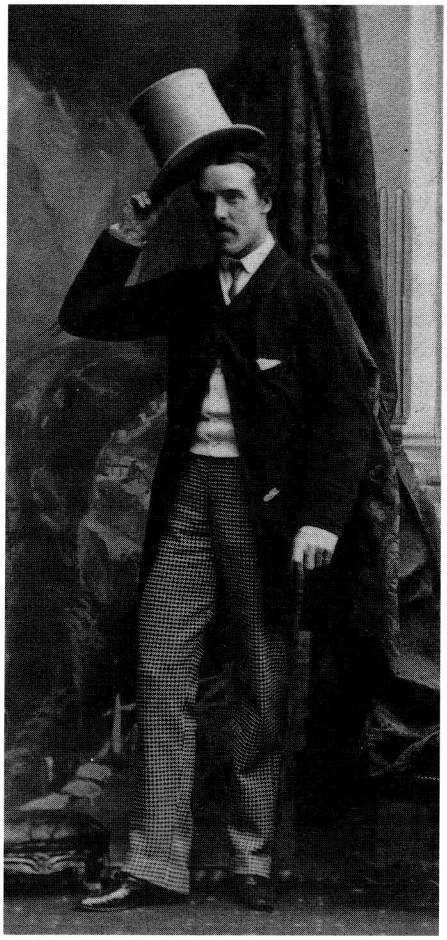

4. Captain Owen Williams
1860
Camille Silvy, London (Daybook 2, no. 1364)

4

In spite of his rather theatrical stance, Lewis Owen Williams is here portrayed at the start of a very successful military career. Born in 1836 and educated at Eton, he entered the Royal Horse Guards in 1854. A captain when this photograph was taken, he later rose to the ranks of colonel (1871) and lieutenant-general (1887). He was also an equerry to the Prince of Wales in the 1870s and MP for Marlow in the 1880s.

Here, Captain Williams wears a fashionable dark morning coat with a lighter waistcoat and narrowly checked trousers. His black-silk top hat, poised beguilingly above his head, reflects the studio lights. His athletic physique lends credence to his entry in *Who Was Who* (Vol. 1, 1898), which lists his recreations as hunting, shooting, yachting and racing. He had residences in Berkeley Square, Anglesey and Buckinghamshire.

5, 6

John, 4th Baron Blaquière of Ardkill, was born in 1812 and pursued a career in the 3rd West India Foot in the 1840s before succeeding as Baron in 1851. He married twice, but left no heir, and was succeeded by his brother in 1871.

Thomas Merthyr and John Montagu were the second and third sons of Sir Josiah Guest, and Thomas was later to marry Lady Theodora Grosvenor, daughter of the 2nd Marquess of Westminster.

All three men wear shooting suits: Lord de Blaquière's is plain and sober; the Guest brothers' are vibrant and patterned. Shooting suits were designed to be warm, loose, practical and comfortable; one wonders if the combined checks of the Guest brothers might not have warned off potential prey at some

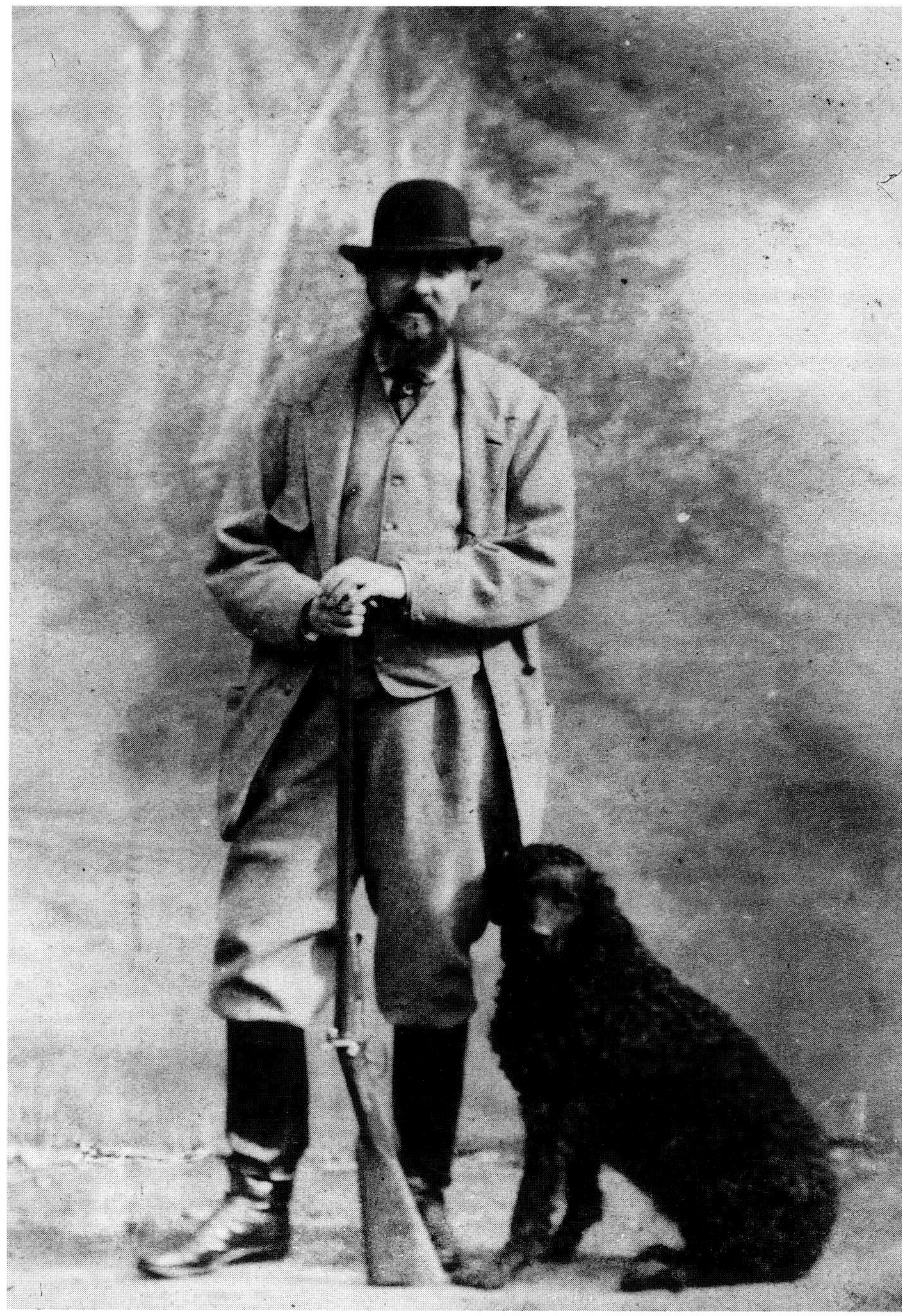

5. Lord de Blaquière
1860
Camille Silvy, London (Daybook 2, no. 1406)

considerable distance.

A 'shooting costume' in *The Tailor and Cutter* for July 1874 has:

> a full cut coat with large pockets in the waist and two outside breast pockets, patch or flaps. Leather on the shoulders, and the coat to button to the waist if required. Large pockets across the inside of the skirt. Breeches should be of cotton cord with leather leggings.[3]

In fact, of the three outfits pictured here, the Baron wears top boots rather than gaiters; and the Guests wear busily patterned woollen socks. Two men wear hard, round, bowler hats, seen here in their original use as protective wear for sport, but which were soon to catch on as fashionable urban wear. The elder Guest brother sports a tweed cap with a large peak.

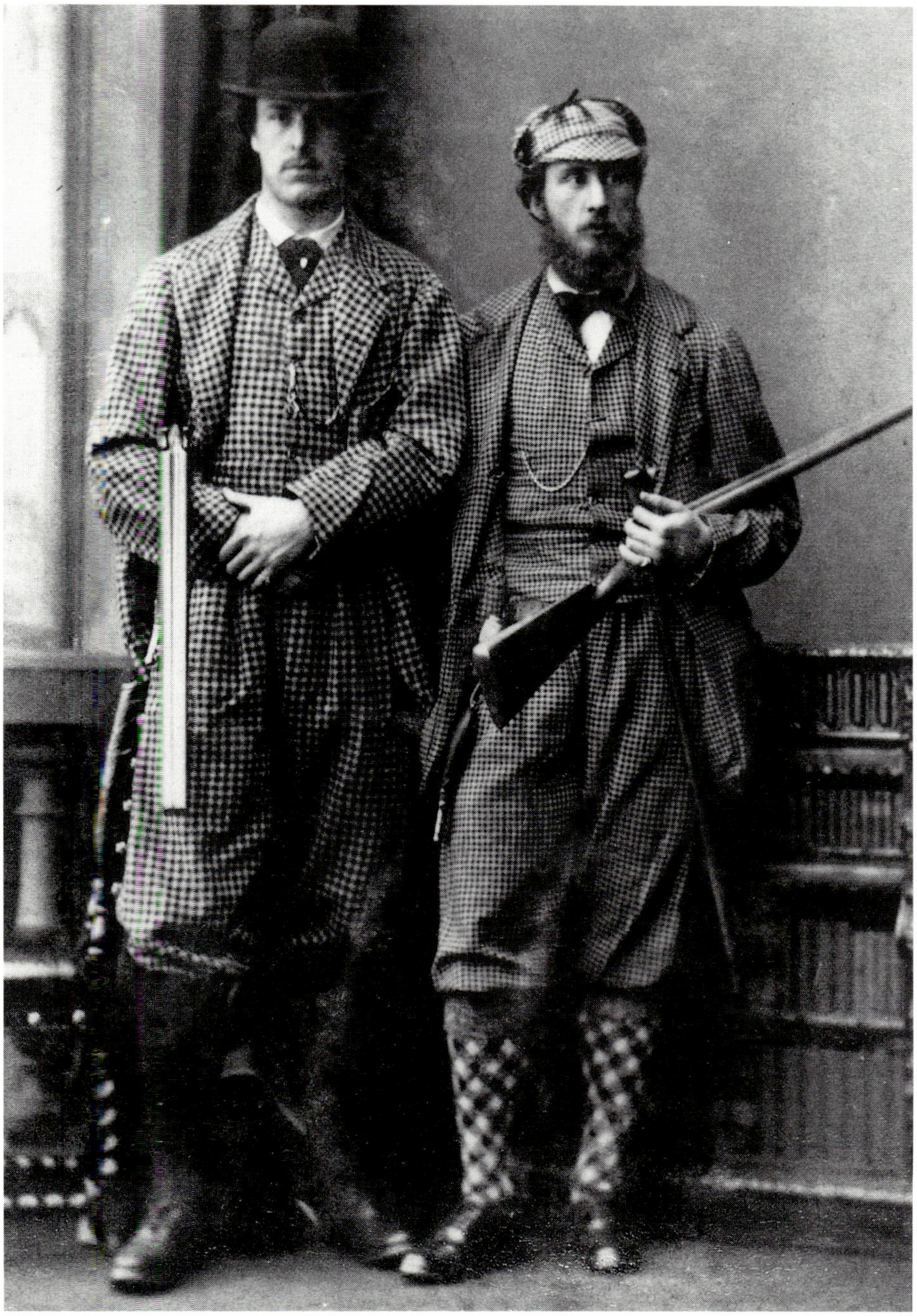

6. Thomas and John Guest
1861
Camille Silvy, London (Daybook 2, no. 2047)

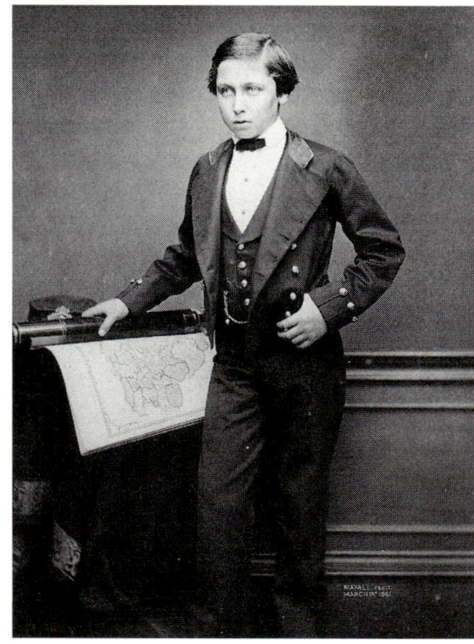

7. Alfred, Duke of Edinburgh
1861
Mayall, London (NPG x 33251)

7

Alfred Ernest Albert, the fourth child of Queen Victoria and the Prince Consort, was born on 6 August 1844 and, unlike his brother Bertie, was a bright, independent and even-tempered child, a favourite with his parents. He was educated with his elder brother by their tutors, Henry Birch and Frederick Gibbs, until about 1857 when they were separated because of Bertie's jealousy and bullying.[4]

Bertie, the Prince of Wales, was provided with a token army career; Alfred, the second son, naturally gravitated to the navy. He is pictured here at the age of sixteen in the dress uniform of a midshipman. The prince had passed his midshipman's exams with distinction in August 1858, aged just fourteen, and had been appointed to the HMS *Euryalus*. His mother had written in her journal: 'He was waiting [at Osborne] in his midshipman's jacket, cap and dirk, half blushing and looking very happy. . . . We felt very proud for it is a particularly hard examination.'[5]

The prince's cap lies on the side-table, with the telescope and an open mapbook showing Great Britain. Apart from the short double-breasted jacket, and the plethora of shiny metal embossed buttons, in essence, the prince wears fashionable formal dress.

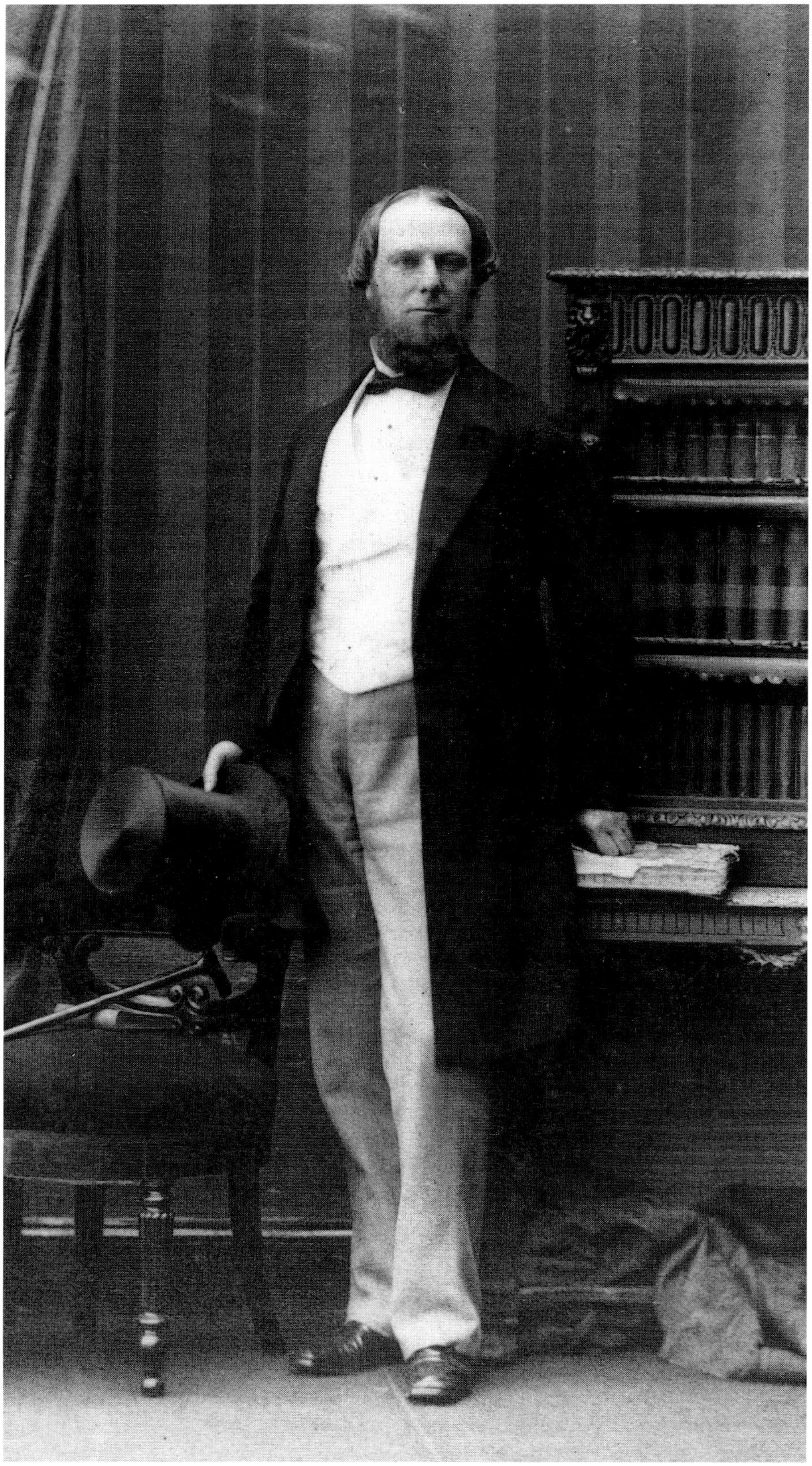

8. The Earl of Kimberley
1861
Camille Silvy, London (Daybook 3, no. 4042)

8

John Wodehouse, 1st Earl of Kimberley, here aged 35, was the British Ambassador to St Petersburg when this portrait was taken.

He wears an open frock coat, worn throughout this period for smart formal wear, replacing the earlier dress or tail-coat. During the 1860s the frock coat became looser and less tailored, giving it a straighter line; it became identified as a hallmark of Victorian respectability.

Lord Kimberley's black frock coat hangs loosely, complementing his aristocratic bearing. *The Tailor and Cutter* for 1 January 1870 includes a plate showing 'a very faithful representation of a well dressed English Gentleman'. This 'gentleman' wears a slightly shorter frock coat than does Lord Kimberley, ending before the knee as was usual in the 1870s; otherwise, it is very similar, and is described as:

> Suited for morning wear or visiting costume. . . . The frock coat is made from superfine black or blue cloth, cut to a medium length in the waist and skirt, the lapels are about three inches wide in the middle.

Underneath is worn a double-breasted 'vest' of checked silk–wool mix. The trousers, which would also suit a morning coat, 'fit close about the body, thighs and down to the knees where they are made from 17 to 18 inches wide, and about the same at the bottom'.[6]

Lord Kimberley wears a double-breasted, pale silk waistcoat with slightly darker, plain cloth trousers. He carries a high black-silk top hat and has laid his walking cane on the nearby chair.

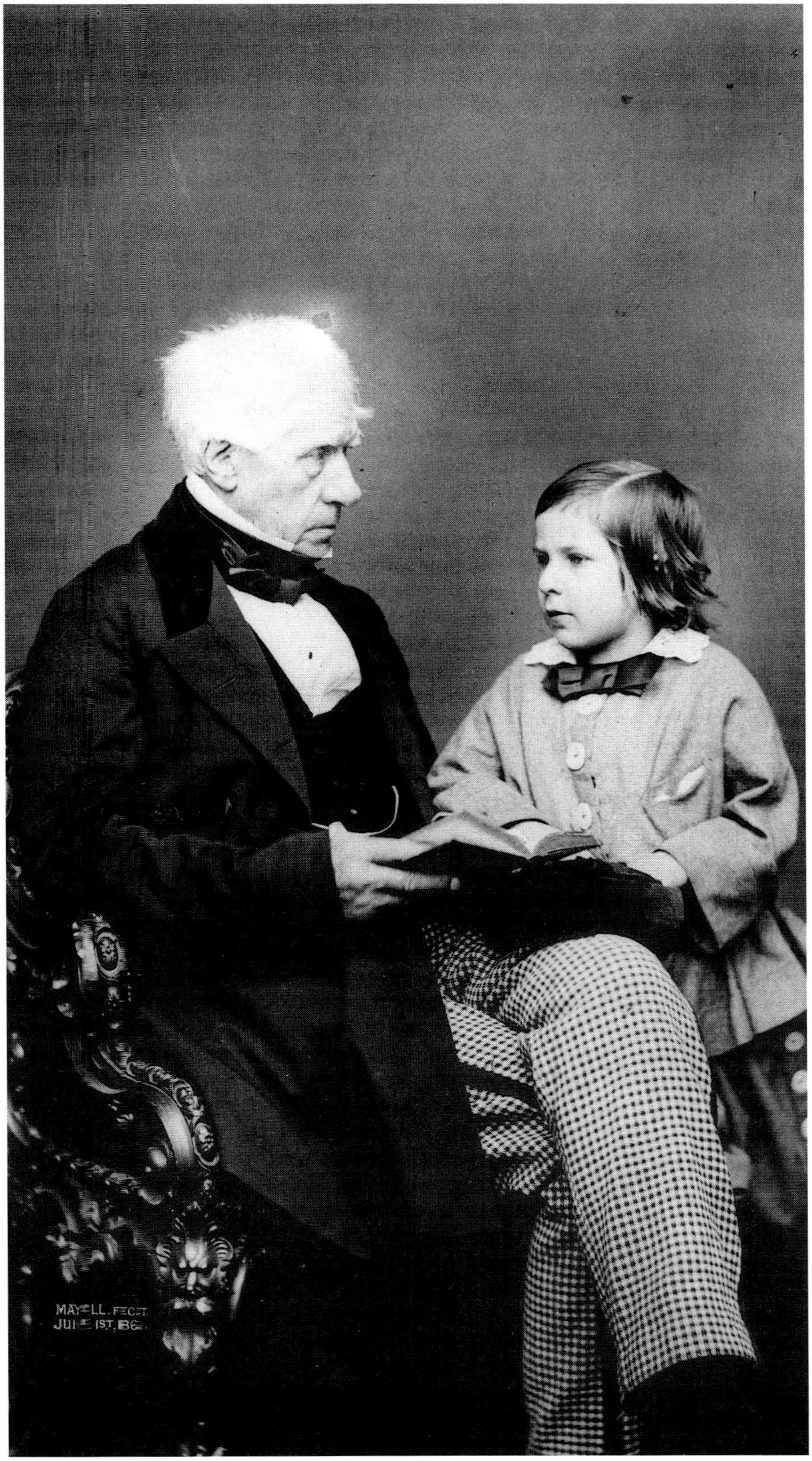

9. **Henry, 1st Baron Brougham and Vaux with his nephew 1861**
Mayall, London (NPG x 4722)

9

Born in 1778 and entering the Commons as a 'Reformer' Whig in 1810, Brougham achieved notoriety by defending Queen Caroline, wife of George IV, at her trial in 1820. Created baron after the death of George IV in 1830, he was to be an active member of the House of Lords until his death in 1868. *The Annual Register* described him, in an obituary, rather unappealingly as 'a man . . . superhuman in his energy and industry'. As he died without issue, the title passed to his brother William, the father of the boy in the photograph.

In this fine-quality published studio portrait, Lord Brougham wears a frock coat with velvet collar and extremely long sleeves bunching at the wrists, in a style popularized some years earlier. His chin rests on a very high collar tied with a black stock. A robust 83 year old with still seven years to live, he is dapper and stylish in appearance.

Lord Brougham's nephew wears a loose-fitting cloth jacket belted in the Norfolk style, with knickerbockers. The jacket is decorated with a lace collar, black neckbow and large, white, pearl buttons with matching buttons down the outer seams of the knickerbockers.

The photograph was issued as a print by the publisher Marion & Co. of 152 Regent Street, a few shops up from Mayall's premises at 224 Regent Street. A popular celebrity, Brougham enjoyed the new proliferation of portrait cartes-de-visite. On passing a shop window in which his photograph was displayed, it was rumoured that he would enquire within as to how well it was selling.[7]

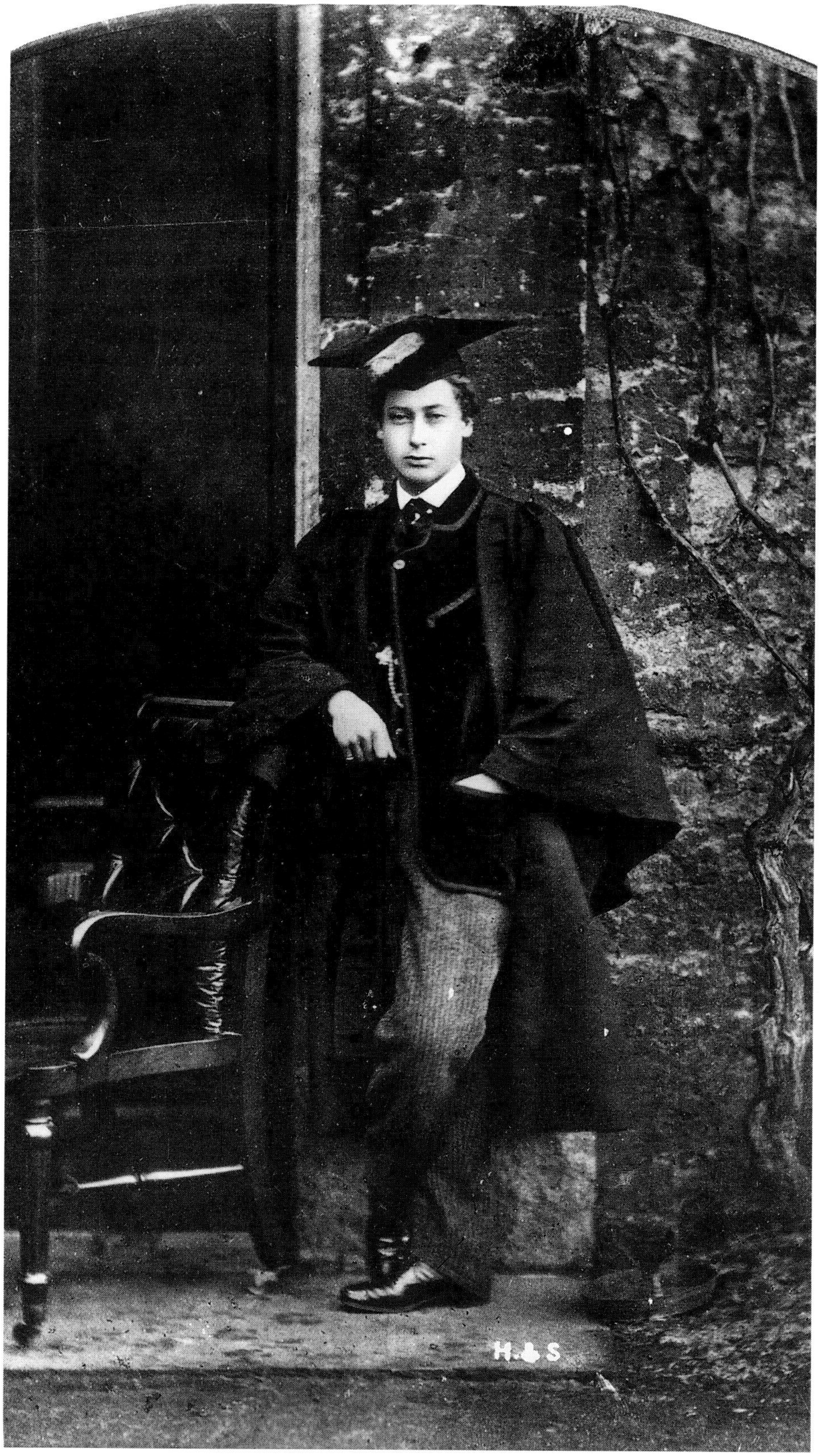

10. Edward, Prince of Wales
1861
Hills & Saunders, Cambridge (NPG x 14382)

10

From January 1861 until his father's death that December, the Prince of Wales attended Trinity College, Cambridge. The 20-year-old prince is seen here standing by a college doorway wearing his academic mortarboard and undergraduate gown, the latter still on display at Trinity College. Below his gown, he wears a black-velvet lounge or 'pea' jacket, buttoned only at the first button and hanging open to reveal his watch-chain.

The Prince of Wales was a rather slow, difficult child, contrasting very unfavourably with his bright and able sister Victoria. Backward in learning to speak and walk, he suffered from jealous rages from infancy. His parents and their nursery staff were liberal for their day, slow to punish and anxious, as the Queen remarked, to bring up their children 'as simply and in as domestic a way as possible.'[8] His tutors, Henry Birch, Frederick Gibbs and finally General Bruce, all experienced difficulties with Bertie's capriciousness.

As his time at Cambridge was clearly not intended to be a period of uninterrupted study, Bertie also visited Germany in the autumn to see military manoeuvres and to meet his future bride, Alexandra. Back in Cambridge, the prince was to receive a visit from his overworked father on 25 November, barely three weeks before he was summoned back to Windsor by his sister Alice, to his father's death-bed.

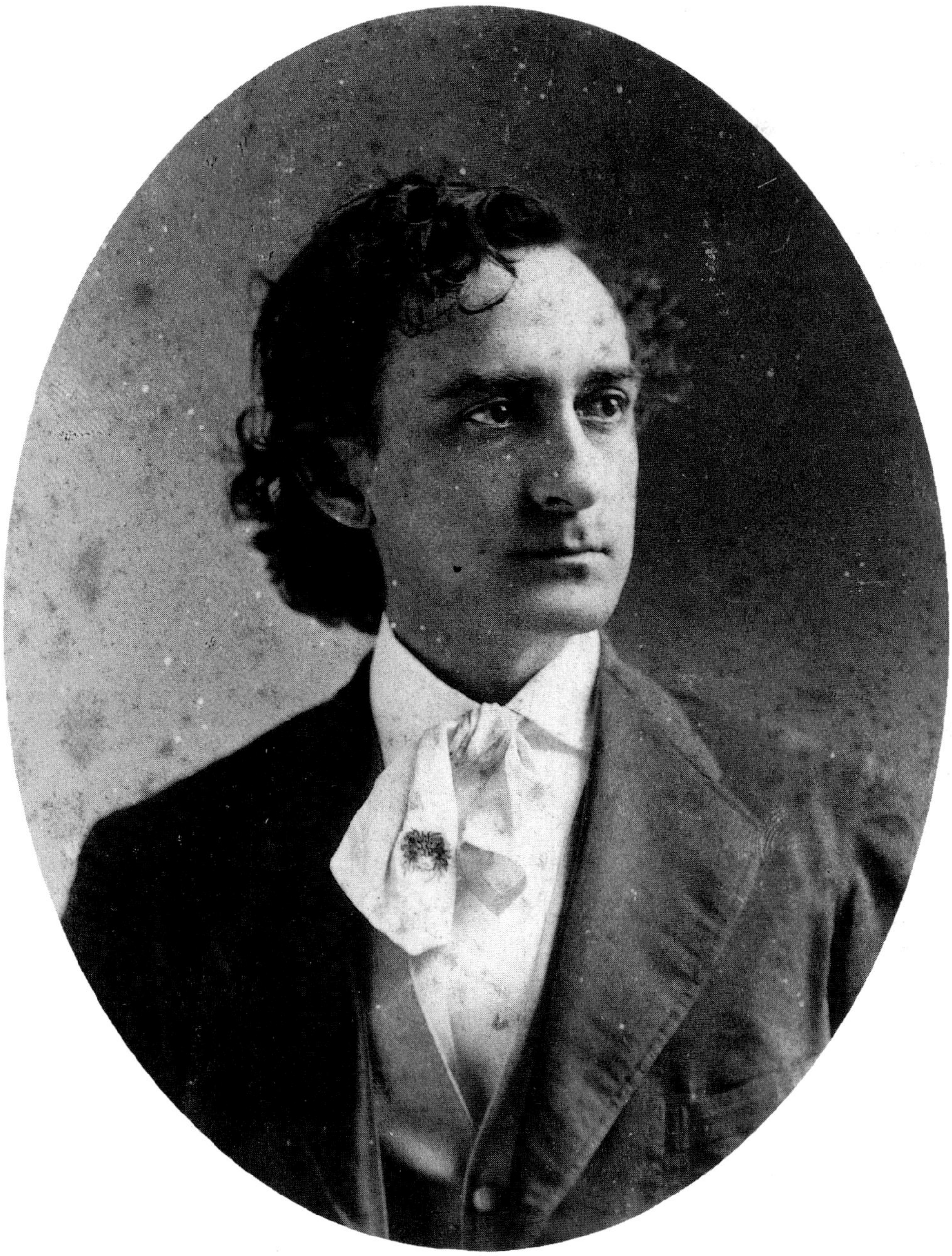

11. Edwin Thomas Booth
***c.* 1861**
London Stereoscopic Company (NPG x 8366)

11

Born in Belair, Maryland on 13 November 1833, Edwin Booth was a famous American tragedian of the 1860s and 1870s. The son of the actor Junius Brutus Booth, he first visited London in 1861, probably the date of this portrait. He returned to the United States to work as Manager of the Winter Garden Theatre in New York (1863–7), before opening his own theatre, 'Booths', in 1869.

Edwin underwent a succession of personal calamities, including the death of two wives and the collapse of his theatre. As a commentator relates, 'his habitual melancholia was aggravated by the madness of his father, second wife and younger brother.'[9]

This famous younger brother, John Wilkes Booth, assassinated Abraham Lincoln in April 1865 in, ironically for his theatre-manager brother, Ford's Theatre, Washington. Obviously enabled to empathize with Hamlet, in 1864 Edwin Booth played one hundred consecutive performances in this role in New York, a record which was to stand until the 1920s.

In this head-and-shoulders portrait, Booth presents an unconventional, artistic appearance, with his rather unruly curly hair and his loosely knotted cravat. Folded kerchiefs were knotted or tied around the shirt collar from the 1790s, usually finished in a bow, although knots were popular too, usually with the loose ends anchored to the shirt front with a tie- or stick-pin.

12

Always a dapper figure, Disraeli is seen here in his middle fifties, in an early carte-de-visite without any backdrop or photographic props. A self-conscious sitter, Disraeli disliked being photographed; in later life he would only do so at the express wish of the Queen, who was perhaps his staunchest admirer.[10]

In this portrait he wears a double-breasted frock coat, with wide lapels, over pale, narrowly cut trousers. As late as 1877, when he was in his early seventies, *The Tailor and Cutter* described his distinctive and 'dandified' costume:

> Lord Beaconsfield, who, in his younger days, was at least a star of some magnitude in the world of fashion, still retains a little of the peculiarity in costume which marked the days when Count d'Orsay flourished. At the reception of the Queen at High Wycombe the other day, the Prime Minister wore a dark blue coat of the sac shape, trimmed with Astrakhan fur, and his trousers were a bright yellow in hue. Now this is precisely the style that suited our fathers, but in these days of extreme neatness, such a get up looked somewhat peculiar and conveyed the impression that the wearer had not forgotten the style in vogue 30 or 40 years since. Notwithstanding that it afforded a contrast to some of the young swells in attendance who wore long Chesterfields buttoning high, and dark trousers, as a rule there was nothing but what was pleasing to the eye in the more showy style of Lord Beaconsfield. It is hard to determine whether the popular taste will ever again run in the direction of colours and a more pronounced style.[11]

Disraeli's coat 'of the sac shape' would have been largely unfitted, cut in a very loose and boxy style. Sacs could be short, as jackets, or longer, as overcoats, and were often belted to provide some shaping at the waist.

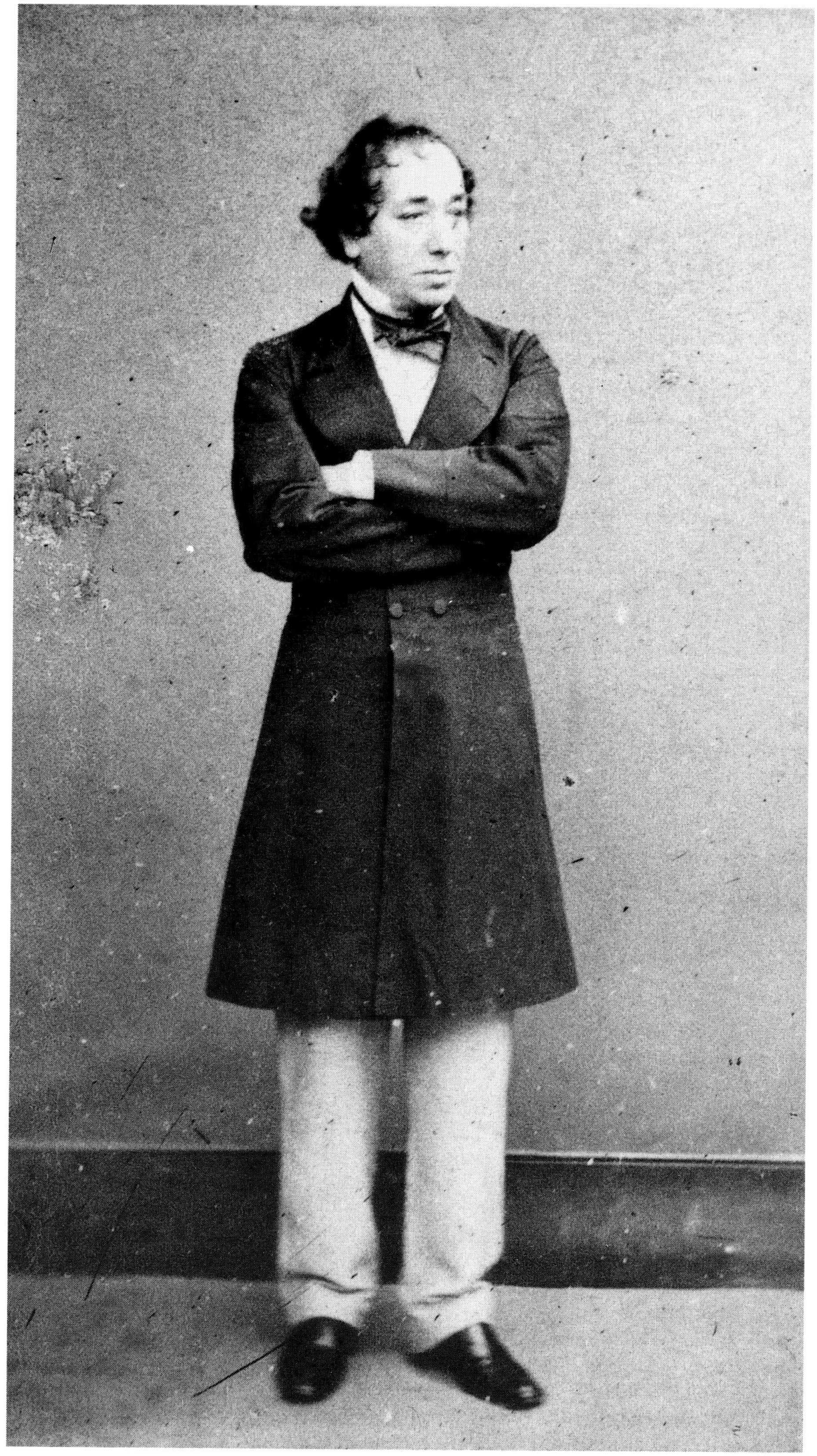

12. Benjamin Disraeli, later Lord Beaconsfield
***c.* 1861**
W. Kilburn, London (Album 102, p. 4a) (NPG Ax 33505)

13

This portrait of Gladstone, from the very early 1860s, shows him as a man in his early fifties and in his second period as chancellor of the exchequer (1852–5; 1859–66). He became prime minister for the first time in 1869 and this led to four subsequent ministries. He had a stormy relationship with his sovereign, Queen Victoria, who disliked both his reforming zeal and his personal demeanour towards her. Her oft-quoted complaint that Gladstone spoke to her as if she were a public meeting, although apocryphal, nonetheless contains a kernel of credibility.[12]

There was a considerable public demand for cartes-de-visite of well-known public figures and political statesmen, and this would undoubtedly have been a published portrait for retail sale. Gladstone chose to wear a black frock coat with a single-breasted waistcoat over a high stiff-collared shirt and black cravat.[13] The plain backdrop serves to emphasize his determined and purposeful expression. A serious and devout man with simple tastes, he found relaxation in his fifties and sixties by chopping wood on his estate at Hawarden. When the royal summons to his first ministry arrived, he was cutting down a tree in his grounds, and he paused only to remark, 'Very significant', before continuing to chop.

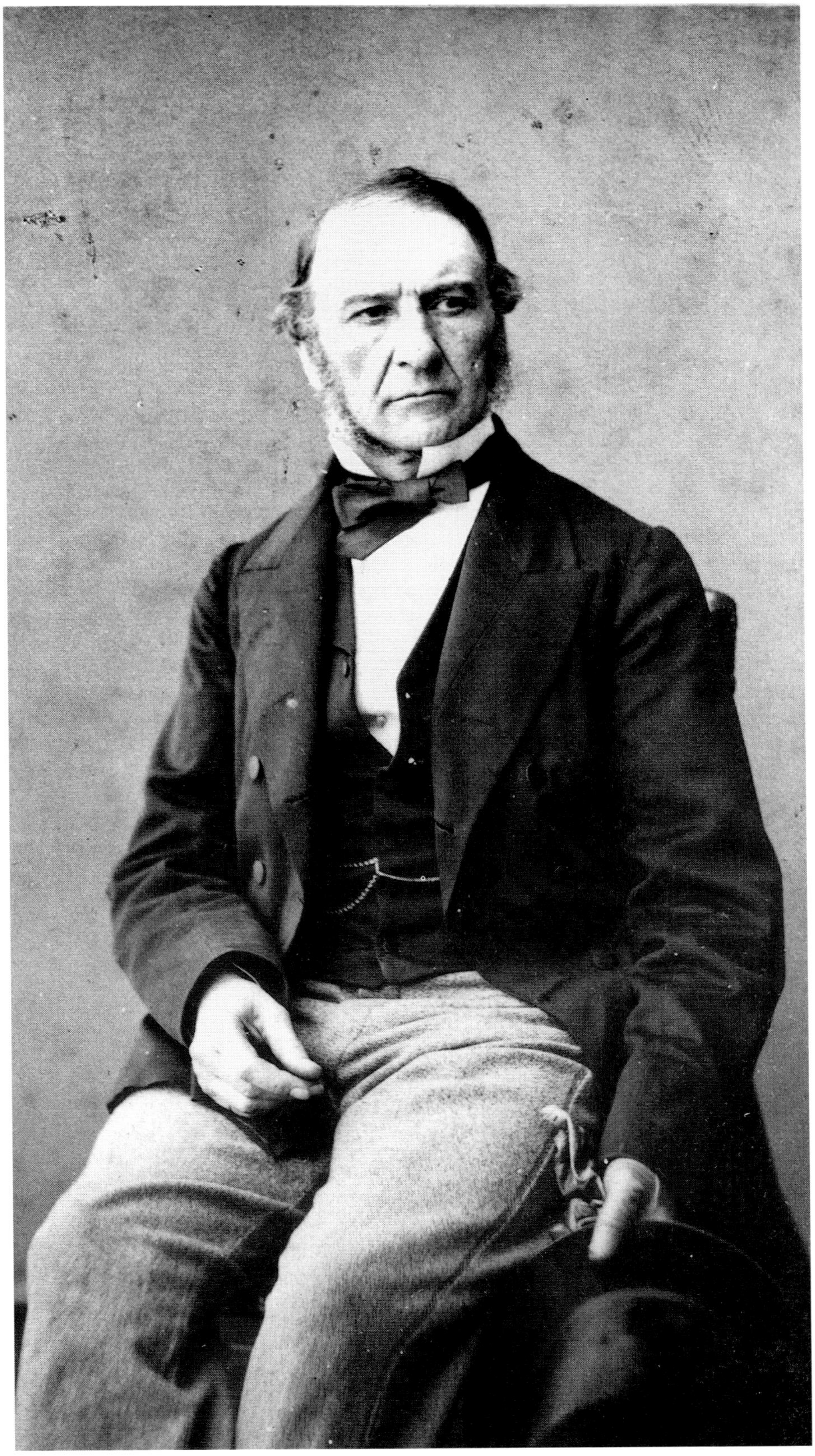

13. William Ewart Gladstone
Early 1860s
W. & D. Downey (NPG x 32945)

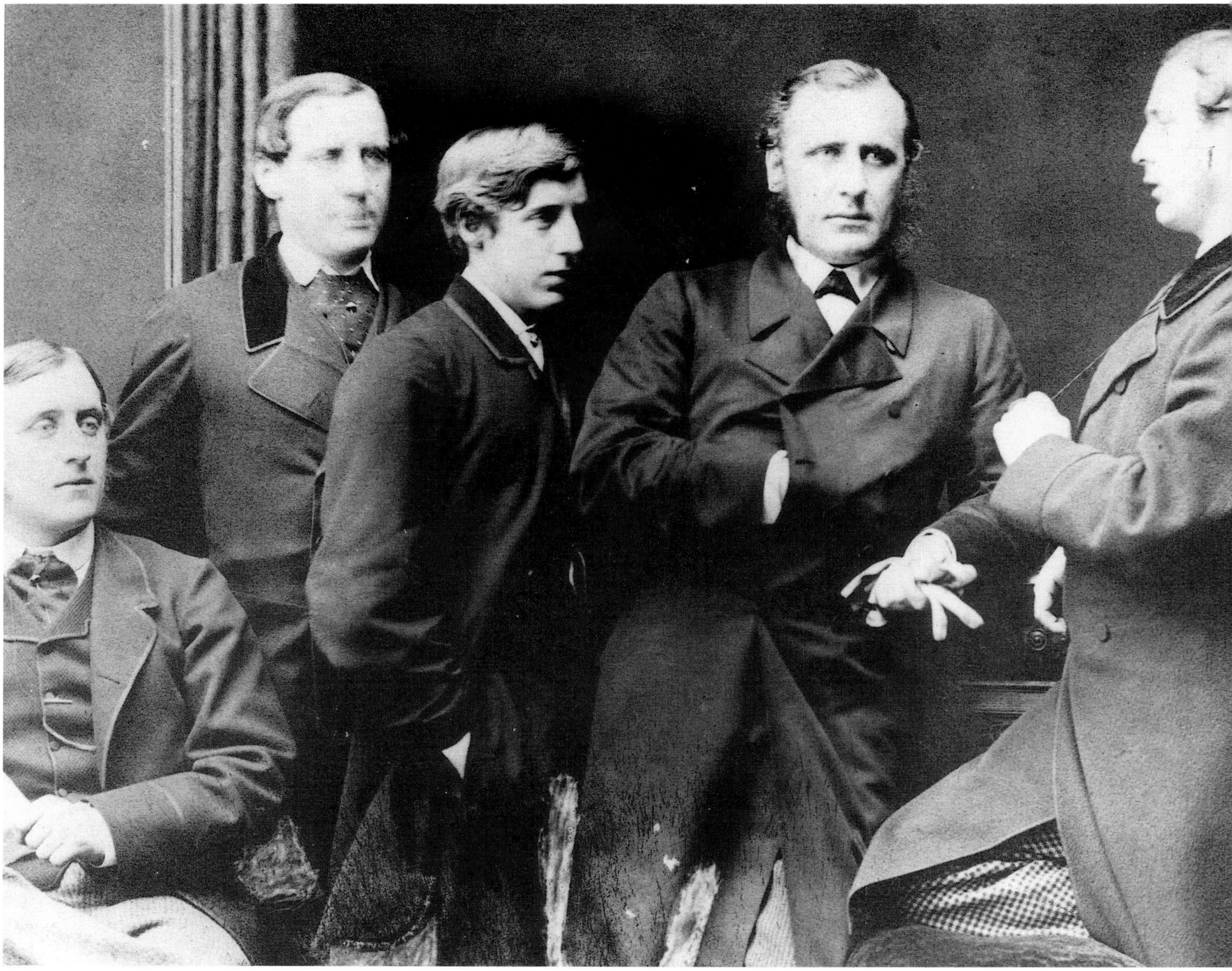

14. The Baring brothers
1862
Camille Silvy, London (Daybook 6, no. 7740)

14

In this atypical Silvy portrait, five of the ten sons of Henry Baring MP, have been photographed in an informal grouping. The brothers here comprise: Edward (b. 1828), Richard (b. 1833), Thomas (b. 1839), Evelyn (b. 1841), and Walter (b. 1844). The Barings were an influential family; Edward was later created Baron Revelstoke, and Evelyn, after a career as consul-general in Egypt, was in 1892 created Baron Cromer, later Earl.

The three elder brothers (all standing) wear double-breasted frock coats with contrasting check or striped trousers. Two of the coats have velvet collars. *The Tailor and Cutter* (24 April 1869) writes of 'a fashionable coat, perhaps the most fashionable – the garment that goes under the name "frock coat", a coat suitable for any occasion.' It goes on to list current innovations including velvet collars and 'silk serge collar and fronts'.[14] Buttoned up, the coat completely obscures the waistcoat and leaves a small triangle of shirt and cravat.

The other two brothers, far left and centre, wear morning coats with matching waistcoats, the edges bound with black braid. All the collars are turn-down, worn with either a neat black stock or a wide expanse of patterned silk cravat held in place by a central tie-pin.

All the hairstyles are relatively long, with left side-partings. The eldest brother, Edward, also sports long side-whiskers.

15

Henry William Pullen was born in 1836, and ordained by 1862 when he became vicar choral at York Minster. He transferred to Salisbury Cathedral in 1863, where he remained until 1875 when he travelled as chaplain on the HMS *Alert* Arctic expedition.

The Reverend Pullen wears a clerical frock coat with a high-cut waistcoat and trousers. The frock coat was worn for ordinary day wear by a majority of clergymen throughout the nineteenth century. During the 1850s and 1860s high churchmen adopted the waistcoat, cut very high, with a band at the neck to support the clerical Roman collar. Low churchmen wore the collar and necktie until the end of the century when they too took to the Roman collar.

The Reverend Pullen carries an ordinary black-silk top hat, and sports luxuriant side-whiskers, sometimes dubbed 'weepers'. He poses in front of a backdrop showing, appropriately, a chantry-like, leaded-glass window.

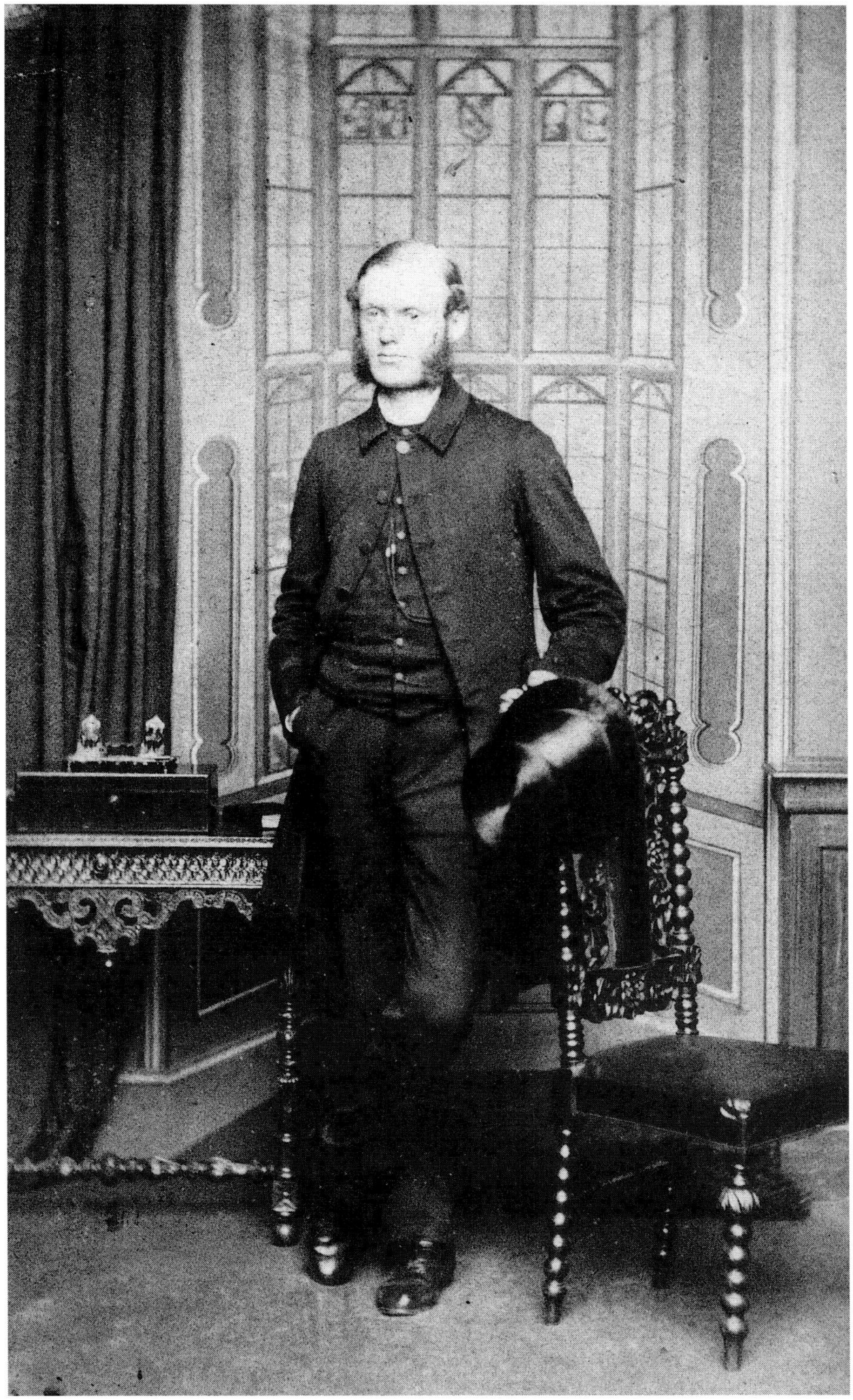

15. Reverend Henry Pullen
1862
W. T. & R. Gowland, York (NPG x 12773)

16

Rather raffish and founded in October 1857, the Savage Club was a literary, social, London club for artists and patrons. Pictured here are the founder members on the occasion of a theatrical performance in Liverpool on behalf of the 'Distressed cotton operatives'.

The founding letter, circulated by George Augustus Sala, read:

> Dear sir, the favour of your presence is requested at a meeting of gentlemen connected with literature and the fine arts . . . at The Crown Tavern, Vinegar Lane, Drury Lane, to confer upon the expediency of forming a social society . . .

The club was later to boast the membership of the Prince of Wales (elected 1882).

The members are seen here in a variety of attire, primarily morning coats with typical contrasting lighter trousers; but also frock coats. The tall 'chimney pot' top hats are primarily black although there is a single paler version (centre back).

They pose in studied casual and artistic mood; Lionel Brough (fifth from the right), in a particularly tall hat, even puffs on a cigar à la Brunel.

17

Born in 1858, and here aged three or four, George Gower is probably about to be 'breeched' and to leave off his infant dress. Seen here perched on a chair in the studio, and steadied by the hand of his nurse or mother, whose dress is visible to the left of the photograph, the boy wears a black-velvet frock trimmed centre-front with 13 black satin-covered buttons. Both the white collar and the scalloped hem of the petticoat are embroidered with broderie anglaise open-work to provide visual alleviation to the uniform darkness of the dress. His black-leather button-boots are worn with turned-down white socks.

Velvet was a favourite fabric for boys' dresses, especially in rich, dark, supposedly masculine colours. *La Belle Assemblée* (February 1862) described: 'A pretty

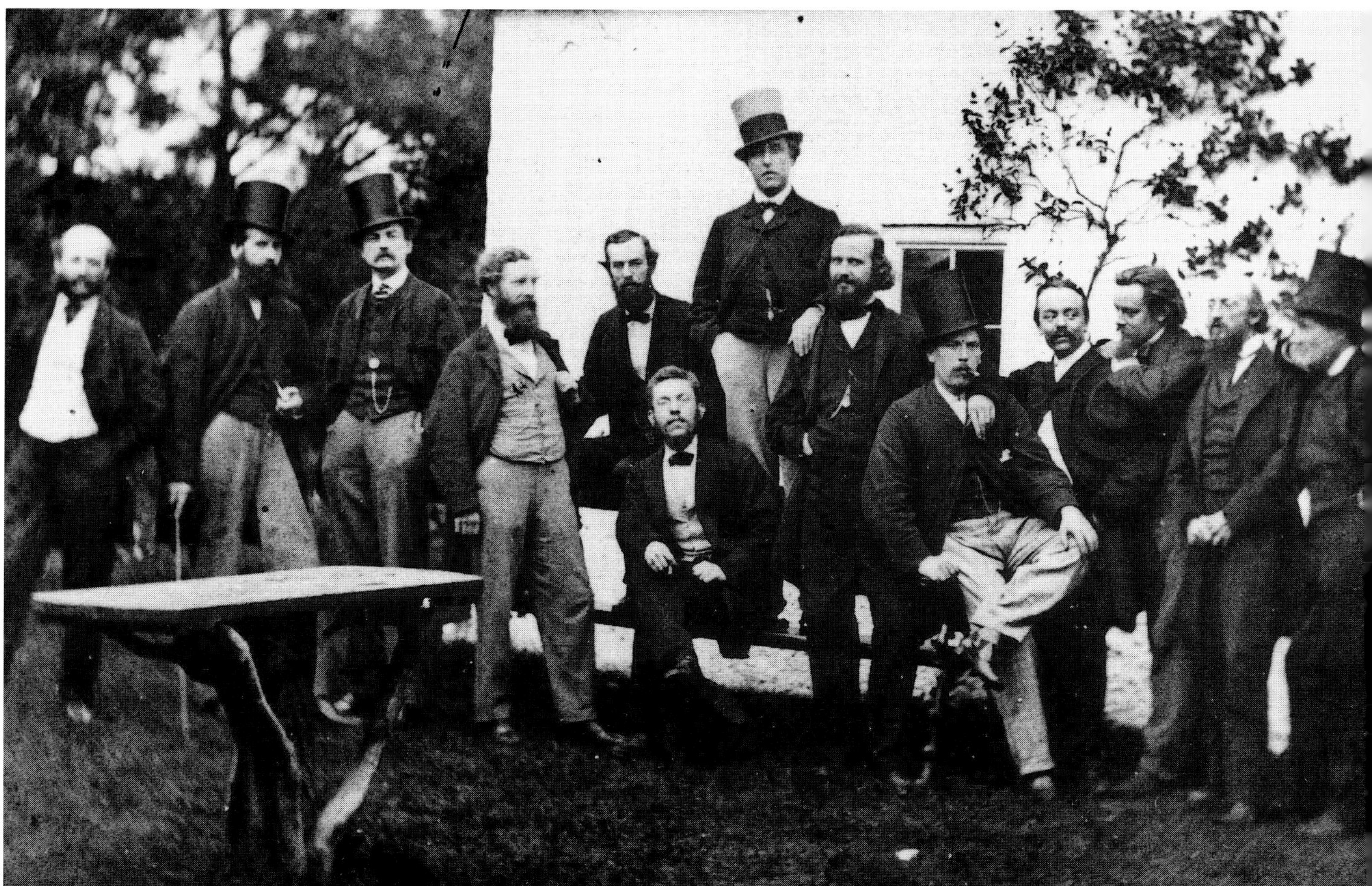

16. Members of the Savage Club 1862
W. Keith, Liverpool (NPG x 22196)

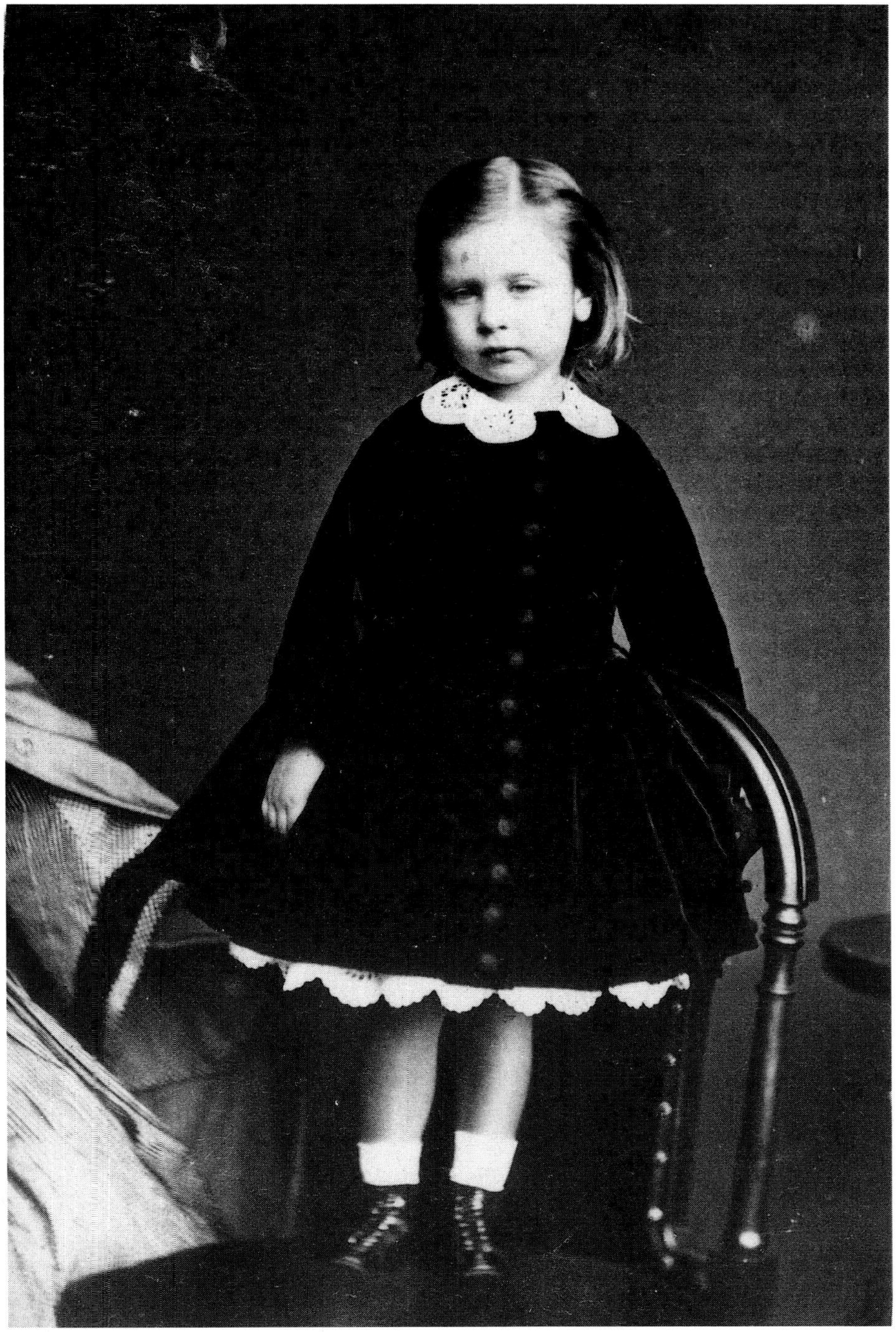

17. George Levenson Gower
1862
Photographer unknown (Jocelyn Album (59) p. 27) (NPG Ax 33519)

little blue velvet dress, suitable for a boy of two years old, was made with a low body, cut square, trimmed round with handsome open embroidery . . .'

Once breeched, boys wore velvet knickerbocker suits which might be 'made entirely of black silk velvet, and ornamented with very large white mother of pearl buttons . . . white silk stockings and patent leather boots . . . and an embroidered collar . . .' (*La Belle Assemblée*, January 1862).

Distinguishing girls from boys at this early age is usually facilitated by examining the hairstyle, which for boys is invariably simple and without bands or ties.

18

A diplomat, George Brackenbury wears a dark-velvet morning coat with contrasting bound edges, lighter cloth trousers and single-breasted waistcoat. *The Tailor and Cutter* (6 March 1869) describes a 'morning or what is more commonly termed shooting coat' as cut with a marked curve in the fronts and with very low lapels. It was sometimes known as 'summer dress'.[15] The lounge jacket which this example resembles had, in the 1860s, higher lapels and was cut shorter in the body.

In 1864, Disraeli wore a fashionable black-velvet morning coat of this type when delivering a famous address at Oxford.[16] The loose cut of Mr Brackenbury's coat is suggestive of a warmer climate, and he carries an umbrella, probably as protection from the sun. He also carries a soft felt hat with its white lining reflecting the studio light back to the camera.

Sporting a full beard, Brackenbury wears a watch-chain or 'Albert'. These had become popular after their introduction in 1849 and were reputedly first worn by the Prince Consort.[17]

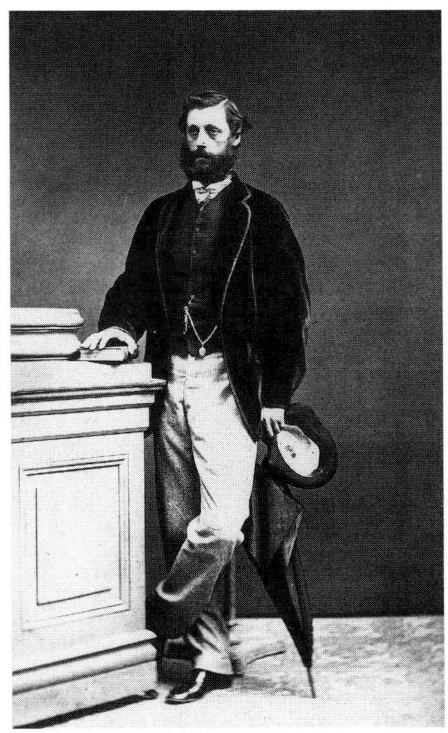

18. George Brackenbury
1863
Silveira and Co., Hong Kong (NPG x 8366)

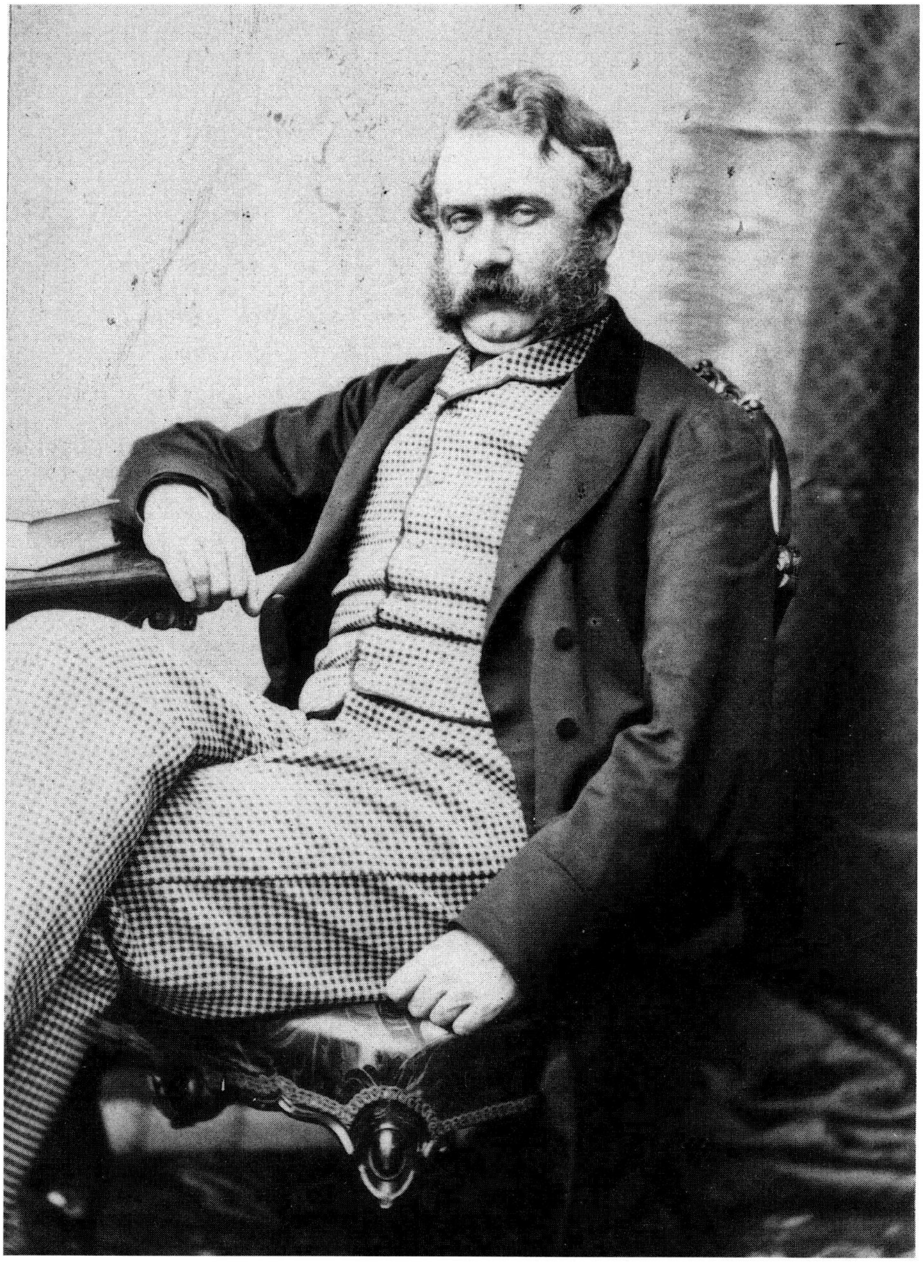

19. Sir William White
1863
J. Johnstone, Birmingham (NPG x 8355)

19

Born in 1824, and educated at Trinity College, Cambridge, William Arthur White entered the diplomatic service in his early thirties, becoming consul general at Warsaw in 1862. He transferred to Danzig in 1864, just after the date of this portrait, and remained in the Baltic until 1875 when he became consul general at Servia. The height of his career came in 1888 when, as Envoy Extraordinary at Constantinople, he was awarded the GCB.

In this seated portrait, a rather quizzical looking Sir William wears a frock coat over stridently checked matching trousers and waistcoat, the latter cut very high, and buttoning up to a turn-down collar. Sir William wears full side-whiskers and moustaches, although not a beard (which might have served to disguise his double chin).

20, 21

Both these boys, aged between five and seven, wear typical cloth knickerbocker suits, the staple boys' outfit from the 1860s onwards. Charles, the younger of the two, was the eldest son of the 3rd Earl of Normanton; he wears a dark suit with ornamental shiny metal buttons, vibrantly striped stockings, and patent-leather shoes, Master A. Wright wears a paler cloth suit with sober stockings and ankle boots.

The Englishwoman's Domestic Magazine (November 1862) declares:

> there is very little alteration in childrens' costume; the knickerbocker suit reigns supreme; it is so comfortable and convenient, and not likely to be surpassed . . .[18]

In the same journal's 'Children's Column', under 'The Fashions for the Month', a large variety of different finishes and cloths for boys' suits were described. In March 1863, a patented suit from Nicolls of Regent Street was described, made of

> cheviot wool . . . a new feature in these suits is that they are braided on those parts that always wear out quickly; namely at the knees and elbows. Mohair braid is used for the purpose, put on in the shape of a fern leaf . . .[19]

Neither of these well-to-do sitters is enduring the indignity of patched ('braided') knees and elbows, a practical if unappealing suggestion.

22

These two portraits of the painter Frederick Walker are separated by five years, and show the sitter in his early and late twenties.

Born in London in 1840, Walker studied at Leigh's Academy and the Royal Academy School before being engaged as apprentice to the wood engraver J. M. Whymper. He was elected a member of the Water Colour Society in 1866 and was made an ARA, in 1871, before his premature death in 1875.

Both prints show Walker in a dark morning coat, the earlier full-length por-

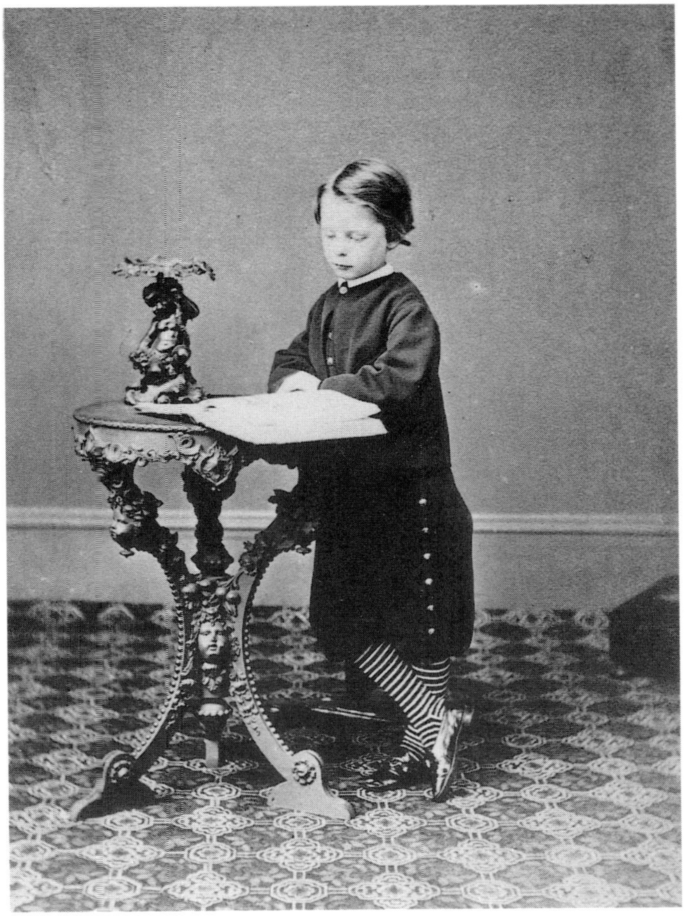

20. Charles Agar, Viscount Somerton
1863
James Russell (Barrington Album, p. 38) (NPG Ax 26277)

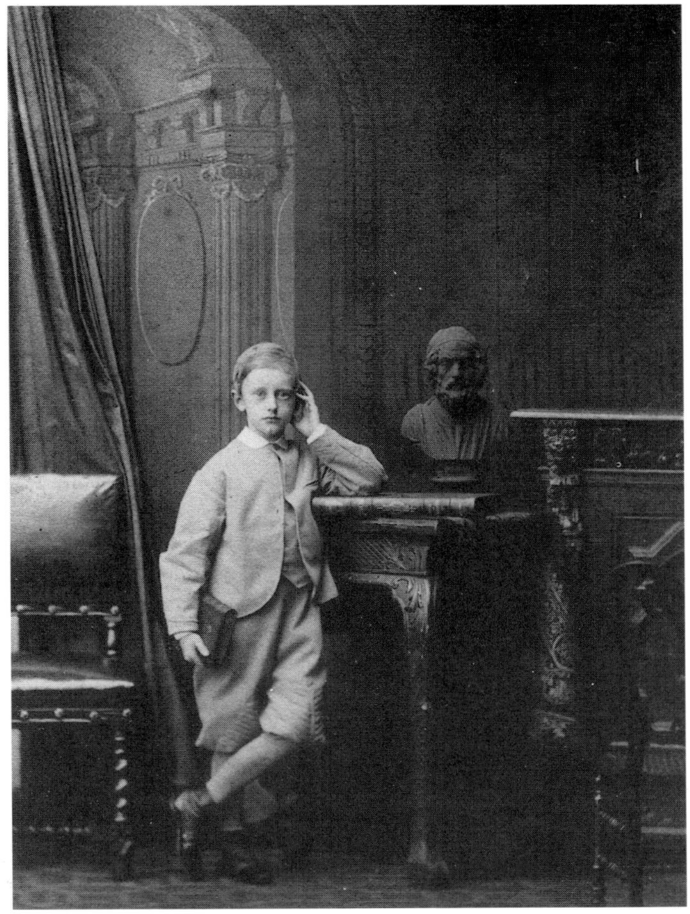

21. Master A. Wright
1865
Camille Silvy, London (Daybook 12, no. 16536)

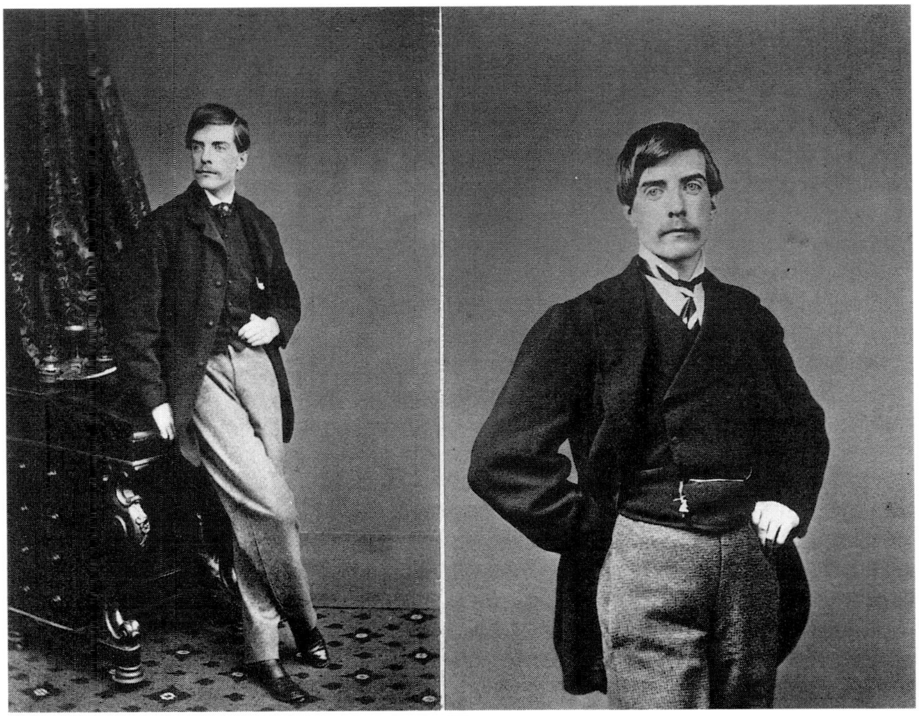

trait showing the narrow, high collar and revers of the early 1860s, worn with a matching waistcoat, cut very high and scarcely allowing room for the cravat. The later three-quarter-length portrait shows a morning coat with much wider collar and revers, the latter descending as low as waist level. There are similar wide revers on the double-breasted waistcoat, which is fastened across a narrow silk tie fastened in the familiar four-in-hand manner. Walker's watch-chain snakes horizontally from the left across his waist.

Although he differs in style of coat and waistcoat, Walker wears almost identical hairstyles and moustaches in both portraits, and very similar narrow-check grey trousers. Facially, he seems to have hardly aged in the intervening five years.

22. Frederick Walker ARA
1863 & 1868
Probably by John Watkins (NPG x 27217)

FEMALE

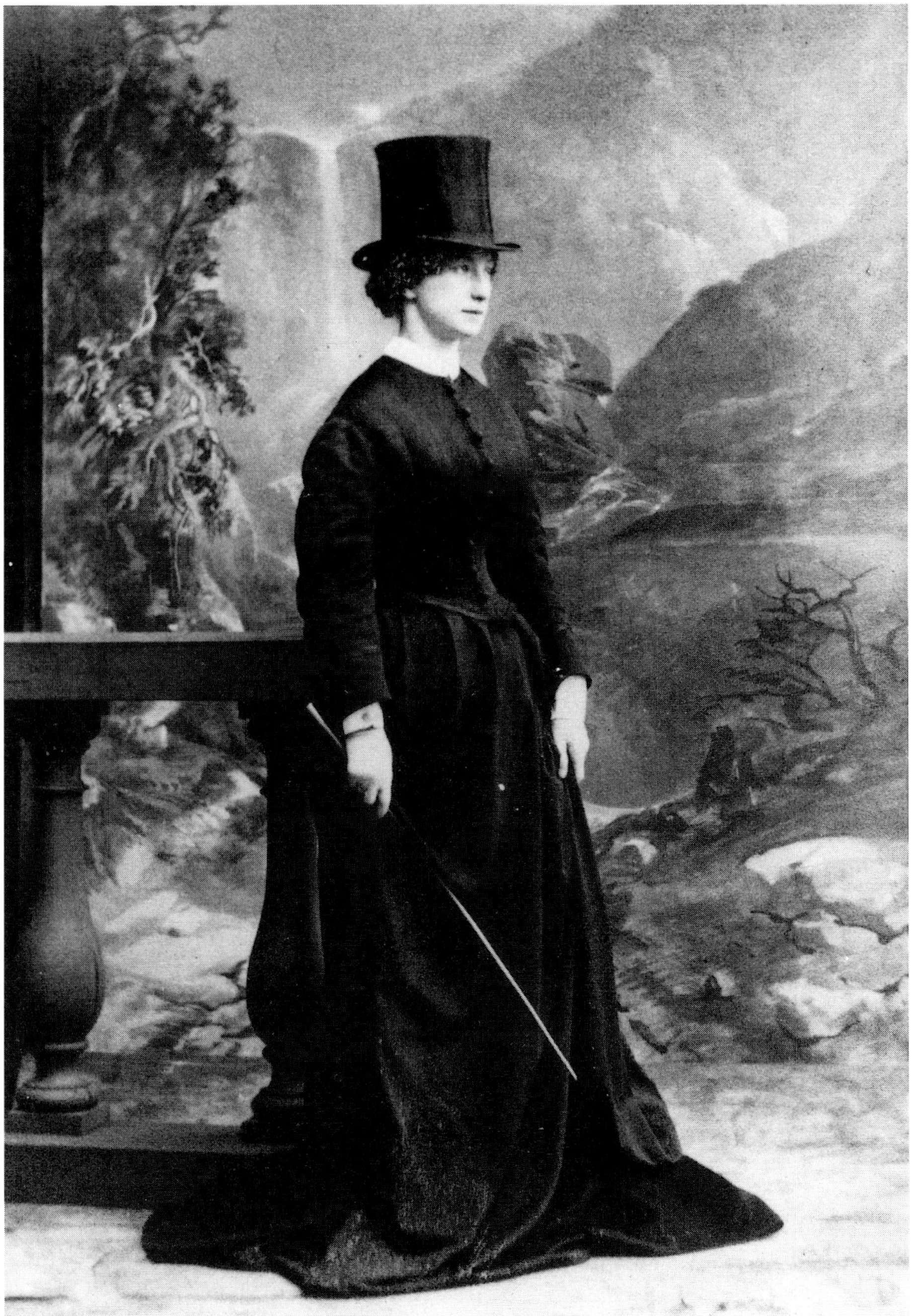

23. Lady Eliza Otway
1860
Camille Silvy, London (Daybook 1, no. 361)

23

Dressed in her riding habit, this is one of three poses of Lady Otway, who had married Sir George Otway, 2nd Bart., in March 1848, and is here aged about 40.

Her dark-cloth habit is worn with a tall, black-silk top hat exactly mirroring similar mens' hats. This was one of two fashionable alternatives for female equestrian wear at this date. Rather more commonly featured in contemporary fashion plates are felt or straw hats with turned-up brims.[1]

Much earlier, *The Young Lady's Equestrian Manual* (1830) directed Lady Otway's mother's generation that:

> to ride in a bonnet is far from judicious. A hat or neat undress military cap, is indispensible to the female equestrian. It should be secured most carefully to the head, for the loss of it would not merely be inconvenient, but perhaps dangerous from the startling effect which its fall might produce on the sensitive temperament of the horse.[2]

Lady Otway's horse was obviously not of so sensitive a disposition since the other two poses by Silvy, taken with his perhaps alarming photography equipment, includes the animal.

For habits, many women stuck to traditional black or dark-brown cloth, matching the skirt. More adventurous riders ventured into more innovative possibilities. *The Gentleman's Magazine* for August 1859 (Plate 2) shows a woman dressed in a buff-coloured cloth jacket-bodice with a contrasting grey skirt. *The Englishwoman's Domestic Magazine* (August 1860) describes 'a riding habit of nankeen quilting trimmed with white cotton braid and buttons'. This costume is completed with 'plain linen collar and sleeves' (like Lady Otway's) and 'lavender-coloured gauntlets'.[3]

24

The fourth daughter of James Hope Vere, Jane married the 3rd Marquess of Ely in 1844, aged 23. Her husband died in 1857, aged only 43, some three years before this portrait, and Lady Ely is still in mourning.

During the first year of mourning for a mid-Victorian widow of means, a concealing black-crape cap would be worn, and the lady would be enjoined to shun all social invitations and places of public amusement. Thus, in her first year of widowhood, Lady Ely would have had no occasion to wear evening dress as she does here. An article in *The World* (June 1875) entitled 'Mitigated Mourning' enumerates the many graduations of mourning etiquette, and decrees that for a widow:

> after two years, mourning may be laid aside although it is in much better taste to wear half mourning for at least six months more. Many widows never put on colours again.

The article goes on to defend the use of mourning dress, and particularly crape, against the members of The Mourning Reform Association who objected to its expense and ostentation:

> The use of crape explains . . . even to those least initiated in the minutiae of etiquette, that the wearer's mourning is for some really near relative . . . supposing that the questioner has not heard of the loss.[4]

Lady Ely was a Lady of the Bedchamber to Queen Victoria from 1851 to 1889 (the year before Lady Ely's death) and must be supposed to have been both well versed in, and a strict adherent to, all the etiquette of mourning. She was also a great friend of Eugénie, ex-Empress of the French, when she lived in exile in England. Lady Ely's obituary in *The Morning Post* (12 June 1890) described her as: 'a handsome woman of imperious character and temper. She brooked no contradiction from anyone, husband, child or friend, and in her large family she was an autocrat . . .'

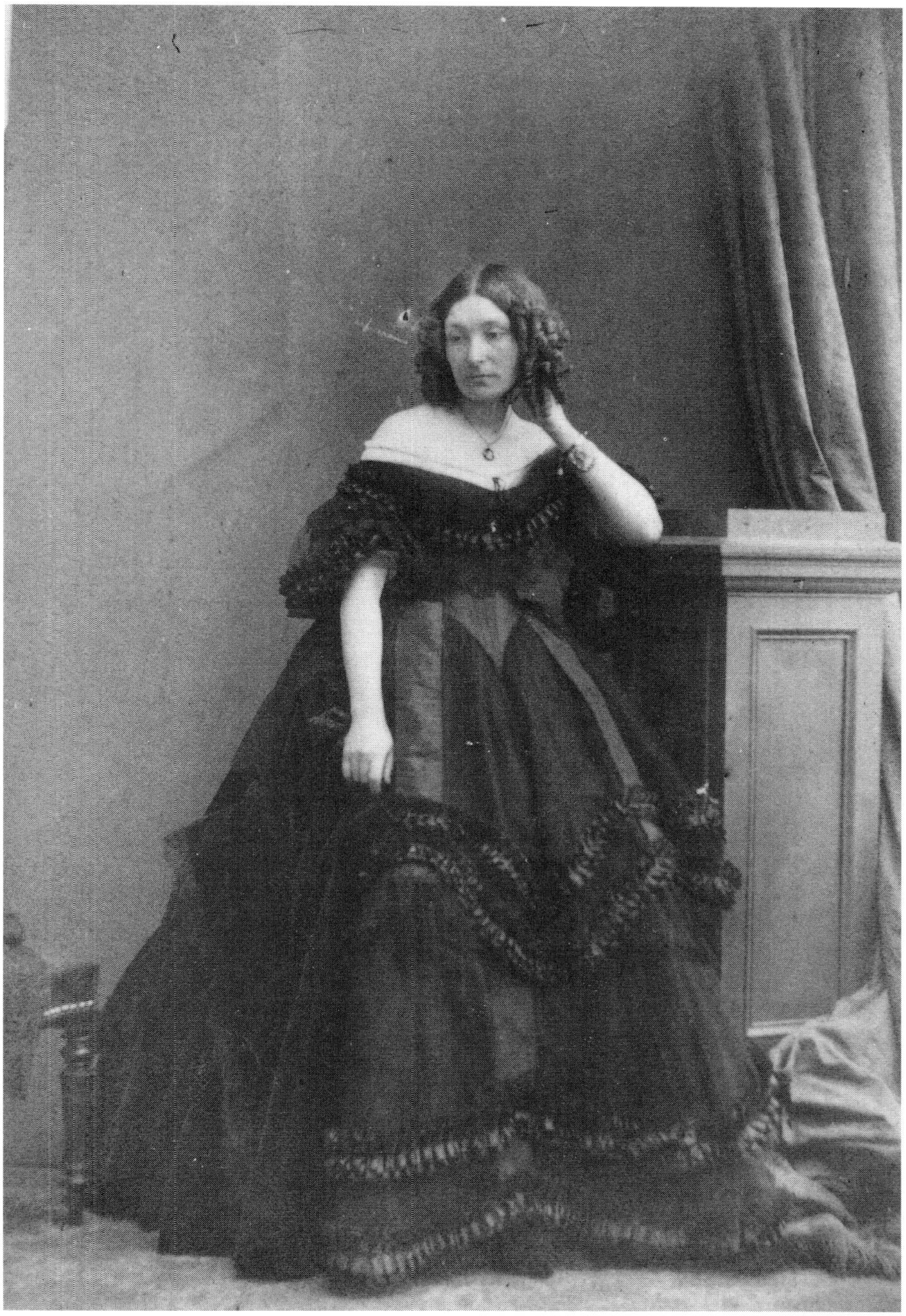

24. Jane, Lady Ely
1860
Camille Silvy, London (Daybook 1, no. 440)

25

Even in a posed and fashionable studio portrait, the cage-crinoline was clearly apparent. Miss Finch wears a wide skirt supported by a crinoline which pushes up slightly at the front. The skirt has five deep flounces woven with contrasting horizontal borders. As early as 1860, fashion writers, particularly male critics and caricaturists, were busy foreshadowing the crinoline's demise. Prematurely, *The Englishwoman's Domestic Magazine* (September 1860) declared:

> the iron reign of the crinoline as some of our gentlemen wags have called it, is undoubtedly but gradually coming to an end . . . at the Sydenham Crystal Palace where perhaps as much of dress in its fashionable mode can be seen as anywhere in these islands, we noticed some leaders of 'ton' entirely destitute of crinoline . . .[5]

Most leaders of 'ton', however, retained their crinolines until well past the middle of the decade. Even *The Englishwoman's Domestic Magazine* was compelled to concede four months later (December 1860) that 'Steel petticoats are still universally worn.'[6] Other fashion journals proved fonder of the crinoline, grudgingly accepting that:

> the crinoline has at least this advantage; it renders the toilette architecturally correct. It gives breadth where it ought to be, at the base of the structure (*Ladies Treasury*, March 1860).[7]

The usual trimming for the wide skirts up to 1860 or 1861 was of a number of flounces. According to *La Belle Assemblée* (August 1860), 'Nothing can be prettier than a robe . . . with flounces festooned with one of the shades in the material . . . .'[8]

Miss Finch's bodice has short pagoda sleeves with white cotton undersleeves beneath. Her hair is centrally parted and drawn into long ringlets at the back.

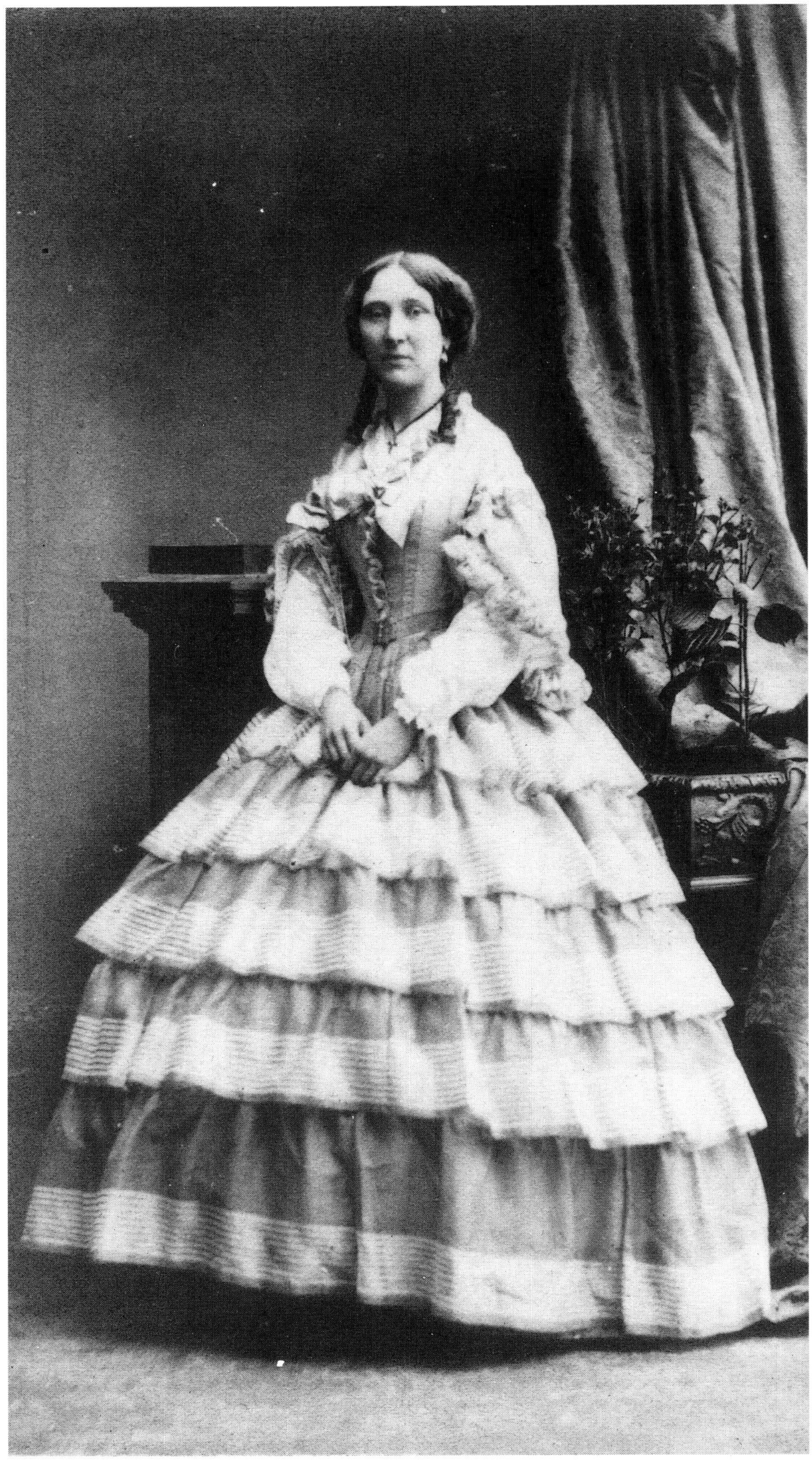

25. Miss Charlotte Finch
1860
Camille Silvy, London (Daybook 1, no. 552)

26

Although white was by no means the norm for all mid-Victorian brides, amongst the wealthy bourgeoisie and gentry (such as who flocked to Silvy's fashionable studio), it was fairly common. Miss Morgan is the first bride, to be photographed by Silvy in London and her dress exhibits most of the usual attributes of wedding outfits of the day.

The body of the skirt is fully trimmed with a deep flounce of lace, with a narrower matching flounce across the bust of the bodice. The voluminous veil is worn pinned to the back of the head as was the fashion in the 1860s, when the fondness for wearing them down over the face had not yet arisen. Lace was usual for veils; Brussels and Honiton being the most costly and prestigious. Valenciennes, Mechlin, and the English point laces were commoner for less wealthy brides.

Miss Morgan's veil is held in place by a wreath of orange blossom, the universal accompaniment to mid-Victorian white weddings. Orange blossom, associated with fertility, first appeared in England during the 1820s and quickly became popular, perhaps as a counterbalance to the virginal attributes of the veil.[9] Brides less elevated on the social ladder wore a best bonnet or hat, which could then be pressed into service for many future Sunday promenades, together with their smart, coloured, wedding dress.

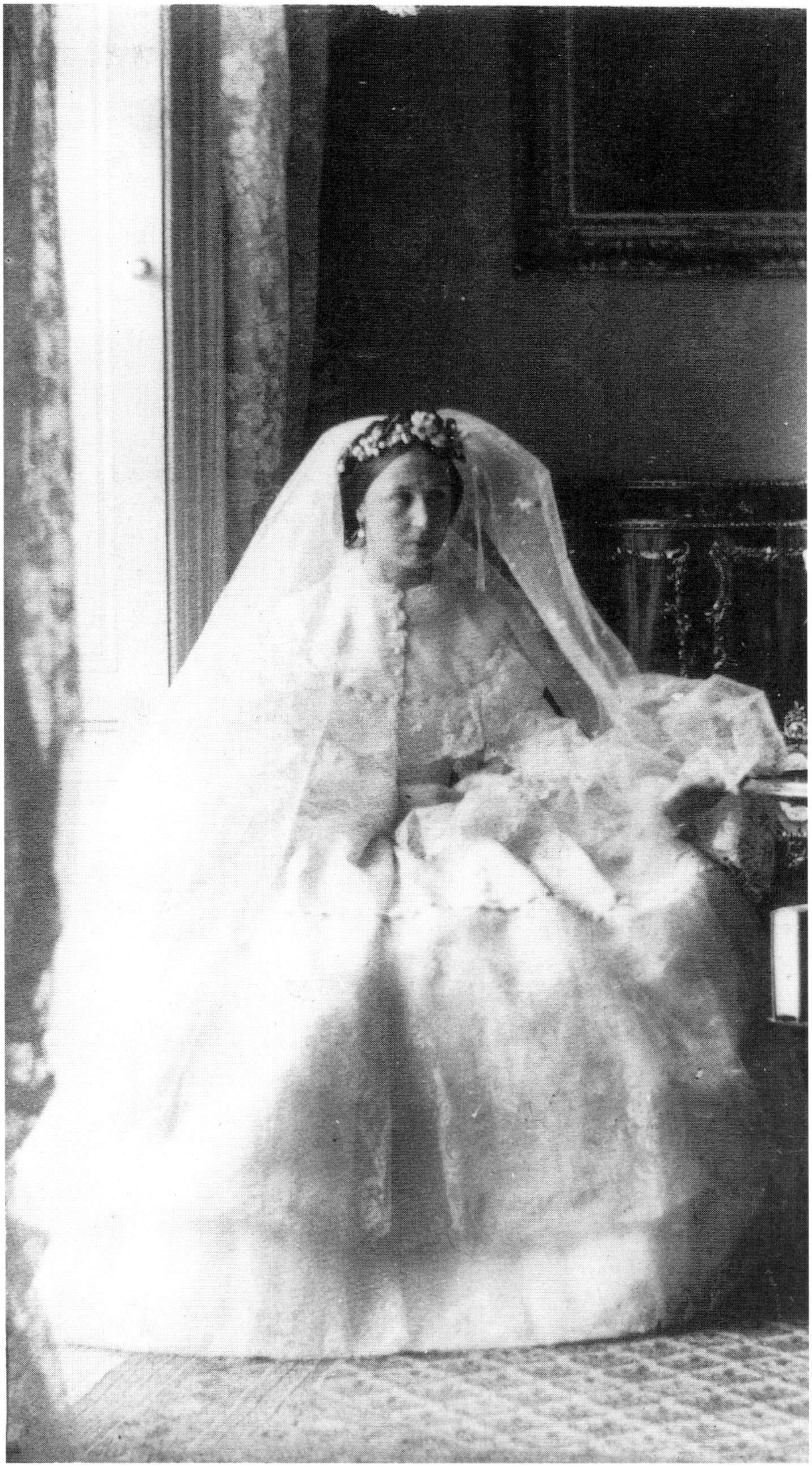

26. Miss Clifford Morgan
1860
Camille Silvy, London (Daybook 1, no. 581)

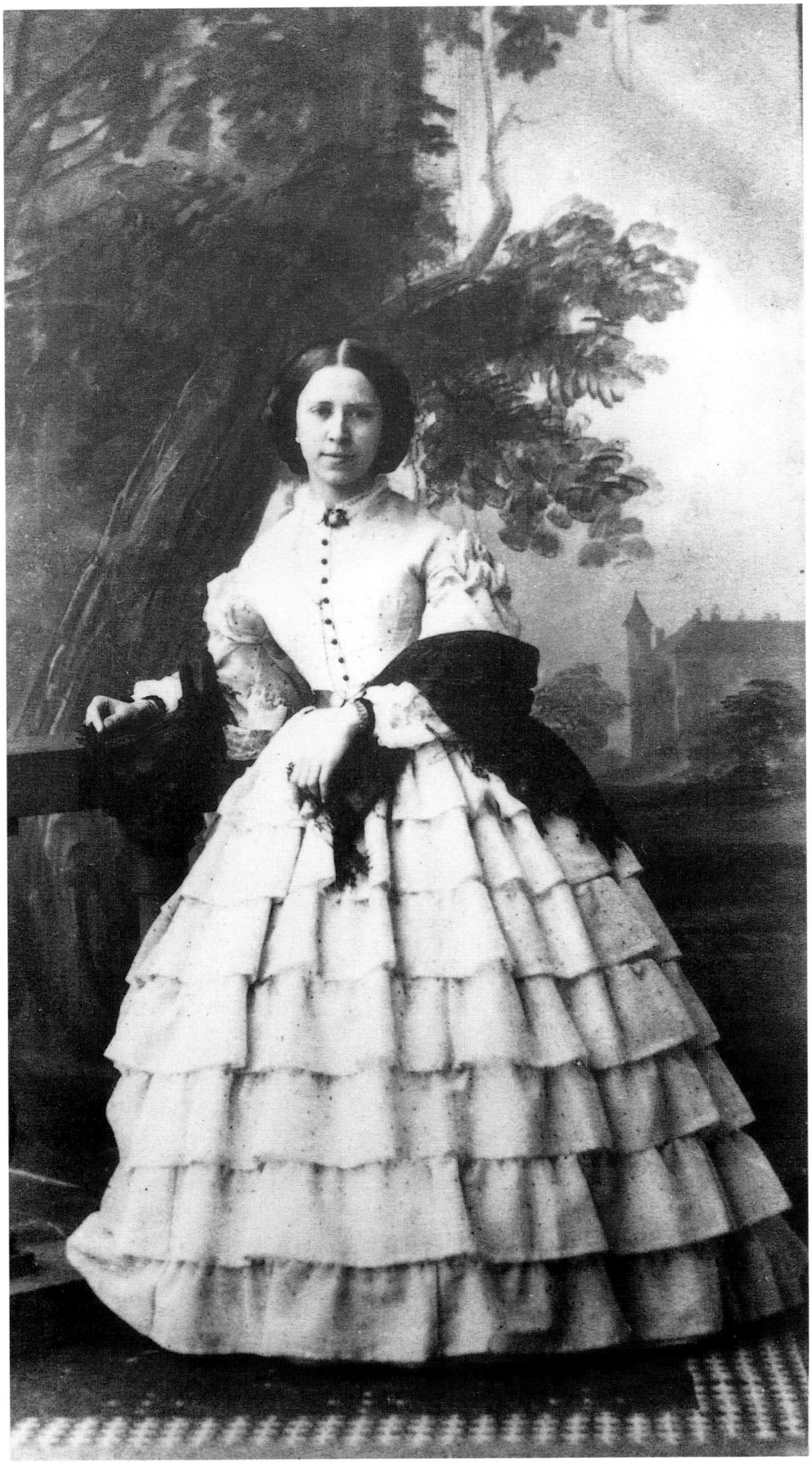

27. Miss Geralupo
1860
Camille Silvy, London (Daybook 1, no. 1138)

27

Miss Geralupo, whose Italian ancestry we can only surmise, leans becomingly on a rustic balustrade before one of Silvy's early, fanciful backdrops.

Her full skirt is supported by her crinoline-petticoat and is decorated with seven broad flounces covering the whole expanse. *The Ladies' Treasury* (October 1860) describes a similar arrangement where 'the flounces may be seven in number reaching to the basque of the jacket . . .'. It goes on to list other possibilities for flounced trimming:

> . . . on skirts, flounces are variously placed; sometimes nine narrow flounces are placed in threes, . . . or the trimming may consist of one deep flounce headed with two or three narrow ones.[10]

The same periodical had shown its great fondness for flounces in the May 1860 issue: 'We are happy to say, flounces have not disappeared. There is hardly any trimming so becoming to the figure as flounces.'[11] Sometimes the dressmaker could be carried away in her delight with flounces: 'We must not forget to mention a grey grenadine dress with sixteen flounces, bound alternately with black and cerise chiné silk . . .', *Englishwoman's Domestic Magazine* (October 1860).[12] Flounced skirts such as these consumed a vast yardage of fabric as *The Ladies' Treasury* (September 1863) related: 'Until lately, flounces went into such extremes that it required twenty or two and twenty yards to make a dress for the wife of a hardworking physician or lawyer . . .'.[13]

Miss Geralupo may seem very subdued by comparison, and indeed, wears a restrained centre-parted hairstyle, and a plain bodice. Her black shawl demonstrates that her ensemble is an outdoor walking outfit.

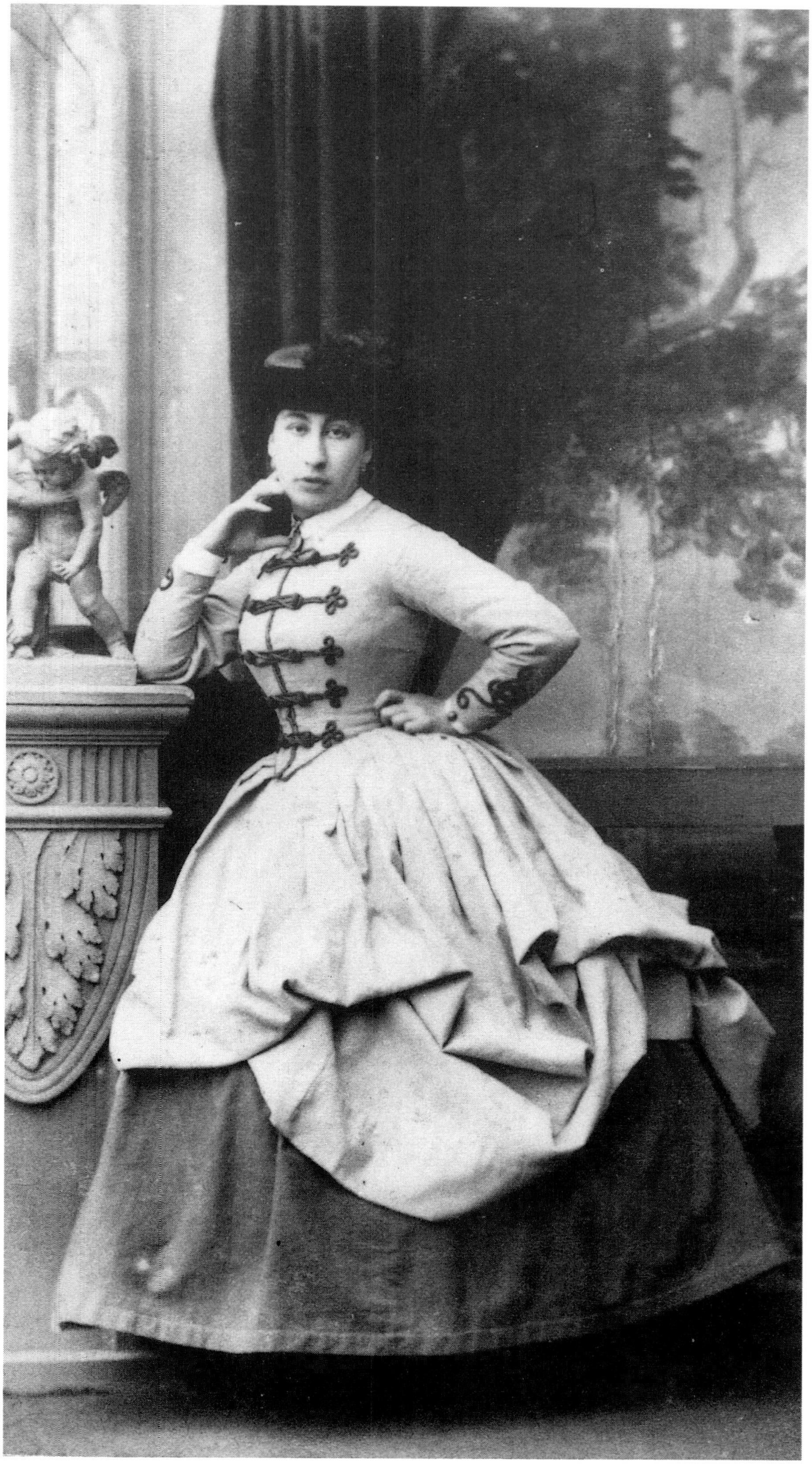

28. Miss Townley
1860
Camille Silvy, London (Daybook 2, no. 1541)

28

Miss Townley rests her arm on a classical column, although the backdrop is contrastingly rustic as though she is poised in some silvan glade. Dressed for walking, her cloth overskirt is looped up *à la polonaise* over a stouter, darker cloth petticoat, protecting it from the dirt and dust of pavement or path.

Her matching cloth bodice is trimmed, military style, with five rows of black-braid frogging with similar serpentine trimming at the cuffs. Her black-velvet 'porkpie' hat sits squarely forward over her forehead, whilst her chignon is securely held in place with a net at the back of her head.

Silvy's sitters are often dressed in very smart day or evening wear and this rather sturdy sitter makes a refreshing change in her fashionable walking dress.

29

This photograph of the 18-year-old Princess Alice serves as an engagement portrait; her betrothal to Prince Louis of Hesse having been announced a few weeks earlier in January 1861. By June, the House of Commons had granted £30,000 for the wedding with an annuity of £6,000 per annum to the Princess. *The World Of Fashion*, in its 'Court and High Life' column, enthused of this popular figure: 'If great talent, majestic spirit and perfect amiability can secure domestic happiness, the married life of the young bride will realize her own fondest expectations.' As in her elder sister's marriage, it was said to be a love-match, and although the groom was a prince, he was only a son of the brother of the Grand Duke of Hesse-Darmstadt.

The period between engagement and nuptials saw the sudden death of the Prince Consort, the bride's father, and consequent prolonged Court mourning. The marriage at Osborne took place in July 1862 in complete privacy with only the Princess's sisters Helena, Louise, and Beatrice, and the uncle and sister of the bridegroom present,.

According to *The World of Fashion*, the 'truly amiable' bride wore a dress of 'crystalline silk with a deep flounce of Honiton guipure lace'.

In this profile portrait, Alice wears a daydress of plain silk trimmed as a border at the hem with appliqué black silk in an inverted vandyking. She carries a woven silk shawl over her left arm; and her naturally wavy hair is drawn back into a chignon.

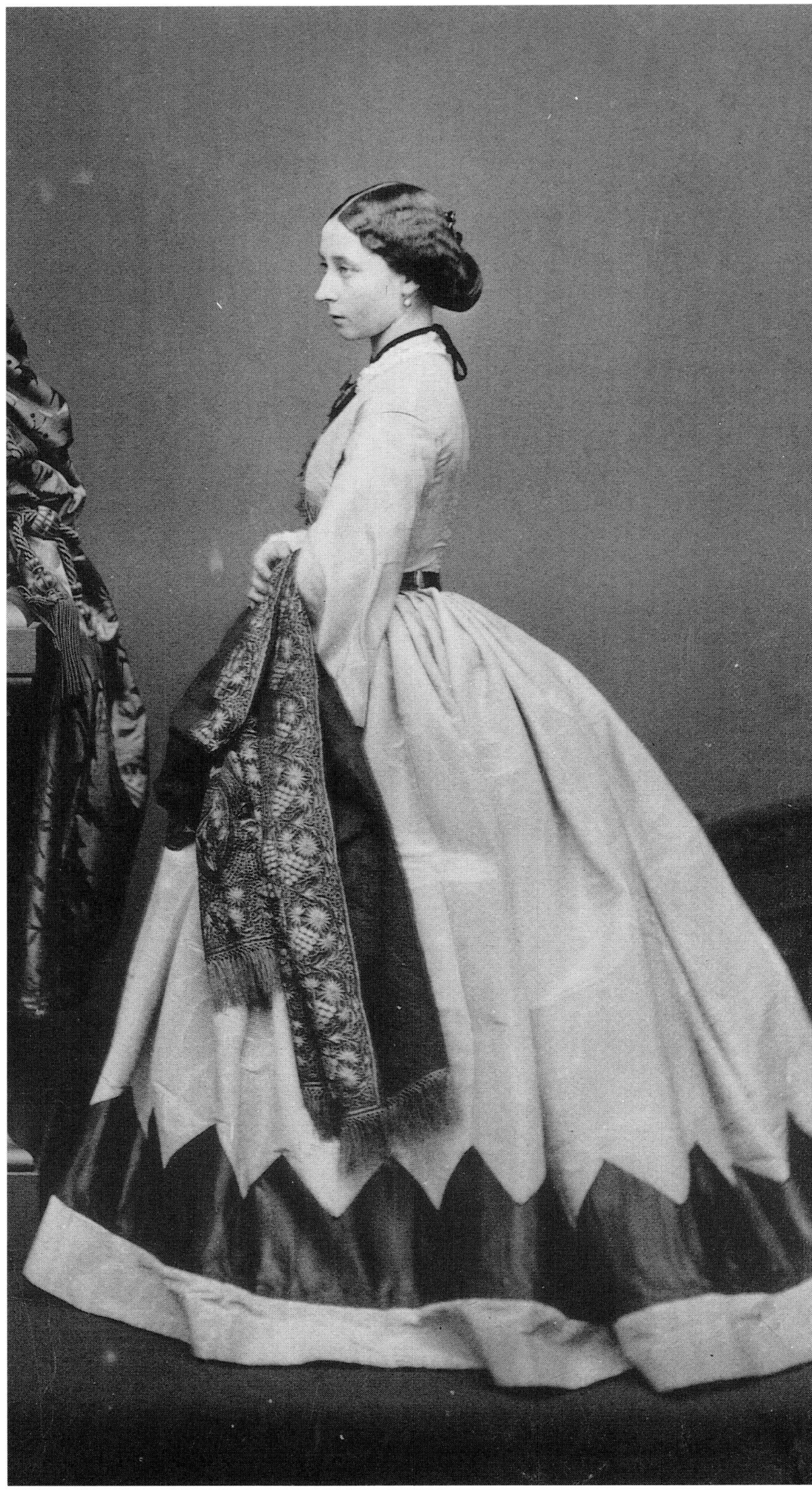

29 Princess Alice
1861
Mayall, London (NPG x 4190)

30

Mrs Benyon is seen here wearing an outdoor walking outfit. Well past the first flush of youth, her rather old-fashioned full bonnet looks back to the previous decade, but otherwise she is dressed conservatively, rather than hopelessly out-of-date.

Over her dark watered-silk dress, only the skirt being visible, she wears a black fur cloak and carries a matching muff. In early 1861 England experienced a severe winter which meant that most women were wearing fur or heavy velvet cloaks. *The World Of Fashion* (February 1861) advised that:

> The severity of the present season renders warm and comfortable cloaks and paletots indispensible for the promenade: velvet sealskin and veloutine or velvet pile are the materials considered the most stylish. Velvet manteaux are made long and full with rich passementeries and black lace – or, which is still more distingué, with fur; light sable being preferred.

The Englishwoman's Domestic Magazine (March 1860) lists a great number of the latest mantles and cloaks, all with very fanciful names: the 'Shanghai', the 'Melazzo' the 'Phoebus', the 'Sultan', the 'Diplomate', the 'Mexican', the 'Titus' etc.

Furs were expensive and generally beyond the means of many women. Jane Welsh Carlyle, in her *Letters* (Vol. 3) writes: 'Lady Sandwich has sent me a sealfur pelisse, a luxury I long sighed for, but costing 20 guineas it had seemed hopeless' (December 1860).

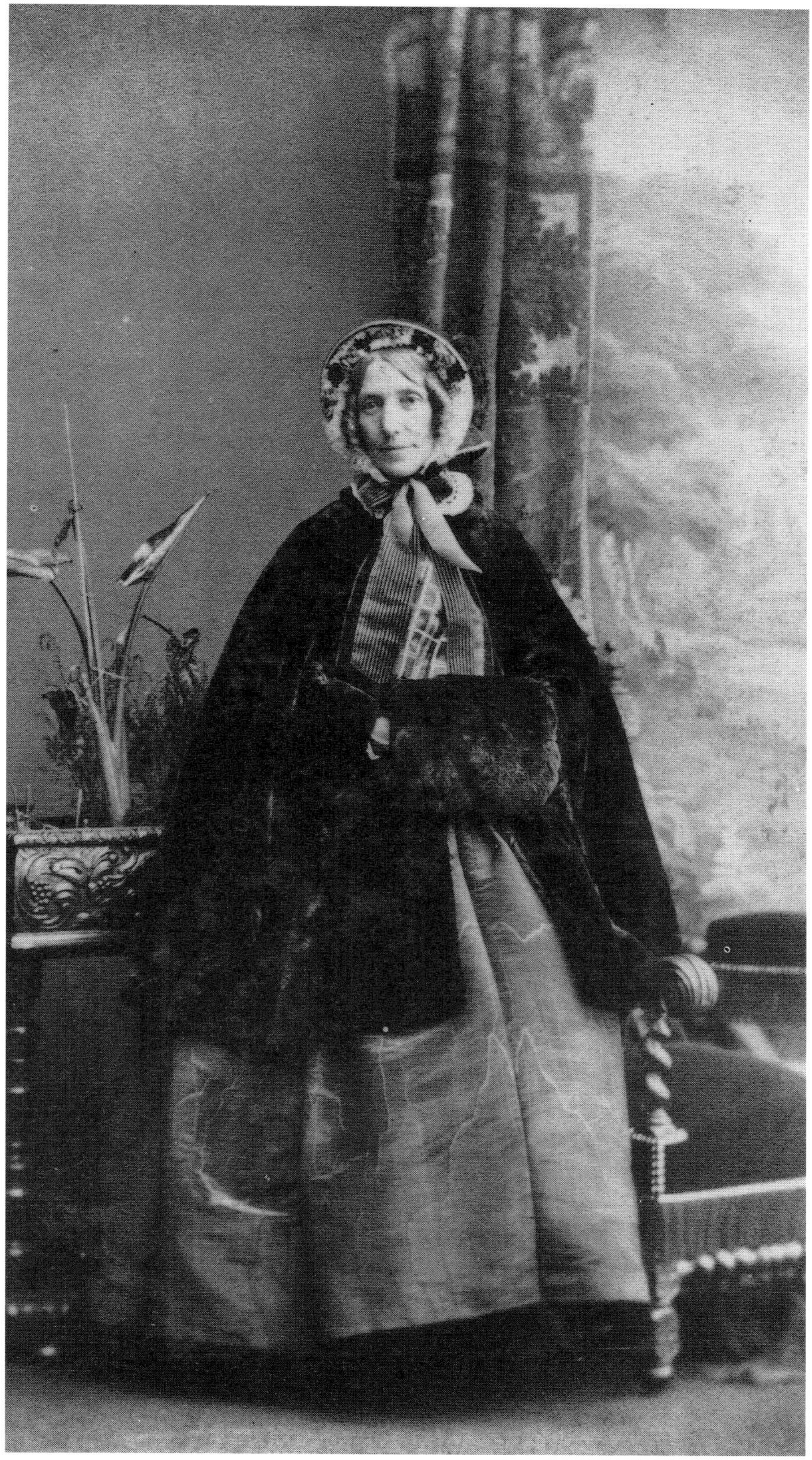

30. Mrs Benyon
1861
Camille Silvy, London (Daybook 2, no. 2406)

31

Mrs Tottenham was the daughter of George Addenbrooke Gore of Co. Kilkenny, and she married Arthur Loftus Tottenham of Glenfarne Hall on 14 June 1859.

The girth of a skirt (such as shown here) supported by a large crinoline was rendered even more massive when a heavy fabric was used. In this portrait, Mrs Tottenham wears a daydress of a stout watered grosgrain silk known as 'moiré antique'. The watering, as in this black silk, was produced by pressing a ribbed fabric in such a way as to flatten part of the ribs and to leave the rest in higher relief. The flattened and unflattened sections then reflected the light differently, providing an irregular, watered effect.[14]

Moiré antiques were popular in the 1860s for all manner of occasions: ball toilettes (ball gowns) or evening gowns as much as walking outfits, and particularly black mourning wear. *The Illustrated London News* includes advertisements from warehouses offering moiré antiques 'in all colours' retailing at about £3 3s od per yard.[15]

Hand colourists working on fashion plates had more difficulty in reproducing the effect of watered silks than with any other fabrics apart from shot silks.

The World Of Fashion reproduces two promenade costumes in November 1862 and January 1863: the first is 'a dress of black moiré antique, the body opening with small revers, and with collar and revers of black velvet'. The second is of 'green moiré velvet, the skirt very long and full, trimmed with rich silk passementerie and two flounces of chantilly lace'.

Mrs Tottenham's dress is very boldly decorated at the front of the bodice and in swags down each side of the skirt with bands of vandyked appliqué white silk.

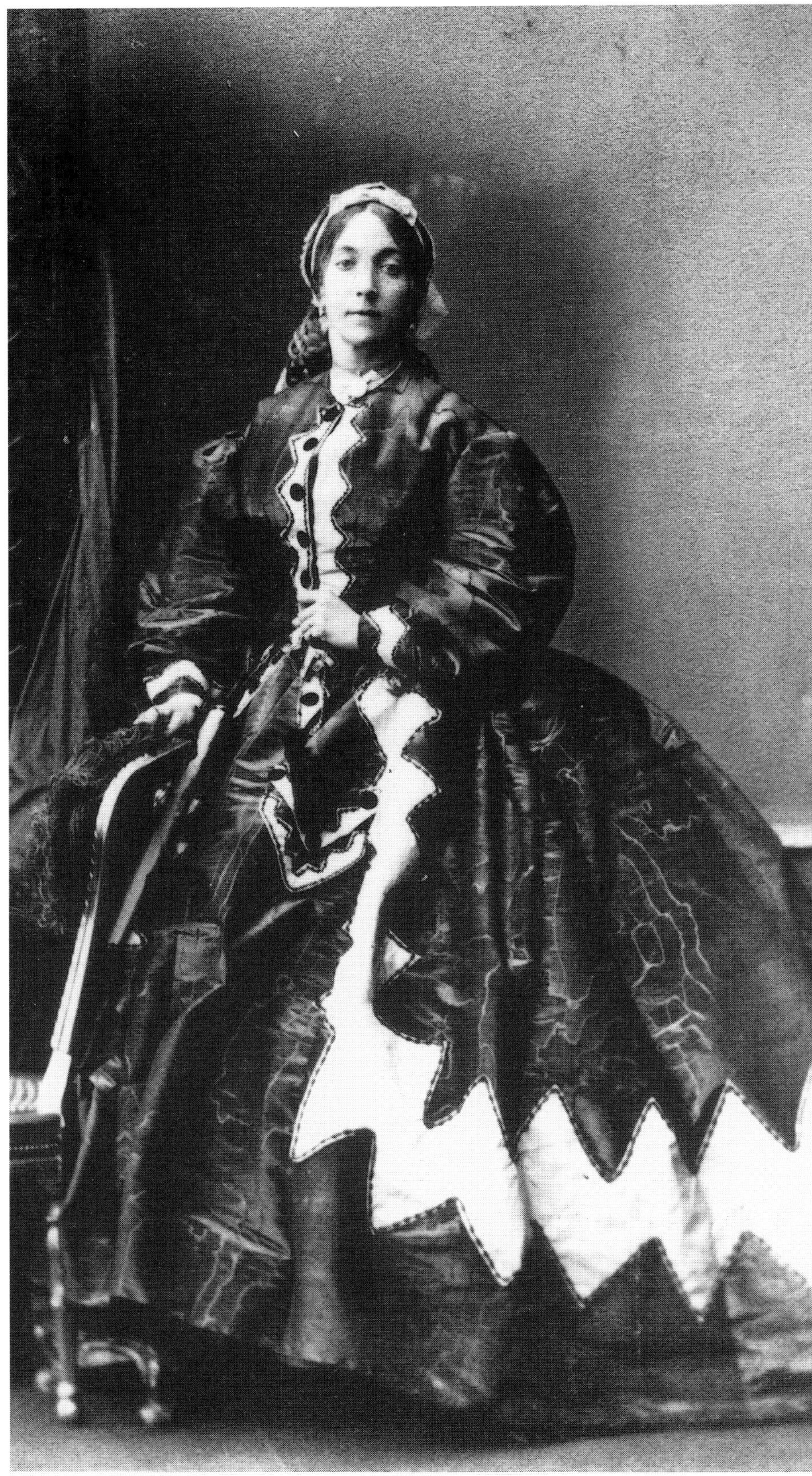

31. Mrs Sarah Tottenham
1861
Camille Silvy, London (Daybook 2, no. 2649)

32, 33

Mrs Duncombe Shafto, née Charlotte Rosa Baring, married Richard Shafto, later MP for North Durham, in 1838. She was the granddaughter of Sir Francis Baring, the 1st Bart.

Silvy often produced prints of more than one pose for his sitters; but rarely did he include views of the back. These two shots of Mrs Shafto provide an unusual all-round picture of a dress, rare in the limited plane of photography. Photographed here in her forties, Mrs Shafto wears a dark, probably black, silk daydress with a voluminous skirt, the fullness pleated into the back waistband. The contrasting tautness of the bodice is seen in the back view, where the creases at the side and shoulder seams demonstrate where the fabric strains at the joins.

During the first years of the 1860s skirts grew to gargantuan proportions, facilitated by larger and larger crinolines. After 1860, flounces became less common as skirts tended to be slightly trained behind. *The Englishwoman's Domestic Magazine* (December 1860) advised:

> Dresses round the bottom of the skirt have rather increased than diminished in size, and those of very handsome materials are usually made plain, that is to say without trimming. . . . Plain deep flounces have almost disappeared.[16]

Wearing a centre parting, Mrs Shafto has conspicuously full and healthy hair, an attribute which would have secured the approbation of contemporary fashion writers such as the journalist in *The Ladies' Treasury* (February 1860) who pronounced that: 'There can be no doubt that luxuriant hair tastefully arranged is the most becoming head-dress'.[17]

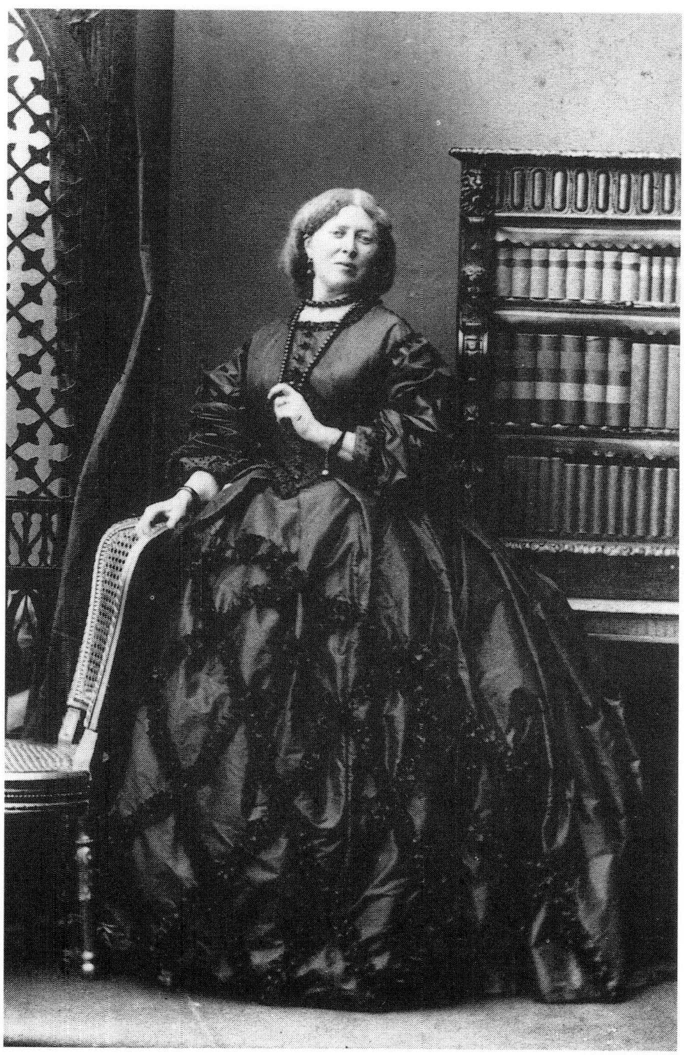

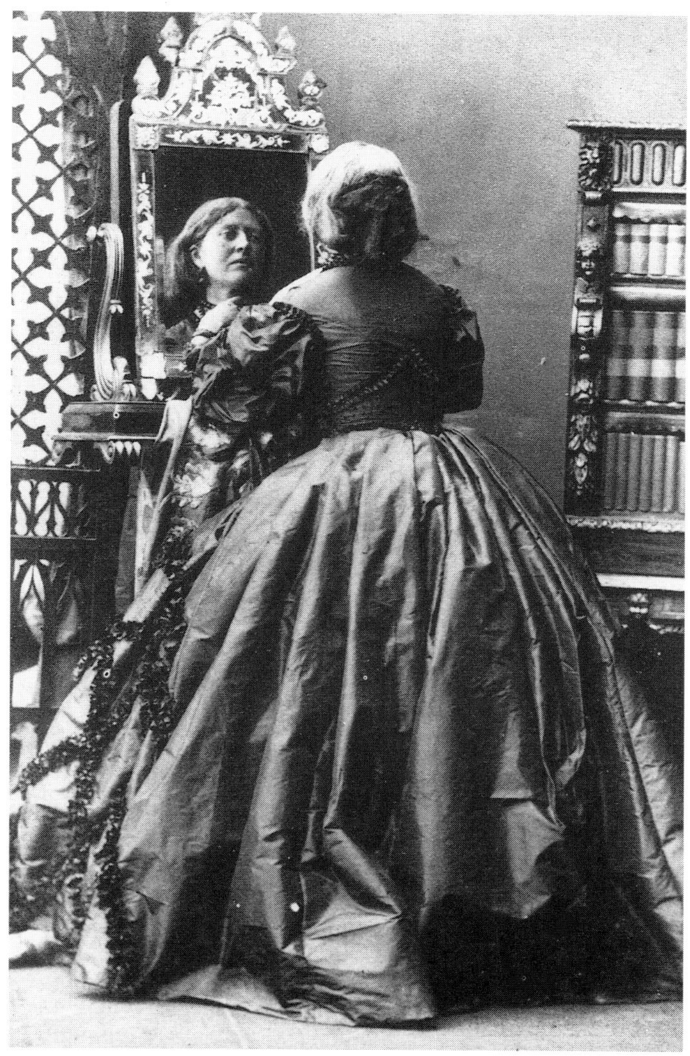

32 & 33. Mrs Duncombe Shafto
1861
Camille Silvy, London (Daybook 2, nos 2665, 2667)

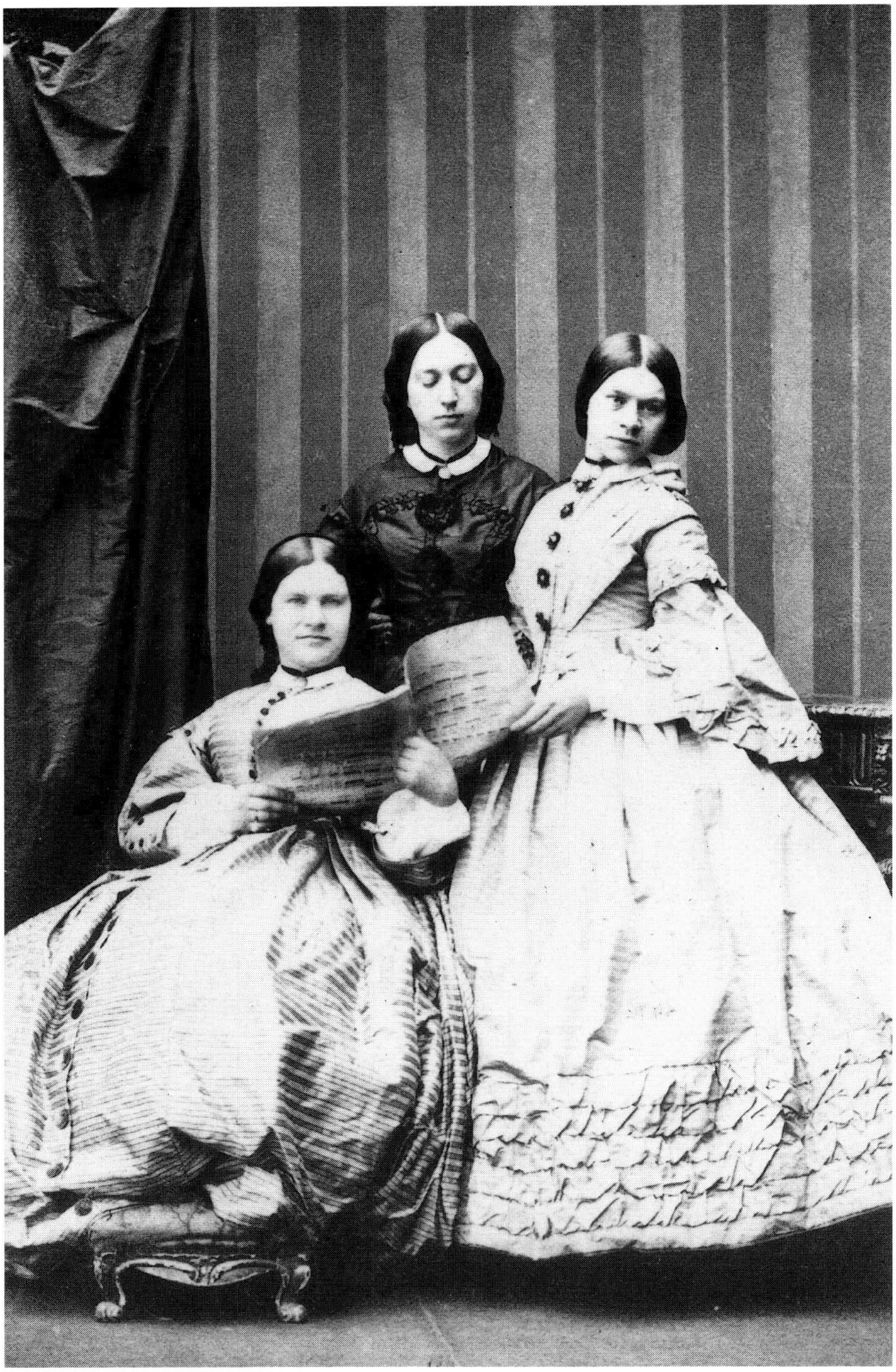

34. The Misses Lambert
1861
Camille Silvy, London (Daybook 4, no. 4220)

34

Poised as if to launch forth into a vocal rendition of some appropriately romantic, Victorian drawing-room ballad, these three sisters pose in their silk daydresses. The narrow horizontal stripes on the front two dresses contrast with the broad vertical striping on the darker wallpaper of the studio. The sisters towards the front of the picture both wear rather conspicuous cage-crinolines, particularly obvious where the seated girl's skirt bunches over the footstool. By 1861, crinolines were virtually universal. Even the Queen had taken to them; the Princess Royal wrote to her mother in July 1858: 'I am indeed not astonished that you wear a cage, what a comfort they are, so cool and light and take no room'.

The Lambert sisters all have similar, centre-parted hairstyles with the fullness of the hair drawn into a single chignon at the nape of the neck.

The general simplicity of the hairstyles appearing in portraits of this time contrasts with the advice given in fashion periodicals which dwelt on elaborate evening coiffures: 'The Marie Antoinette style is with the hair waved in front, rolled back over frisettes, and terminating in the long hair behind falling in two long curls' (*The Ladies' Treasury*, May 1861.)[18]

Certainly, however, for ordinary daywear the majority of women wore their hair as simply as the demure Miss Lamberts.

During the 1860s, for ladies less fortunate than these three sisters, vast quantities of false hair were imported to London to help to bulk out chignons and to ensure that no fashionable young belle seemed without a plentitude of luxuriant tresses. Paris was the centre of this market, exporting about 100 tons of French and Italian hair per annum by 1862.

35

Here aged about ten, the Hon. Miss Smith affects a rather strange pose, with her breakneck-handled parasol leaning at a crazy angle over her shoulder. Parasols of the 1860s were similar to those of the previous decade, with very narrow ivory or wooden shafts of perhaps only three-eighths of an inch in diameter. They were often spiral-turned or chip-carved, and frequently were hinged centrally to facilitate carrying. The shades were made of silk (plain, moiré or *chiné*), printed cotton, or alpaca, and were invariably either fringed, or completely covered with black or white lace, usually Chantilly, Bedford, Honiton or Brussels.

The Englishwoman's Domestic Magazine (June 1862) remarked:

> a little lace trimming may with advantage be introduced on a perfectly plain glacé silk parasol; for instance, a row of broad black Maltese lace laid on

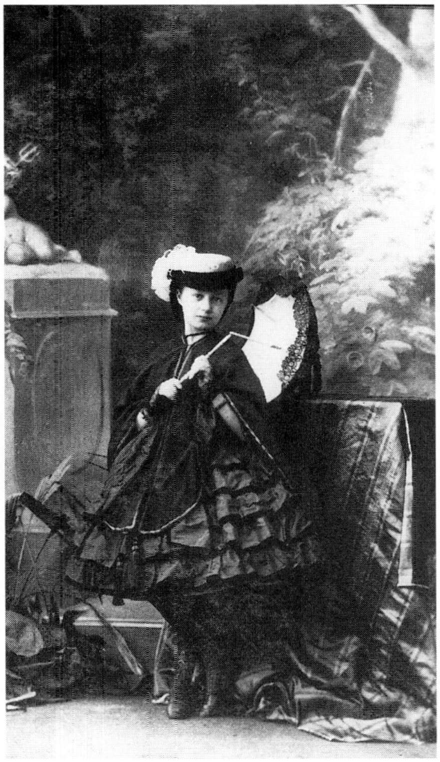

35. The Honourable Rosalind Smith
1861
Camille Silvy, London (Daybook 4, no. 4495)

three inches from the edge and another row of narrower lace placed almost at the top. This ornamentation any lady may arrange for herself and for lighter parasols, somewhat soiled and fanés, this kind of trimming may with a little trouble be put on to completely cover the silk.[19]

A month later in July, the journal declares that: 'nothing is so suitable and distingué as black or white lace made up over a bright coloured or white parasol.'[20]

Miss Smith wears a flounced dress, ending at the knee and showing her black wool stockings and button boots. She has black lace mittens and black mantle or paletot, with a straw hat trimmed with velvet and a white ostrich feather. This is identical to an example for a little girl of eight or nine as illustrated in *The Englishwoman's Domestic Magazine* (May 1860): 'a straw hat with turned up edges trimmed with green velvet. A feather is fastened in the front and falls over the back on the left side'.[21] It also precisely reflects fashionable millinery for women.

36

For summer wear, 1861 saw the widespread introduction of a wide boned belt or corslet which could be worn over a dress, or more commonly, with a blouse or sleeved *chemisette*. These were known as 'corsages suissesses' or 'Bernese waistbands' and Mrs Fitzgerald wears a black-velvet example. *The Englishwoman's Domestic Magazine* (April 1861) explains the novelty: 'Le Corsage Suissesse is a sort of corslet which may be made in silk, velvet or gimp. These bodies are worn over high dresses and reach as far as a low body would.'[22] *The World of Fashion* (August 1863) shows a typical example; made of black velvet like Mrs Fitzgerald's and worn over a pearl-grey silk skirt 'without any trimming' and a 'Garibaldi shirt' in scarlet. Another figure in the same plate wears a black-silk *ceinture* over a coffee-coloured skirt and a spotted-white cashmere Garibaldi.

Mrs Fitzgerald's full skirt is supported by a crinoline and there is a noticeable seam at the centre-front. The fabric is of a crisp, black, silk taffeta woven with a small spotted all-over trefoil motif.

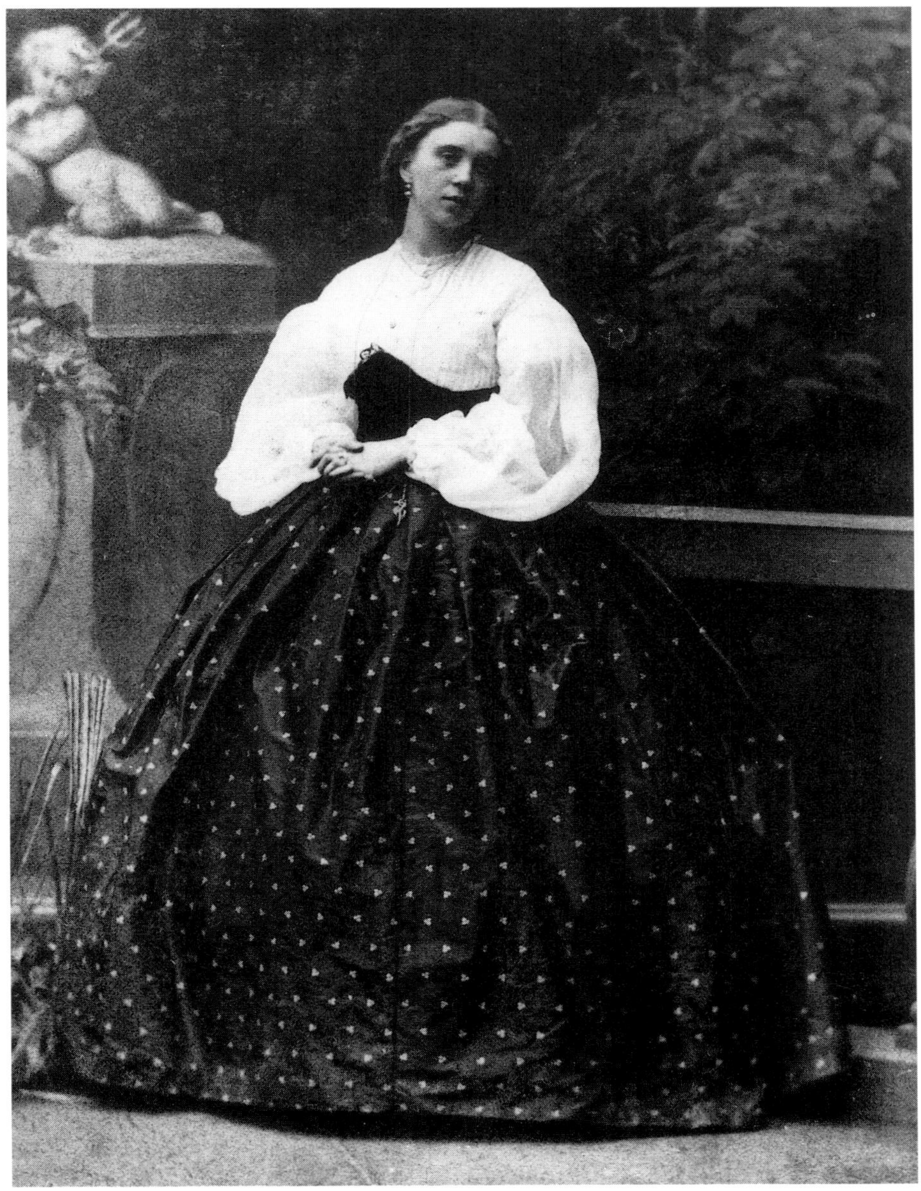

36. Mrs Fitzgerald
1861
Camille Silvy, London (Daybook 4, no. 5147)

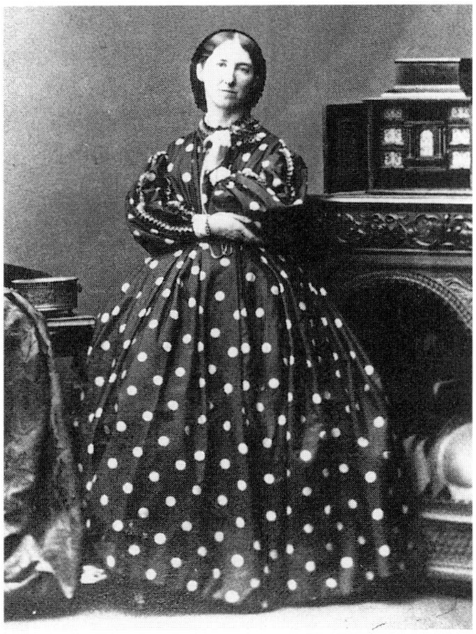

37. Miss Dudin Browne
1861
Camille Silvy, London (Daybook 5, no. 5639)

37

Very dark colours, especially black, contrasted with white, were popular and striking combinations often seen in studio portraits in the early 1860s. They could be used in either a woven or a printed pattern, or else in trimmings of lace, braid or frillings. *The Ladies' Treasury* (January 1861) relates that:

> The mixture of black and white is one of the remarkable fancies of the day. Thus a stylish visiting dress is made as follows – the robe of black taffeta, the skirt trimmed en tablier with five flounces piped with white . . . we do not think this rage for the magpie mixture of white and black is likely to last . . .[23]

The fashion plates rarely show any designs as bold as Miss Browne's or even printed patterns, but fainter sprigged or dotted motifs do appear. *La Belle Assemblée* (January 1863) describes 'a full dress toilet for a young lady . . . of Empress blue Mexico silk, dotted with black . . .'.

Miss Browne's bishop sleeves and diagonal pleating to the centre-front waist are very fashionable for 1861, as is her severe hairstyle with a netted chignon at the back. She stands amidst the clutter and paraphernalia of Silvy's early studio, where fabric and ornate furniture jostle with the sitter for the viewer's attention.

38

A widow, Mrs Bainbridge is in first mourning for her husband and wears a skirt entirely covered with nine deep flounces of black crape or *barège* and a heavy, black lace shawl, worn as a thrown-back veil, exposing her face. So as to avoid the vanity of looking directly at the camera, Silvy has shown his sitter's face only as reflected in a dressing-table mirror glass. Mourning wear was, of course, a poignant and all too common requirement for most Victorian women and fashion magazines included the appropriate advice:

> To those of our readers who require mourning toilets, perhaps the following

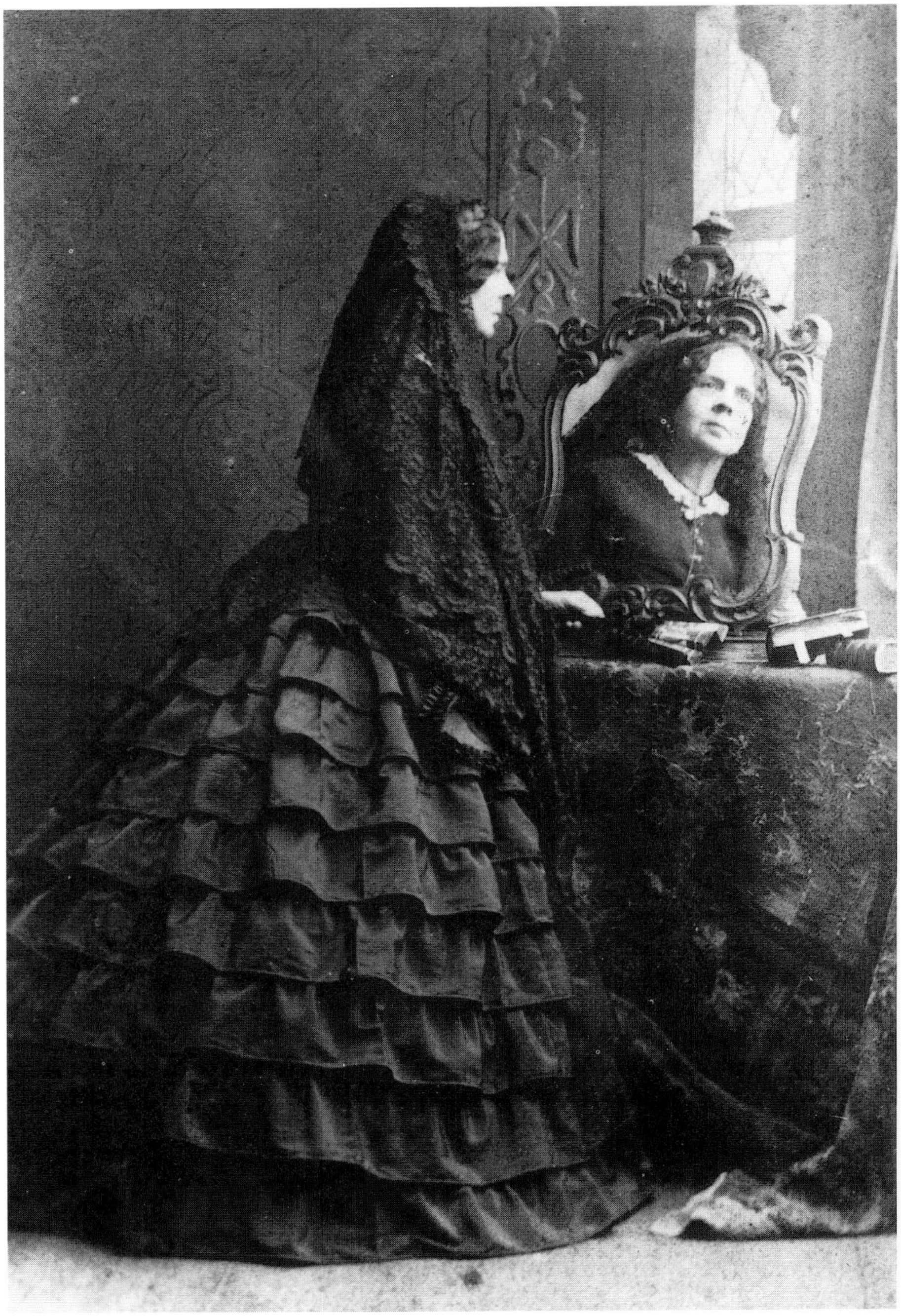

38. Mrs Henry Bainbridge
1861
Camille Silvy, London (Daybook 5, no. 6086)

> suggestions may be useful: a black crinoline bonnet trimmed inside and out with branches of black lilac; with the bonnet, a black barège or grenadine dress with very tiny flounces, and a shawl of the same material. (*The Englishwoman's Domestic Magazine*, May 1861.)[24]

Barège and grenadine were mixtures of silk and wool gauzes, resembling crape and very suitable for full mourning. 'Deep mourning' outfits for 'two young ladies' as related in *The Englishwoman's Domestic Magazine* (July 1861) were of black grenadine with black silk trimming and 'a piece of white tartalane or crepe tacked in round the neck and wristbands'.[25] Mrs Bainbridge wears a similar trimming at her collar and it provides the only relief to her otherwise uniformly black and sombre appearance.

39, 40

Vicky, the eldest child of Queen Victoria and the Prince Consort, was born in 1840. Betrothed at the early age of 14 to the Crown Prince of Prussia, she was married on 25 January 1858, aged 17.

The Crown Princess is shown here in two poses from the same sitting: the single portrait is from the National Portrait Gallery Archive; the view with her two children is from the Gallery of English Costume's collection.

Prince Wilhelm, the future Kaiser, is the elder child, and was born in January 1859 after a very difficult birth during which mother and baby nearly died. As it was, the Prince was left with a withered arm, always carefully concealed in photographs. The Crown Princess holds her second child, Charlotte, who had been born in 1860, and she was already expecting her third child. Four more were to follow.

The Crown Princess is in mourning for her grandmother, the Duchess of Kent, Queen Victoria's mother, who had died in March that year. Within a month she was to be in prolonged mourning for her father, the Prince Consort. Three broad bands of pleated crape trim her skirt, whilst Prince Wilhelm, aged nearly three, wears a black dress, and the baby has a black sash and a white crape bonnet to match her mother's black one.

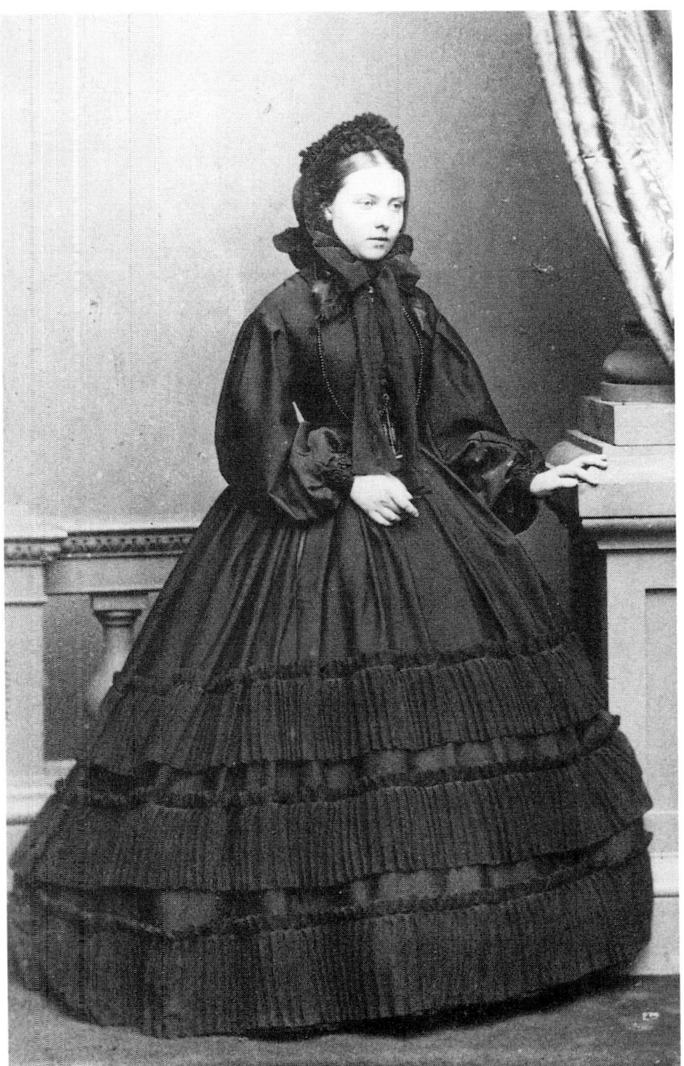

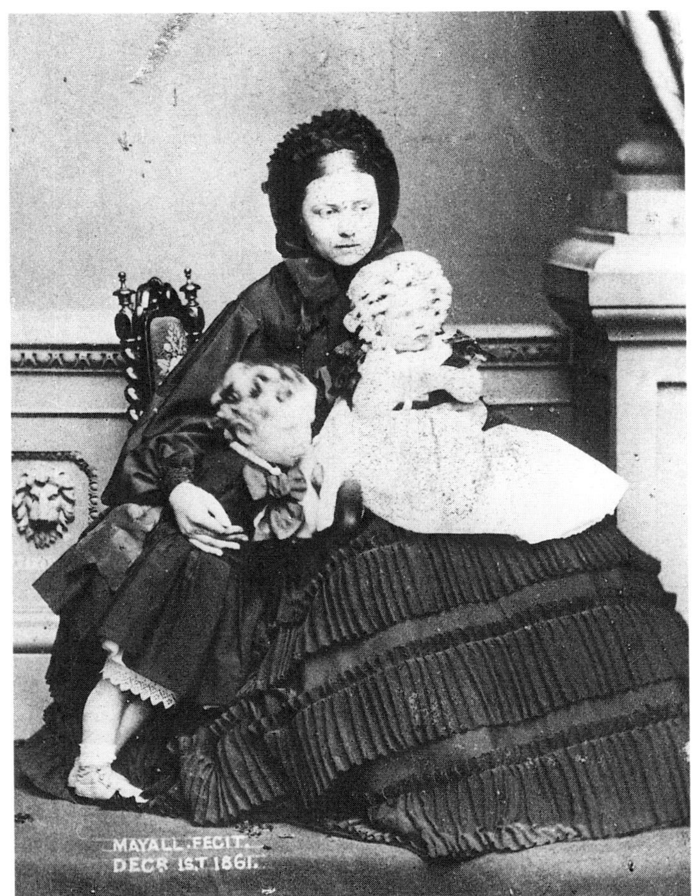

39 & 40. Victoria, Crown Princess of Prussia
1861
Mayall, London (NPG Ax 33506)

41

Perhaps the most celebrated coloratura soprano of the nineteenth century, Adelina Juana Maria Patti was born in 1843 in Madrid, reputedly just after her mother had completed the evening performance of Bellini's *Norma*.

A musical prodigy, Adelina could sing before she could speak, and on being scolded by her mother would apparently reply: 'Dear Mamma, it is so easy to sing, and so difficult to speak'.

Appearing in public as early as 1851, she made her operatic début, aged only 16, as Lucia in Donizetti's *Lucia di Lammermoor*. In May 1861 (the date of this photograph), she made her London début at the Royal Italian Opera in Covent Garden in Bellini's *La Sonnambula*. It was an immediate triumph, elevating her overnight to the status of idol of an adoring public. A contemporary critic went into raptures about her performance:

> during the whole opera, they were spellbound by the magic of her acting, so full of truth, refinement and simplicity; by the charm of her voice, so fresh and lovely . . . and by the most marvellous powers of execution . . . she is in short, a heaven born artist . . .[26]

In this studio carte-de-viste Miss Patti, aged only 18, wears a dark-ground watered silk dress over a medium-sized crinoline. Her hair is in the severe style of the very early 1860s: a centre parting with the body of hair drawn into a chignon at the back. She stands before a suitably grandiose and theatrical backdrop representing some baronial mansion, as perhaps depicted by Donizetti or Rossini.

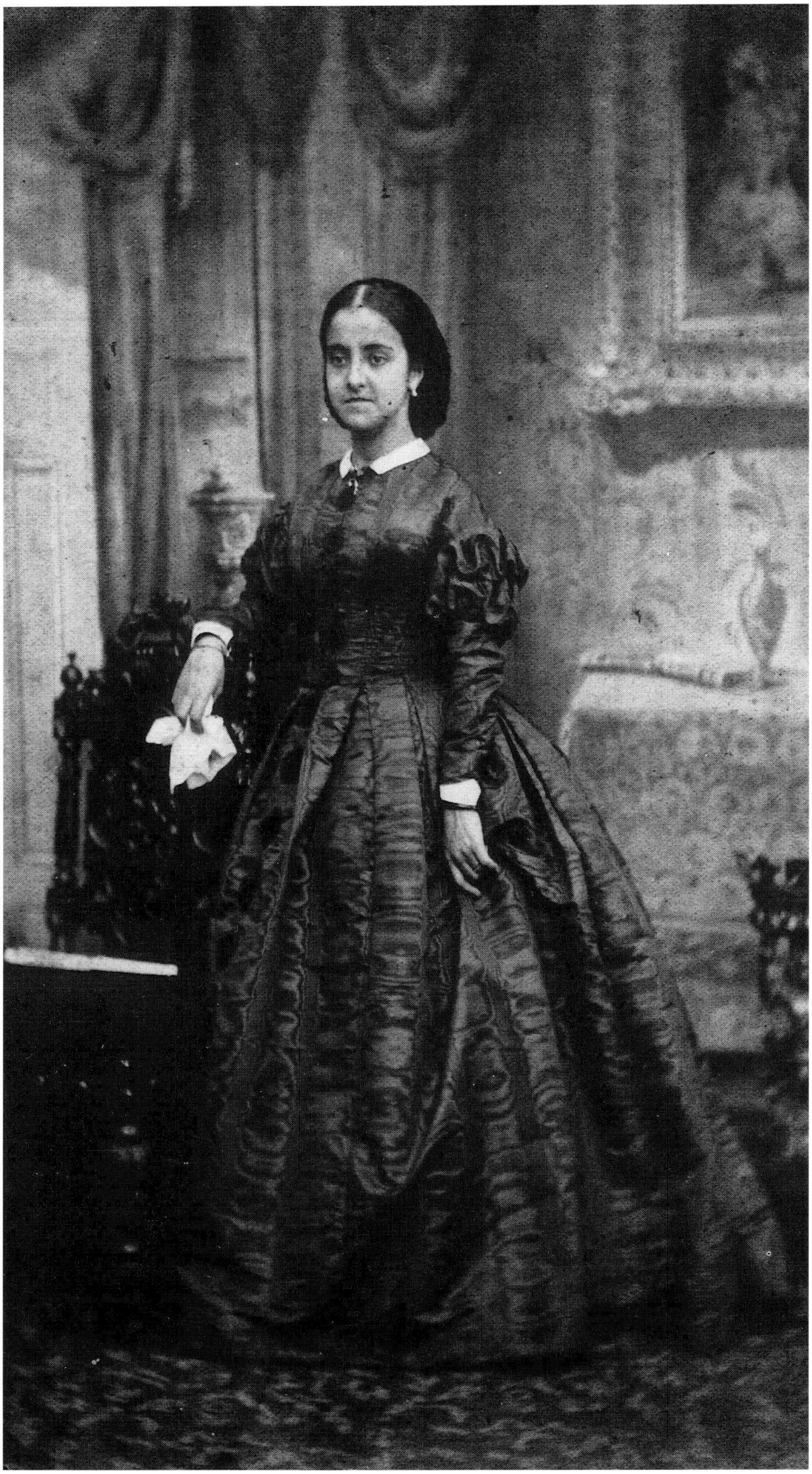

41. Adelina Patti
1861
Adolphe Beau, London (NPG x 31027)

42

In 1815, William Shore inherited the estates of his great-uncle Peter Nightingale, and changed his name in gratitude. A Classical enthusiast, his travels in Italy ensured that his two daughters were called after their Italian birthplaces: Parthenope (the Roman name for Naples, in 1819) and Florence (in 1820).

Despite her privileged background, Florence insisted on training for nursing, travelling to the Kaiserswerth Institut near Düsseldorf, and in 1853 being appointed Superintendent of the Hospital for Invalid Gentlewomen in Upper Harley Street. She was well-placed, therefore, when the Crimean War broke out the following year, to answer the plea from *The Times* correspondent, William Russell, at Scutari. Florence recruited 40 nurses and journeyed to the Crimea, arriving in early 1855. Overcoming obstructiveness, lack of supplies, gross filth and overcrowding, and the overwhelming numbers of injured, she established an efficient hospital and reduced the medical mortalities from 42 in every 100 in February 1855, to 2 in every 100 by June 1855. She remained in the Crimea until the war finished in July 1856.[27]

She subsequently published her 800-page *Notes on Nursing* (1859) in which she includes her comments on dress for women:

> the dress of women is daily unfitting them for any 'mission' or usefulness at all . . . compelled by her dress, every woman now either shuffles or waddles . . . her skirts (and well they do not throw down some piece of furniture) will at least brush against every article in the room if she moves . . . fortunate is she if she does not catch fire . . .[28]

In this photograph of a few years earlier, Florence wears a sensible dark watered-silk daydress, not by any means devoid of fashion, but plain and uncluttered, and clearly not using a crinoline petticoat.

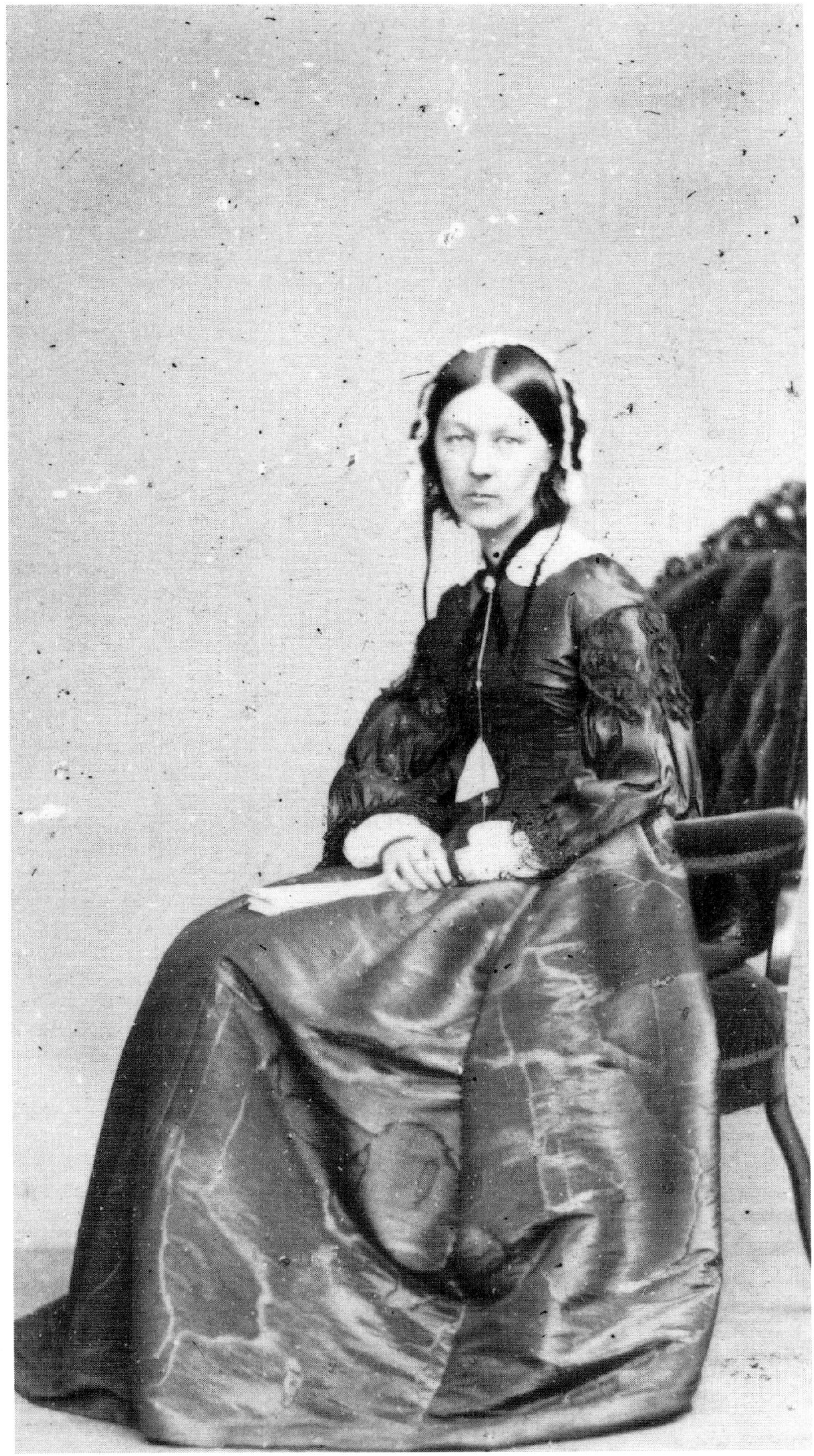

42. Florence Nightingale
1854 (re-photographed as a carte-de-visite *c.* 1861)
W. Kilburn, London (Album 102, no. 30) (NPG Ax 27595)

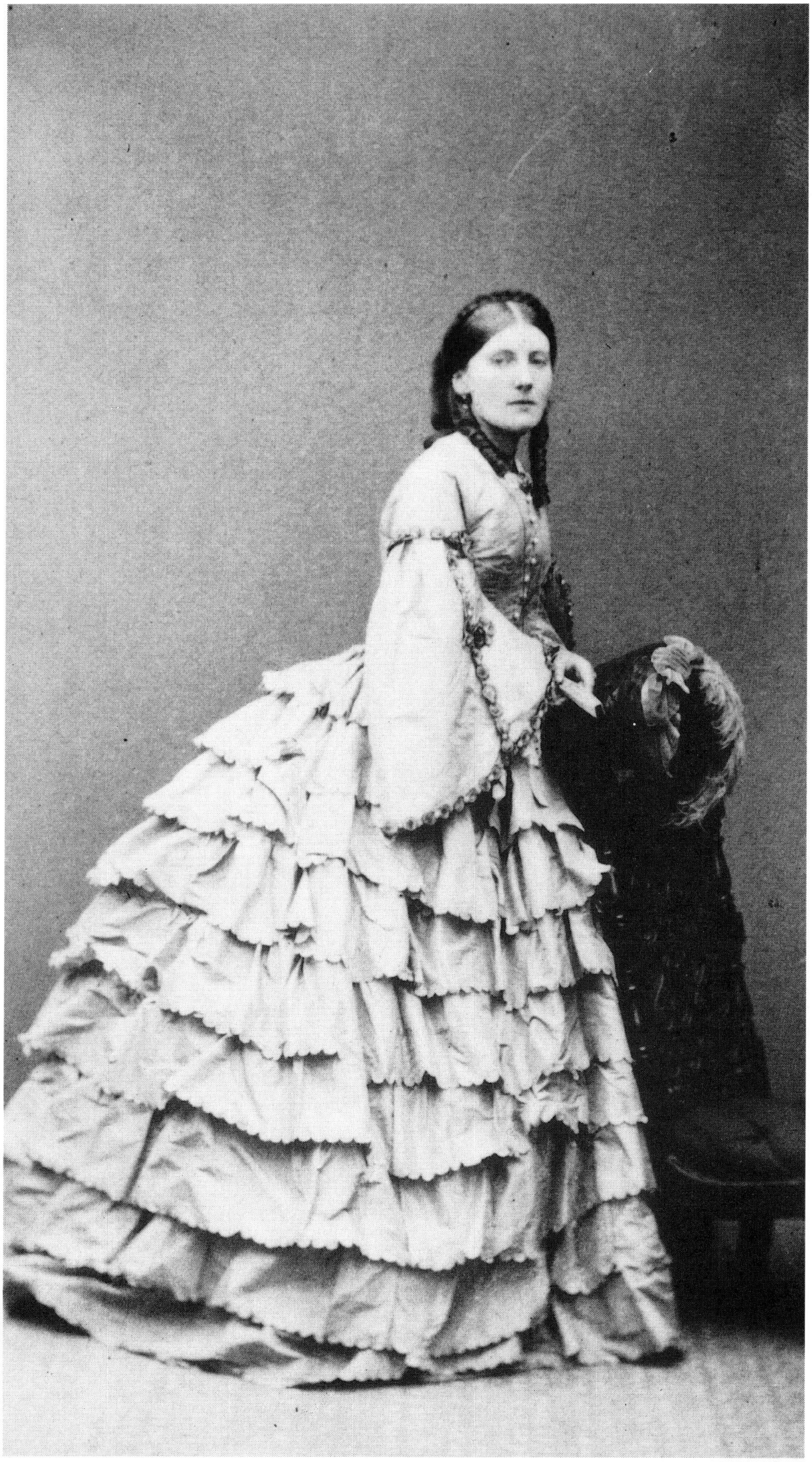

43. Louisa, later Lady, Esmonde
***c.* 1861**
Hennah & Kent, Brighton (Eykyn Album 42, p. 10) (NPG Ax 33507)

43

The daughter of Henry Gratton MP, Louisa married John Esmonde in 1861, about the date of this portrait. Her husband, MP for Waterford from 1852 until his death in 1876, became the 10th Baron Esmonde on the death of his brother Thomas in 1868. Lady Esmonde was to have six children before her early death in 1880.

She wears a pale, silk dress which exemplifies many of the features of fashionable daywear in the very early 1860s: a full, long skirt, trailing slightly on the floor, worn over a crinoline, and trimmed with nine equal self-fabric flounces with pinked, scalloped edges. Above this, there is a tightly fitted bodice with a row of tiny decorative buttons centre-front and very full pagoda sleeves, edged with braid.

Flounces reigned supreme for skirt trimming by 1860, usually applied to cover the whole expanse of the fabric: 'For walking dresses, I notice that flounces have completely dethroned the double skirts: three, five, seven, nine, eleven, even thirteen or more, are worn . . .' (*La Belle Assemblée*, October 1859). This effusive correspondent cannot restrain her enthusiasm when describing a pretty flounced ball toilette: 'Imagine a toilet of tarlatane, white and rose coloured, the shades the daisy carries . . . over the whole skirt, nine coquettishly quilled flounces, alternatively of white and rose . . .'.[29] A 'dinner costume for home' illustrated in *The World of Fashion* (September 1861) shows: 'a dress of India muslin, the skirt with eleven scalloped flounces . . . a canezou of tulle . . . the sleeves of the form pagoda with two bouffants at the top . . .'.

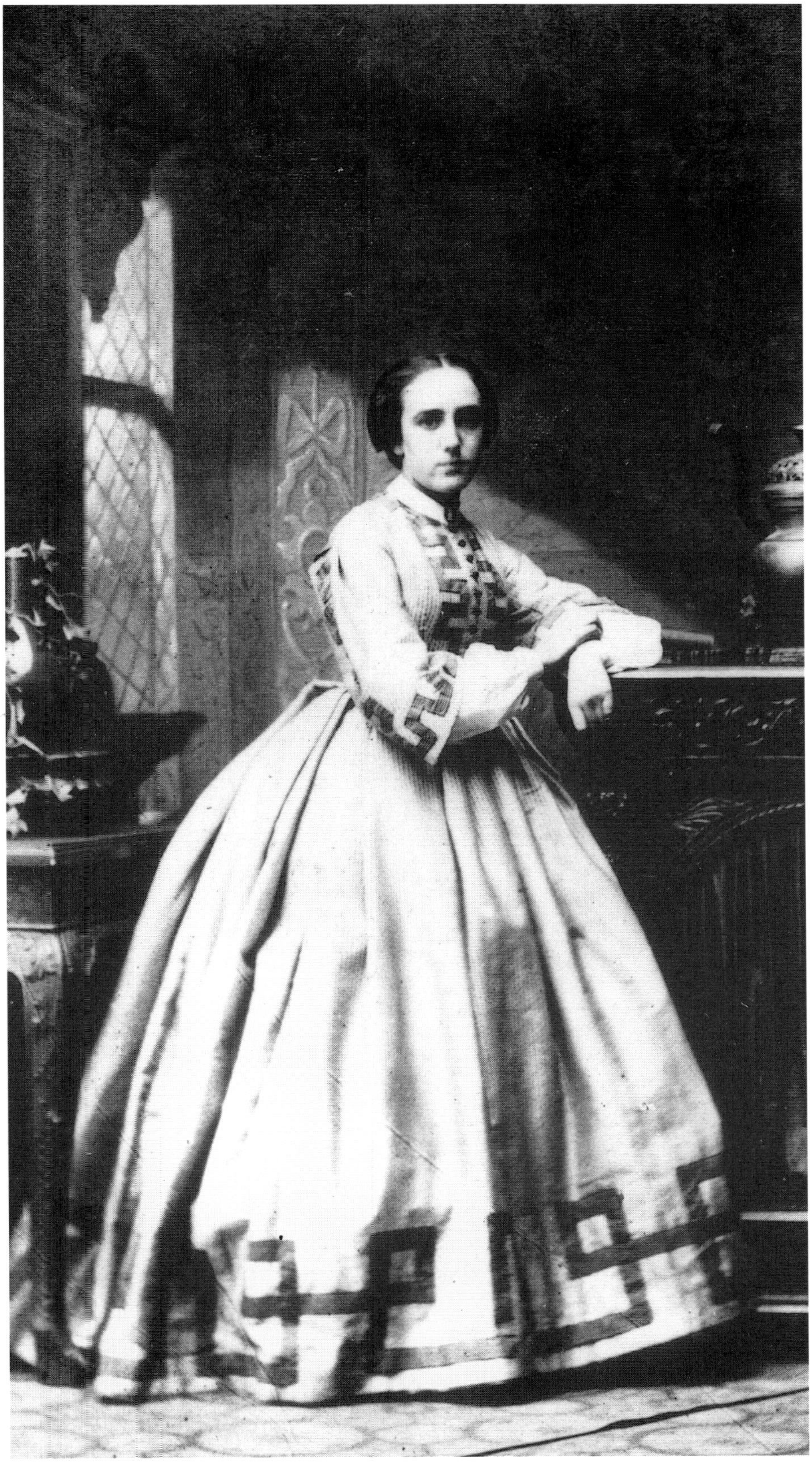

44. Miss De Murreta
1862
Camille Silvy, London (Daybook 6, no. 8161)

44

Miss De Murreta wears a cloth walking dress trimmed, on the front of the bodice, the cuffs, and the skirt hem, with appliqué black-velvet ribbon.

From 1861, flounces used as trimming on skirts grew less popular; they were superseded by a variety of decorative borders used often in striking combinations. The Greek Key pattern, as used on the hem of Miss De Murreta's skirt, was extremely popular until the middle 1860s. *The Ladies' Treasury* (March 1863) called the design Greek or Egyptian: 'The trimmings [on skirts] are generally ruches put on in a variety of designs, the Greeque [*sic*] or key pattern being the most general.'[30] and in August 1863 described 'a ball dress of white tartalane . . . with a transparent jacket of Greek form, having a small Egyptian or Greek key pattern embroidered in gold round it.'[31] *The World Of Fashion* for December 1861, the month of Prince Albert's death, directed that:

> skirts are worn very long and full, the breadths gored towards the top: various styles of trimming are much worn, the Greek border in several rows of narrow velvet is likely to be the most fashionable.

Broad, bold, appliqué trimmings such as these, 'run on in the Greek pattern', were effective for enlivening dull and plain fabrics; and also simple and quick to apply. Their vibrancy made them particularly appropriate for walking and outdoor wear.

45

Mrs Hood wears a striking matching parure in black jet comprising necklace, pendant earrings, bracelet and head ornament. Geometric motifs, as seen in the heavy star-pendants of Mrs Hood's jewellery, were particularly popular in the 1860s whereas simpler, large, bulky designs, as in her bracelet, were common throughout the middle of the nineteenth century.

Probably in half mourning, Mrs Hood wears the only permissible jewellery: jet, probably from Whitby where, by around 1870, nearly 1,500 men and boys were employed to excavate, cut, polish and finish the stone.[32]

Mrs Hood wears an evening dress, not permitted in the first stages of mourning. The black silk is trimmed as a bertha at the neckline with vandyked white lace. Three bands of white lace radiate down the skirt-front from a point at the waist.

A 'ball costume' in *The World Of Fashion* (January 1862) shows a dress of white tartalane trimmed with narrow Honiton lace and similar to Mrs Hood's: 'a low body à pointe, the bertha trimmed with lace and three frills of tartalane . . .'. The ball coiffure is also similar, but instead of jet has: 'a Couronne pompadour of marquesite'.

The tiny residual point to the bodice front is shortly to disappear as the waistline settles higher and eventually becomes completely horizontal.

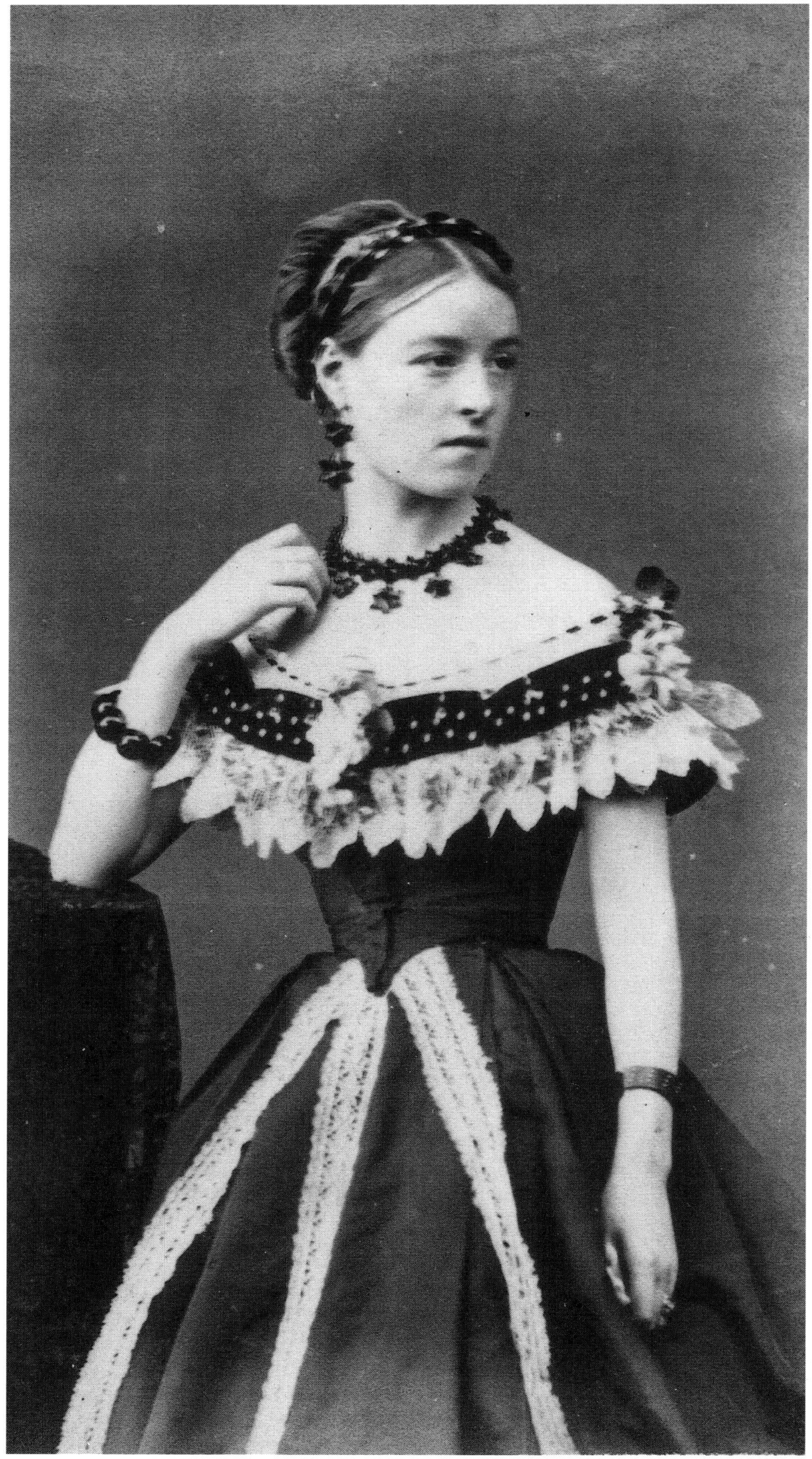

45. Mrs Hood
1862
Camille Silvy, London (Daybook 8, no. 9726)

46

Miss Compton was photographed to record her Court Presentation at the Drawing Room of 6 March 1863, only a week before the wedding of the Prince of Wales at Windsor. As *The Queen* (7 March 1863) relates, because of the death of the Prince Consort, it had been 18 months since the last Drawing Room and 'the sight was almost a novel one, consequently it attracted large crowds of well-dressed people into St. James Park'.

Queen Victoria was represented by her daughters the Princess Royal (visiting from Prussia) and Princess Helena; *The Queen* report continues breathlessly:

> No less than two hundred and fifty ladies were presented to her Royal Highness besides five hundred others who attended the Reception. Many of the Presentations included young ladies whose first introduction into society took place upon that day. These were principally dressed entirely in white: white glacé silk, elaborately trimmed with white tulle; white glacé trains ornamented with white satin ribbon and flowers, such as snowdrops, white azaleas, lilies of the valley, hyacinths, white lilacs, white roses, camelias etc.; white tulle veils and drooping feathers and headdresses and pearl ornaments.[33]

Some young ladies wore pink, blue or 'maize'-coloured dresses but white predominated, as with Miss Compton, whose voluminous dress is coloured only with trailing floral sprays and headdress, and a bold, dark-stone, double-strand necklace Her low, almost horizontal neckline is also threaded with a narrow, dark ribbon, as if to differentiate between the twin snowy whites of fabric and shoulders.

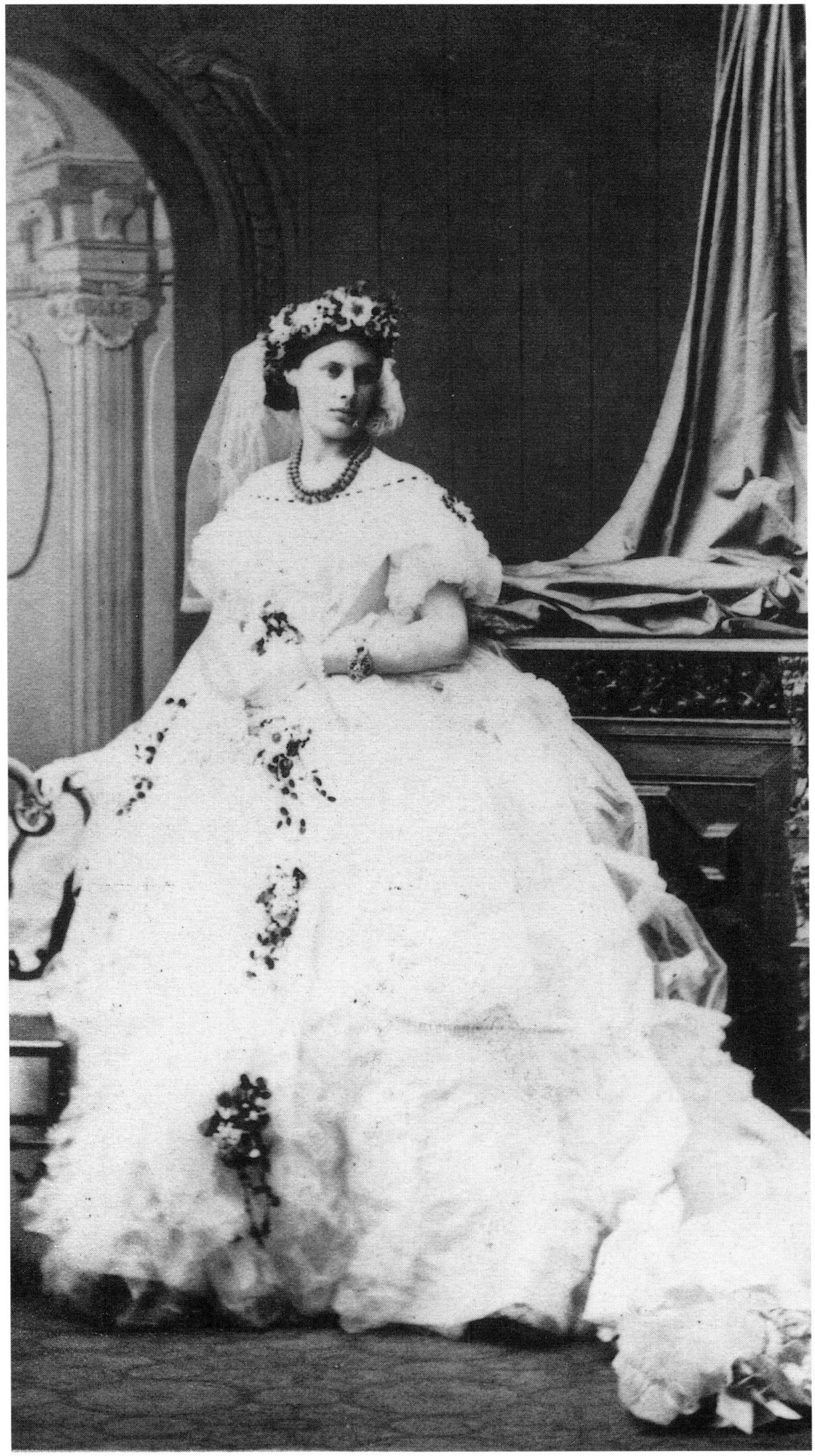

46. Miss Compton
1863
Camille Silvy, London (Daybook 10, no. 12780)

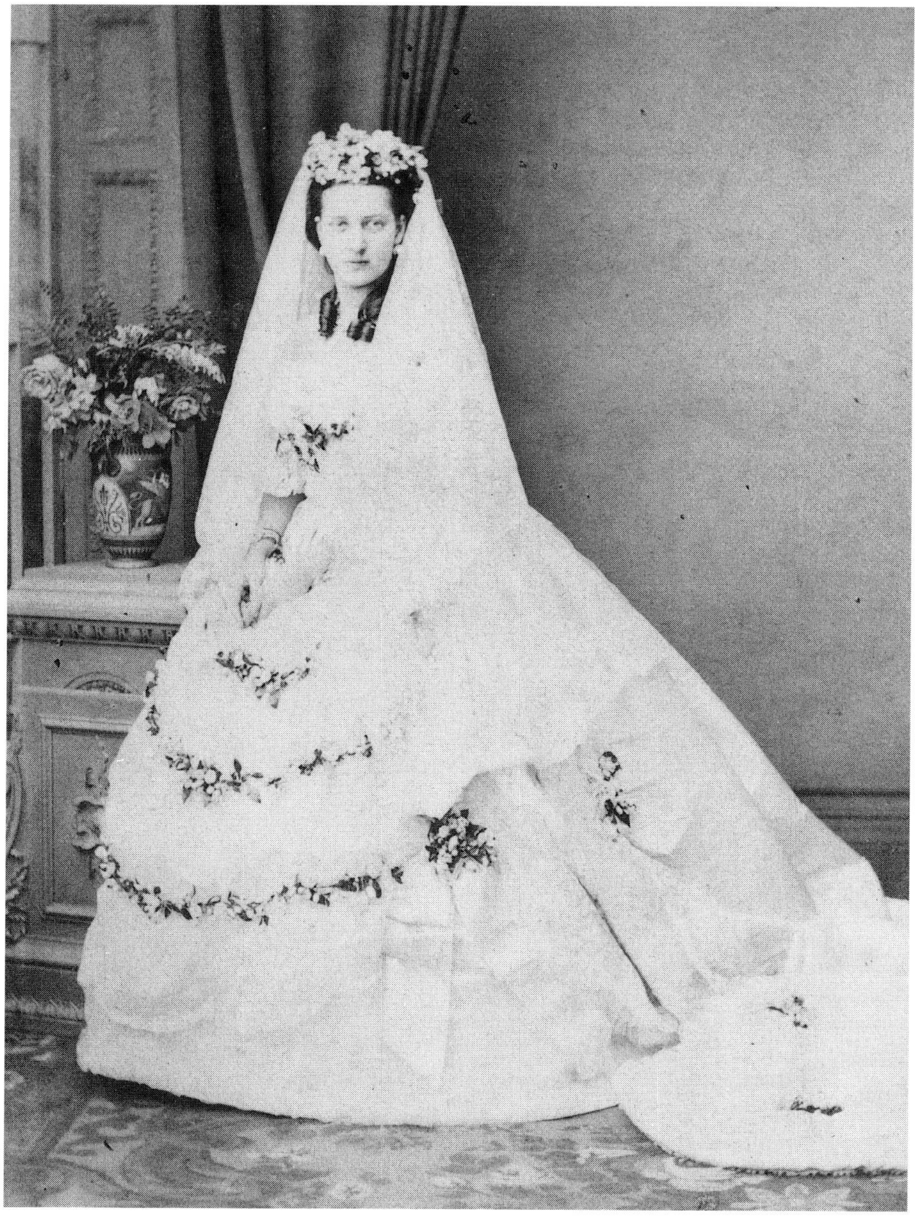

47. Alexandra, Princess of Wales 1863
Mayall, London (NPG x 42028)

47

Princess Alexandra, daughter of Prince Christian IX of Denmark, married the Prince of Wales in St. George's Chapel, Windsor on 10 March 1863, the first royal marriage solemnized there since that of Edward the Black Prince in 1361.

Her dress, photographed here, was of white satin trimmed with bouffants of tulle and Honiton lace. Across the skirt there are four great swagged flounces of Honiton lace, specially designed by a Miss Tucker from Branscombe and including cornucopia filled with thistles, shamrocks, and roses.[34] The bodice and skirt are decked with swags of orange blossom and myrtle, and the train is of silver moiré silk. Her vast Honiton-lace veil is surmounted by a wreath of orange blossom and a diamond coronet given by the bridegroom.

The Princess was also weighed down by an array of jewellery at her wedding: her necklace, earrings and brooch, in pearls and diamonds, were a gift from the bridegroom, who had reputedly spent over £15,000 on jewels as well as £5,000 on the trousseau. Her *rivière* of diamonds, valued at over £10,000 was the gift of the City of London; and her three bracelets of varying opals and diamonds were presented by the Queen, and the ladies of Manchester and Leeds.[35] All this ostentatious wealth was a considerable change for the Princess, who had been raised in the impecunious, if idyllic, Danish court.

A beautiful, tactful, and immediately popular bride for the future King, Alexandra was greeted with ecstasy in London and the provinces on her arrival. She was even rhapsodized by Lord Tennyson:

> Sea-King's daughter as happy as fair,
> Blissful bride of a blissful heir,
> Bride of the heir of the Kings of the
> Sea, . . .'[36]

48

In order of social rank, the bridesmaids can be listed as follows: Lady Victoria Scott, daughter of the 5th Duke of Buccleuch; Lady Diana Beauclerk, daughter of the Duke of St Albans; Lady Georgiana Hamilton, daughter of the Marquis of Abercorn; Lady Elina Bruce, daughter of the 8th Earl of Elgin; Lady Agneta Yorke, daughter of the 4th Earl of Hardwicke; Lady Victoria Howard, daughter of the Earl of Suffolk; Lady Feodora Wellesley, daughter of the 1st Earl Cowley; Lady Eleanor Hare, daughter of the Earl of Listowell.

Dressed to complement the bride, they wore white glacé silk, covered with tulle and gathered at several points with blush roses, shamrock and heather; and wreaths to match. They were not, of course, selected for their beauty; a point not lost on some contemporary observers:

> The bridesmaids looked well in their uniform dresses when their backs were turned; they were hideous when in full view, excepting Lady Di Beauclerk who looked as if she had just stepped off the stage of the opera.

Thus wrote the decidedly ungallant Lord Granville to the Duchess of

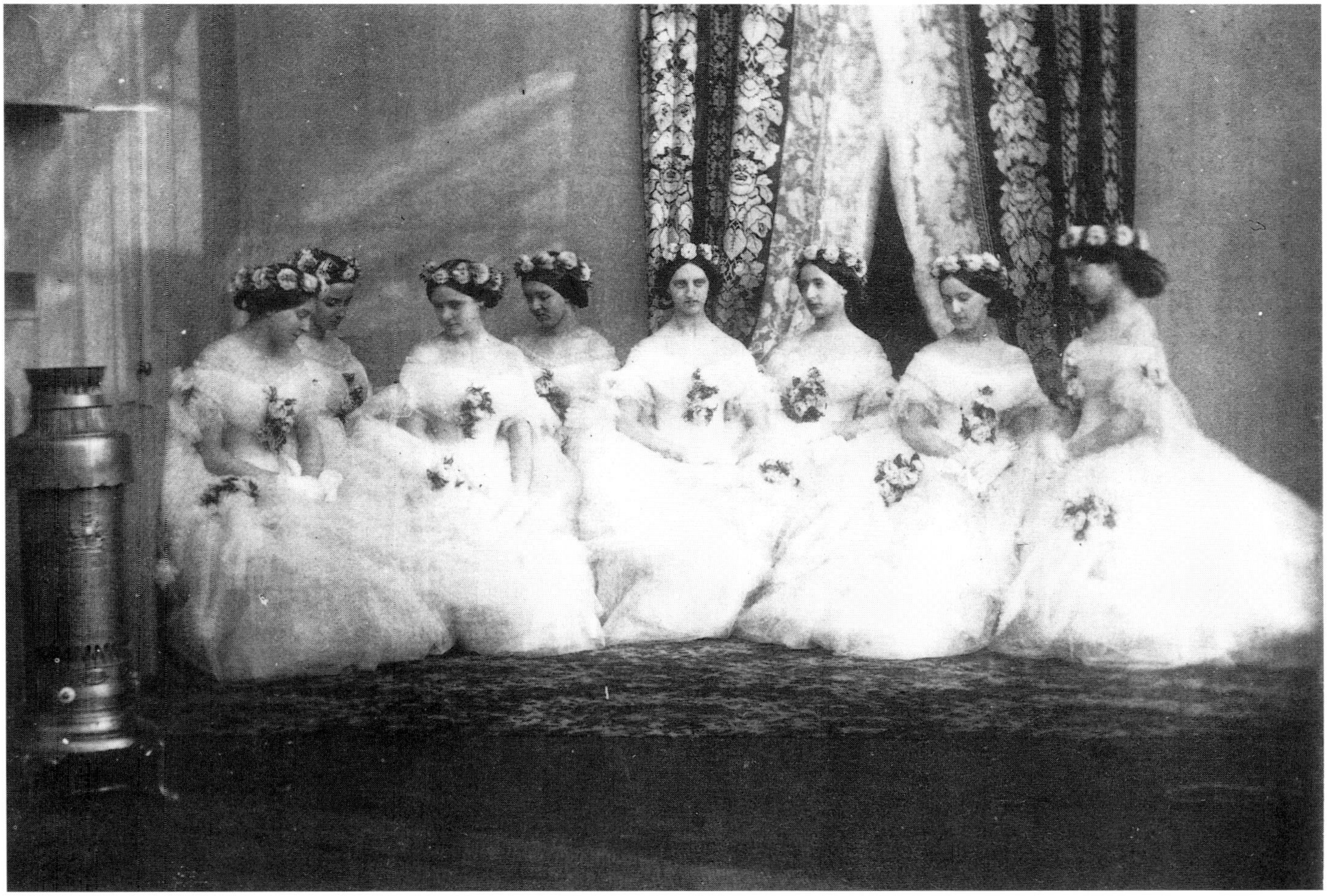

48. The eight bridesmaids of the Princess of Wales
1863
Photographer unknown (NPG x 33255)

Manchester.[37]

Multiple bridesmaids were common for aristocratic brides by the mid-nineteenth century, although often not dressed in white.

This photograph shows the bridesmaids before a draped window, with a prosaic paraffin heater to the extreme left, demonstrating how the room was warmed, and subsequently to be trimmed from the print.

49

Miss Lehmann, later Mrs Barry Pain, was the daughter of Rudolph Lehmann. She stands attentively watching her young charge perched on an early push-chair or perambulator. The first modern perambulator was produced in New York by Charles Burton in 1848, and baby carriages caught on in England after Queen Victoria ordered one. The early models were all for seated infants or toddlers; the first model for a prone baby did not appear until 1870.[38]

The little girl with Miss Lehmann holds her doll, dressed in broderie anglaise finery, and herself wears a typical tartan dress tied at the waist with a tartan silk sash. Scottish influence in children's wear became popular in the 1840s and 1850s, particularly after the Royal purchase of Balmoral, and it could not have been more widespread in the 1860s. Full Highland dress, including kilt, was worn by boys; for instance by the four young brothers of the Princess Royal at her wedding in 1858.

Tartan or plaid dresses were worn commonly by girls, often with matching sashes. Tartan sashes for partywear were all the rage, with any sort of fabric, including the perennial white piqué.

Miss Lehmann's costume consists of a light-coloured cloth paletot or burnouse over a dark skirt, probably of alpaca. Her very large crinoline supports her skirt a good six inches above the floor and pushes outwards and upwards at the back to compensate for the pressure at the front where she leans against the perambulator.

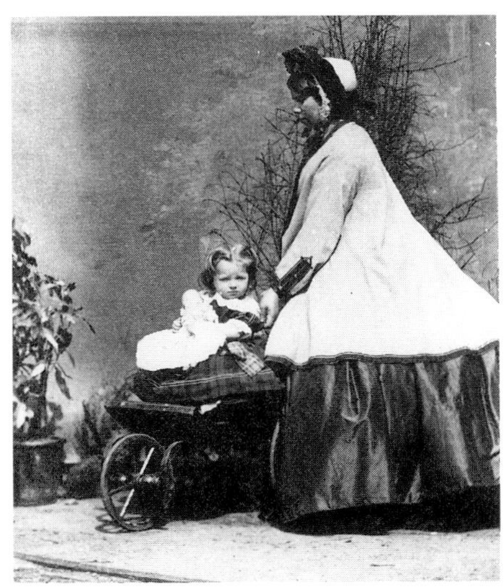

49. Miss Nina Lehmann
1863
Camille Silvy, London (Daybook 10, no. 13065)

50

Catherine Frances Drummond, the wife of Admiral the Honourable Sir James Drummond, stands prepared for a walk. Her dark alpaca or mohair dress is trimmed only with a band of black velvet across the bust and at the wide open sleeves. The narrow width of the fabric can be seen easily between the two vertical seams on the skirt-front. Lady Drummond carries a straw-chip hat and wears a lightweight woollen shawl.

Wools, ornamented with braid or bands of silk or velvet trimming, were usual materials for walking or 'country' outfits in the 1860s:

> For country toilets, the stuffs most in vogue are foulard, alpaca or mohair. With these fibres, it is marvellous what coquettish toilets are created, which preserve at the same time an exquisite simplicity. I have seen a very pretty robe of mohair ornamented at the bottom of the skirt by an undulation formed by three bias pieces of Mexican blue silk . . . (*La Belle Assemblée*, September 1863).[39]

Lady Drummond's dress veers decidedly more towards simplicity than to coquettish tastes, but it is nonetheless fully in fashion.

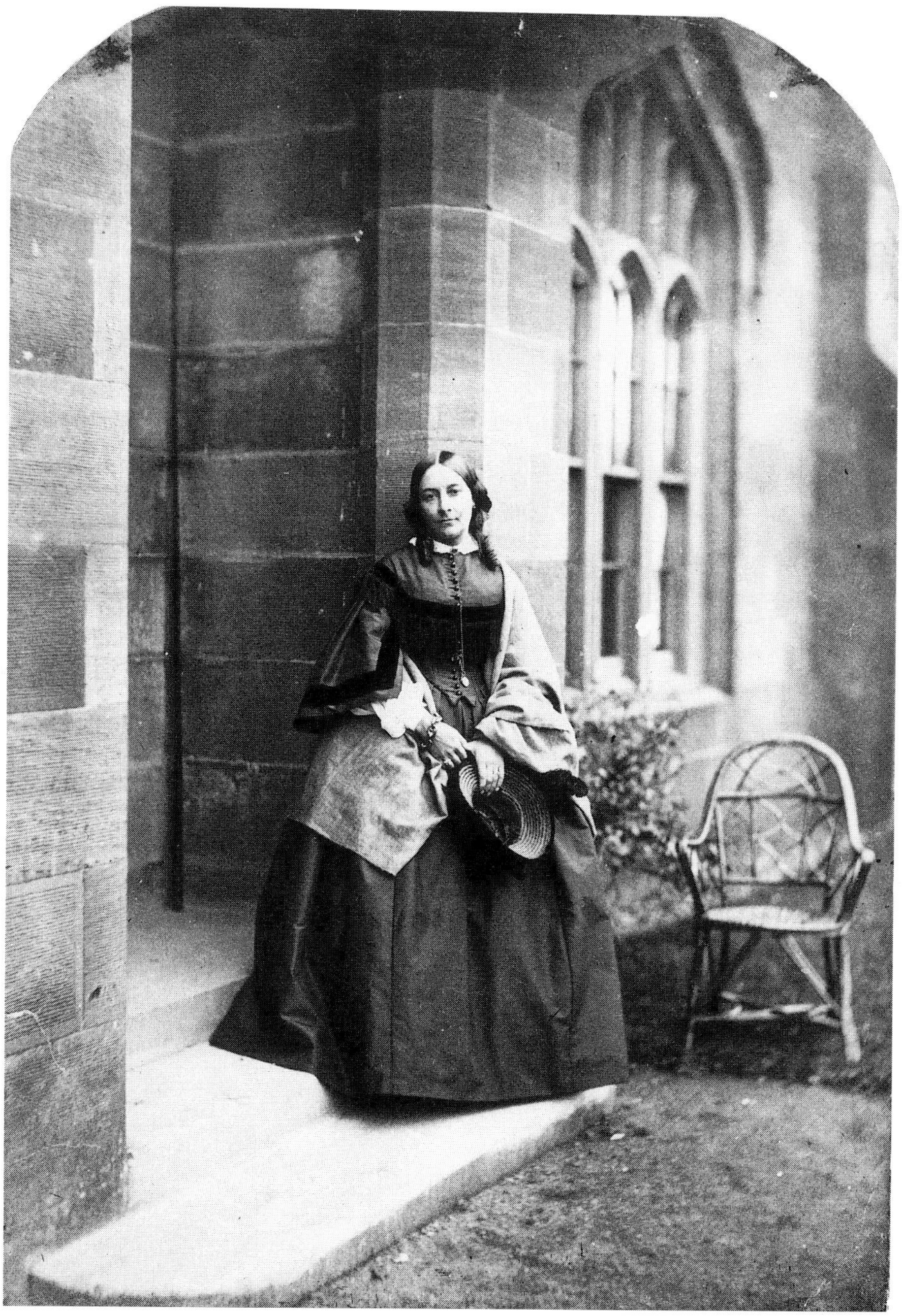

50. Lady Catherine Drummond
Early 1860s
Photographer unknown (Jocelyn Album (59) p. 36) (NPG Ax 33527)

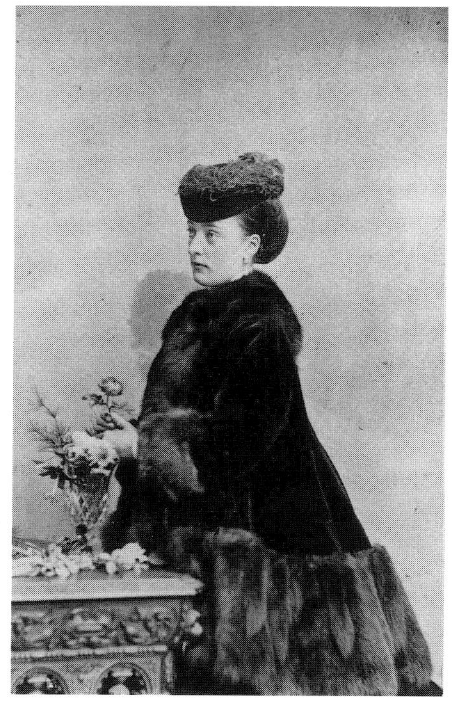

51. Frances, Lady Hastings
Early 1860s
Lambert Weston and Son (NPG x 32947)

51

Born in 1829, the daughter of the 1st Viscount Canterbury, the Honourable Frances is here aged in her mid thirties. She had married Delaval Loftus, the vicar of East Barsham, in 1848 and he inherited the Barony of Hastings in 1871, only a year before his death. Lady Hastings had two sons, born in the 1850s, before her premature death in 1874, aged 44.

The Honourable Frances Hastings, pictured here in the early 1860s, wears a black velvet mantle, profusely trimmed with broad bands of fur at the hem, collar, cuffs, and fronts. Her hair is dressed into a netted chignon with a 'porkpie' hat tipped forward at the front and decorated with a curled ostrich feather. Velvet and fur were, of course, perennials for winter coats and mantles and seemed to be particularly popular in combination in the mid 1860s: 'For out of doors costumes, mantles and paletots of black velvet are the most stylish; these are sometimes trimmed round with fur which makes them very costly . . .' (*World of Fashion*, January 1863).

A month later, the same journal related that:

> For paletots and sleeved cloaks, furs are considered the most stylish trimming: sable, marten, and 'vison' [*sic*] are worn on black velvet; for violet, blue and claret velvets, ermine and chinchilla are more suited . . .

52

Seaside costumes are a feature of fashion magazines during the summer months throughout the period 1860 to 1880. Similar to walking or croquet outfits, they often include a jaunty allusion to naval dress, a theme more overtly popular in children's dress.

Mrs Field, carrying a small pair of binoculars, wears a very full, loose, thick wool skirt with a paletot or jacket above. Fashion plates portray their belles in less practical silk seaside costumes but in similar and equally plain styles. *The World Of Fashion* for August 1865 includes plates from *Le Monde Elégant* and has a number of 'Seaside Outfits'. Primarily, these are dresses of plain, untrimmed silk worn with a cashmere 'burnous' or 'short tight fitting casque or paletot with hood'.

Mrs Field wears a straw boater which carried very direct nautical connotations and which caught on in the 1860s, having originated in children's wear. *The Englishwoman's Domestic Magazine* (September 1861) noted this new fashion:

> A sailor's hat in brown straw, trimmed with black ribbon, with bow and ends . . . has even been adopted by many fashionable ladies at some of the French watering places . . . ,[40]

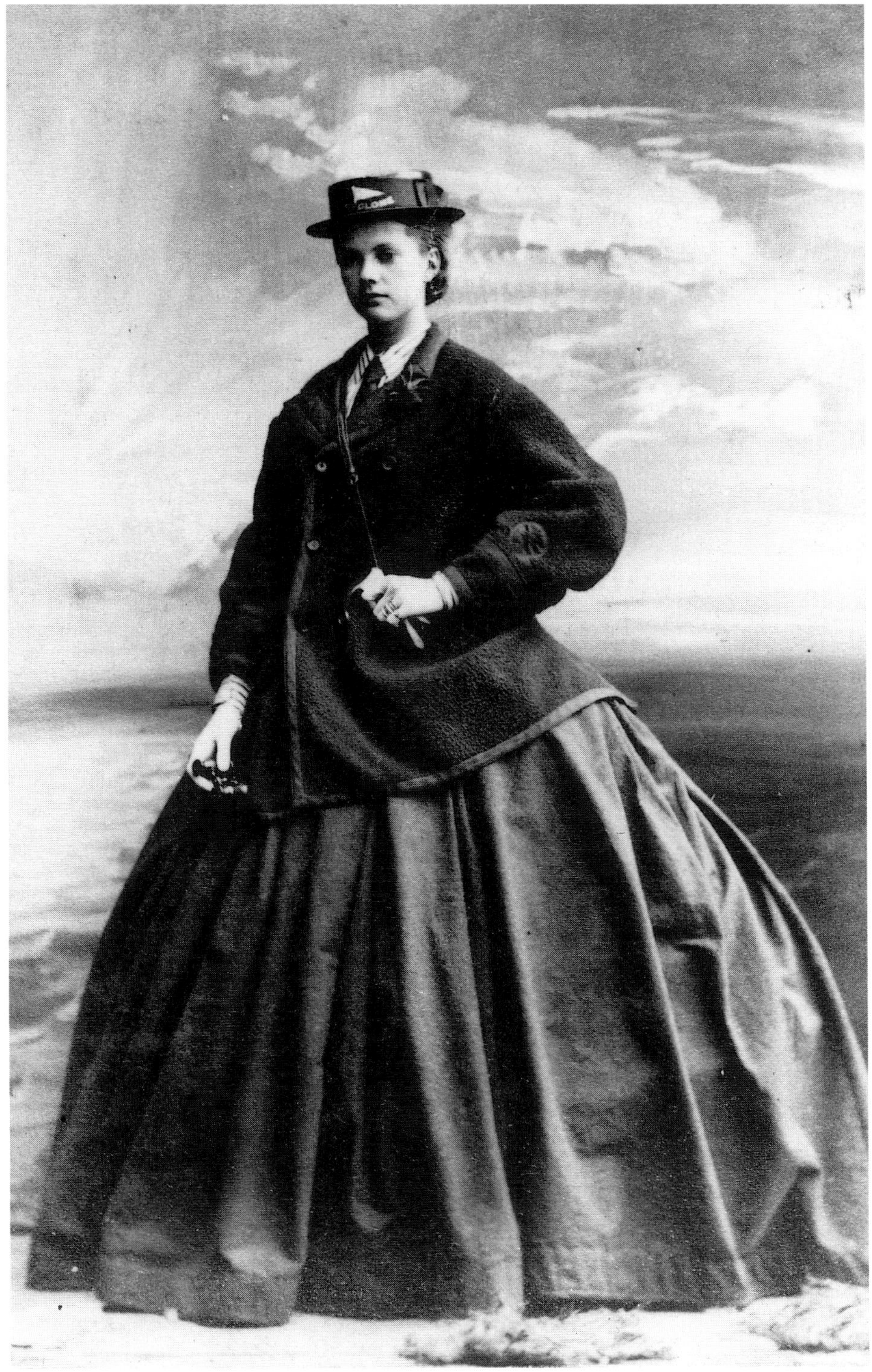

52. Mrs Telford Field
1864
Camille Silvy, London (Daybook 12, no. 15929)

and was doubtless shortly to reach English watering spots too. Apart from boaters, other straw hats with round crowns and turned-up brims were popular and also often called sailors' hats. *The World Of Fashion* (August 1865) shows a hat of white straw trimmed with a feather and black velvet and calls it 'a chapeau de matelot'.

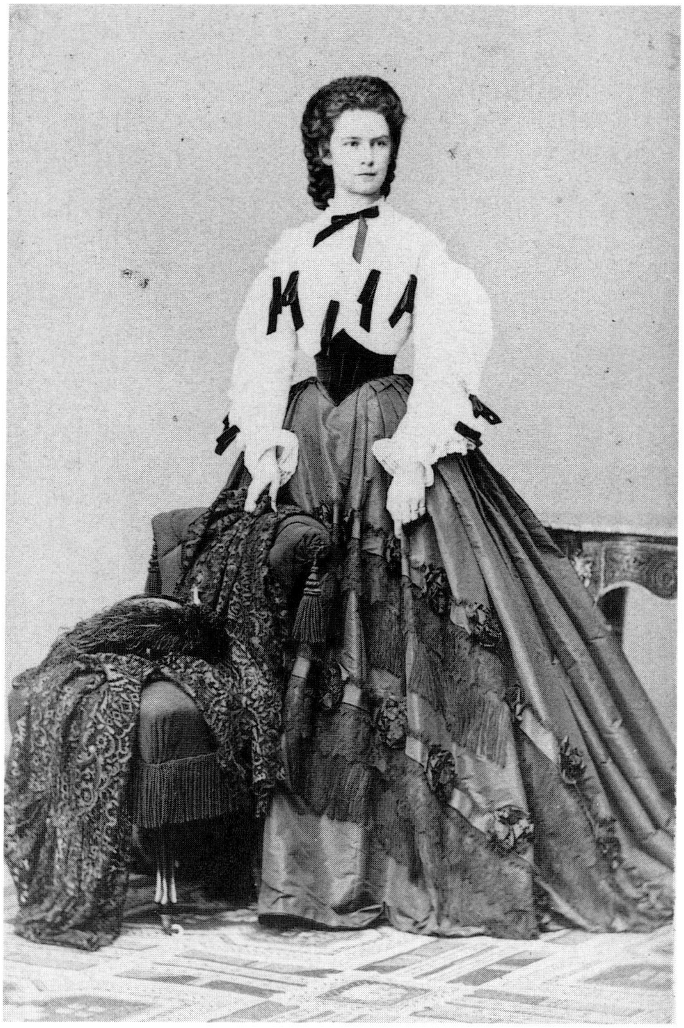

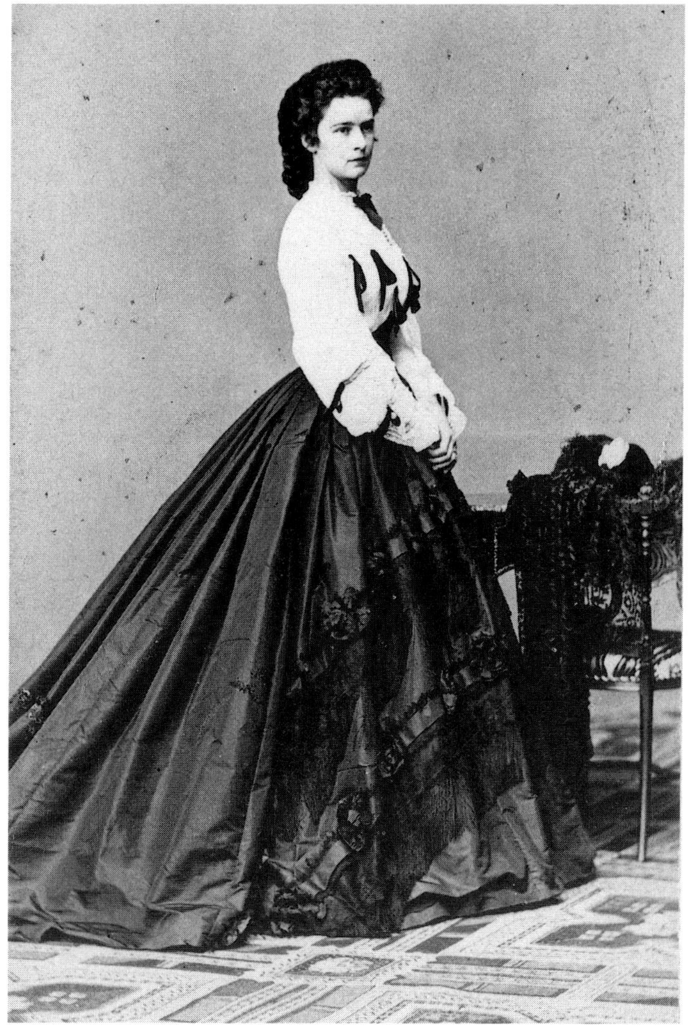

53 & 54. Elizabeth, Empress of Austria *c.* 1864

Angerer, Vienna (NPG x 5822)

53, 54

One of the celebrated beauties of her age, the Empress is in her late twenties in this portrait. A Wittelsbach, and related to the King of Bavaria, Elizabeth had married her first cousin, Franz Joseph of Austria, in 1854 at the age of only 16. She disliked the rigid Court etiquette in Vienna and, after the birth of three children, she turned increasingly to hunting and travel. She was holidaying in Geneva in 1898 when she was assassinated by an Italian anarchist.

The Empress wears a separate bodice and skirt joined with a broad black-velvet Swiss belt or 'ceinture Suissesse'. Her type of bodice went under a variety of names in the 1860s; 'blouse' was not one of them. *The World Of Fashion* has separate plates for bonnets and bodices, and calls the latter 'canezous', 'senorita bodies' or 'chemisettes' when made of white muslin or cotton. These are often worn with Swiss belts.

The most striking element in the Empress's bodice is the bold, tabbed decoration in black-velvet ribbon across the bust and at the cuffs. Similar pendant-tab trimming can be seen in fashion magazines of this date: *The Young Englishwoman* (February 1865) shows a French fashion plate with trimming 'of hanging gimp tabs and cord' to the bodice front and sleeves.[41]

The Empress poses here in Angerer's studio. She was as frequently photographed as she was painted by the Court painters. Winterhalter painted her three times between 1864 and 1865, the date of this sitting, and was sent two photographs of her to assist in securing her likeness in Paris.[42]

55

On 30 May 1864, a few years before this portrait, Marie Isabelle, the 16-year-old daughter of the Duc de Montpensier, married her cousin Louis Philippe, the Count of Paris. In exile, they married at the Roman Catholic Chapel at Kingston, reported *The Queen* (4 June 1864). This report talks of the bride's 'finely chiselled features, a countenance as clear as alabaster . . . her dignified yet modest mien . . .'. It also reflects on her great maturity for a 16-year-old, and this is also apparent in this photograph, which shows her in an imperious three-quarter-turn pose.[43]

Her dark-silk evening dress has a tight bodice with a high horizontal waist, typical of the mid 1860s, as is the low, curved *décolletage*, later to become squarer and higher. The bodice and waist are trimmed with pendant jet beads and fringing, a popular fashion. *The Young*

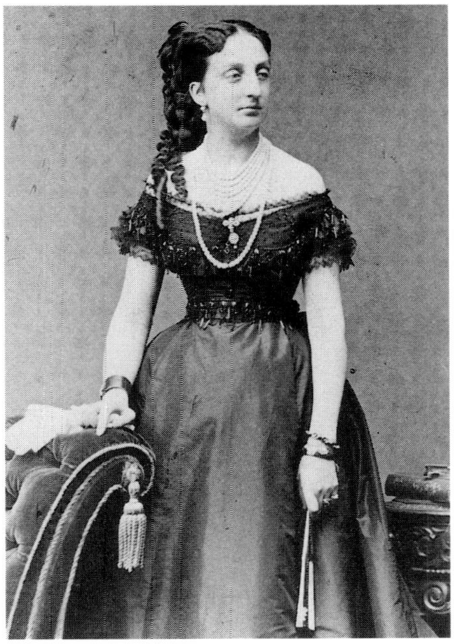

55. The Countess of Paris
***c.* 1864**
Angerer, Vienna (NPG Ax 33514)

Englishwoman (January 1870) shows a similar evening dress

> of imperial blue silk, made with a plain gored skirt and a train behind. Bodice arranged with a short round waist . . . the top of the bodice and the sash and ends are trimmed with a handsome edging and fringe of white jet, now a very favourite style of ornamentation for ladies' garments.

The Countess's wealth of jewellery, including a six-strand pearl necklace, helps to reinforce her aristocratic position. After the death of Louis Philippe, ex-King of the French, in 1850, his grandson the Count of Paris was left as the focus for Royalist exiled supporters. At this time, the Countess of Paris was in exile in England, as later the Empress Eugénie was to be.

56

Born in August 1832, Louisa was the daughter of the organist and composer James Kendrick Pyne. A precocious singer, she appeared in public with her sister Susan from 1842, and at the Princess Theatre from 1849. After a triumphant three-year tour of the United States in the mid 1850s, she formed a London company for the performance of English operas; not, one might have thought, in great supply. Her voice was reputedly 'a soprano of beautiful quality and great compass and flexibility; she excelled in the florid style of which she was a perfect mistress . . .'.[44]

A few years after this studio portrait, Louisa married the baritone, Frank Bodda, in 1868.

Here, she wears a dark-cloth riding habit, plain except for braid trimming at the cuffs. The bodice has 30 front fabric-covered buttons which conceal the hook and eye fastenings. It is worn with narrow, white cotton (or linen) collar and cuffs, and fits over a long trailing skirt. By the 1850s, skirts were worn over riding 'trousers' of cloth or chamois leather, which matched the cloth of the habit from the knee down.[45]

An early manual of about 1830, *The Young Ladies Equestrian Manual* decrees in its chapter on 'Personal Equipments' that 'the habit should fit the bust without a crease; but beneath the waist it ought to be, not only long, but somewhat full and flowing.'[46]

Miss Pyne carries a riding crop and wears a black-silk top hat, only the bunched veil distinguishing it from male attire. Riding dress at this time was plain and, once mounted, functional; as the same manual advises: 'all that is gaudy, needless or elaborate, is vulgar. Perfect simplicity is expected of every well-bred female equestrian.'

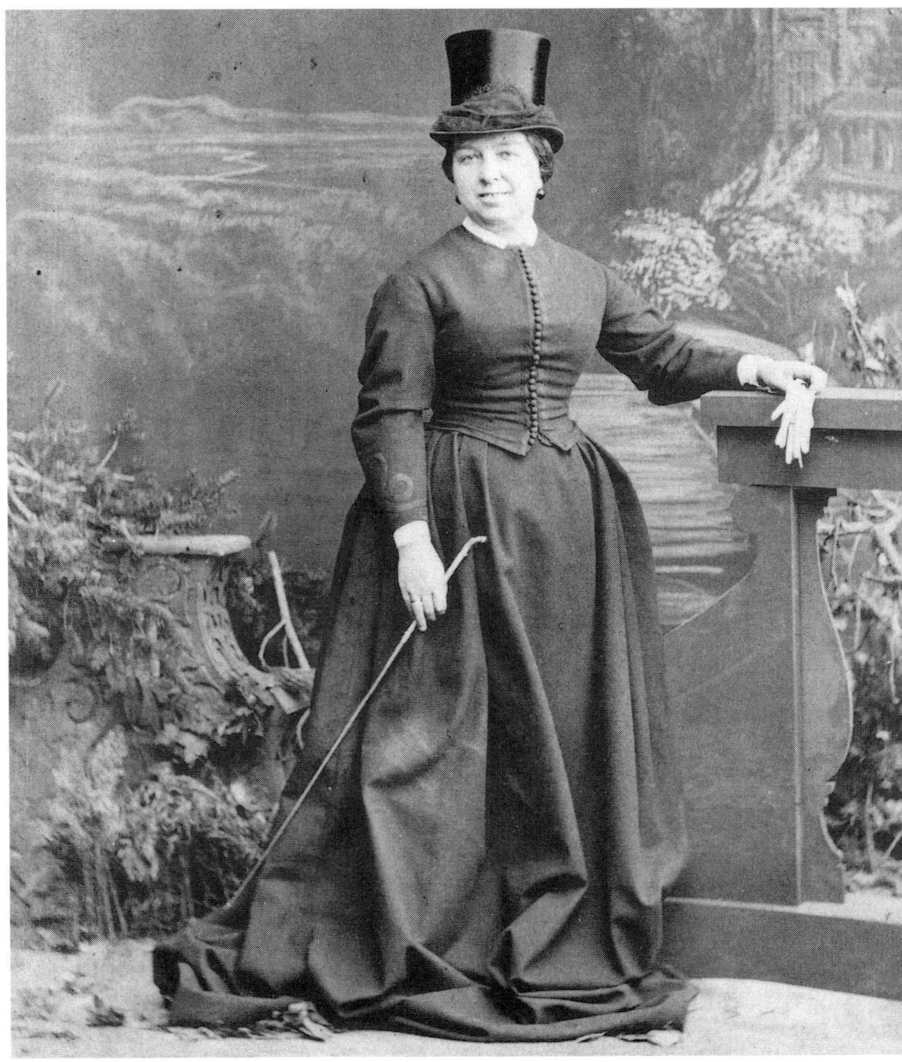

56. Louisa Pyne
***c.* 1864**
Southwell Brothers, London (NPG x 12777)

GROUP

57

Silvy has apparently not succeeded in relaxing his three glum young sitters, peering at the camera whilst held in position by surrounding chairbacks and stools.

The two young sisters both wear cotton dresses of white piqué, very popular in the 1860s, and rivals to lighter cottons and muslins. Piqué presented a much stiffer and fuller silhouette and like all cotton, washed easily and was simple to starch and iron.

The usual decoration, as in these matching dresses, was of a striking dark braided trimming, often as a border at the hem and at the collar and cuffs. Similar braiding was extensively used in women's daydresses also, in bold geometric patterns such as the cross lattice-work here, or the celebrated Greek Key motif.

The younger Devaux sister, aged perhaps three or four, wears her dress reaching to just below the knee and reveals, beneath the dress hem, the broderie anglaise white-work edging to her drawers. Her elder sister shows nothing of her underwear, and sports a more sophisticated hairstyle, held back from her forehead by an 'Alice-band' and falling in ringlets on either side of her face.

Their elder brother wears an early form of the popular Norfolk knickerbocker suit and is here aged six or seven, having been breeched at four or five. The loose Norfolk shirt or blouse buttons to the throat and is belted below the waist. His knickerbockers are held in place below the knee by knitted stockings. *The Ladies' Treasury* (March 1860) tells us that 'dresses for children are still very fanciful. The knickerbocker, the "Costume Bretonne" and the Highland suit are all advisable.'[1] In November 1861 Queen Victoria wrote to her daughter, the Princess Royal in Prussia, telling her of her little brother Leopold who was aged eight: 'Leopold had a nice dark grey jacket, waistcoat and knickerbockers which is what little boys wear so much now'.

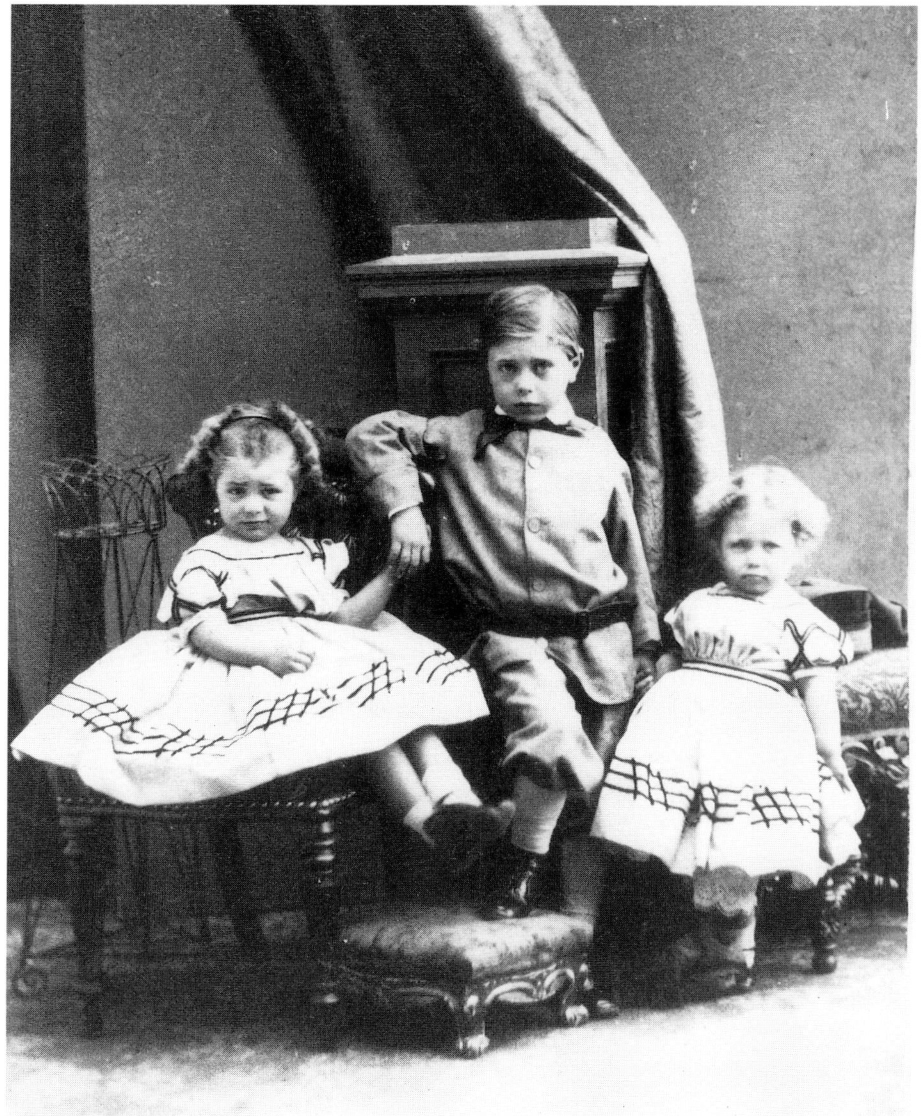

57. The Devaux children 1860
Camille Silvy, London (Daybook 1, no. 475)

58

Mrs Duncan, an estate worker at Balmoral, sits in a doorway with her three daughters and young baby. Her hair, coiled over her ears and partly concealed by a lace day-cap, is in a rather out-of-date style much favoured in the 1840s.

Her eldest daughter's hair is far more fashionably dressed, drawn into a netted

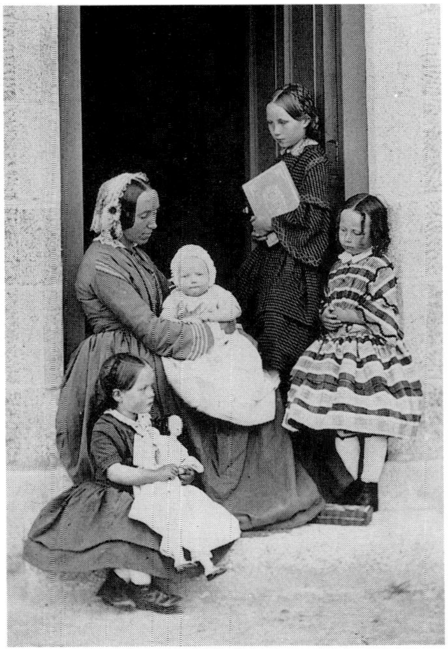

58. Mrs Duncan and four children 1861
George Washington Wilson, Balmoral (Balmoral Album P22(21))

chignon at the back. The two elder girls both have striped cotton dresses with full pagoda sleeves and short crinolines; and all three girls wear ankle-length black-leather boots with white stockings.

The baby, appearing admirably confident in front of the camera, wears a white cotton robe with white cap. Both the baby and the youngest girl's doll exhibit the limitations of photography in the 1860s: all detail of dress and trimmings is lost in a bright white blur or blotch.

Photographers at Balmoral did not have an easy time in the early days; accommodation was at a premium in the vicinity, and facilities outside the castle itself were primitive. Although this portrait is by Wilson, the Queen favoured William and David Downey for her Balmoral photographs. When first summoned by Royal command, the photographers found that they were unable to find shelter anywhere but in a labourer's cottage. Apparently, on hearing of their plight, the ever amiable Prince of Wales (whose character had greatly improved since childhood), 'knowing of the strait the photographers were likely to be in, drove over in a waggonette to see them and good naturedly sent up provisions and wine . . .'.[2]

59

Major-General Trollope's upright and rigid bearing, his rather condescending expression, and his vast moustache and whiskers, all indicate a military man. He wears a dark-cloth frock coat with matching double-breasted waistcoat with turn-down collar and revers. His neat, black cravat tied as a bow tie is worn with a starched, upright shirt collar. His dark woollen trousers are woven with a narrow-spaced window-pane check. *The Tailor and Cutter* (March 1869) reported that 'stripes and checks are all the rage' in trousers.[3]

Mrs Trollope's skirt is probably made of *barège*, a silk and wool mixture, with a separate, dark Garibaldi shirt and a short jacket with pagoda sleeves. Her hair is gathered into a chignon at the back, enclosed in a crochet net, later known as a snood. Similar nets were often worn with velvet porkpie-style hats or with turned-brim straw hats, for walking or croquet outfits. *Le Monde Elégant* fashion plates in *The World Of Fashion* (June 1862) show a sequence of bonnets and hats and include a net for a chignon, which it grandly calls 'a straw coloured résille'.

This restrained, respectable, middle-aged couple is typical of the type and calibre of Silvy's sitters.

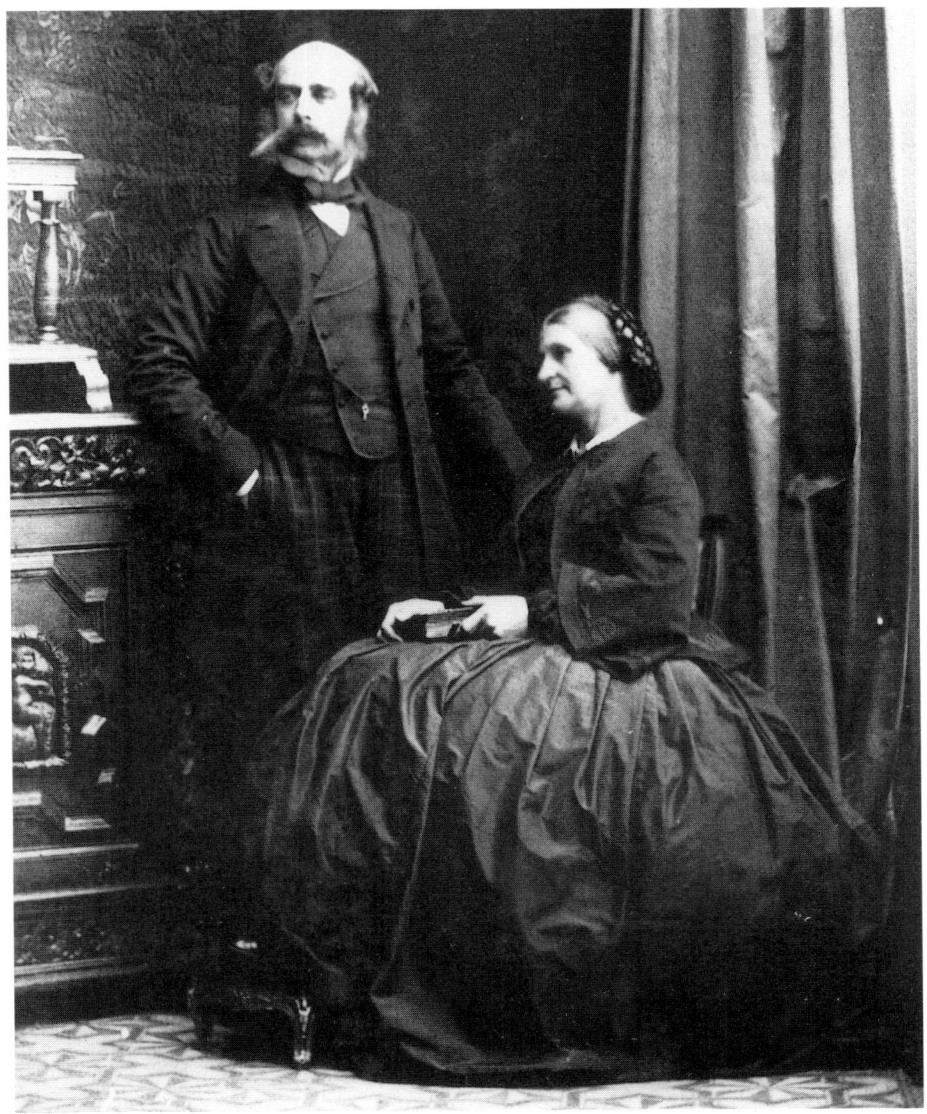

59. Major-General and Mrs Trollope 1862
Camille Silvy, (Daybook 6, no. 7656)

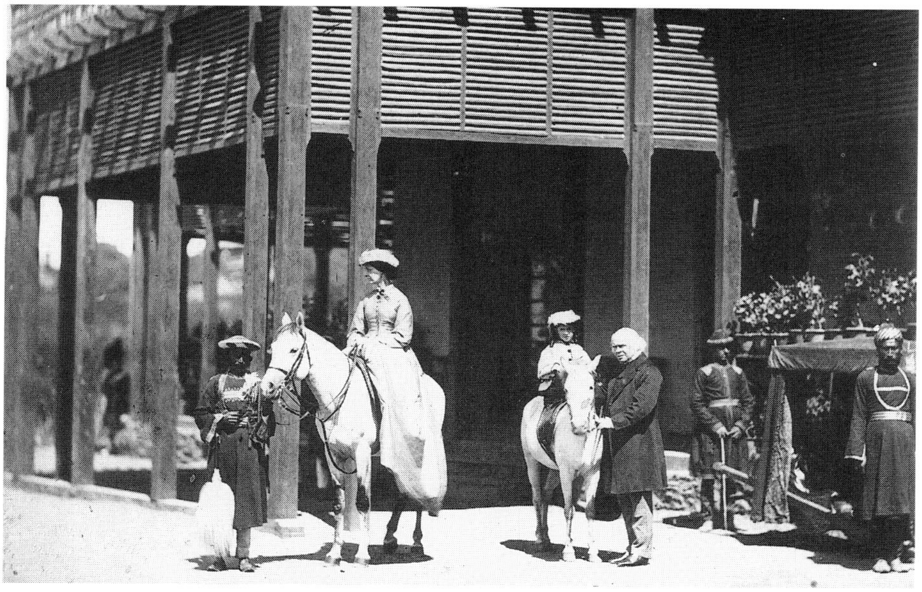

60. **Lord and Lady Elgin with their daughter**
1862
Schwarzchild of Calcutta (Strachey collection) (NPG x 12645)

60

James Bruce, 8th Earl of Elgin, was born in 1811 and, after an education at Christ Church, Oxford, began a successful diplomatic career. Governor-General of Jamaica (1842) and subsequently Canada (1846), he was appointed Governor-General and Viceroy of India in 1861, arriving there with his second wife in March 1862. Lady Elgin, née Lady Mary Lambton, was the daughter of the 1st Earl of Durham; her daughter, also pictured, was born in 1856.

Posing for the Calcutta photographer Schwarzchild, beside a vast wooden verandah, the family is attended by three Indian servants. Lord Elgin stands beside his young daughter's pony, dressed for business and allowing himself only a short break from paperwork. Looking far more elderly than his 50 years, Lord Elgin was to die, only a year later, of a heart attack at Dharmsala. Lady Elgin, returned to the healthier English climate and outlived him by some 35 years.

In this photograph, Lord Elgin wears a dark-cloth frock coat, whilst his wife and daughter wear much lighter coloured dresses, far more practical for outdoor wear in India. Both ladies have fashionable straw hats, trimmed with feathers, to help shade their faces from the sun.

61

The Princess wears her wedding dress as described in Plate 47; the Prince wears the blue-velvet mantle of the Order of the Knights of the Garter which he wore for his marriage. He also wore the decorations of the Golden Fleece and the Star of India; and below he wears the scarlet uniform of an army general.

The Queen, still in deepest mourning for the Prince Consort, took no part in the ceremony, observing the marriage from the separate Royal Closet in St George's Chapel. The Princess was led in by her father Prince Christian of Denmark, and by the Duke of Cambridge, and accompanied by her eight bridesmaids. The band and organ performed

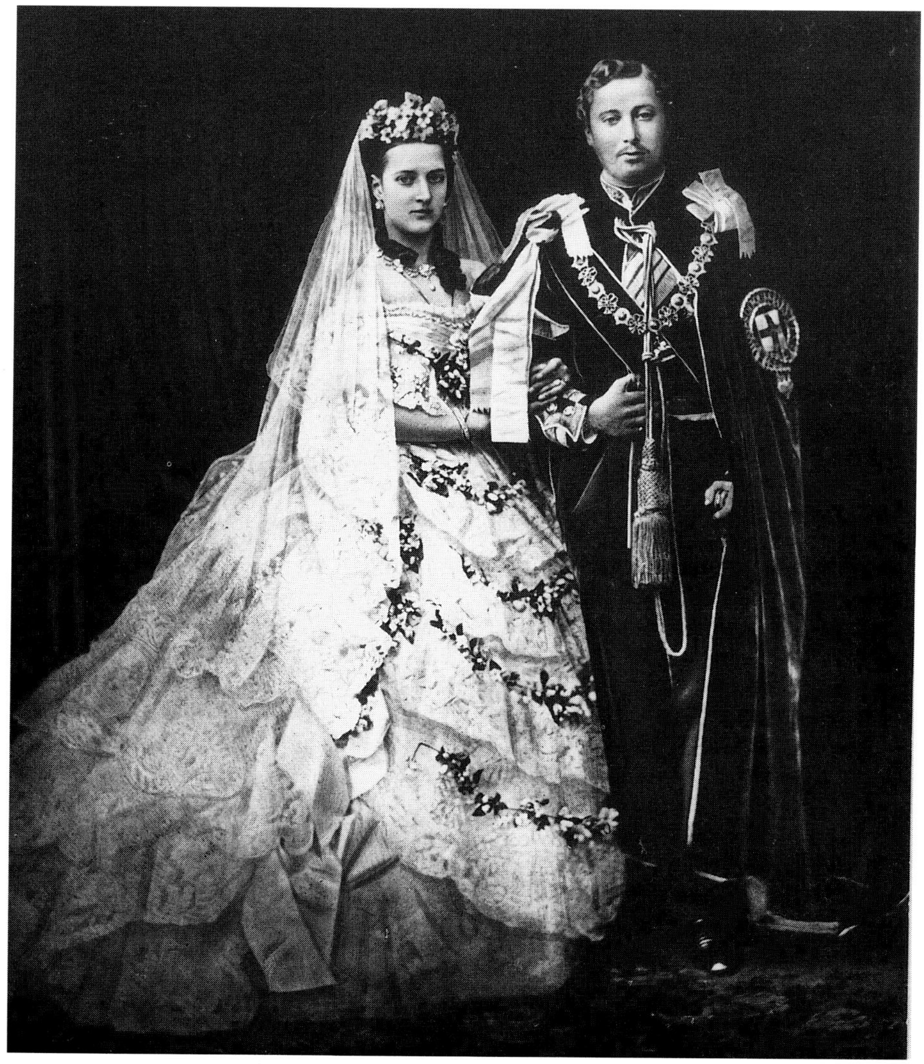

61. **The Prince and Princess of Wales**
1863
Mayall, London (NPG x 9182)

Handel's 'Processional March' from *Joseph*, which was followed by the choir's rendition of a chorale by the late Prince Consort. The couple left to the rousing 'Hallelujah Chorus' from Beethoven's *Mount of Olives*.

After a wedding breakfast for 38 in the dining-room at Windsor, and for 400 in St George's Hall, the Prince and Princess left for Osborne. The subsequent exodus of guests resulted in chaos, especially when the general public were allowed to throng on to the station platform to view the special train to London. According to Lord Malmesbury's diary, the Duchess of Westminster 'had on half a million pound's worth of diamonds' and could only find a place in a third-class carriage, along with Lady Palmerston. Count Livradic had his diamond star torn off and stolen by ruffians.[4]

Rejoicing of a more or less boisterous nature took place throughout the nation and, after a week's honeymoon at Osborne, the bride and groom returned to London to hold the first of very many courts at St James's Palace on 20 March 1863.

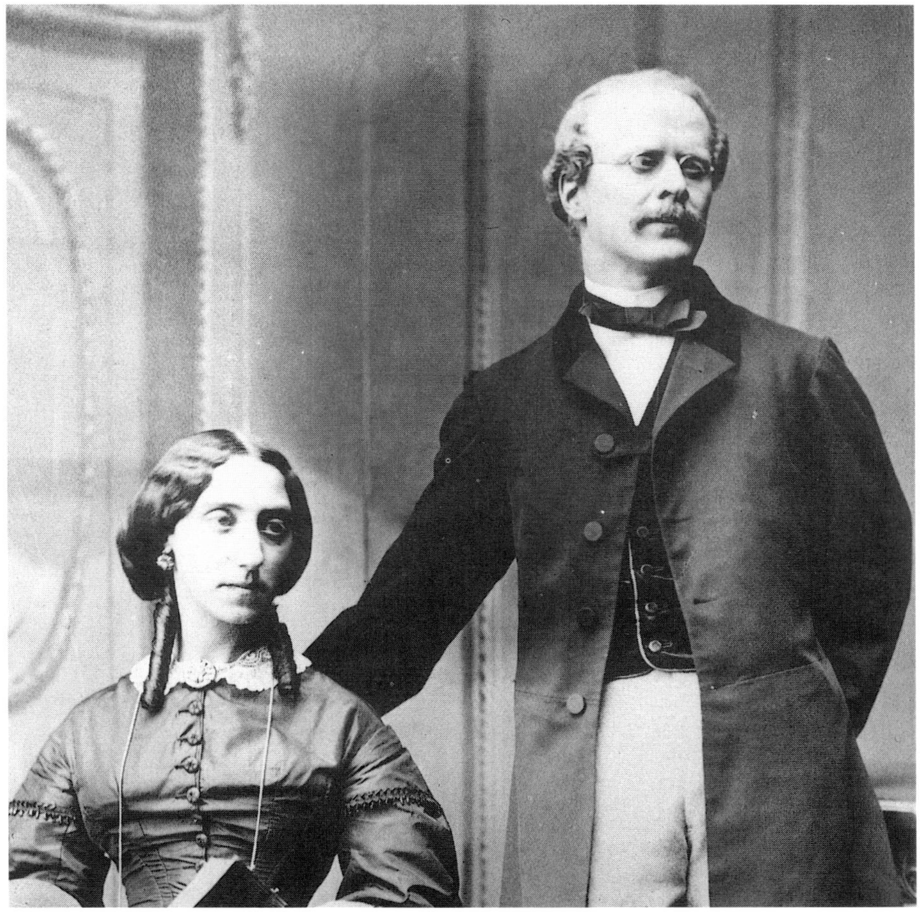

62. Mr and Mrs Raphael
1863
Camille Silvy, London (Daybook 10, no. 12929)

62

In this conventional half-size double portrait Silvy has the husband standing behind his wife, although it was more usual to reduce the discrepancy in height by seating the man. Mr Raphael wears a black frock coat with a tab fastening to the top button and a black-velvet collar matching his velvet waistcoat. He wears spectacles, typical for the 1860s, with small elliptical lenses and narrow, wire frames. Spectacles were seen as medical accessories and there were no fashionable styles. The anonymous author (named as 'a Countess'), of an etiquette book entitled *Good Society* (1860), wrote 'If spectacles are necessary, they should be of the best and lightest make, mounted in gold or blue steel. For weak sight, blue or smoke-coloured glasses are best; green glasses are detestable'.[5]

Mrs Raphael wears a day bodice with fashionable dropped-shoulder bishop sleeves trimmed with a band of black glass or jet. The tautness of the bodice across her diaphragm is emphasized by the horizontal creases across the two long curved darts either side centre-front.

Her hair is still styled with a centre-front parting and with the body of the hair drawn into a chignon or low bun at the back with a long, tight ringlet over each shoulder.

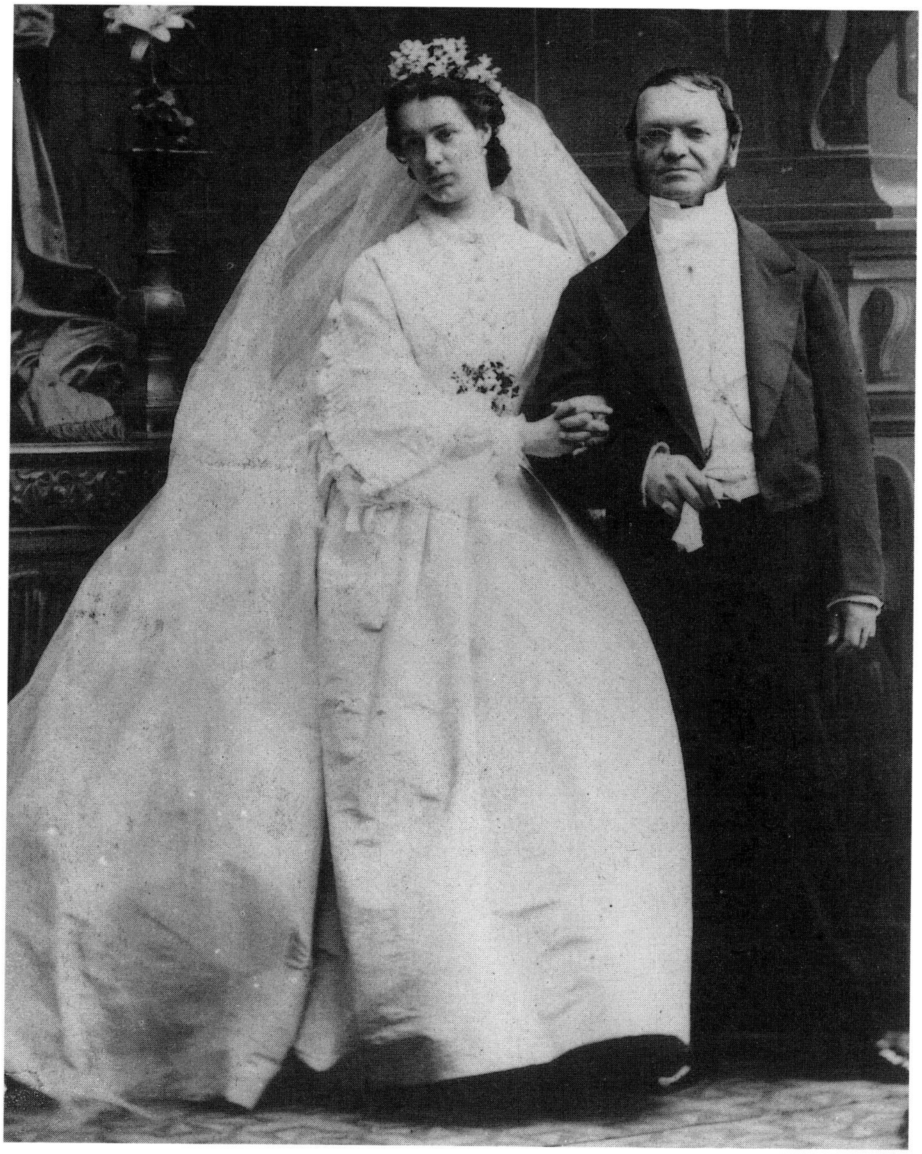

63. Mr and Mrs Faure
1863
Camille Silvy, London (Daybook 10, no. 12989)

63

Small of stature but benign in appearance, Mr Faure wears a respectable, if slightly unfashionable, tailcoat for his wedding photograph. On the whole, older bridegrooms of the period favoured tailcoats, whilst their younger contemporaries wore frock coats. In a particularly formal situation, such as the wedding of Princess Alice to Prince Louis of Hesse in July 1862 when the Court was in deepest mourning for the Prince Consort, then the bridegroom would also wear a tailcoat. Black was by far the most popular colour, although fashion periodicals urged more imagination for weddings: 'a short blue frock coat with velvet collar and edging of silk cord, dove grey trousers, lavender gloves and light blue tie' (*Westend Gazette of Fashion*, 1869).

Advice was showered on receptive bridegrooms-to-be by contemporary etiquette books:

> If all goes well, when the settlements are finished the lady names the wedding day . . . a licence is purchased by the gentleman; he also buys the ring. The trousseau, breakfast and wedding cake are given by the bride's family . . .' (*Etiquette for Ladies*, c. 1870).

Interestingly, the manual instructs that the mother of the bride should remain safely at home for the whole service and that at the reception the cake should be cut 'by the nearest gentleman', not necessarily the bridegroom.[6]

Mrs Faure's vast skirt is supported by a crinoline which lifts up noticeably at the front hem; her net veil is floor-length, attached to her chignon at the back by an orange-blossom wreath.

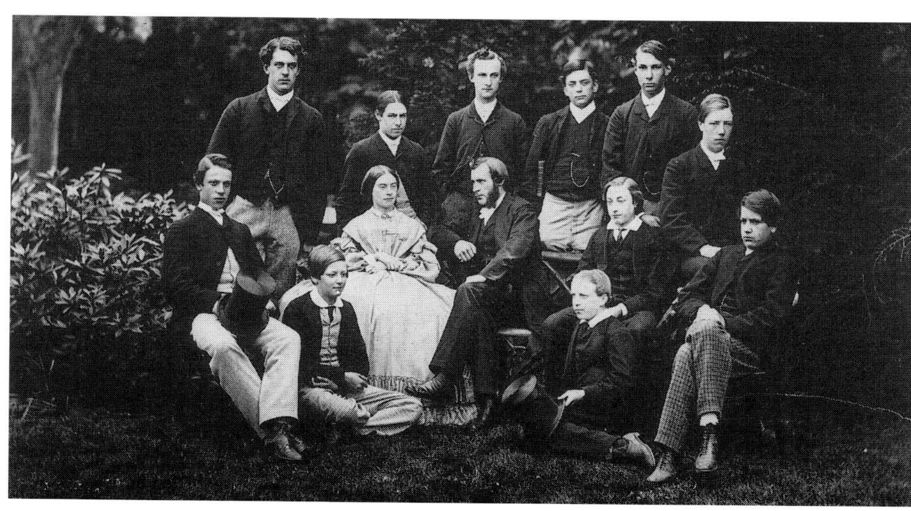

64. The Reverend and Mrs St John Thackeray with schoolboys at Eton
1863
Photographer unknown, Windsor (Barrington Album (182) p. 36) (NPG Ax 26261)

64

Assistant Master at Eton College from 1858 until 1883, the Reverend Thackeray is pictured here with his wife of three years, Louisa Katherine, and 11 boys from his House.

The Reverend wears a formal, dark frock coat whilst the elder boys wear black morning coats fastened mostly at the top button. The three youngest boys at the front wear short Eton jackets with typical deep lapels, over distinctive, round turn-down collars and narrow black ties. A variety of hairstyles is in evidence, with left, right, and centre partings; although each style is roughly the same length, just covering the tops of the ears. Most of the elder sixth-form boys wear black waistcoats, with their watch-chains snaking across to the left; and two tall, black silk hats are on view.

Surrounded by juvenile masculine company, Mrs Thackeray looks relaxed and wears a pale-silk daydress with a bodice featuring an attached bertha-cape panel dipping to a point centre-front. This effect was known as trimming with 'capes à bretelles' and was common at the end of the 1850s, and sporadically through the early 1860s.[7] Her wide skirt has two flounces towards the hem and is spread out as she sits, providing a foil to the uniform inky black of the men's dress.

65

This family group is photographed outside the family seat at Hooton in Cheshire; Sir Rowland was the Deputy-Lieutenant of Northumberland.

Seen here in his early fifties, Sir Rowland poses in the prone position, in a rather artistic shooting outfit, comprising black-velvet lounge jacket, waistcoat, and breeches; black patent boots, and a dark straw boater. His rifle lies beside him, and his gamekeeper stands discreetly in attendance to the extreme left of the photograph. The three sisters, aged a little on either side of 20, wear dark-silk walking outfits, possibly in second-degree mourning. Venetia, standing, was later (1867) to marry Viscount Pollington, who became the 5th Earl of Mexborough. She wears a dark-silk daydress with full bishop sleeves, and a wide-brimmed straw hat, trimmed centre-front with a large black rosette.

The seated sister, Claudine (to the left), was to die only a year or so after this photograph, in July 1864, and she is similarly dressed, but with a velvet jacket-bodice and a porkpie-style hat.

Ethel (to the right) wears a looped-up walking skirt over a paler skirt trimmed at the hem with two rows of black velvet as a border. She also wears a black-velvet jacket-bodice and holds her hat in her lap.

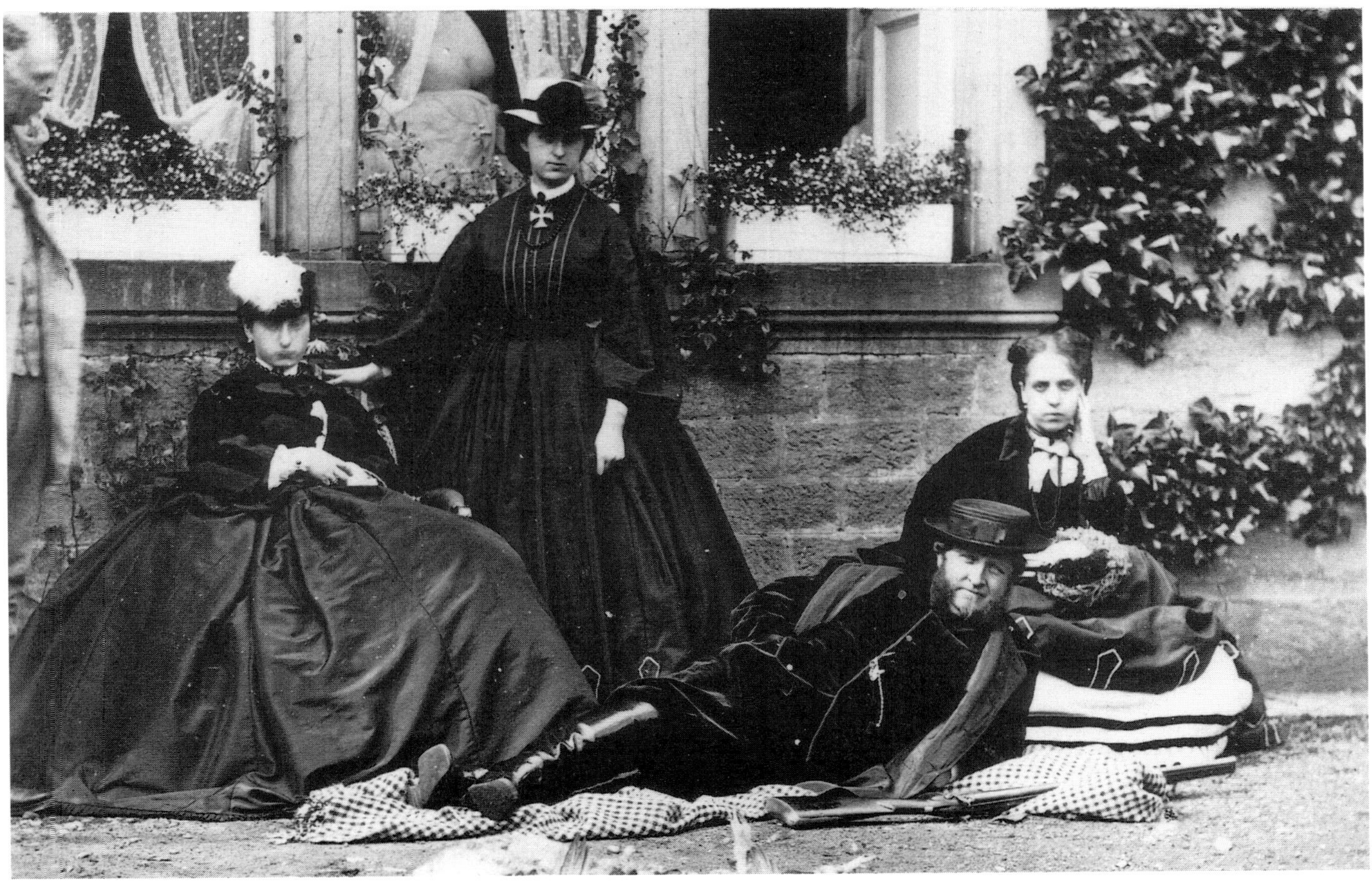

65. Sir Rowland Stanley Errington with his three daughters
Early 1860s
J. P. Gibson, Hexham (NPG x 32946)

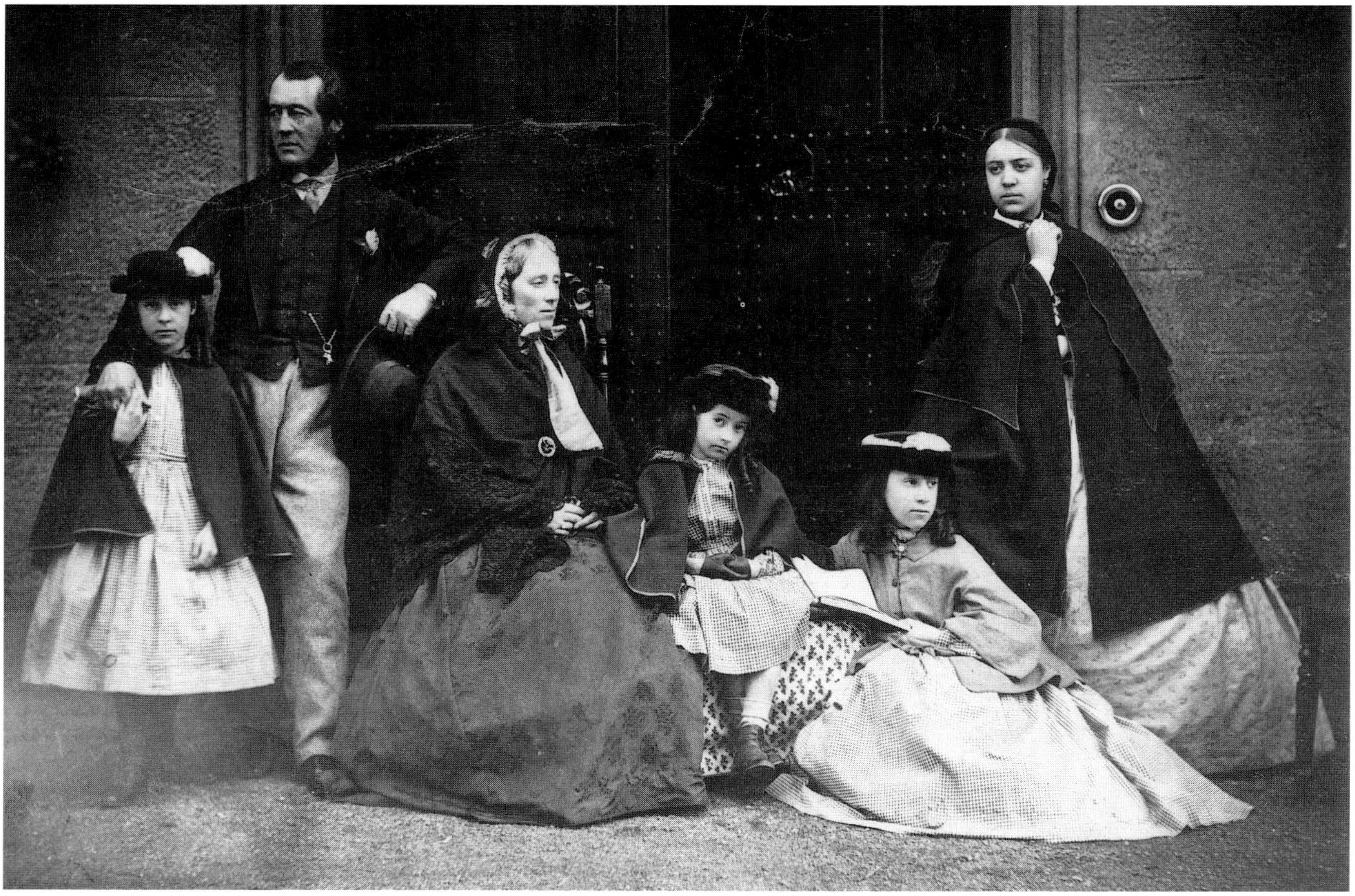

66. The Honourable Sir George and Lady Elliot, with their four daughters: Elizabeth, Nina, Hersey, and Olivia Early 1860s

Photographer unknown, Midlothian (Jocelyn Album (59) p.2) (NPG Ax 33528)

66, 67, 68

Born in 1812, George Elliot was the son of the 1st Earl of Minto and married Hersey Wauchope in 1842. They were to have a succession of daughters, beginning with Elizabeth Georgiana Frances, posing here on the far right of the group portrait. She wears a black-cloth, hooded and caped cloak, over a pale printed-silk dress. She was to marry the 9th Earl of Northesk shortly after this photograph, in 1865.

The next eldest sister, Nina Helen, shown kneeling in the group portrait, is also shown in Plate 68, with her pet parrot. For both photographs, she wears a checked-cotton summer dress over a crinoline petticoat, with a slightly darker, plain, loose paletot. For the parrot portrait, she wisely wears a pair of suede gauntlet gloves to afford some protection against a sharp beak. She was to marry Captain Sir Thomas Butler in 1871.

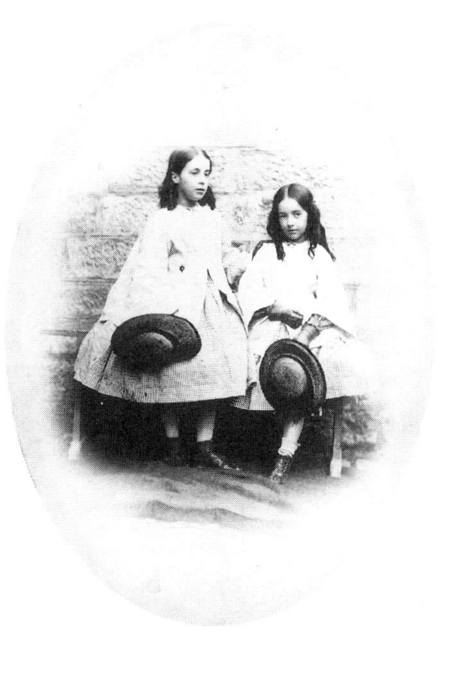

The two youngest sisters, Hersey Cecilia and Anna Maria Olivia, are shown as a pair in Plate 67 and also in the group, wearing matching checked-cotton dresses. In the family portrait they wear dark cloth capes and round straw hats; on their own, they have pale pagoda-sleeved paletots and carry wide-brimmed straw hats.

The girls' parents, aged about 40, pose with them outside the main entrance doorway at the family seat of Niddrie Hall in Midlothian.

67. Hersey and Olivia Elliot Early 1860s

Photographer unknown, Midlothian (Jocelyn Album (59) p.5) (NPG Ax 33517)

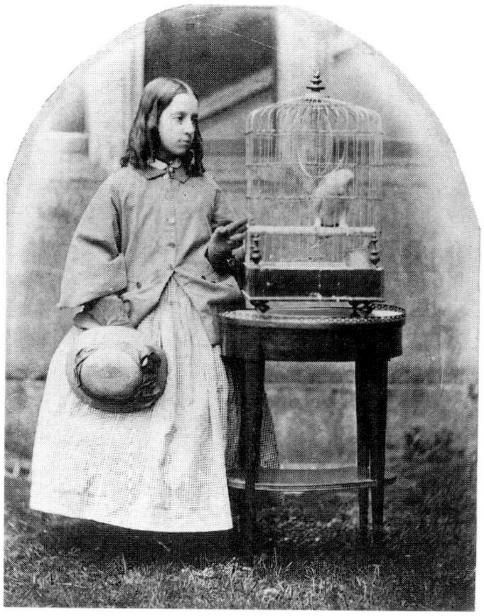

68. Nina Elliot
Early 1860s
Photographer unknown, Midlothian (Jocelyn Album (59) p.17) (NPG Ax 33529)

The Englishwoman's Domestic Magazine (December 1864) relates that

> little boys, as soon as they leave off short frocks and pelisses, are clothed in jackets and knickerbockers; and the plainest style is the best – that is, some pretty grey or drab cloth trimmed with braid or buttons of exactly the same shade.[8]

It goes on to assure the reader that 'little girls' dresses give more scope to taste and fancy'. The same periodical in August 1864 had advised that

> Little girls wear almost universally for the summer, the white bodice with a sash or Swiss band, and a skirt for walking, the paletot to match the skirt . . . the embroidery in many colours, Oriental style is the newest for trimming white or maize coloured frocks in piqué, mohair or foulard . . .[9]

69

Mrs Emma Reeves, to the left of the photograph, poses with her five children and her mother. Formerly Emma Lucombe the soprano, she had married the tenor John Sims Reeves around 1850. The children are, from left to right: Herbert, Ernest, Constance, Maud, and Percy, and are dressed in a nice array of juvenile fashion. Herbert (on the far left) wears a dark-velvet knickerbocker suit fastened full-length down the centre-front. Next to him, Ernest wears a Highland suit as popularized by the royal princes in the 1850s, and complete with a sporran.* Constance (seated), the eldest child, wears a white cotton piqué dress trimmed with black braid in vertical bands at the front. On her knee, Maud is dressed in a light muslin dress with flounces and ruching. The final boy, Percy, not yet breeched, wears a matching waistcoat and skirt with a darker, short, collarless jacket fastened only at the neck, and similar to the fashionable 'Zouave' jacket worn by women.

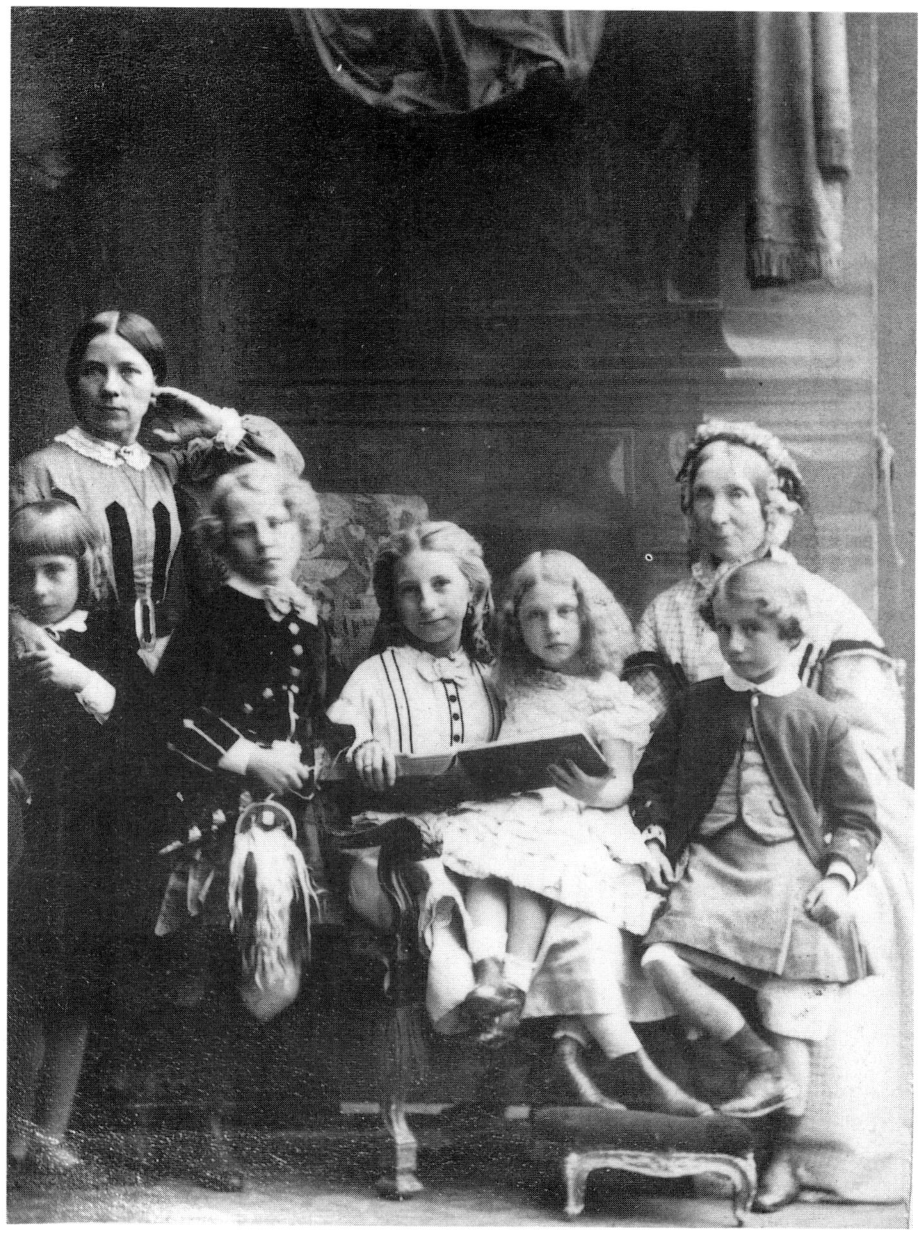

69. The family of John Sims Reeves
1864
Camille Silvy, London (Daybook 12, no. 15986)

PART TWO: 1865-69

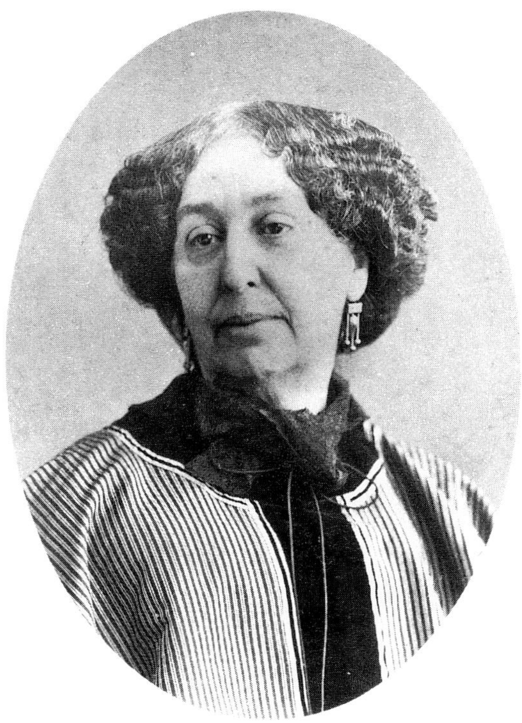

MALE

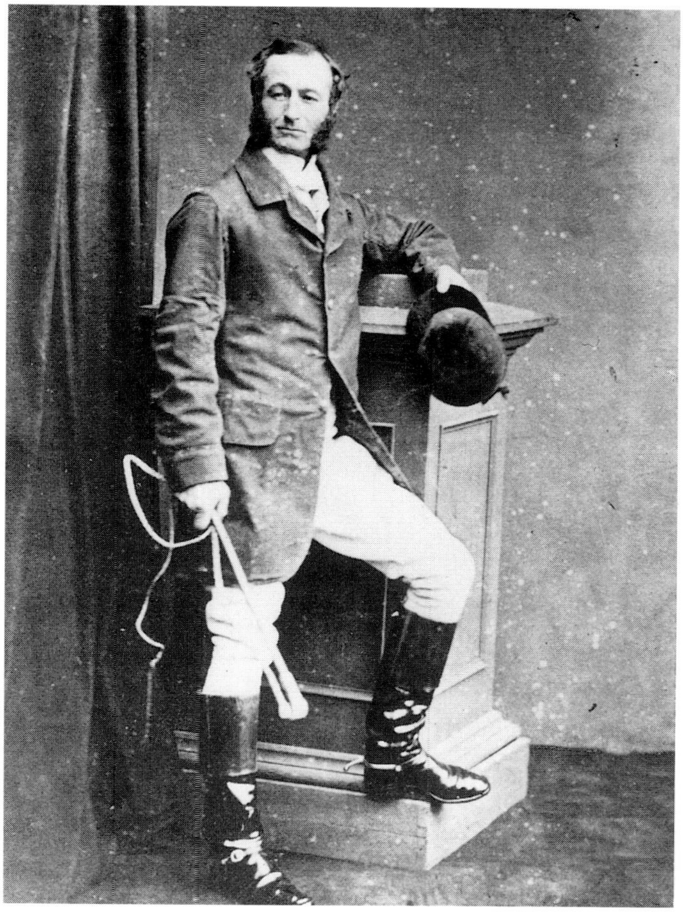

70. John Henry, 4th Baron de Robeck
1864–5
T. Crawfield, Dublin (Album 42, p. 6) (NPG Ax 33508)

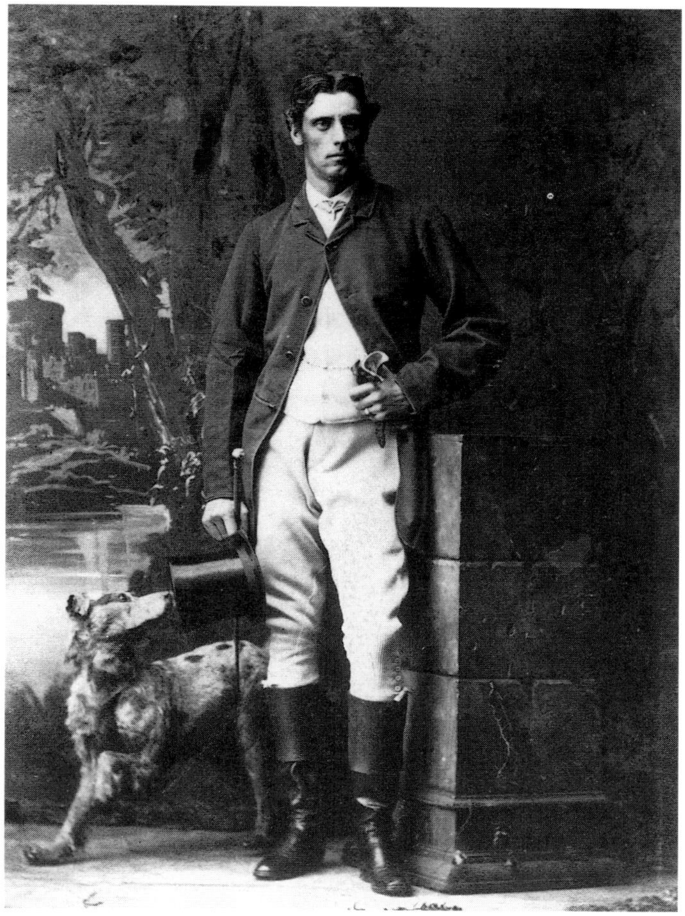

71. Henry Hall
1865
Camille Silvy, London (Daybook 12, no. 16327)

70, 71

John Henry Edward Fock was born in 1823 and is here in his early forties. He was a military man by profession and later became a high sheriff in Ireland.

Both the Baron de Robeck and Mr Hall wear hunting coats, the one with hard hat and whip; the other with top hat, gloves and attendant stuffed, studio-prop dog. A 'hunting coat' dated a little later in *The Tailor and Cutter* (31 October 1868) is of scarlet cloth with a velvet collar:

> the coat is formed to button to the top, with a turn down or Prussian collar, five club buttons on the front and two behind, inside breast pocket in the waist seam, and large pockets across the skirt facings, put high and to lay well back so that the contents may keep well clear of the thighs.

With their hunting coats, both men wear breeches, probably in white or buff Bedford cord, and either front-fall or fly fastening, both being common. Top boots are also worn; these were usual for hunting from the 1820s.

The top hat was the usual headgear up until the middle years of the century, but by the 1860s, the round hard hat or jockey cap, which had formerly been worn only by hunt servants, caught on, primarily for safety reasons. By the 1870s, the bowler became the popular, fashionable compromise for the hunting field.

Regular members of a hunt, such as (presumably) the Baron, wore scarlet; other, less serious huntsmen could wear green, brown, or black coats. As they needed to be extremely robust, these coats were difficult to make:

> The making up of these kind of coats requires more than [the] usual amount of skill and attention on the part of the workman; not the least important is firmness in the putting together, the stayings, tackings, and every stitch put in, with the view to stand rough usage. (*Tailor and Cutter*, 31 October 1868.)

72, 73

Both gentlemen are dressed in black-cloth morning coats, with much paler-cloth trousers and collarless waistcoats.

The Honourable Richard, third son of the 1st Baron Denman, a successful barrister, and seen here aged about 50, wears checked-cloth trousers and waistcoat over a stiff, upstanding collar and spotted silk cravat. Mr Mehul has plain, light-coloured trousers, a plain waistcoat, with a more modern looking turn-down collar and four-in-hand tie.

Although these two dapper individuals show that both variety in pattern and contrast in textures were still

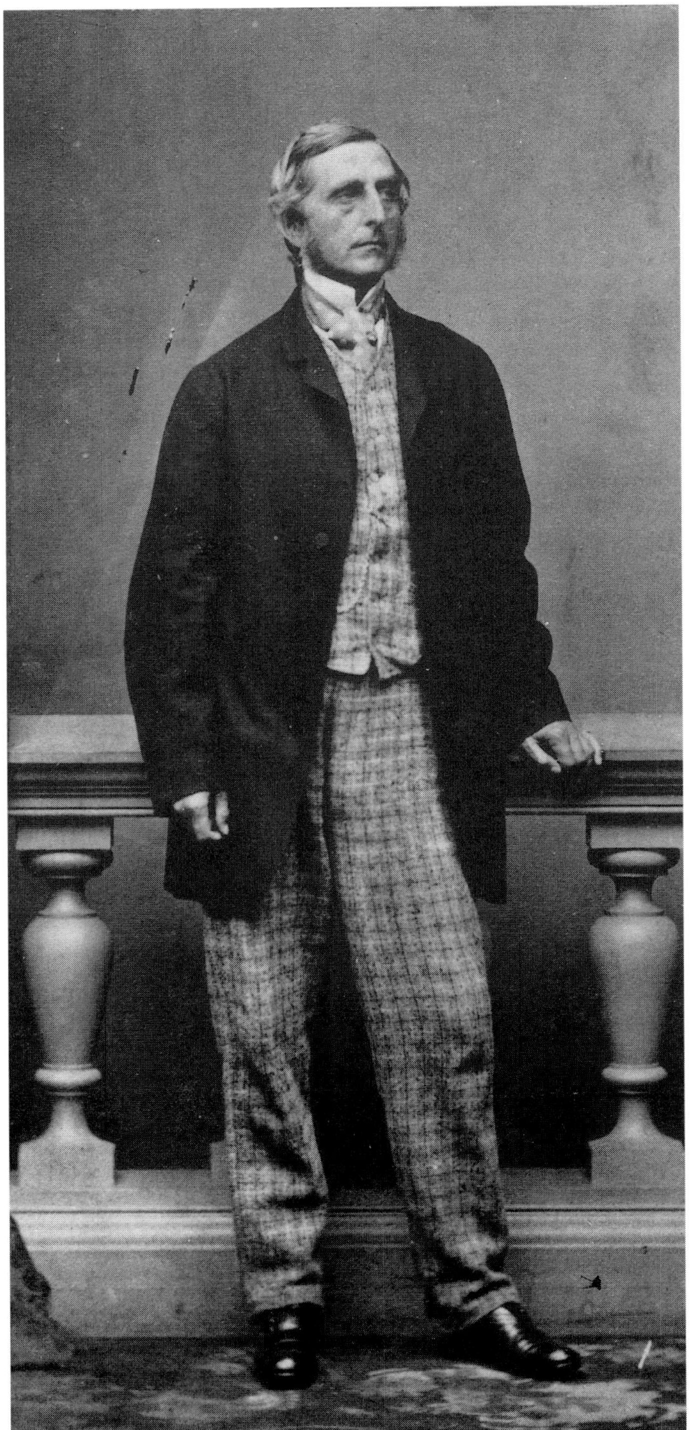

72. The Honourable Richard Denman
1864–5
Photographer unknown (NPG Ax 9560)

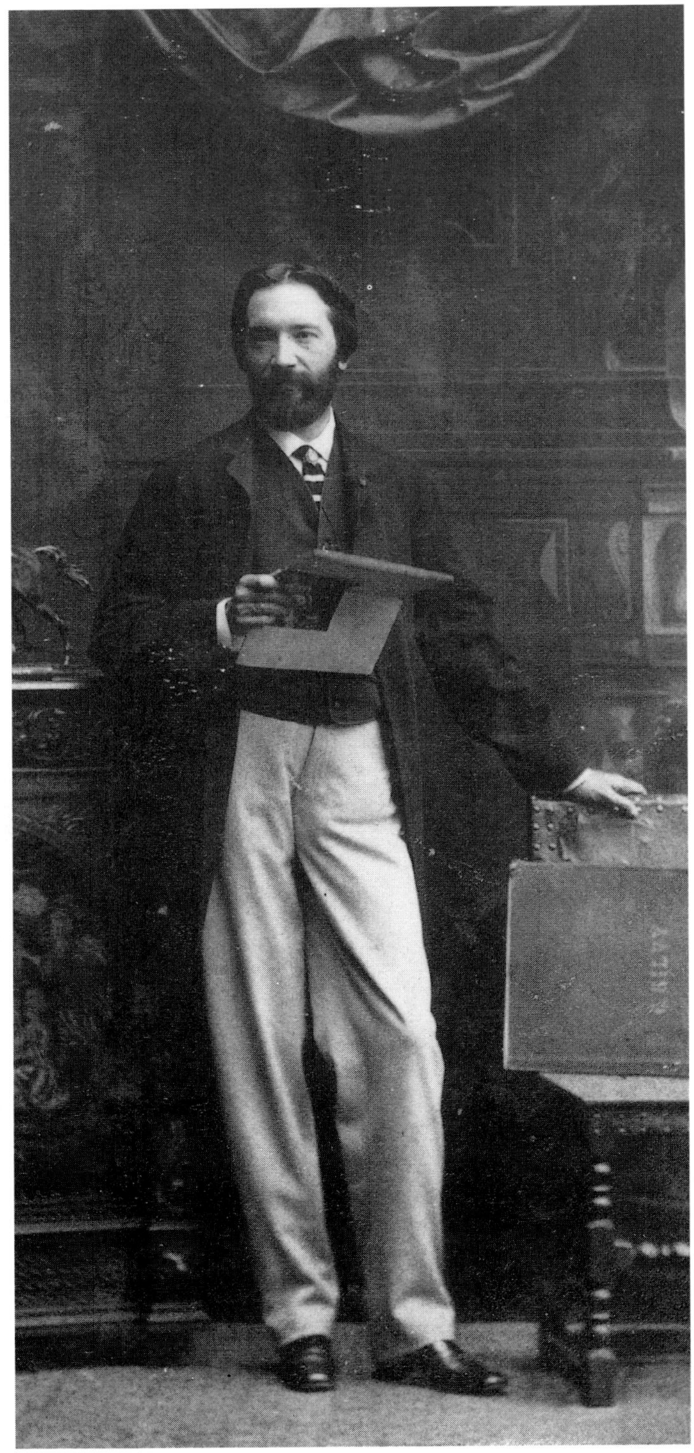

73. D. Mehul
1865
Camille Silvy, London (Daybook 12, no. 16366)

common in men's daywear for the 1860s, ten or fifteen years later, the fashion was less relaxed:

> The four staple colours for men's wear are black, blue, brown and olive. Other colours such as drab, grey, mixed etc. being so far as principal garments go what are termed fancy colours, should be very cautiously used. . . . It is a very high compliment to any man to tell him that black becomes him . . .[1]

This manual, quoted above, entitled *Complete Etiquette for Gentlemen*, of about 1880, reflects the prevailing lack of individuality and adventurousness in men's wear by the last decades of the nineteenth century. 'Drab' and 'grey' have become 'fancy' colours to be avoided by the cautious and respectable.

74

The sons of Frederick Chichester, and grandsons of the 1st Baron Templemore, these two brothers are photographed amidst the incongruous nautical rigging in Silvy's studio.

During the 1860s, both the knickerbocker suit and the sailor suit became staple wear for young boys. The Prince of Wales had been painted by Winterhalter in a sailor suit as early as 1846. The sailor's blouse or shirt, as worn by the Chichester brothers, could have either a square-cut or revers collar, and was worn with either long bell-bottom trousers, or knickerbockers.

Sailor hats, too, were popular, usually in the style of yachting hats with low, flat crowns. *The Englishwoman's Domestic Magazine* (September 1861) describes 'a sailor's hat in brown straw trimmed with black ribbon with a bow and ends, suitable for a little boy from six to seven years of age . . .'.[2]

The young sons of the Prince and Princess of Wales wore sailor suits regularly in public in the 1870s and consolidated the fashion's popularity. The Royal connection with the Navy had, of course, always been strong, and was continued by the career of Prince Alfred, who joined as a midshipman in 1861 (*see* Plate 7).

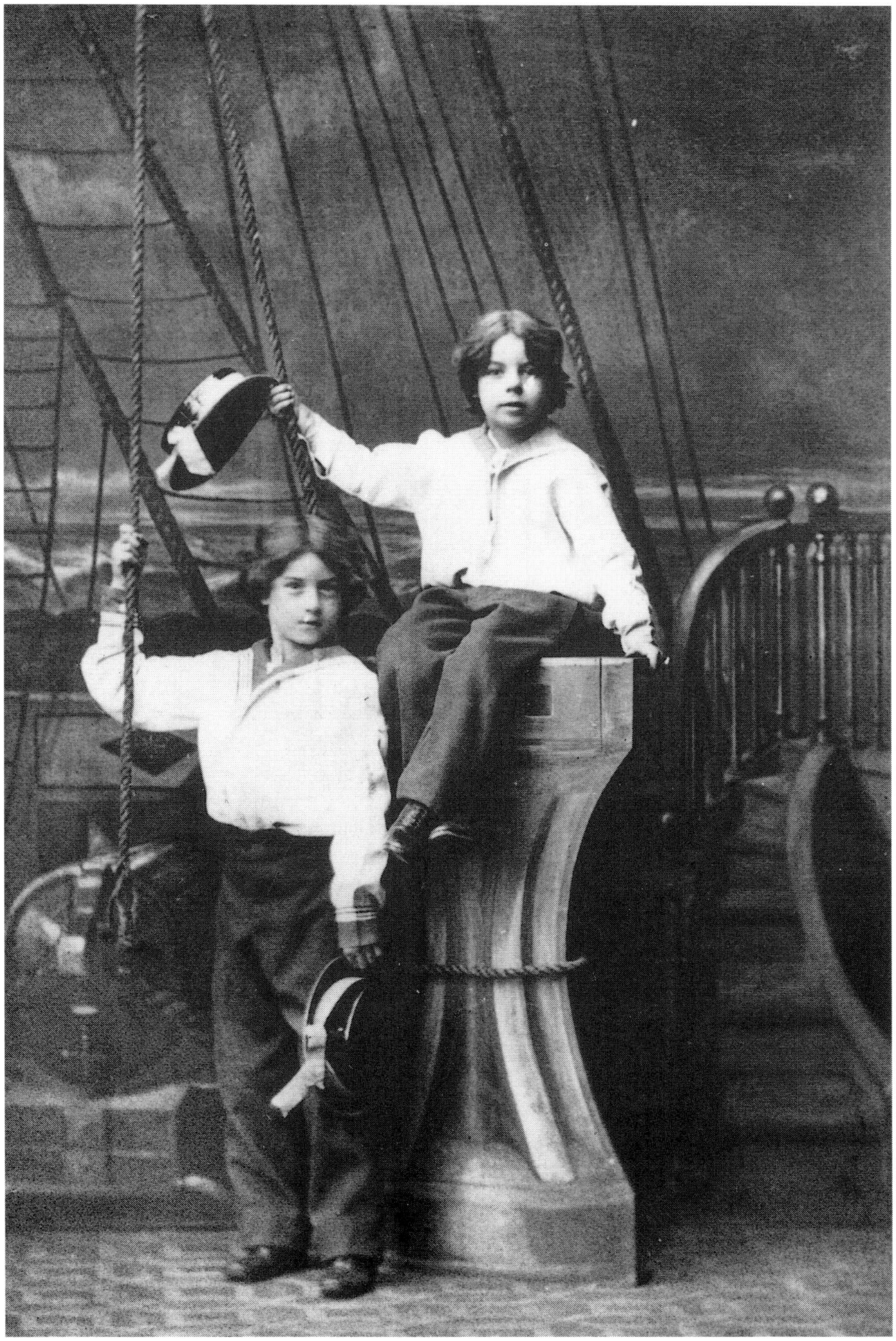

74. Alan George and Ernest William Chichester 1865
Camille Silvy, London (Daybook 13, no. 16622)

75

A celebrated actor-manager, Buckstone adopts a rather theatrical stance in this anonymous studio portrait.

Born in 1802, and first appearing on the London stage in 1823, Buckstone rapidly secured a reputation for distinctive comedy roles in contemporarily famous productions such as *Popping The Question* and *Good For Nothing*. He settled down as Manager of the Haymarket Theatre from 1853 to 1876, and died in 1879.

In this photograph, Buckstone wears a double-breasted frock coat, quite tight fitting and showing the distinctive front crease marks caused when the wearer sat down with his coat fastened. The coat has a prominent waist seam level with the bottom button, and the cloth has a glossy nap, which has caught the photographer's light. The frock coat was universal men's wear in the 1860s, as *The Tailor and Cutter* (24 April 1869) declared: 'A superfine black frock coat can be worn on a wedding day, or to attend a funeral; it is suitable for any occasion . . .'

This sitter wears a patterned waistcoat, barely visible above the coat collar, a high, starched collar and a satin cravat. The juxtaposition of the extremes of light and dark in this portrait – the black of the coat and trousers with the white lining of the top hat, the white shirt and pale face – exemplifies the stark contrasts with which the studio photographer of the 1860s had to contend, and of which he most complained.

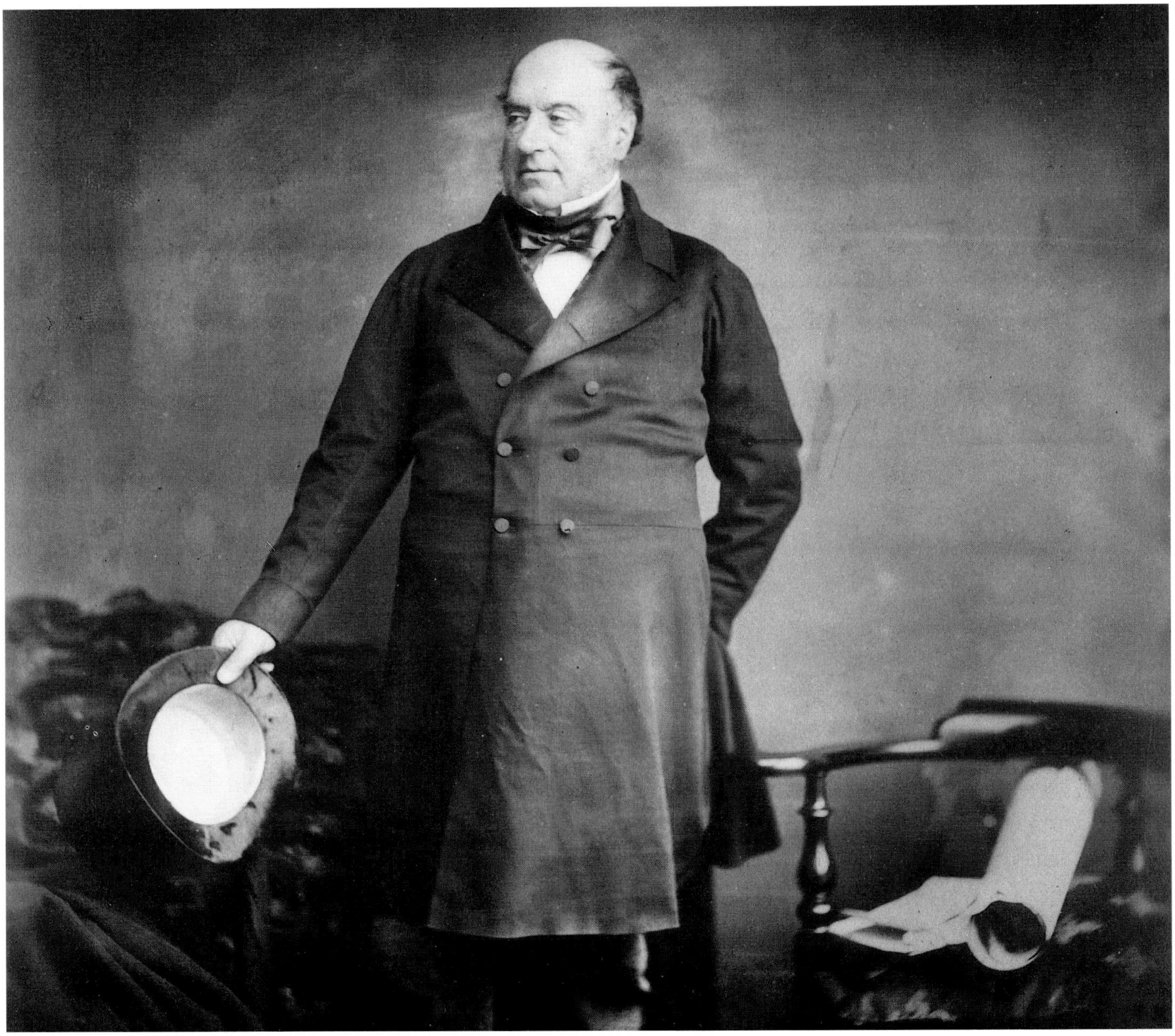

75. John Baldwin Buckstone
***c.* 1865**
Photographer unknown (NPG x 6421)

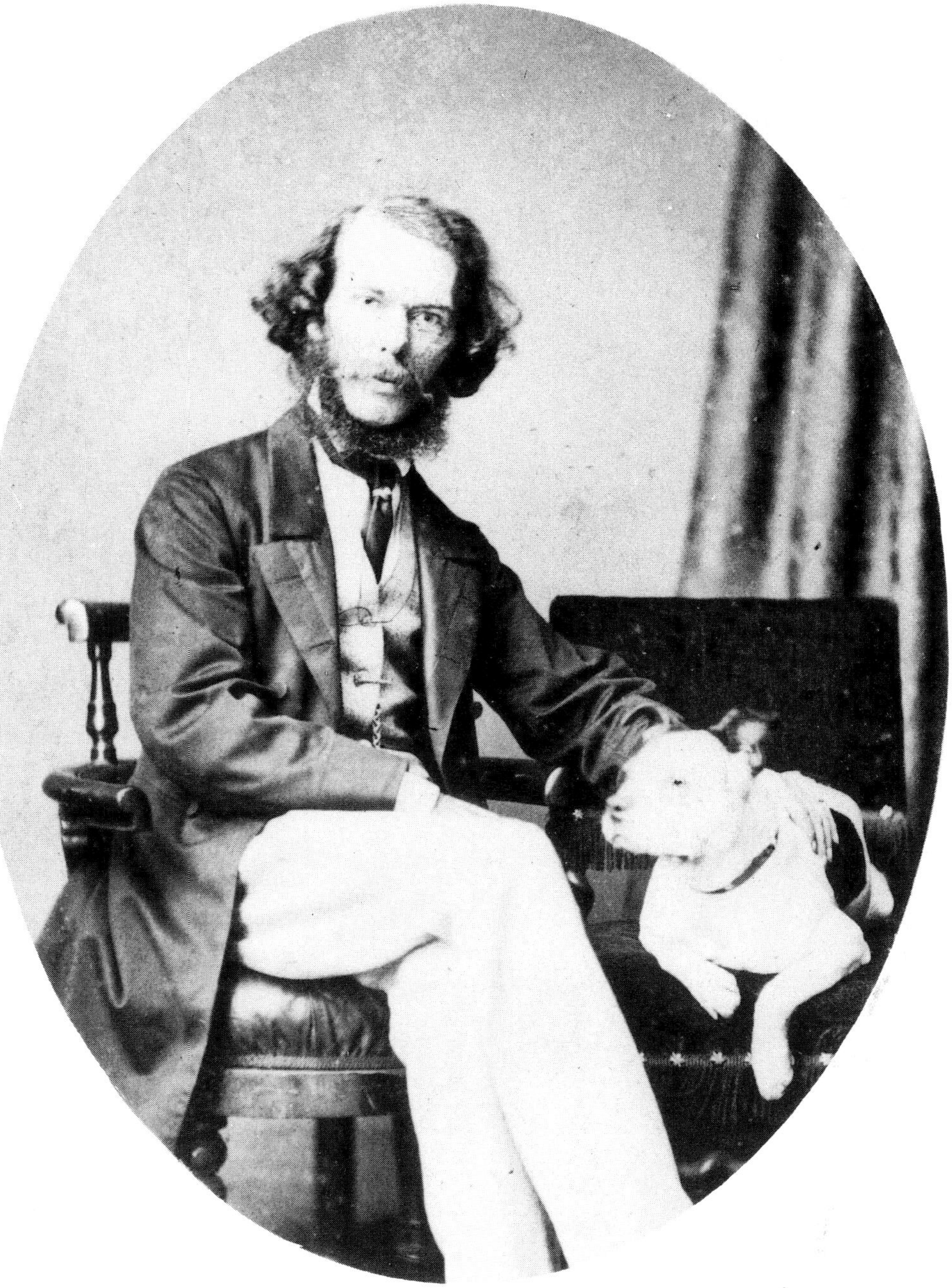

76. George H. Lewes
***c.* 1865**
John & Charles Watkins, London
(NPG Ax 7530)

76

A famous writer, critic, and editor, Lewes was also notorious for his longstanding relationship with Mary Anne Evans, or George Eliot as she is better known. Born in 1817, he was Editor of *The Leader* in 1851, when he met George Eliot, by which time his wife Agnes was showing the first signs of her progressive insanity. Although he had three sons by his wife, he left his family in 1854 to live on the Continent with George Eliot. They remained together until his death in 1878.

In this carte portrait, Lewes wears a fashionable frock coat with wide, satin-faced collar and revers. His lighter-cloth waistcoat matches his trousers in hue, and is worn with a high, stiff winged collar, and a tie fastened in the four-in-hand way.

He has bushy hair, and side-whiskers meeting below the chin. Luxuriant side-whiskers, known as 'Dundrearies' and usually worn with full, drooping moustaches, became very popular after the celebrated portrayal of the character Lord Dundreary by E. A. Southern in the 1861 stage production of Tom Taylor's *Our American Cousin*.[3]

Relaxed, if attentive, Lewes rests his hand affectionately on his pet bull terrier as they sit on their separate chairs for their photograph.

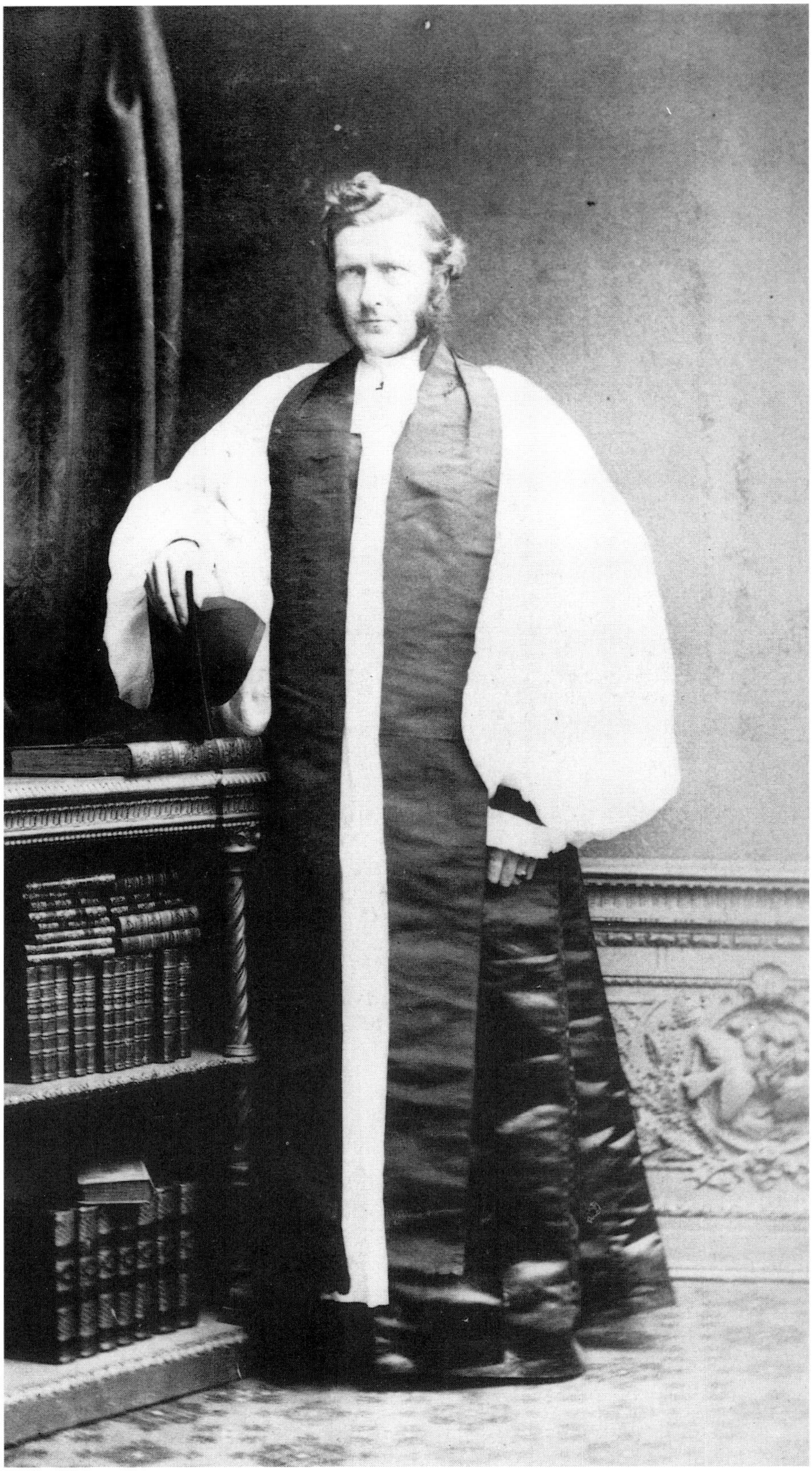

77. Right Reverend William Tozer, Bishop of Honduras Mid 1860s
C. T. Newcombe, London (NPG x 6421)

77

The Reverend Tozer wears his clerical rochet and chimer and carries his square cap or academic 'mortarboard'.

The bishop's rochet is a full-length gown or robe of fine, white linen or lawn with very full sleeves gathered into frilled cuffs, and with a band of black (or sometimes red) silk.

The chimer of black (or red) silk taffeta, is a sleeveless gown worn over the rochet. With these two are usually worn a hood and tippet (or scarf): the hood as part of academic dress; the full-length tippet hanging loosely over the chimer. The tippet was a largely nineteenth-century innovation and was common by the 1860s and 1870s. It distinguished the clergy from the laity in choir dress, when all were wearing cassock, surplice, gown, and hood.

78, 79

Both bishops display 'low church' leanings in their choice of dress. The Rev. Ellicott, standing, wears a black, clerical frock coat over black vest and trousers, with a high, white cravat. He carries a black-silk top hat. The Rev. Gray, seated, wears a short cassock held at the waist with a broad sash and worn with black breeches and a clerical frock coat. Both men wear long side-whiskers.

'Broad' and 'low' churchmen were dressed more casually than their 'high' brethren; in garb more akin to ordinary, formal, lay dress. A 'high' churchman would usually have been clean-shaven, and more of an aesthete in appearance than these gentlemen.

The Rev. B. J. Armstrong in his *Norfolk Diary* (22 February 1864) wrote that, 'Dr Vaughan, the vicar, is 'Broad' church which his secular coat in the photographs in the Doncaster shops fully confirms – double breasted frock coat and high shirt collar . . .'.[4]

By 1864 trousers had replaced the customary breeches, unless worn with a cassock. Most Anglican clergy wore dark suits for everyday wear and cassocks for preaching, services, and formal occasions (including studio portrait sittings). Roman Catholic clergy were forbidden to wear cassocks outside church.

The distinctive white bands were also losing favour by the 1860s, although some bishops fought a rearguard action to save them, seeing them as representing position and prestige, and allying the clergy with lawyers and parish clerks. The white cravat, stock, or collar remained obligatory wear.

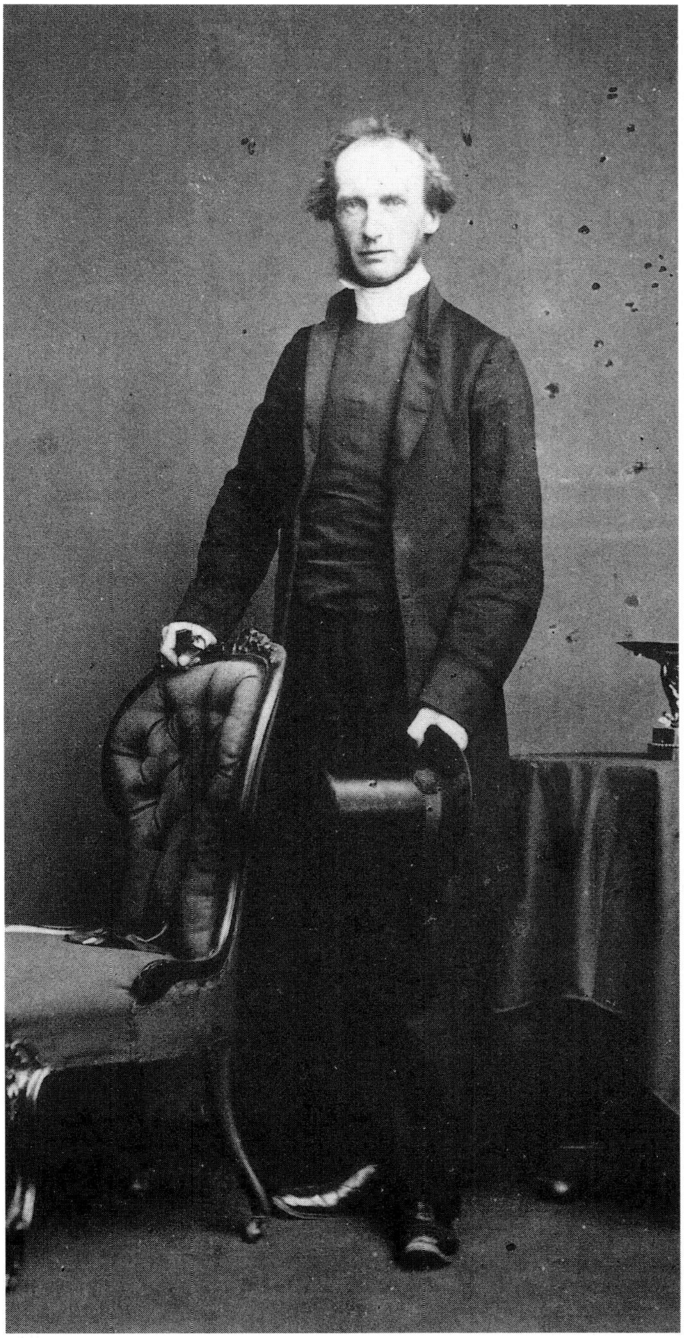

78. Right Reverend Charles Ellicott, Bishop of Gloucester
Mid 1860s
Photographer unknown (NPG Ax 9811)

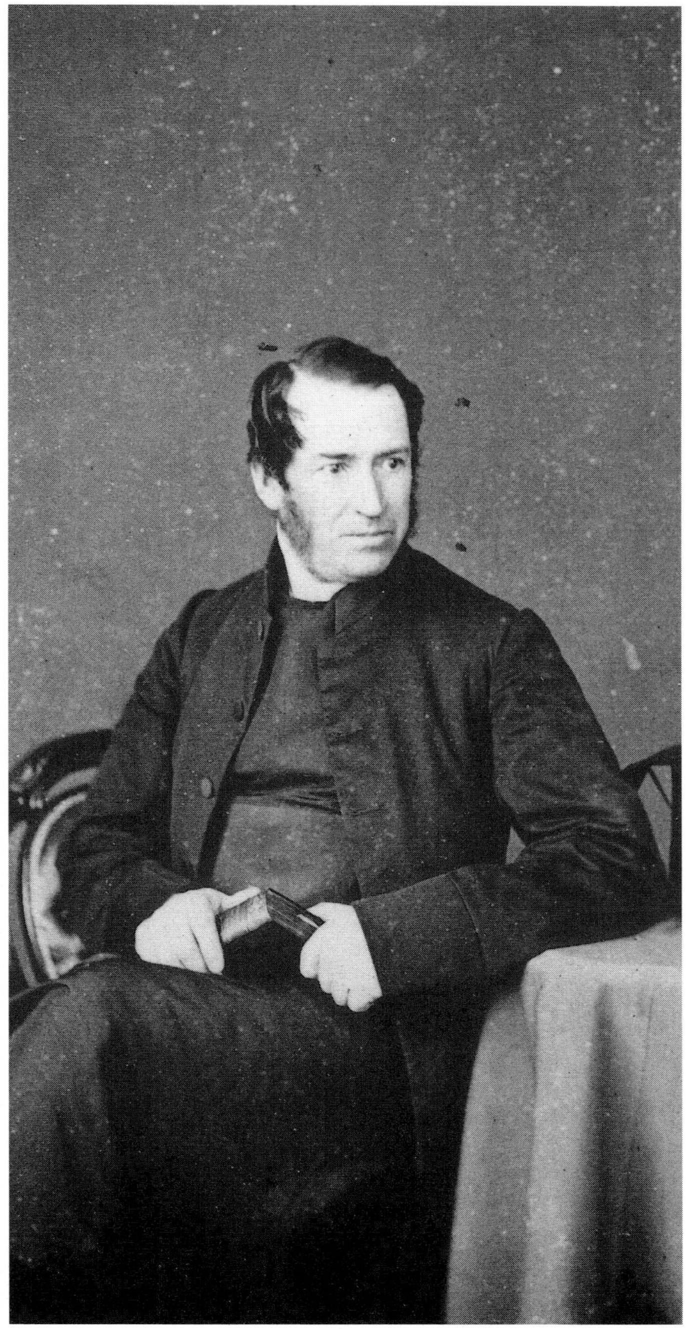

79. Right Reverend Robert Gray, Bishop of Cape Town
Mid 1860s
H. Hering (NPG Ax 9815)

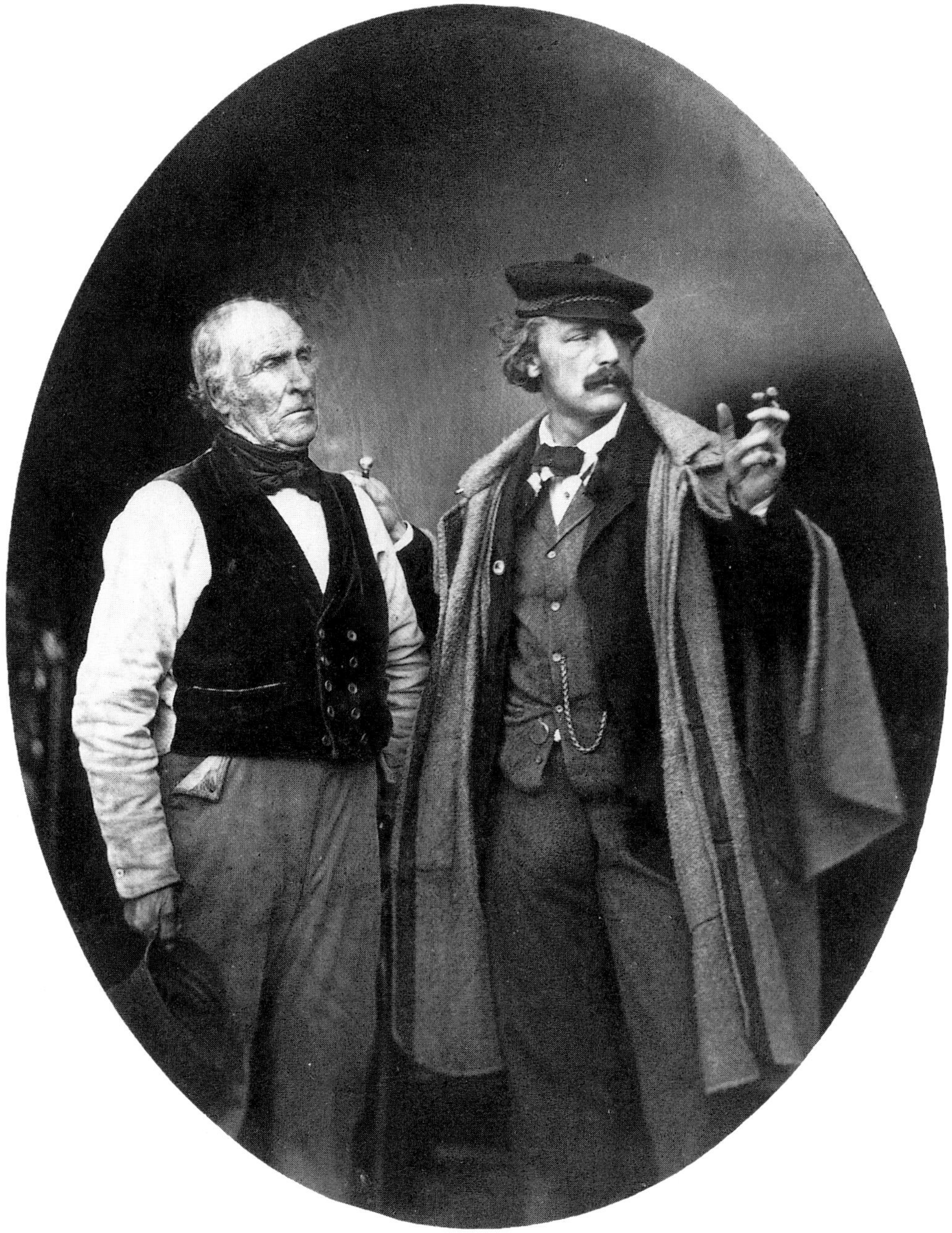

80. Sir Coutts Lindsay and Peter Drummond
Mid 1860s

Photographer unknown (Jocelyn Album (59) p. 41) (NPG Ax 36075)

80

Sir Coutts Lindsay, soldier, artist and art-lover, poses in rather 'Bohemian' attire with his head gamekeeper. Lindsay, born in 1824, achieved fame as the founder of the Grosvenor Gallery in 1877, some ten years after the date of this portrait. This gallery exhibited the work of many contemporary artists, including such figures as Holman Hunt and Burne-Jones. Before this venture, Sir Coutts Lindsay had reached the rank of Captain in the Grenadier Guards and had fought in the Crimean War. He also painted, exhibiting ten works at the Royal Academy between 1862 and 1875. In 1864, just pre-dating this photograph, he married a daughter of Mr Henry Fitzroy by whom he had two daughters.

His obituary in *The Times* (9 May 1913) suggests that his commercial interests in the famed Grosvenor Gallery were allowed to overreach themselves, thus contributing to the institution's demise. Mention is made of obtrusive, vulgar announcements 'incompatible with the dignity of art'.

In this portrait, Sir Coutts Lindsay is in a woollen cape worn in the artists' manner, with a peaked, flat hat and a casual lounge jacket.

Peter Drummond, the gamekeeper, wears the typical working dress of an estate worker: sleeved velvet (or 'velveteen') waistcoat, fall-front cloth trousers, wound, black cravat tied in a simple double knot. He carries his black peaked hat, out of deference to his master.

81

Photographed here in his early twenties, in the middle 1860s, Prince Alfred cuts a stylishly casual figure. His straw boater, worn slanted, represents usual outdoor summer wear, as does his short double-breasted morning coat. Straw or 'nautical' hats were worn with sporting and walking outfits, as were early bowlers. Black-silk top hats, fashionable in the 1840s and 1850s, were rapidly acquiring the stamp of formality and, indeed, they were little worn for fashionable day wear by the 1870s, particularly by younger men like the Duke of Edinburgh, who preferred informality. *The Graphic* (20 February 1875) ran an editorial entitled 'Modern Masculine Dress' in which it declared:

> The great institution of British respectability, the tall black hat, along with its equally respectable adjuncts, the frock coat and all the attributes of what is called 'morning dress', totters to its fall. Already there are signs of disaffection among its most enthusiastic adherents. Loungers in the Park last season, might have noticed how frequently they encountered men dressed in suits of tweed and 'billy-cock' hats, and people similarly attired might have been often observed in many of the more fashionable thoroughfares of the metropolis . . .

The article goes on to recommend the adoption of the ever popular lounge suit for all daytime activities: 'For business, for study, for lounging, for walking, for riding, there is nothing better than the modern costume of a country gentleman . . .'. Royalty photographed in such casual attire only helped to reinforce this trend to informality in men's wear, albeit a cautious and slow-moving current.

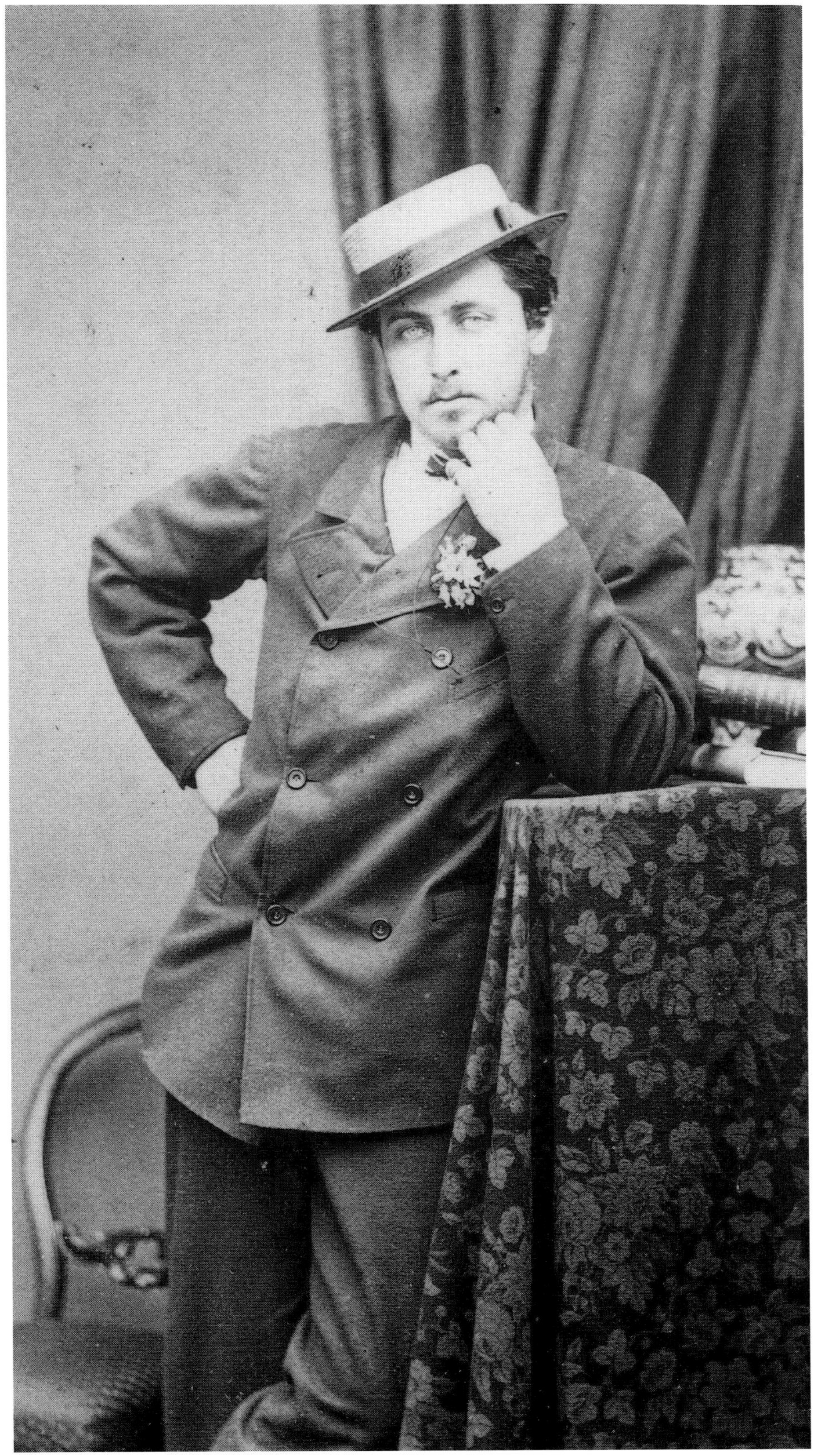

81. Alfred, Duke of Edinburgh
Mid 1860s
J. Russell & Sons (NPG Ax 33504)

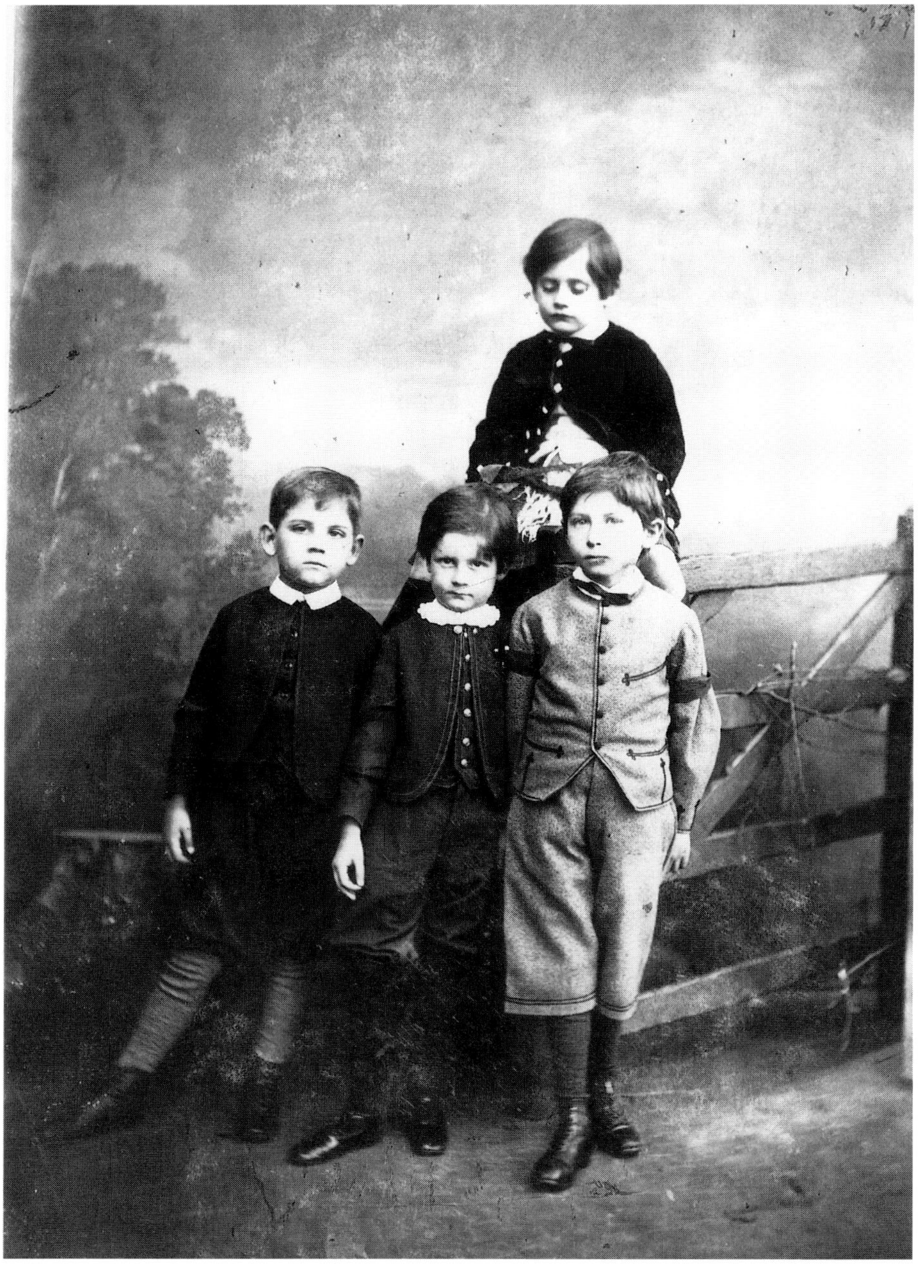

82. Richard and Andrew Rendel, Trevor and Johnnie
***c.* 1867**
James Ross, Edinburgh (Strachey Collection) (NPG x 33256)

82

This group of four boys, probably two pairs of brothers, dates from about 1867 and shows the variations available in the perennially popular knickerbocker suit.

The two standing boys, to the left of the photograph, both wear dark-cloth suits with matching breeches and short, round jackets fastened only at the top button. Similar suits abound in the fashion plates of the 1860s: *The Queen* (6 October 1866) includes

> a costume for a boy between six and eight, being loose and easy, and not impeding climbing propensities – a prominent characteristic among schoolboys. The material of the entire suit is dark grey tweed cloth . . .[5]

The boy illustrated wears calf-length boots, rather than ankle-length ones as worn by the boys in this portrait, and the account declares that these 'Polish boots' have 'a more pleasing effect with a knickerbocker suit than short boots.'

The eldest boy, in the lighter coloured suit, to the right of the group, wears a suit with buttoned jacket and open-leg, loose trousers rather than knickerbockers. *The Englishwoman's Domestic Magazine* (May 1867) shows a variation 'in brown cloth, with short loose trousers to match the jacket . . .'.[6]

The Queen for a year previously (18 August 1866) shows a

> pretty costume for a boy, made up of grey and black check tweed cloth – the trousers and jacket being cut from the same material. The jacket is bound with black braid and fastened with fancy grey pearl buttons.[7]

The youngest boy, aged about five, seated on the gate, wears a Highland suit with black-velvet jacket and tartan kilt. All four boys wear black crape mourning bands on both arms, presumably for a mutual relative.

83

In a portrait from the time when the prince was the proud father of a young and expanding family, Edward wears a

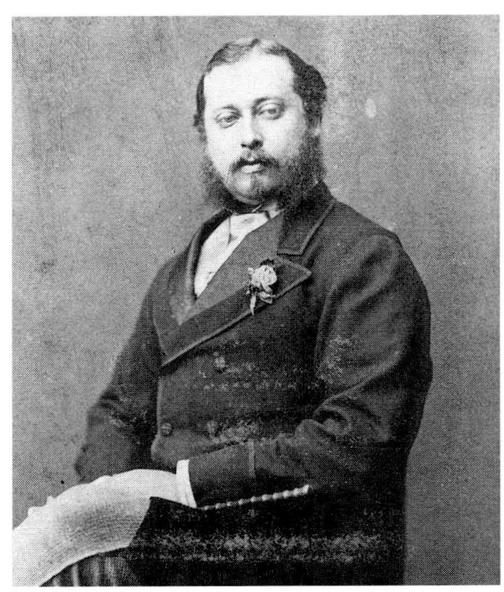

83. Edward, Prince of Wales
***c.* 1869**
W. & D. Downey (NPG x 32937)

frock coat with wide collar and revers, partially faced with black satin. His large silk cravat is pinned in place, completely obscuring his shirt front.

Never as noted for his good looks as was his beautiful wife for hers, the prince was nonetheless extremely particular about his dress, and usually sartorially immaculate. Several styles of jacket were ascribed to his name, including one of this date appearing in *The Tailor and Cutter* (21 November 1868) and described as 'the jacket usually worn by the heir apparent . . . a loose double breasted jacket, greatly patronised by the West End bloods at present . . . showing the figure off to better advantage . . .'.[8] Smarter and more formal for his photography sitting, the prince has exchanged his loose jacket for a tight and constricting frock coat.

The father of five children by 1869, the Prince of Wales is already beginning to acquire the heaviness of jowl and fullness of figure of a middle-aged man. His full side-whiskers run low on his cheeks, practically meeting under his chin, and were soon to blossom forth into his characteristic beard, so useful in concealing his unprepossessing double chin.

84

The Harrow versus Eton annual cricket match was a feature of the social season by the middle of the nineteenth century.

Dressed in their cricketing 'whites', this XI wear matching peaked caps in dark-blue and white stripes, the colours of Harrow School; two-tone sporting shoes; and sashes tied at the waist. Their shirts are a variety of collared and collarless, only Mr Law, at the back, wearing his white blazer.

The Illustrated London News (17 July 1869) reported on the match and concluded that Harrow made a rather poor showing, being forced to follow on, and only scoring 218, 19 short of Eton's first innings. However, it continues to remind its readers that, since the matches began in 1805 (annually from 1822), Harrow had still scored one more victory in total than Eton.[9]

Whether photographed before or after their rout at the hands of their opponents, the team have a somewhat dejected air. A few years later, at the 1876 match, *The Queen* reported on the typical 'toilettes' in evidence amongst spectators:

> We noticed that the younger ladies favoured thick white striped muslin dresses with white sashes. Hot as it was, silks were the prevailing thing, and there were even velvets trimmed with feather and fur trimming. Light and dark blue appeared chiefly in bows, fans and rosettes, not much in the dresses . . .'.[10]

This portrait, taken outside a clubhouse, has unfortunately suffered from some deterioration over the years.

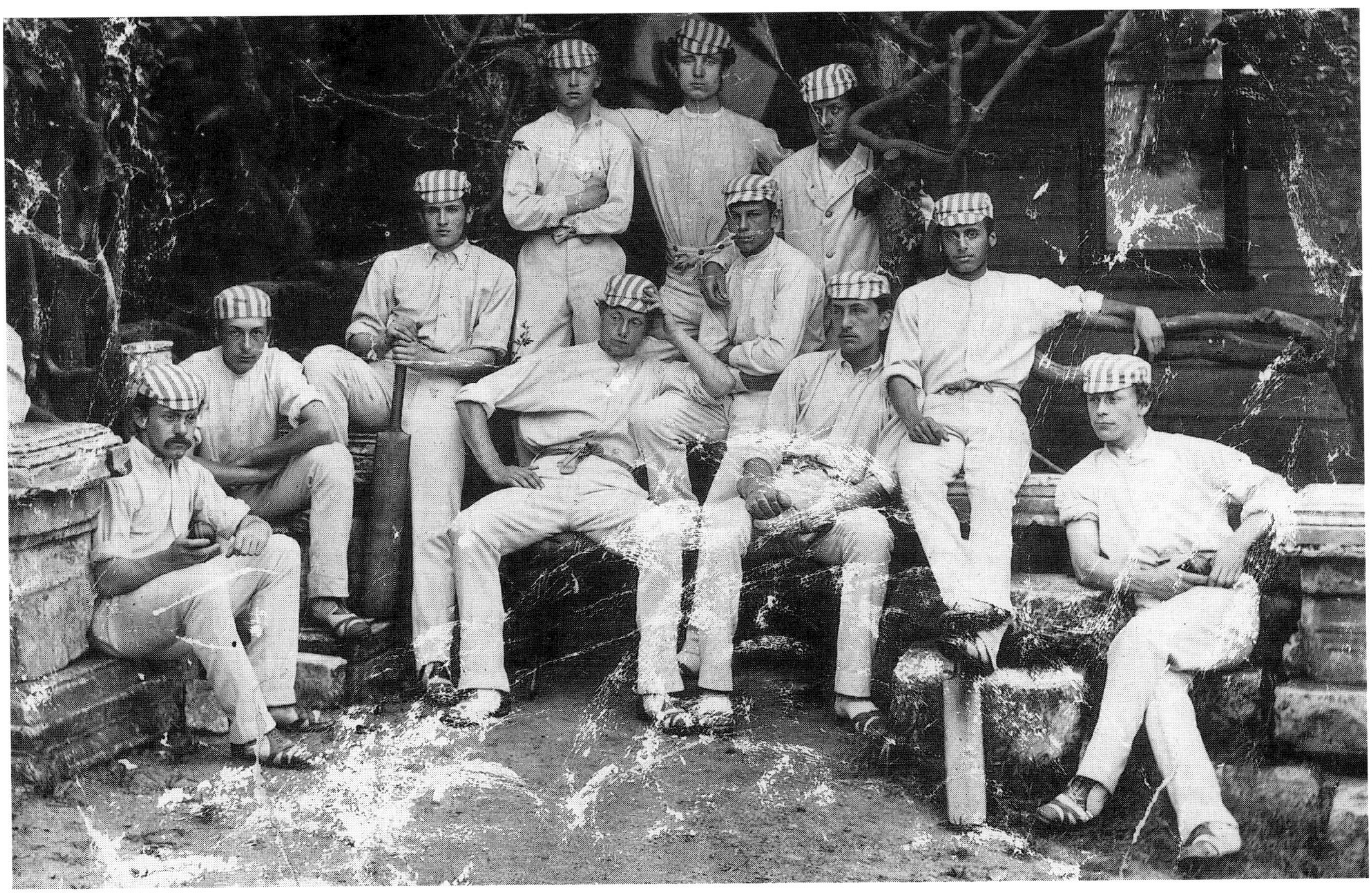

84. The Harrow School Cricket Eleven 1869
Photographer unknown (NPG x 4333)

FEMALE

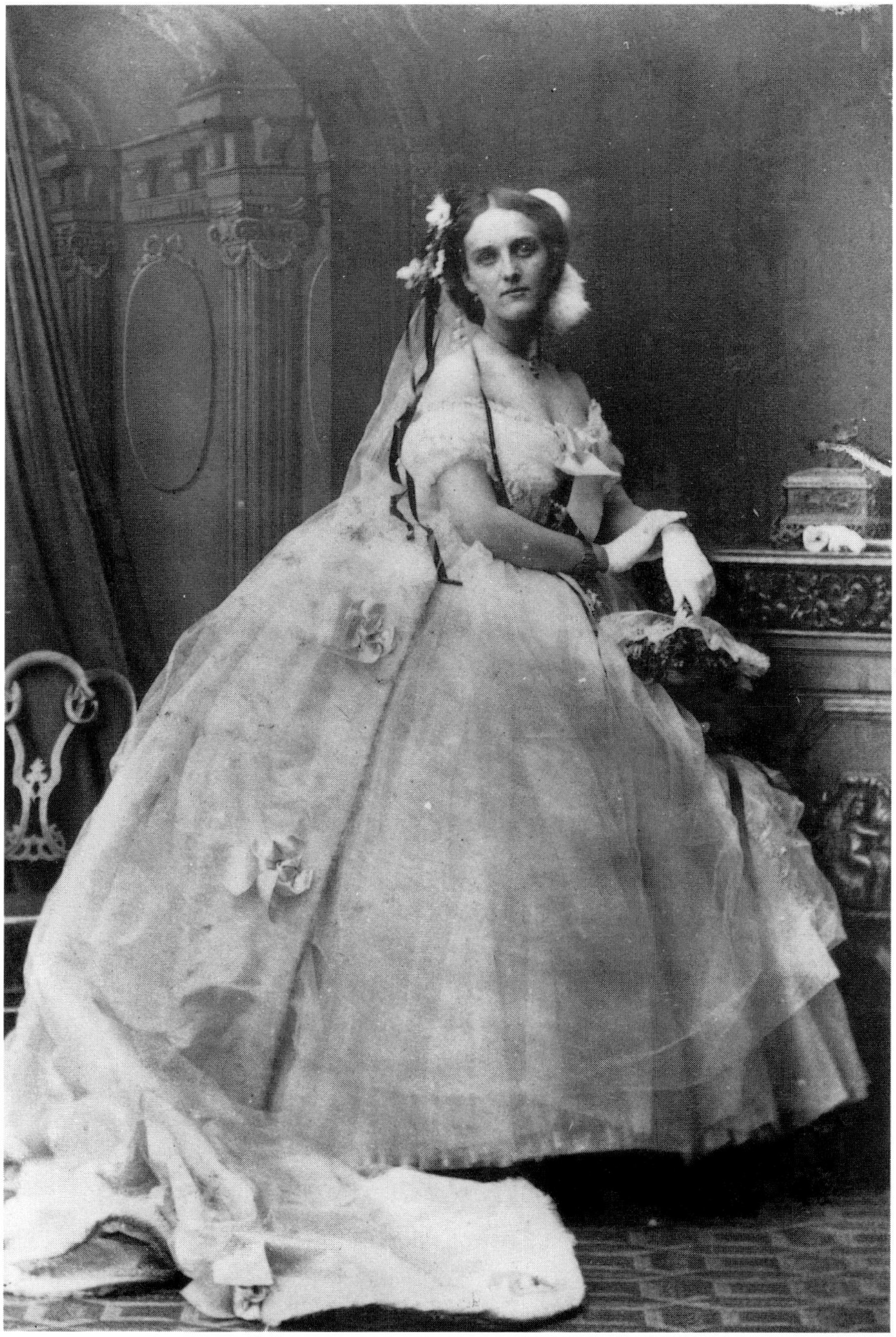

85. Miss Emily Pringle
1865
Camille Silvy, London (Daybook 13, no. 16352)

85

Miss Pringle wears a white-silk court presentation dress entirely covered in a cloud of white tulle. Other features include a veil, voluminous train, white gloves, ostrich-feather head ornament, very low neckline, and a presentation bouquet.

Drawing Rooms were usually held in March, May, and August, and were the occasions on which the Queen, or her representative, held Presentations. They were governed by strict regulations and attendance represented a considerable social distinction. Applications for presentation were made on 1 January for the following Season, by a sponsor who had already been presented. *Etiquette For Ladies*, a manual of 1870 published by 'Warne's Bijou Books' advised that: 'Only certain professions are admitted at court after the nobility and squirearchy. The wives and daughters of the clergy, of naval and military officers, of physicians and barristers . . .', not, it continues, those of solicitors or merchants 'though wealth and connexion have proved a passport thither of late years'.[1]

The 18 May 1865 Drawing Room was held by Princess Helena on the Queen's behalf. The early years after the Prince Consort's death (1861) saw the Queen delegating such official functions entirely to her daughters and daughter-in-law. This Drawing Room was one of the very last held at St James's Palace; in the same year the ceremony was moved to the rather more spacious Buckingham Palace.

Miss Pringle's train, which bunches at her feet, was probably about seven or eight feet in length, and considerable skill would have been required in negotiating the ceremony itself, particularly the exit from the royal presence, which had to be engineered backwards out of the 60-foot throne room.

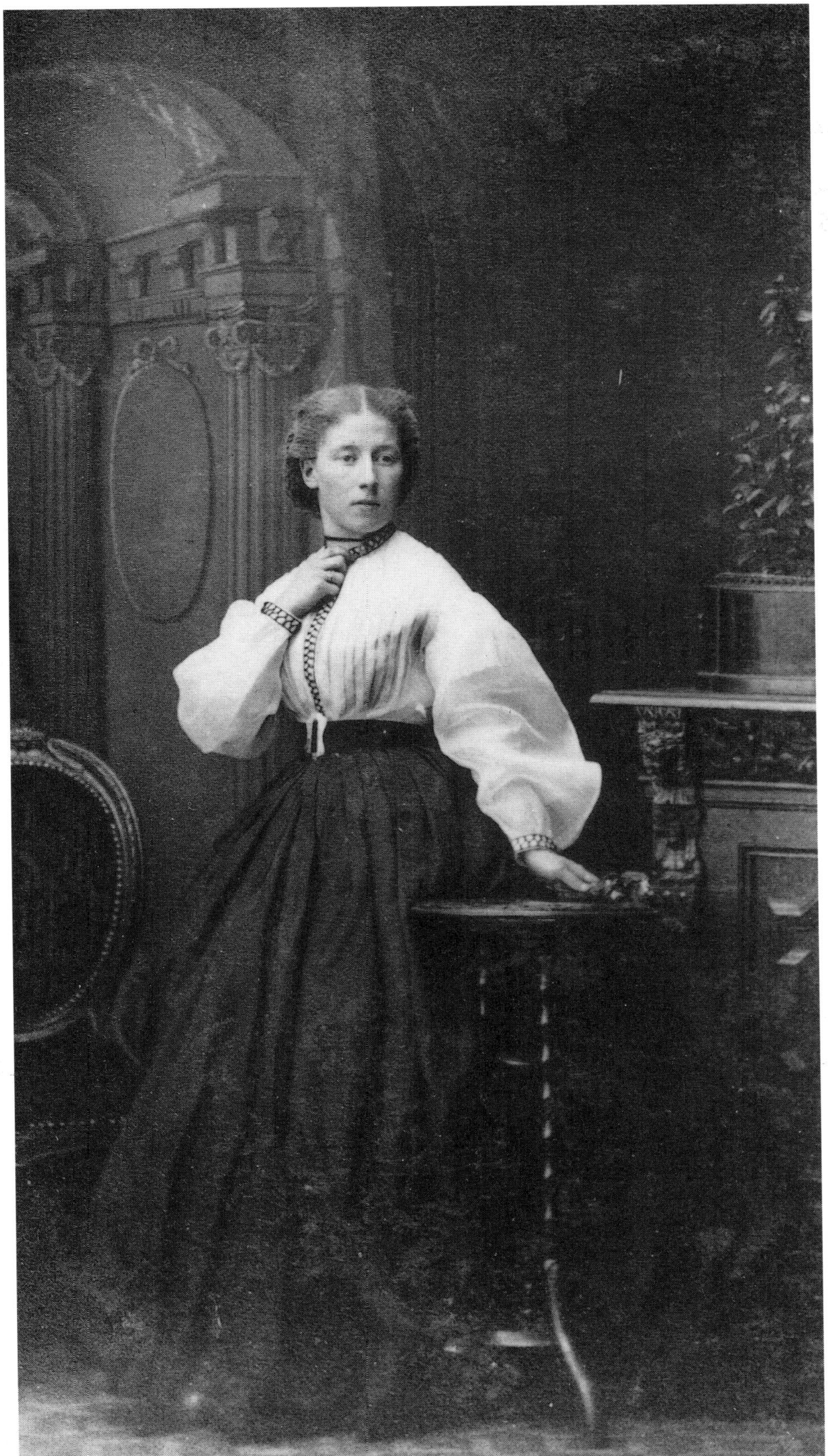

86. Miss Gordon
1865
Camille Silvy, London (Daybook 12, no. 16466)

86

The Miss Gordon photographed here is the sister of General Gordon who, 20 years later, was to lead the ill-fated expedition to the Sudan and to meet his death at Khartoum in January 1885. He achieved the status of patriotic martyr immediately, and the whole nation grieved for him, none more so than the Queen, who wrote a letter of sympathy to his sister on 17 February 1885 when the news reached England.[2]

Miss Gordon is seen here in earlier and happier days, and wears a white muslin 'canezous' or *chemisette* with full bishop sleeves, trimmed at the collar, fronts, and cuffs with narrow, black, criss-cross braid. She wears a full skirt, widely pleated to the waist and fastened with a black belt with metal buckle. This blouse and skirt ensemble represents an unusual indoor outfit for the 1860s, illustrative of future developments. The spring and early summer of 1865 were unusually warm, as *The World Of Fashion* (July 1865) related: 'The brilliant sunny weather with which we have been favoured during the past month, has occasioned the adoption of light summer Toilettes at an unusually early period . . .'.

87

The daughter of the 2nd Baron Wenlock, Miss Lawley poses in a pale summer dress composed primarily of diaphanous, ribbed-silk tulle. Bands of darker-silk fringed braid trim the cuffs and shoulder seams and run as a border above the hem and its three, narrow flounces. The fullness of this skirt, worn over a wide crinoline, made it both difficult to manoeuvre and also an alarming fire and accident risk. The women's journals were peppered with gruesome accounts of fatal accidents: *The Ladies' Treasury* (1 April 1864) carried an article entitled 'Our Iron-Clads':

> A statement has appeared in the public papers that 40,000 women have lost their lives by accidents, attributable to crinolines.... Two more victims, within the last week, have been publicly added to this number.... One infatuated victim wore two crinolines, and these coming in contact with fire, she was burned to death. One horrifying circumstance connected with this disaster was the fact that in the endeavour to put out the fire by wrapping a blanket round her, she at once tore it from her. The inference is that the steels of the crinoline were red hot and that the blanket pressed these against her person . . .

The second 'terrible fatality' occured in Carlisle when a certain Miss Nelson was dragged by her skirt and crinoline into an Archimedean screw machine at a biscuit manufactory and was:

> . . . dragged in by a leg and whirled round again and again; in truth, she was torn and mangled and dead in less than a second . . . and all this within two minutes of the entry of the party through the mill gates.[3]

The Honourable Caroline Lawley, however, managed to escape such a dreadful fate, and indeed, lived until 1934.

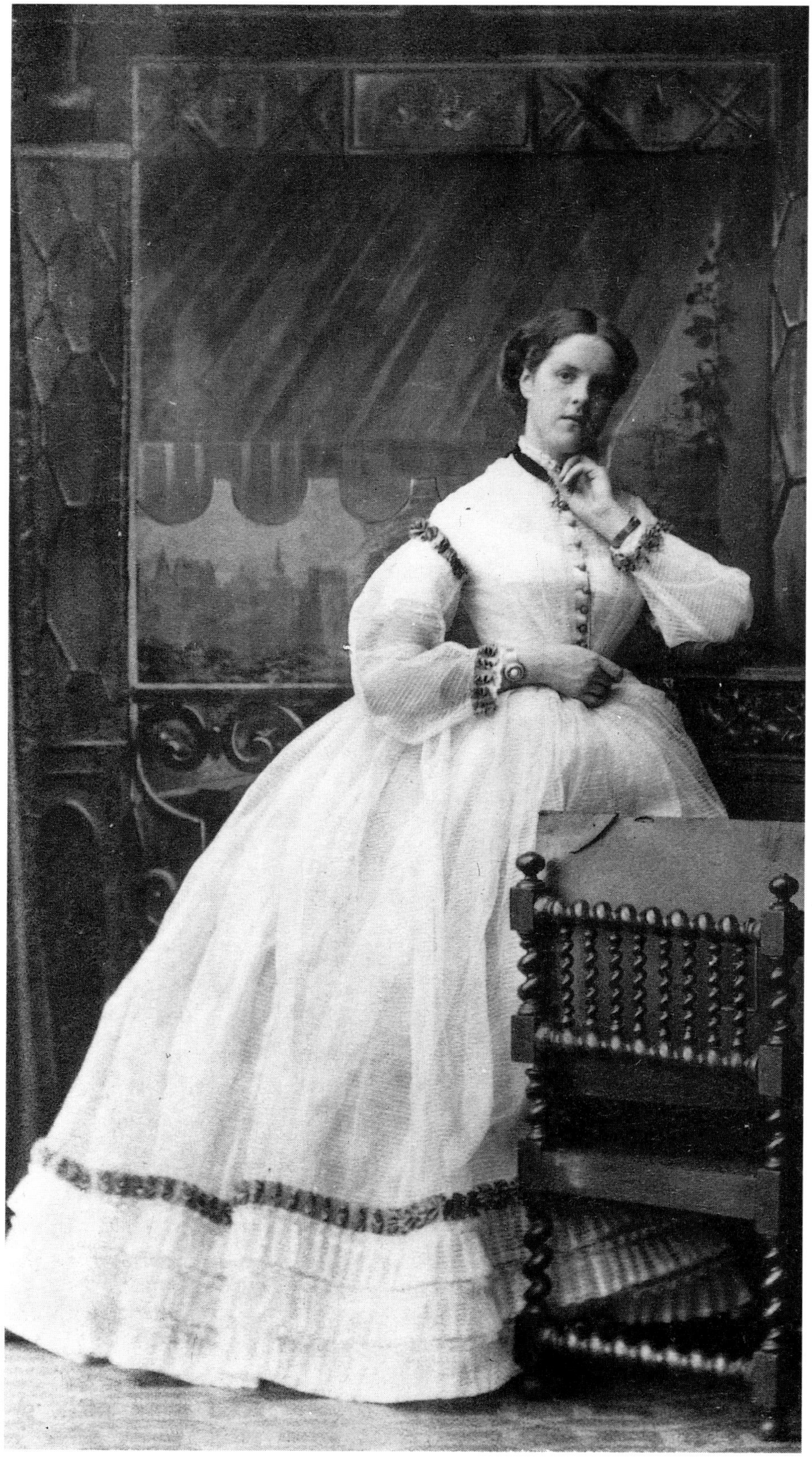

87. The Honourable Caroline Lawley 1865
Camille Silvy, London (Daybook 12, no. 16517)

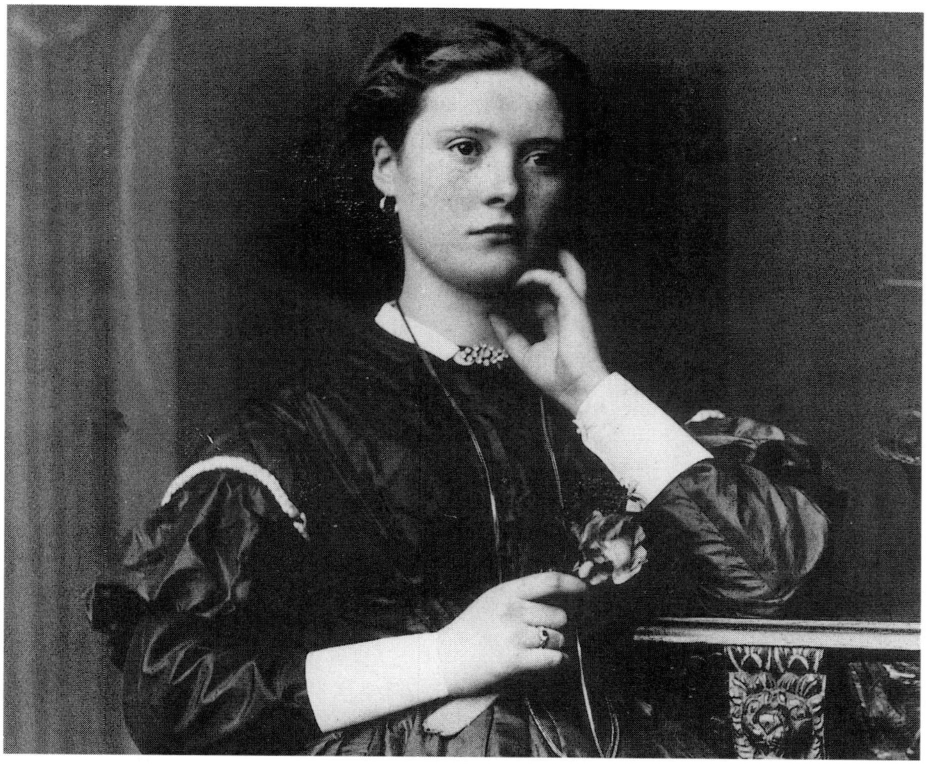

88. **Miss Brown**
1865
Camille Silvy, London (Daybook 13, no. 16530)

One of the most significant features of Miss Timenez's photograph is that it has been considerably retouched, presumably at the sitter's request, in order to trim her figure. This has involved redefining the line of the bodice at each side and particularly on her left; and also the scratching out of areas of the waist itself, which has left a rather noticeable 'shelf' effect to the top of the skirt, again on the sitter's left.

Retouching to reduce figures or to remove blemishes was very common with cartes-de-visite, although not so common for Silvy's sitters. Indeed, this is the most obvious example of this practice seen in all the 17,000 portraits left in the Silvy Daybooks.

88, 89

These two half-length portraits show the young women (about whom we know nothing more than their names) in dark daydresses (possibly made from alpaca) with full skirts pleated into the waist in deep knife pleats all the way round. Both women have plain, white cuffs and collars, with neck brooches. Miss Brown's cuffs are particularly long and worn over her dress cuffs. Miss Brown wears half puffed 'Medici' sleeves with a piped, white band of braid at the shoulder seam. Miss Timenez wears a bodice decorated at the front and on the sleeve cuffs and epaulettes with appliqué black velvet in cross-tabbed motifs. Both women wear their hair dressed into back chignons, thus exposing their earrings.

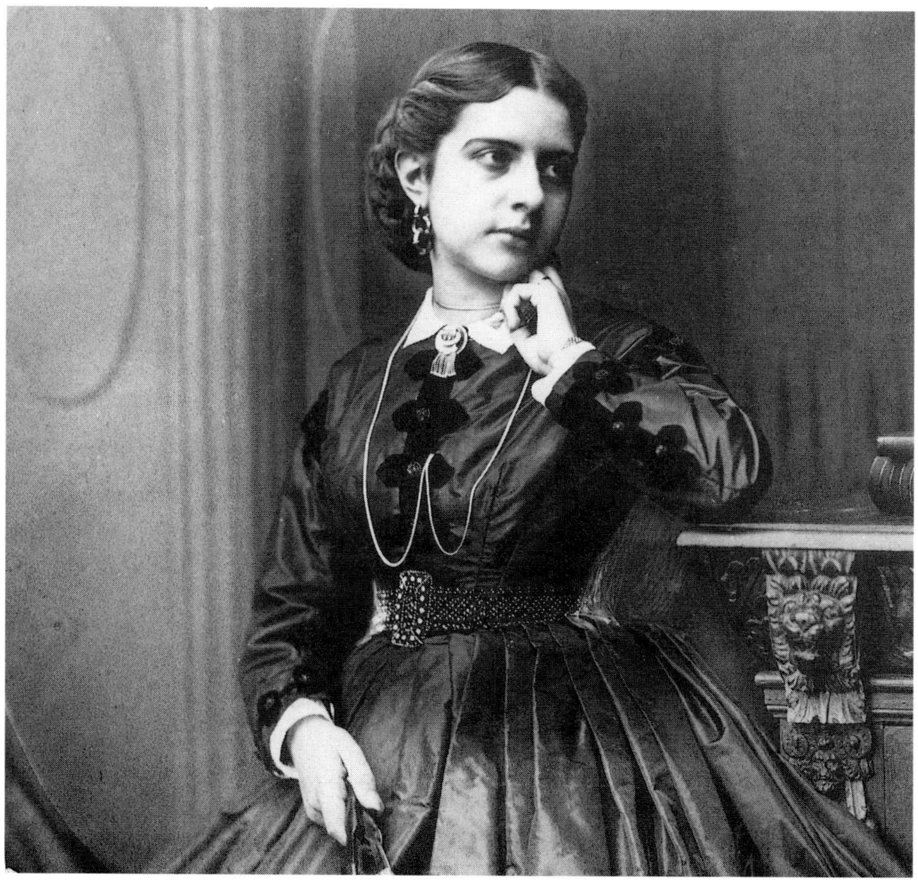

89. **Miss Timenez**
1865
Camille Silvy, London (Daybook 12, no. 16581)

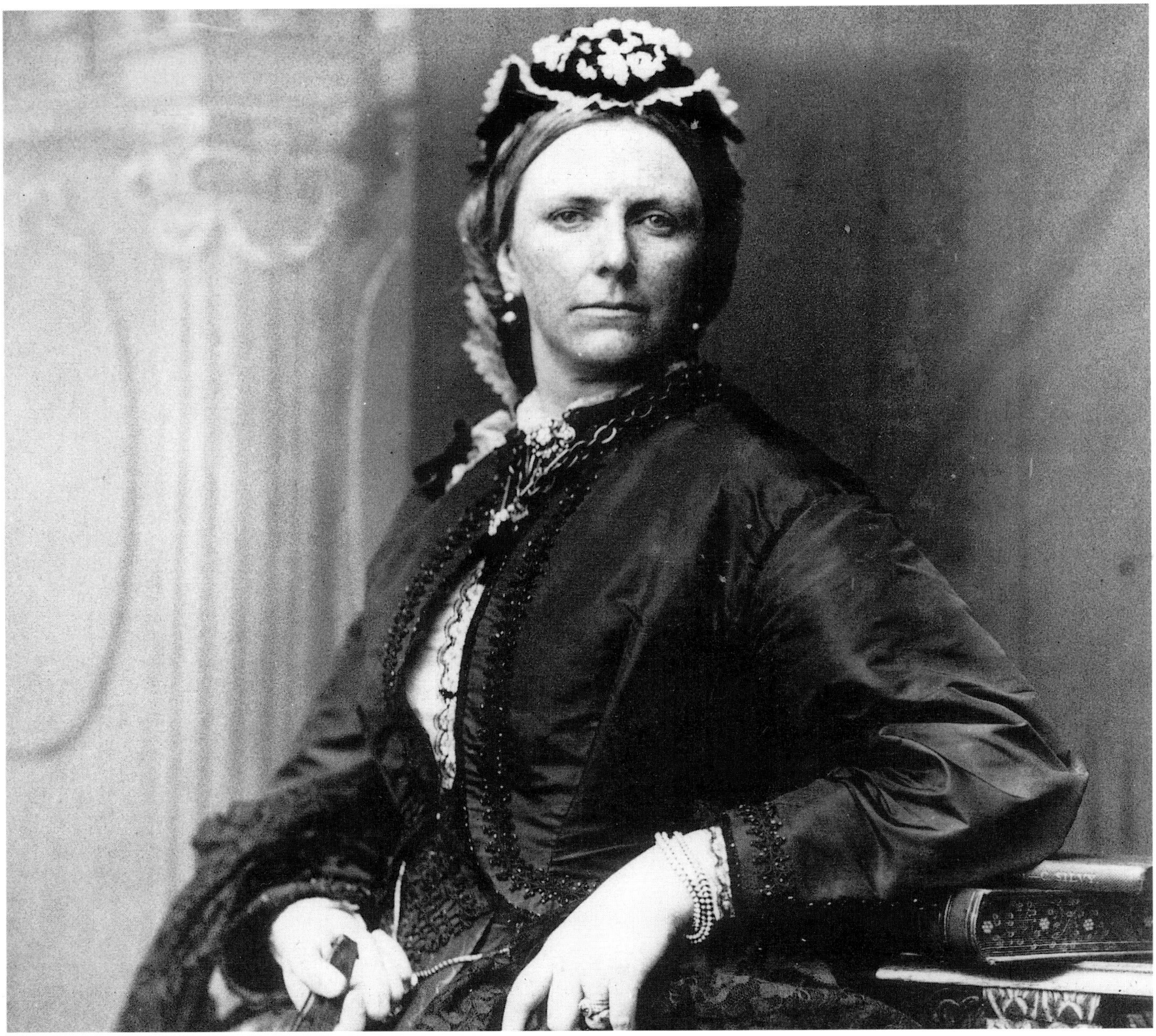

90. Lady Eden
1865
Camille Silvy, London (Daybook 13, no. 16580)

90

Elfrida Susanna Harriet Iremonger married Sir William Eden in 1844. She bore him eight children: William, Morton, Charles, Caroline, Helen, Edith, Blanche, and Rose. Rather poignantly, this portrait was taken only a few days before the youngest two daughters were to die, on 10 and 11 August 1865.

In this half-length photograph the imperious looking Lady Eden wears a black-silk bolero jacket. Known by a variety of names in the 1860s, these short jackets were tremendously popular, particularly in walking ensembles. 'Zouave' was the most usual term and derived from the appearance of the uniform jackets worn by the Algerian Zouave troops in the Franco-Italian War of 1859.[4]

The Ladies' Treasury (March 1860): 'The Zouave jacket is still in favour for morning dress. These may be of cashmere or cloth; if the latter, we recommend dark braid, but for the former, the gayest *passementerie* is advisable . . .'[5] Lady Eden's Zouave jacket is of black silk and trimmed at the fronts and cuffs with black-glass bead or jet *passementerie*.

The 'Senorita' jacket was another term for these boleros: 'The short Senorita jacket will be a great favourite as it is suited to be worn either with a ceinture suissesse or with a plain buckle belt' (*The World Of Fashion*, March 1865). *The World Of Fashion* also describes these jackets as 'Caracos Suisses', as seen in a black velvet example in a fashion plate for March 1862.

Lady Eden wears a black and white trimmed 'Marie Stuart' cap as popularized by the widowed Queen Victoria in the 1860s. She holds a fan in one hand and a black, Chantilly lace shawl in the other.

91

Nurses, like governesses, were expected to present a neat and demure appearance, in accordance with their respectable, almost genteel, position in the servants' hierarchy. Mrs Gregory's unnamed nurse wears a plain silk dress, neatly buttoned at the bodice front, with a discreet black hat and a black cape fastened at the neck with a cameo brooch. She succeeds in merging into the background, thus allowing attention to centre on her young charge, splendidly attired in a christening robe and frilled white bonnet. The long skirt of the baby's robe is carefully spread out over the nurse's knee to exhibit the white-work decoration to its full advantage. Four, broad, horizontal bands trim the front skirt, each one composed of eight, narrow, parallel tucks. The hem and edges are embroidered with broderie anglaise white-work with a scalloped edge.

Christening robes described in fashion periodicals of a similar date show like decoration: *The Englishwoman's Domestic Magazine* (April 1867) illustrates a robe

> of fine jaconet, pleated and trimmed with embroidery insertions forming a berthe to the collar, and revers down the front of the skirt which is terminated by two jaconet flounces.[6]

The Queen for five months later describes a robe

> of clear muslin, enriched in front with five long tabs composed of bouillonnés, embroidered insertions and guipure . . . the bodice is composed of narrow tucks alternating with rows of guipure insertions and trimmed at top and bottom with rich guipure edging.[7]

Undisturbed by the photographer, this infant sleeps peacefully by the cradle, itself lavishly trimmed with white muslin and bobble fringing.

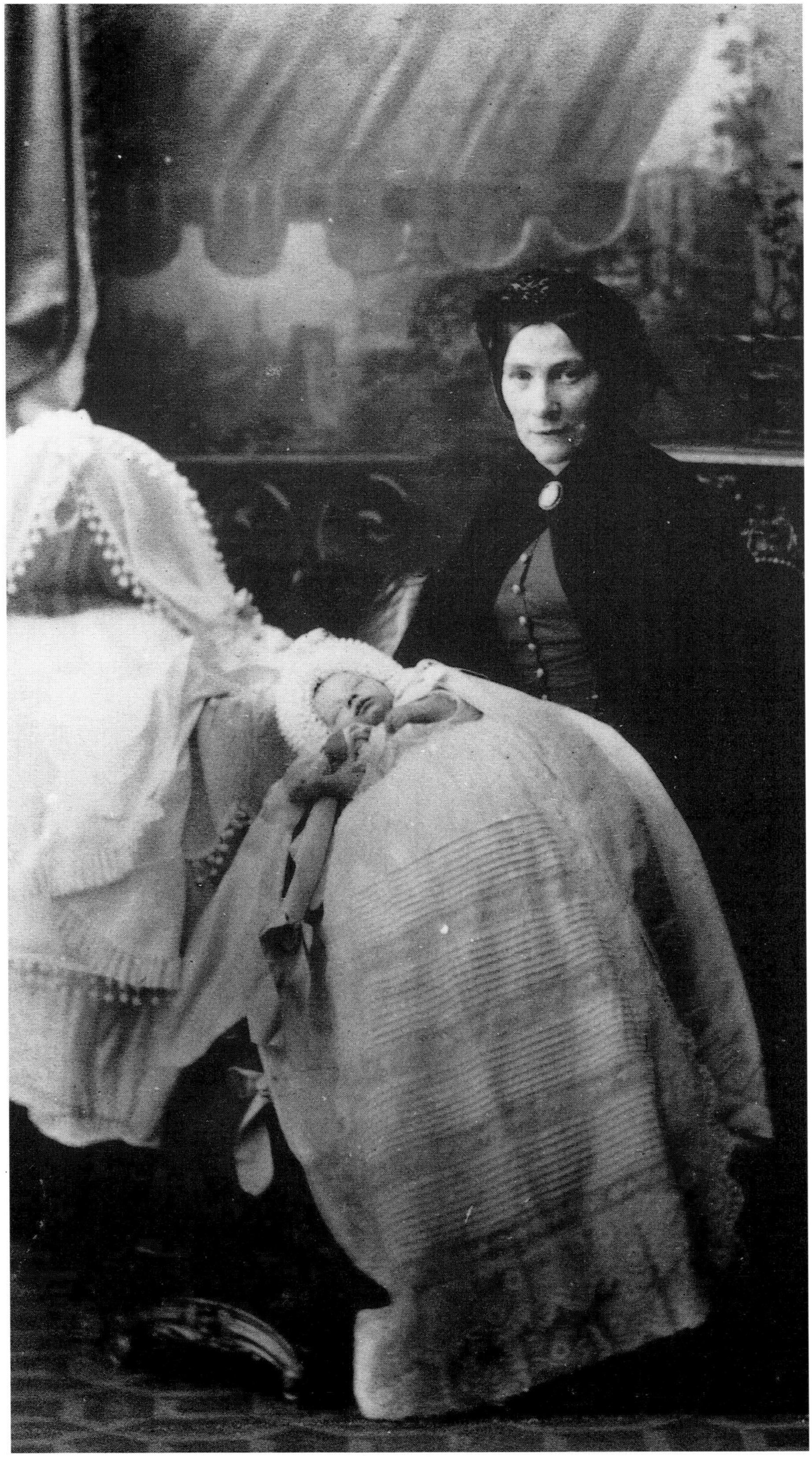

91. Mrs Gregory's nurse and baby 1865
Camille Silvy, London (Daybook 13, no. 16635)

92

Matching bridesmaids were the order of the day at a society wedding by the 1860s, although it was not usually possible to have them all with the same name as well. Presumably assisting at the marriage of another sister, the Misses Mercers wear matching white-silk dresses with tulle overskirts, over-sleeves, and veils. Vibrant, black-chenille braid trimming snakes round each collar and centre-front to form a bolero or Zouave jacket. Similar trimming edges the cuffs, and forms a 'V' below the waist where a Swiss belt effect is provided by the under fabric. Large chenille rosettes are appliquéd at each shoulder, and at

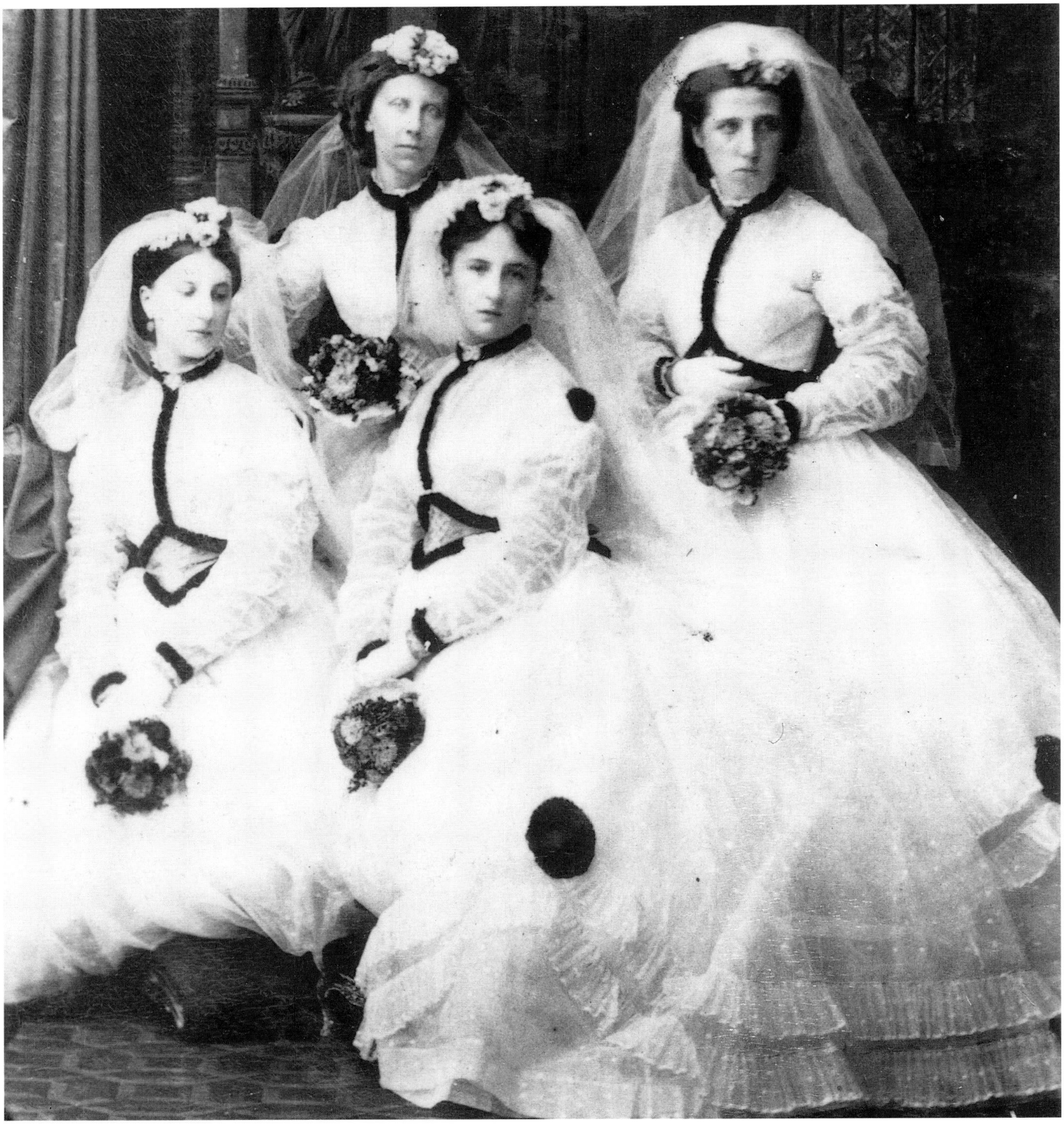

92. The Misses Mercer
1865
Camille Silvy, London (Daybook 13, no. 16655)

points towards the hem of each skirt where the overskirt is caught up into swags. Each girl wears short, white kid gloves, and a waist-length veil attached to the back of the floral head-wreath. Each also carries a floral posy. Bridesmaids had little to do except look appealing, particularly when appointed in considerable numbers. The chief bridesmaid was required to attend the bride on her trousseau shopping expeditions, and on the day of the marriage, she removed the bride's gloves when the priest began the service (and kept them as a perquisite). She also held the bride's scent bottle and witnessed the signatures in the register.

The 1870 manual *Etiquette For Ladies* related nothing about duties, but laid down that:

> the number of bridesmaids varies from two to eight. If the bride is young, the bridesmaids should be young also; if the lady be middle-aged, her bridesmaids also should be middle-aged. A widow has no bridesmaids . . . .[8]

93

In August 1865, Queen Emma, Dowager of the late King Kamehameha IV of the Sandwich Islands (latterly known as Hawaii), paid a visit to England. Staying with Lady Franklin, and with the ostensible aim of publicizing the needs of Hawaiian Christians, she visited such bodies as The Society For The Promotion Of Christian Knowledge. Born in 1822, and here aged 43, the Queen was of mixed race; her father being a native chieftain; her mother of English extraction. She married the King in 1856 and had only one child, who died in 1862. The throne passed to her brother-in-law, Kamehameha V.[9]

A year into mourning for her husband, the Queen wears a dress fully covered with black crape. Dress fabrics used during mourning included grenadine, *barège* and paramatta, all sounding as mournful as their status.

The Queen is also wearing a full mourning cap or bonnet in the style beloved of her fellow monarch Queen Victoria. The first degree of mourning for a widow, for the first nine months, directed that the dress should be entirely swathed in a single piece of crape. The next three months allowed the crape to be worn in two deep tucks. The cap and this crape covering should be worn for a year and a day. As was also stipulated, Queen Emma's outdoor cape is trimmed with black crape and devoid of any fur or velvet trim.

Another year of lesser mourning followed, with black silk trimmed only with crape and jet. Finally there was half-mourning for the last six months. The wife of a reigning monarch, at this time, would probably have been expected never to wear colours again.

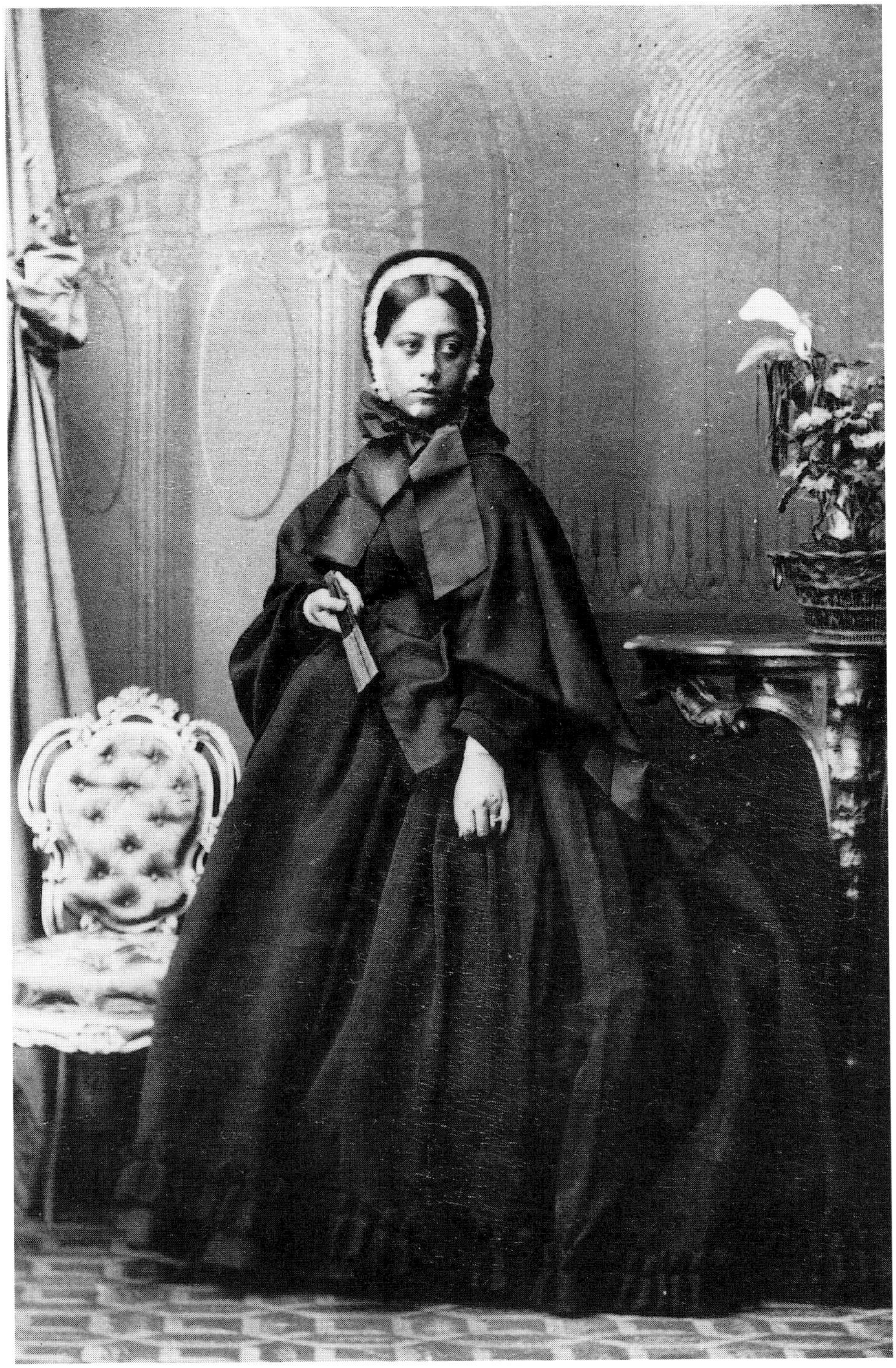

93. The Dowager Queen Emma of Hawaii 1865
Camille Silvy, London (Daybook 13, no. 16660)

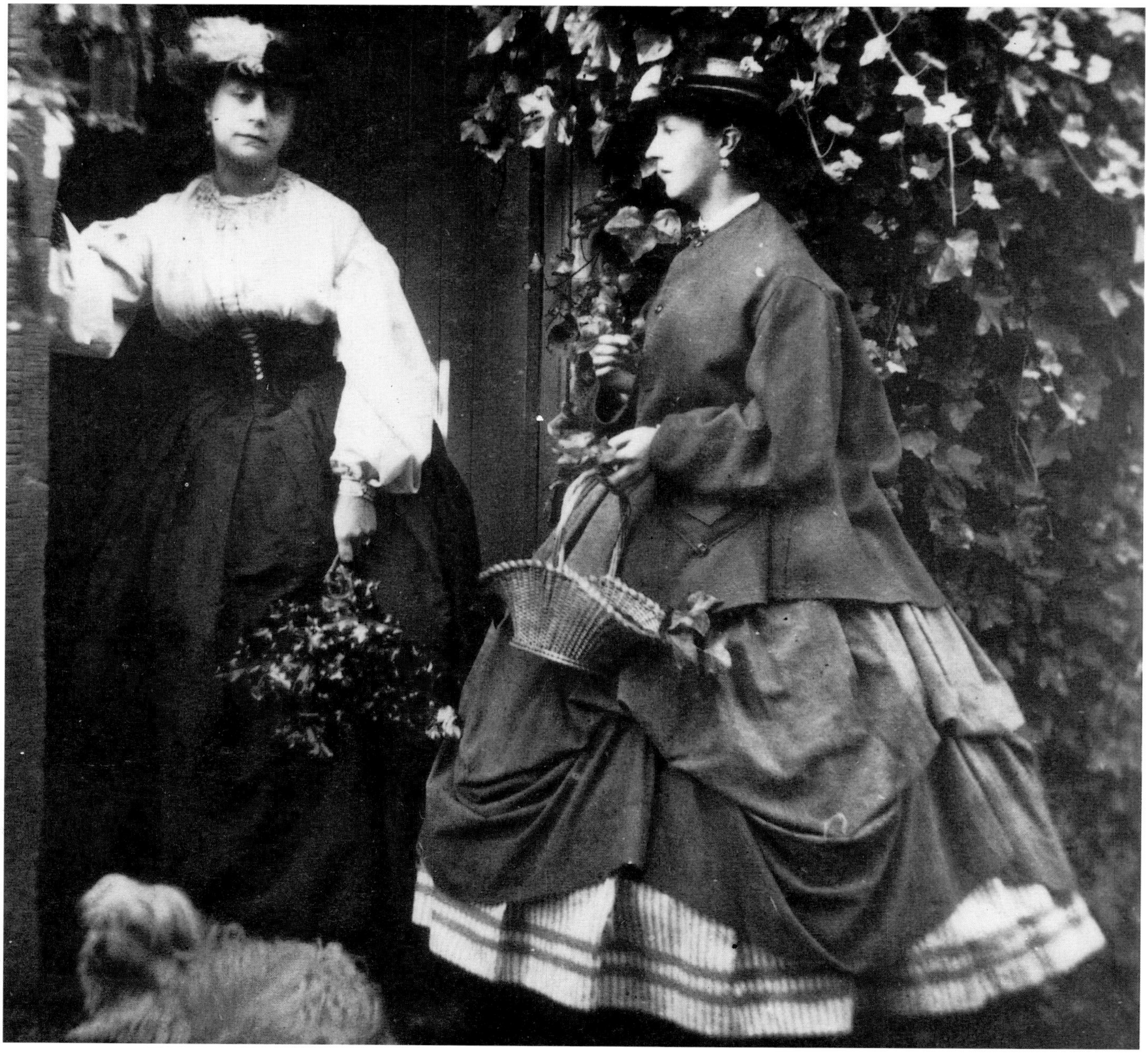

94. Cecilia Mary Elliot and Alice Drummond
1865
Photographer unknown (Jocelyn Album (59) p. 4) (NPG Ax 33516)

— 94 —

The 'Jocelyn Album' was assembled by Cecilia Mary ('Ceci'), the youngest daughter of Admiral Sir George Elliot KCB, the second son of the 1st Earl of Minto. Shortly after the date of this photograph, she was to marry (in 1866) the Honourable William Nassau Jocelyn, son of the 3rd Earl of Rodea. Her friend, Margaret Alice Drummond, is the daughter of the 7th Viscount Strathallan. Both women were born in the early 1840s.

Ceci, to the left, wears a white cotton 'body', known as a 'canezou' or a *chemisette*, joined to her contrasting dark skirt with a fashionable Swiss belt. Similar outfits, often termed 'costume for home', pepper the fashion plates of the early 1860s. *The World Of Fashion* (July 1864) shows a similar ensemble which is described as having 'A body of white muslin, forming narrow plaits, covered by a 'corsage suissesse' which is in fact nothing but a broad ceinture pointed top and bottom.' This costume includes a vast crinoline petticoat, whereas clearly, Ceci Elliot has left off her crinoline. Holding a few sprays of holly, she wears a straw hat tipped down over her forehead and trimmed with a white ostrich feather. This style of hat is variously dubbed 'casquette' or 'helmet hat' in *The World Of Fashion* for this date.

Alice Drummond wears a walking outfit comprising woollen paletot, looped-up cashmere overskirt, and striped wool skirt below. She wears a round straw hat, and carries a decorative straw basket for gathering ivy.

95

This unusual half-turn, three-quarter-length portrait provides the viewer with a useful picture of the construction of the back of a daydress, in this case made in a strikingly striped silk. Silks such as this were popular in the middle 1860s: see, for example, *The World Of Fashion* (April 1866) in which it was stated that 'Striped silks will be very fashionable this season; . . . the dresses trimmed with silk cord or tassels to match are very "distingué" . . .'. Miss (or Mrs) Whytock's bodice is constructed with a narrow back section, with typical, deeply curving side-back seams and low-set diagonal shoulder seams. Effort has been expended on matching the pattern at the side-back seams, but not on the shoulder seams. The skirt, worn over a number of petticoats, but not a cage crinoline by this date, is pleated into the waist in wide knife pleats, the waist seam being concealed by a wide, black belt with pendant black-glass or jet beads.

The sitter's hair is dressed back from a centre parting to a large bun, or fashionably high chignon. 'Comfortably' fashionable, she could not be accused of demonstrating the extremes of style in *coiffure* so condemned by contemporary fashion commentators. Eliane de Mersey in *The Queen* (1867), condemned the prevalent lack of moderation:

> Some ladies wear their chignons ridiculously high and of an exaggerated size, with two extravagantly long curls at the back in place of ribbons. It is far better taste to accept the decrees of fashion in moderation instead of adopting these eccentric extremes . . .[10]

A vast majority of English women would have followed this advice, as demonstrated by Patey Whytok's prudent example.

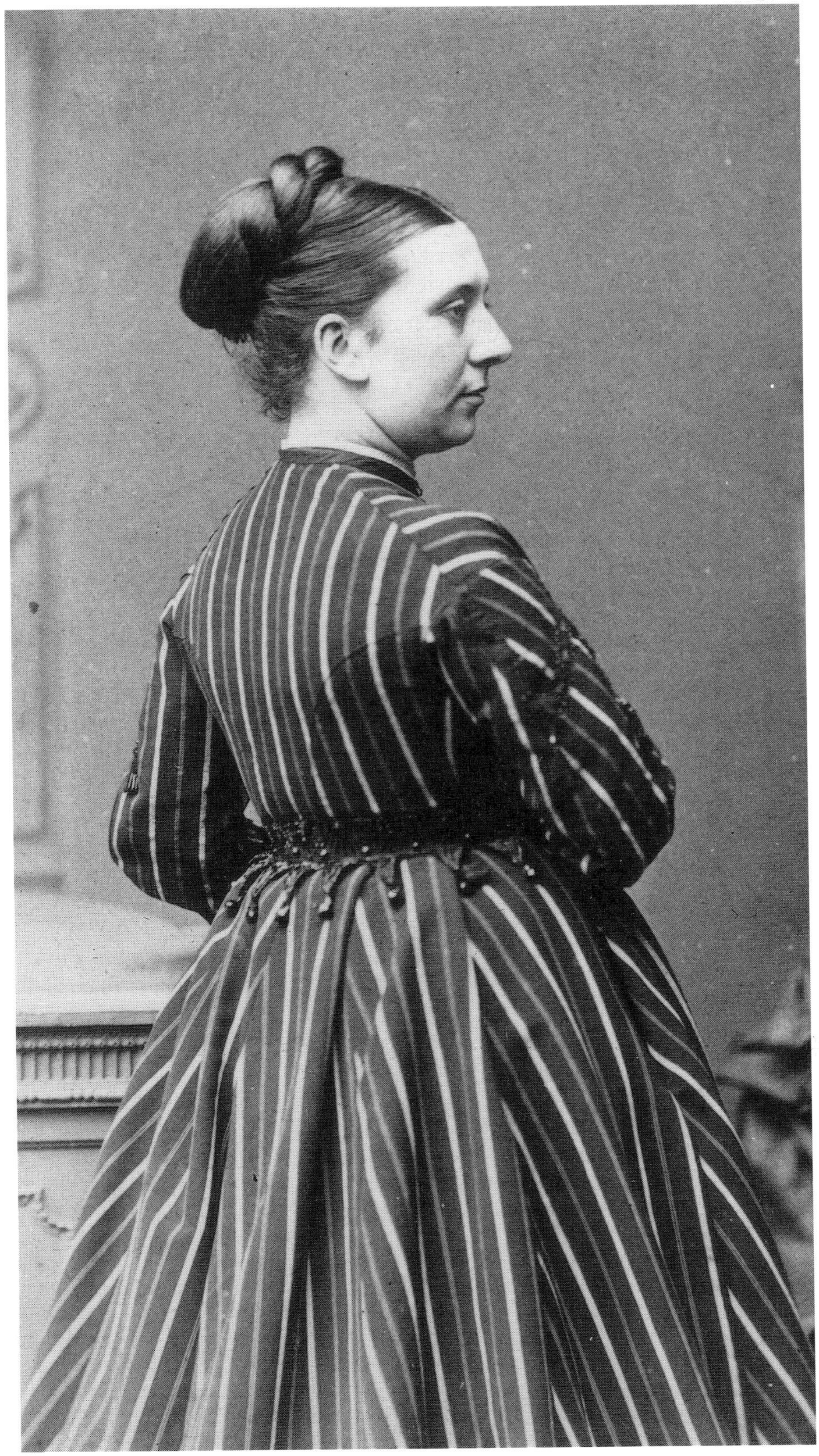

95. Patey Whytock
Mid 1860s
R. W. Thrupp, Birmingham (Album 102, p. 20a) (NPG Ax 33515)

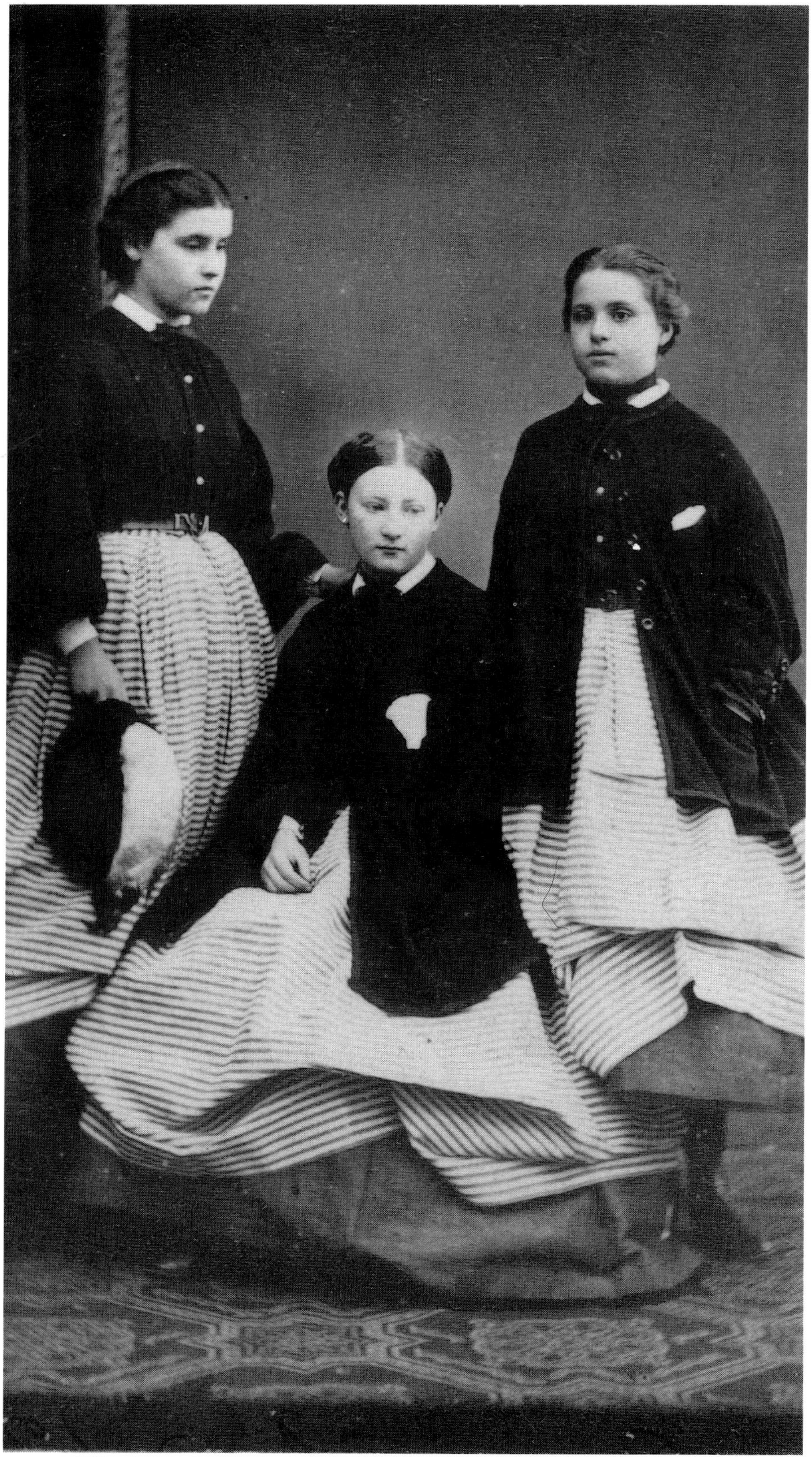

96. Constance, Evelyn, and Florence Barrington
Mid 1860s
Photographer unknown (Barrington Album (182) p. 37) (NPG Ax 26273)

96

From left to right, Constance (born 1847), Evelyn (born 1848), and Florence (born 1850) were the daughters of George William, 7th Viscount Barrington and his wife Elizabeth. There were no sons of the marriage and on the death of the Viscount in November 1886, the title passed to his brother Percy. Of the daughters, Constance married the 2nd Baron Haldon in 1868; and Evelyn, the 3rd Earl Craven; whilst Florence remained single. All three died in the 1920s in their late seventies.

Here dressed identically, they wear black, bishop-sleeved bodices with matching wool paletots, and striped cashmere overskirts looped up *à la polonaise* for walking, over thicker, woollen skirts below. Their black bodices contrast with the three, white, centre-front buttons and with the plain white collars, cuffs and paletot breast-pocket handkerchiefs.

In their later teens, the sisters wear skirts a good ten inches or so above the floor, in a style practical for walking; their looped-up skirts have a similar purpose, and were recommended in fashion plates for 'promenade', 'croquet' and 'sea side' costumes.

Their father was the Conservative MP for Eye from 1866 to 1880 and sometime Private Secretary to the Earl of Derby when he was Prime Minister.

97

Half-length portraits often show greater detail of the sitter's costume than the commoner, full-length photographs. Mrs Bealey's fine lace collar and undersleeves, and her gold locket and brooch can clearly be seen here.

She wears a pale-silk daydress with a bodice incorporating an over-panel pleated diagonally to the centre-front waist, in a style known as 'à bretelles'. The sleeves are decorated with two, large, silk-cord arabesques with pendant-fringe ends. Arabesques and complex bow motifs were often used to trim pockets and sleeves in the middle 1860s, on both dresses and mantles, and in either contrasting or matching hues. *The World Of Fashion* for February 1864 illustrates a

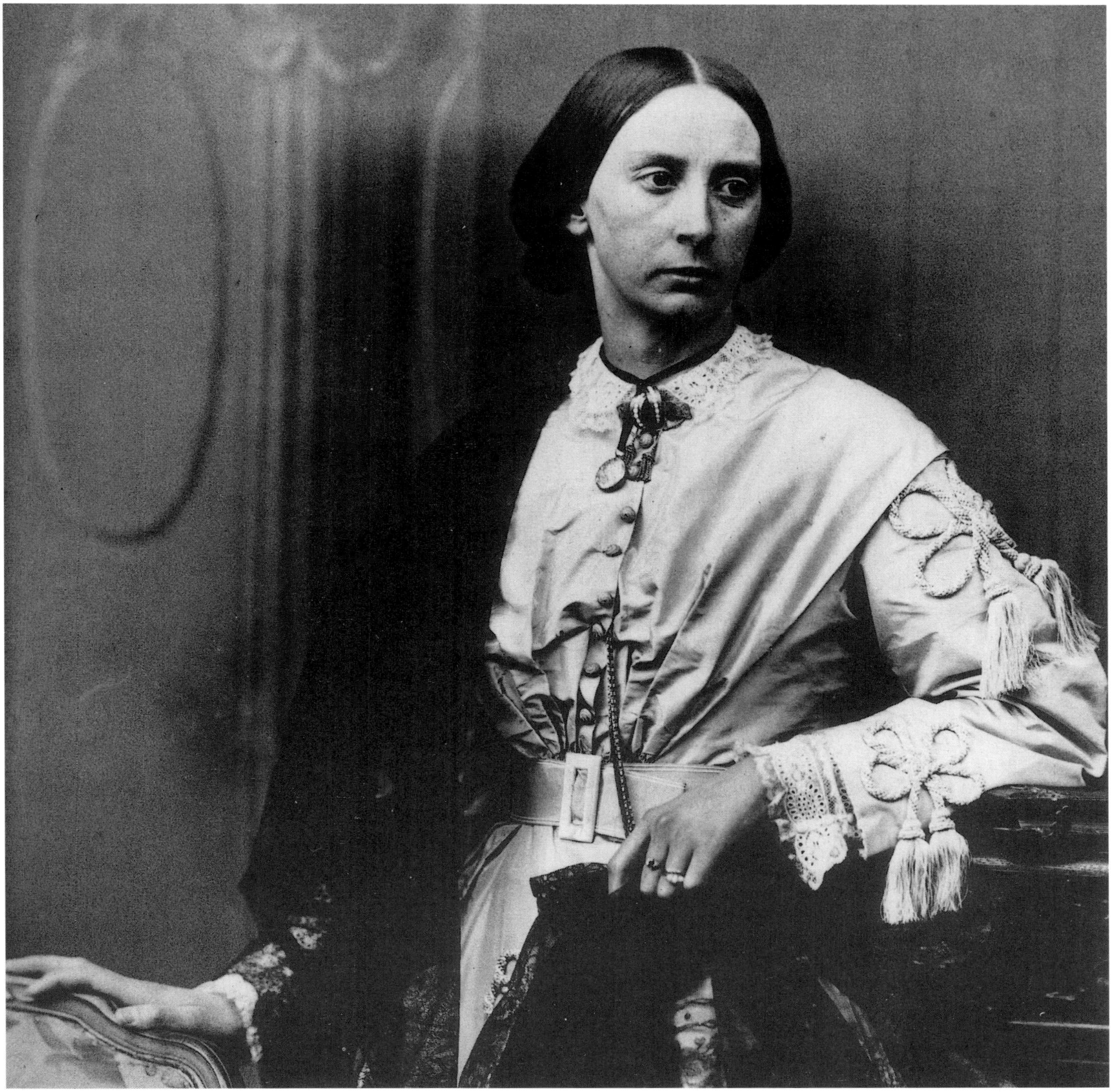

97. Mrs Bealey
1866
Camille Silvy, London (Daybook 13, no. 16907)

paletot of rich silk plush, the colour warm brown or Havanna . . . there are two pockets at the waist, placed lengthwise, and these are trimmed by a passementerie forming an Arabesque pattern. A similar Arabesque is also placed at the bottom of each sleeve and another on each shoulder [see Mrs Bealey] with three tassels . . .

A little later, (March 1866) the same periodical shows a dress of 'imperatrice blue silk' again with pockets 'ornamented by rich Arabesques of silk cord with floss silk tassels . . .'.

Mrs Bealey carries a black Chantilly lace shawl, loosely draped over her right shoulder, and drawn across her back to her left hand.

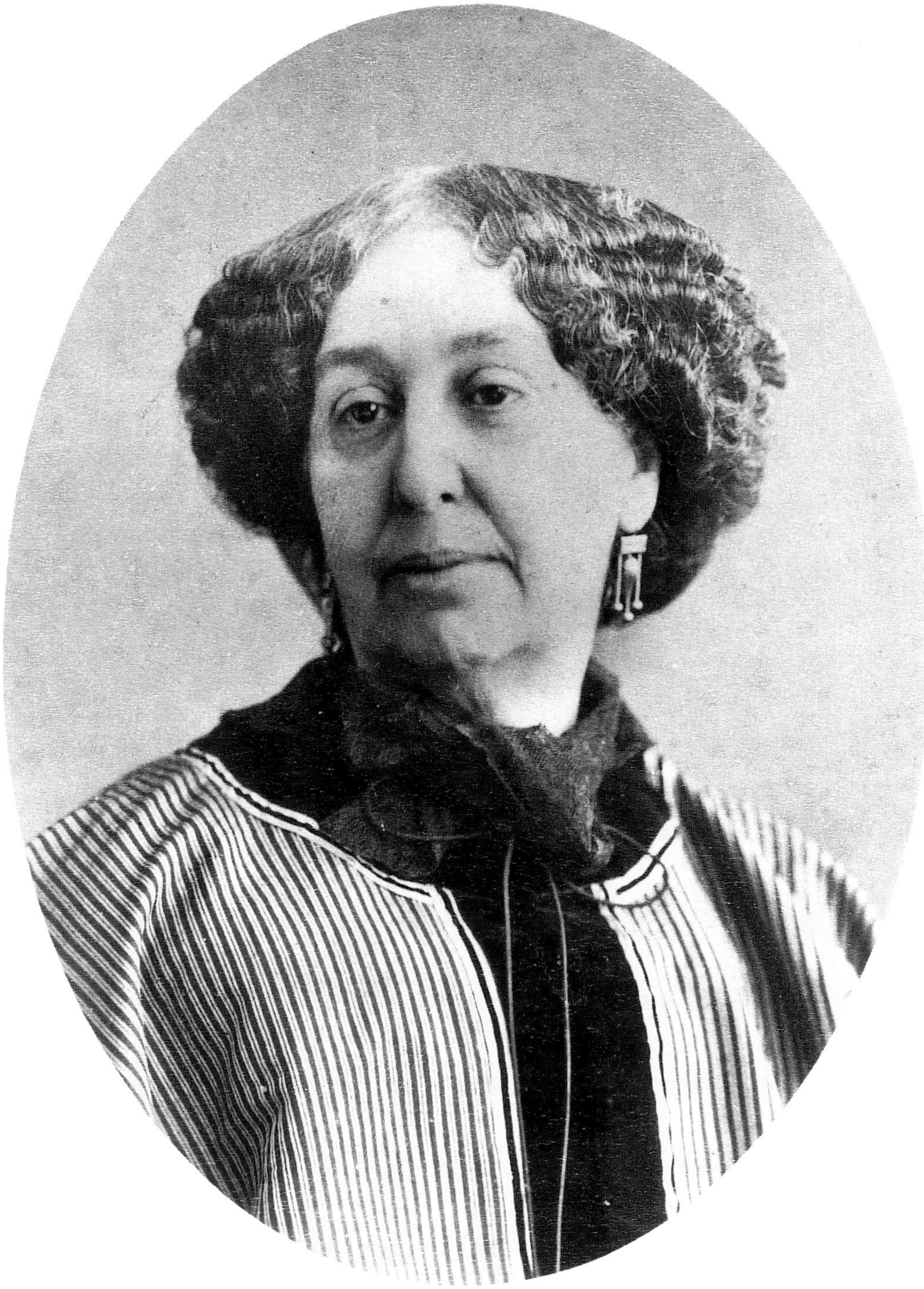

98. George Sand
1866
Nadar, Paris (NPG x 9190)

98

George Sand was born Amandine Dupin in July 1804, the only child of a misalliance between the Marquis Maurice Dupin de Franceuil and a lowly born birdseller's daughter. After the death of her father, when she was only four, she was brought up by her grandmother, from whom, in 1822, she inherited the Chateau Nohant and a considerable fortune.

After a brief, respectable interlude, during which George Sand married the Baron Dudevant and bore two children, she left for Paris, and eventually divorced her husband in 1836. She quickly established a notorious public reputation, openly practising sexual permissiveness, taking lovers – including Frederick Chopin – and espousing political radicalism. She achieved fame with her novels, beginning with the immensely successful *Indiana* (1832), which she published under the pseudonym of George Sand.

Always controversial, she liked to dress as a man, although by the date of this portrait, when she was 62, she had long since eschewed masculine attire.

An article devoted to her in *The Young Englishwoman* (July 1875), less than a year before her death, exemplifies the respectable response to a life so flouting of narrow conventionalism: 'there are some lives which fascinate us by their interest, but of whose course we cannot approve. This is one of them. The impulses of genius are not always identical with moral strength . . .'.[11] Indeed, in the early 1870s, Edmond de Goncourt told of her 'eating late suppers, drinking champagne, fornicating and carrying on like a forty year old student . . .'.[12]

This photograph is by the famous French artist Nadar, who was an ardent admirer of George Sand. Indeed, George Sand was godmother to Nadar's son Paul.

99

The stately Mrs Alward poses in court presentation dress before a suitably grandiose backdrop in Silvy's imposing studio. Her gown shows the obligatory features of presentation dress: low *décolletage* (in this case almost horizontal at the neckline); short sleeves; full train fastened at the waist; and ostrich-feather head-dress (in this case incorporating a 'Marie Stuart' cap). It was an established custom for society brides to be presented again, by a member of their new family and, for that occasion, the wedding dress might be worn, suitably adapted to comply with the regulations for short sleeves, low neckline and train.

White was the favourite colour for presentation dresses, particularly for unmarried girls; often in tulle net over silk, satin, or moiré. Mrs Alward has allowed herself a coloured-silk fringing below her neckline.

Low evening-style necklines ensured that many young presentees shivered from more than understandable nervousness when being ushered into the royal presence. Two months before Mrs Alward's presentation, on 23 March 1867, *The Queen* related that 'The poor belles at the Court on Tuesday seemed to suffer a great deal from the excessive cold'.[13] This is not surprising, as no shoulder covering whatsoever was allowed. An 1870 manual entitled *Etiquette for Ladies* directed that, at presentations, 'Everything in the shape of a cloak or scarf, even of lace, must be left in the carriage'.[14]

Young ladies were often exhausted, as well as cold and apprehensive. They had to make the long progress through the Great Hall, up the Grand Staircase, through the First Saloon, and through a succession of further rooms to the Throne Room, carrying their weighty trains over their left arms.

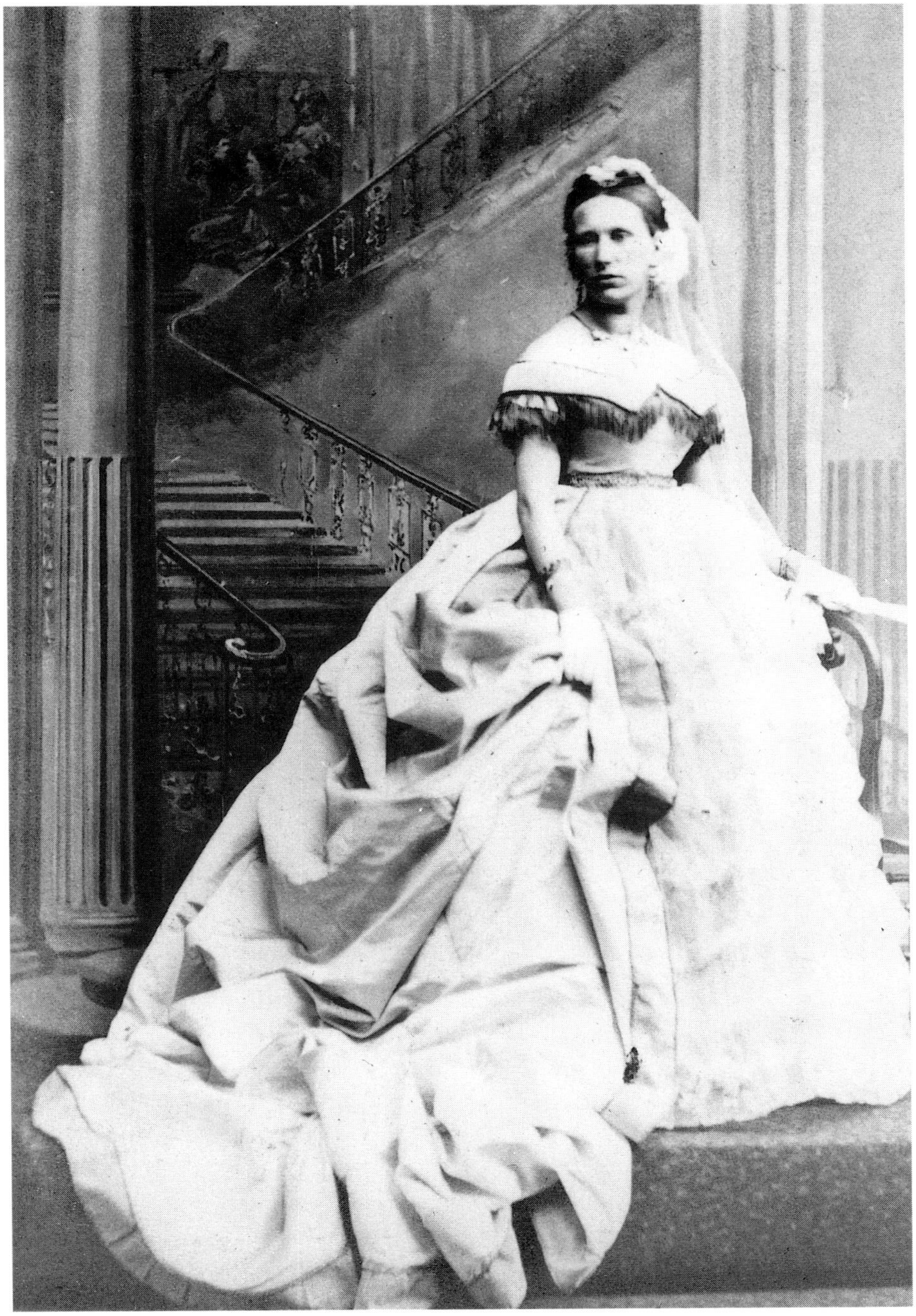

99. Mrs Alward
1867
Camille Silvy, London (Daybook 8, no. 9978)

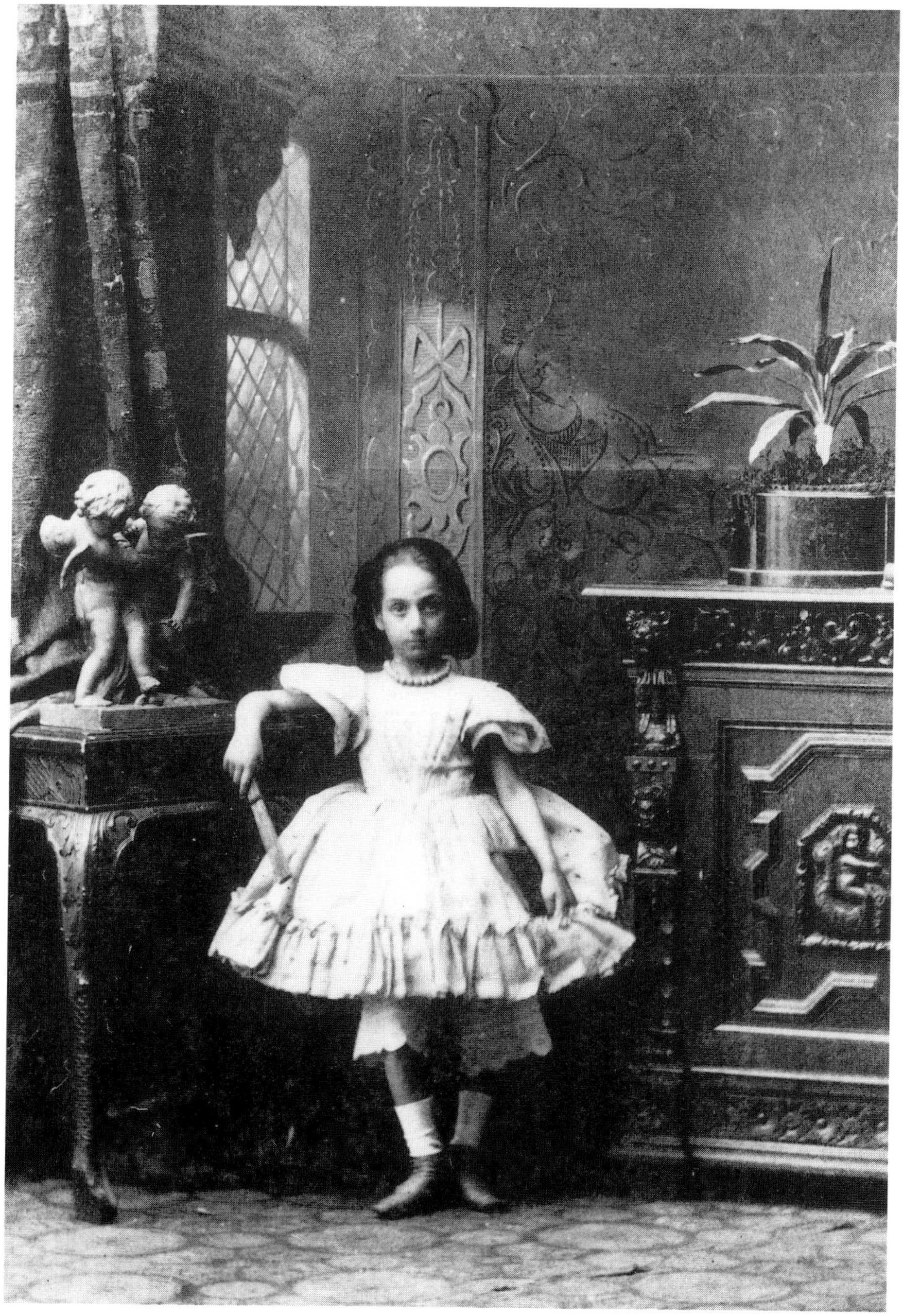

100. Miss P. Ralli
1867
Camille Silvy, London (Daybook 9, no. 11815)

100

Positioned next to a table-top sculpture of a pair of wrestling cherubs, Miss Ralli seems dwarfed by the ornate furniture and furnishings in Silvy's studio.

This young sitter, probably aged seven or eight, wears a short, full skirt, clearly showing the broderie anglaise openwork on the legs of her white drawers. Judging by its bulk, the dress would seem to be of a pale-coloured wool, with a full pleated flounce at the hem. The 1860s saw a large variety of fabrics gain popularity for use in children's dresses as well as in women's. *The Queen* (June 1867) carried two columns of 'children's toilettes' with a total of 11 outfits. Fabrics include poplin (a corded silk and wool mixture); foulard ('the soft India silk' as it was described in *The Englishwoman's Domestic Magazine* of January 1865); alpaca, mohair, and 'sultane' (all mixtures of goat hair with silk, and resembling each other); flannel; velvet; and such exotic sounding material as 'mousse marine' (a lightweight wool) and 'leno' (a fine linen gauze).[15] *The Englishwoman's Domestic Magazine* (December 1866) has similar variety: a red-and-white checked poplin; a grey rep; a white-and-blue checked linsey. As for construction, it advises only that 'little girls' dresses are made with gored widths, but not entirely plain; there is one large double pleat to give the required fullness at the back . . .'.[16]

101

The daughter of John Fortescue and granddaughter of the 1st Earl Fortescue, Elizabeth was to marry the Reverend Leigh Thomas Rendell in 1877. Here aged about 20, she is pictured in a striped-silk evening dress with a train bunched at the back. Her bodice is very *décolleté*, with a slight point to the centre neckline and falling fully off her shoulders. A similar

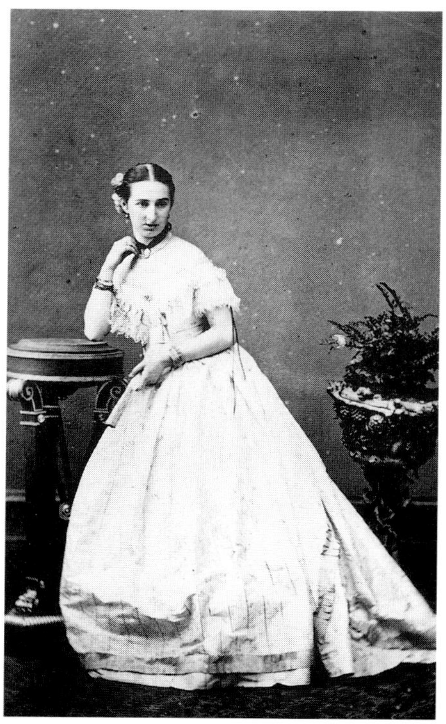

101. Elizabeth Fortescue
1867
Hills and Saunders, London (Wilberforce Album, vol. 1, p. 15, no. 7) (NPG Ax 33522)

'evening toilet' illustrated in *The Young Englishwoman* (March 1867) is described as

> a low bodice of white muslin, arranged in cross pleats, trimmed with guipure lace and rosettes of narrow ribbon velvet upon the shoulders; waistband of velvet. Skirt of striped coloured silk. Pearl necklace. Coiffure ornamented with loops and lappets of black ribbon and a bunch of roses.[17]

Like Miss Fortescue, the fashion model wears two fairly substantial bracelets and drop earrings, and carries a closed fan. Miss Fortescue also wears a locket as a choker-necklace tied with wide, black ribbon.

The sister's crinoline hoop can be detected towards the front hem of her dress where she leans against the tripod table. The death knell for the crinoline sounded throughout 1867 although it just hung on until 1868, when skirts finally collapsed into flat fronts and long, trailing skirts.

102

Born in 1858 and 1859, these two daughters of the 8th Viscount Strathallan, wear matching, white piqué dresses, black patent shoes, cloth gaiters, and striped-cotton stockings. They are differentiated only by hairstyle; the younger sister Mary Virginia sports a more infantile front fringe than her elder sibling Kate Gertrude, who has a plain, adult, swept-back style.

Their dresses, trimmed with rows of contrasting black braid, typify children's wear for this period. White piqué, or indeed, pale cashmere or alpaca, trimmed with fancy black braid provides a staple for the 1860s: a 'Mignonne' costume for a girl of eight or nine in *The Queen* (19 October 1867) shows a dress 'of Bismark poplin, trimmed with black gimp, arranged round the skirt so as to form vandykes, and on the bodice and sleeves to similar revers, and a 'folie' collar.'[18] The two Miss Drummonds' braid decoration also imitate revers and cuffs.

The Queen (2 May 1863) includes a full-size pattern for a braided dress to be made of white or nankeen piqué, or coloured cashmere, and suitable for a three year old. To facilitate ease of construction, the description gives practical details of hems, margins, and making-up, as well as advice on the type of braid, and the tracing of the pattern on to tissue paper.[19]

Mothers wore similar decoration: again, in *The Queen* (14 September 1867), an 'indoor toilette' is shown, composed of 'white sultane, ornamented with black braid arranged above the hem in a fanciful design . . . the waistband bordered with black braid . . . and the cuffs and sleeves . . .'.[20]

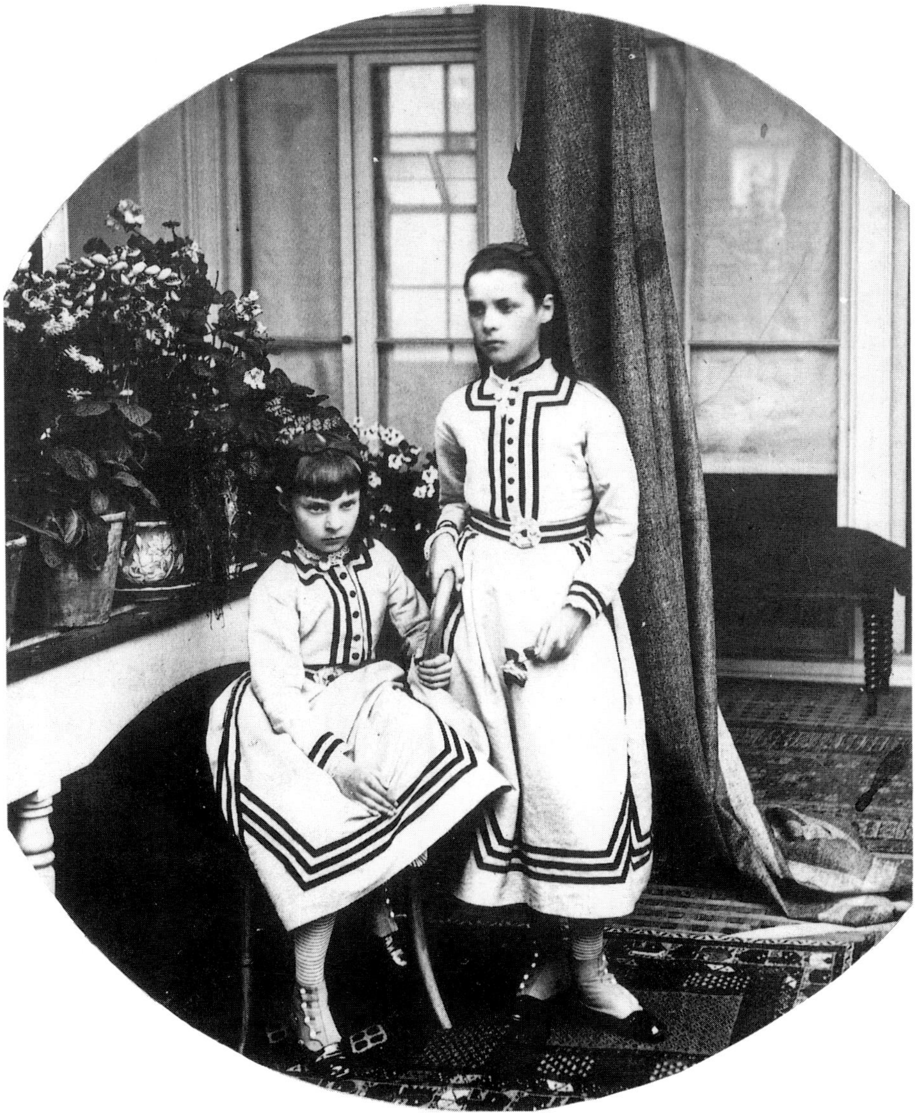

102. Kate and Mary Drummond 1867
Photographer unknown (Jocelyn Album (59) p. 24) (NPG Ax 33518)

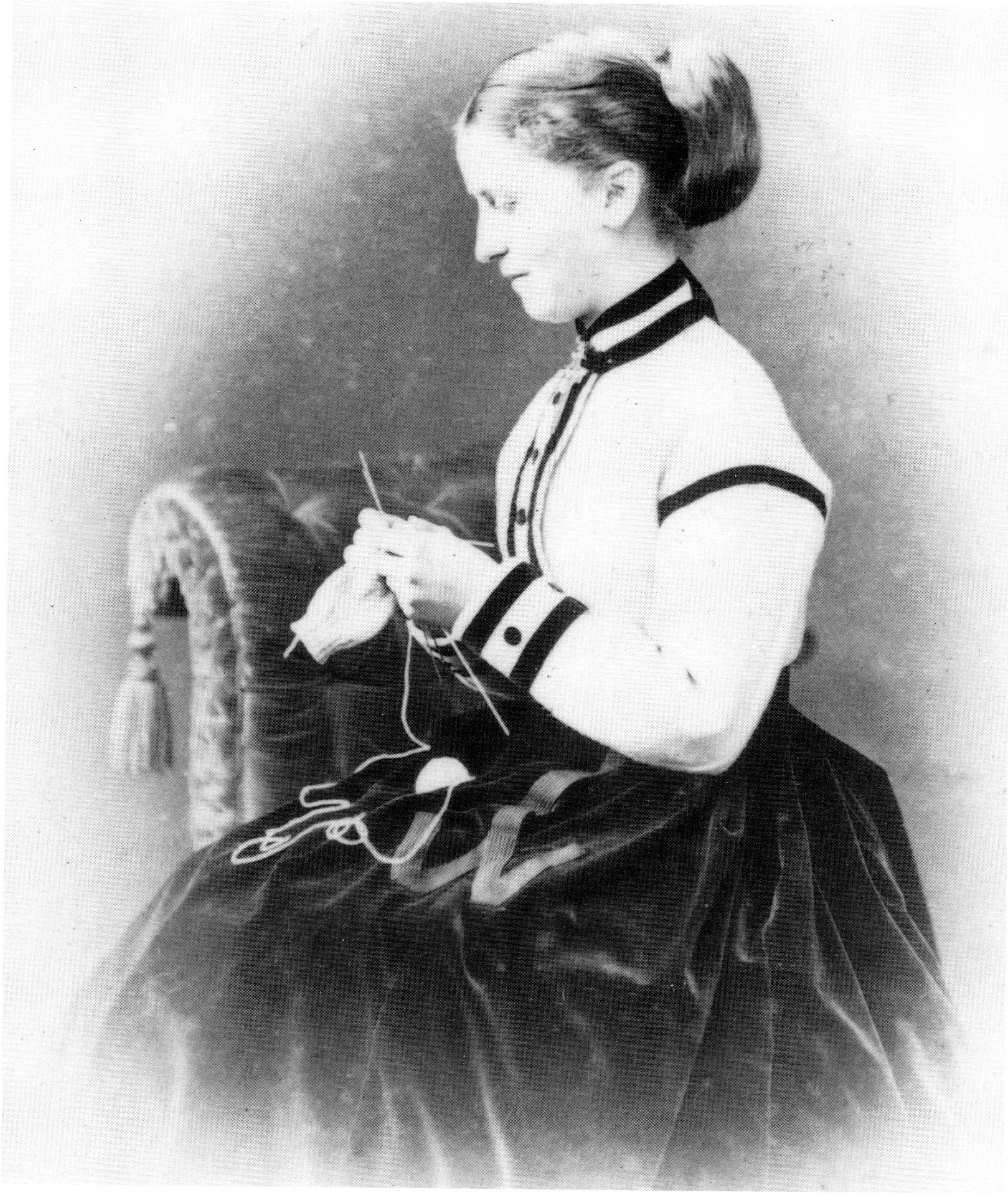

103. Elizabeth (Betty) Denman
***c.* 1867**
Photographer unknown (Wilberforce Album, vol. 2, p. 10, no. 6) (NPG Ax 33520)

103

This portrait shows Miss Denman posing in the activity of knitting, probably a sock. She wears a white cashmere bodice trimmed at the neck, front, cuffs, and dropped shoulder seam with contrasting black ribbon and with decorative black buttons. Her skirt is of black velvet, ample and fairly high waisted.

Knitting was a very popular pastime in the 1860s, seen, like sewing, to be a productive, useful, but also genteel occupation for well-bred women. Domestic magazines, such as *The Ladies' Treasury, The Englishwoman's Domestic Magazine*, and *The Queen*, show a large variety of patterns for knitting, crochet and 'tricot', ranging from the ever popular scarves, mittens, and socks, to more adventurous designs for children's vests and over-drawers, pelerine-capes, and men's jerseys 'such as sailors wear'.

The Lady's Knitting Book by a certain 'E.M.C.', and published in 1879 by Hatchards, has a total of 216 'receipts' for a range of items, including antimacassars, knee-caps, muffetees, sofa-cushions, and Shetland shawls.

104

Mrs Scott-Siddons, the Anglo-Indian actress, here strikes a theatrically reproving pose from one of her public readings. The great-grand-daughter of the renowned actress Mrs Siddons, Mary began her professional career in London in 1867, aged 23, with public readings in Hanover Square followed by a stage début at the Haymarket Theatre as Rosalind in *As You Like It*. This portrait dates from this time and we can, perhaps, agree with the *Daily Telegraph* review (10 April 1867) which declared her to be 'possessed of a fine expressive face which may be called classical in its profile, and endowed with the advantages of a neat symmetrical figure . . .' Shortly after her London début, Miss Scott-Siddons left on an extended tour of the United States, and did not return for two years.

She wears a dark-silk daydress with a full, bertha shawl-collar in white lace, with matching pleated cuffs. The sleeves have a theatrical look to them, with an open outer seam tied with bows at four points to reveal the black-lace lining. The full skirt has a long back over-panel with a shorter apron front, both edged with black machine lace and narrow black quilled frilling, which matches the skirt hem. Her hairstyle is extremely full; a wide plait of false hair encircles the front and falls in long, loose tresses at the back.

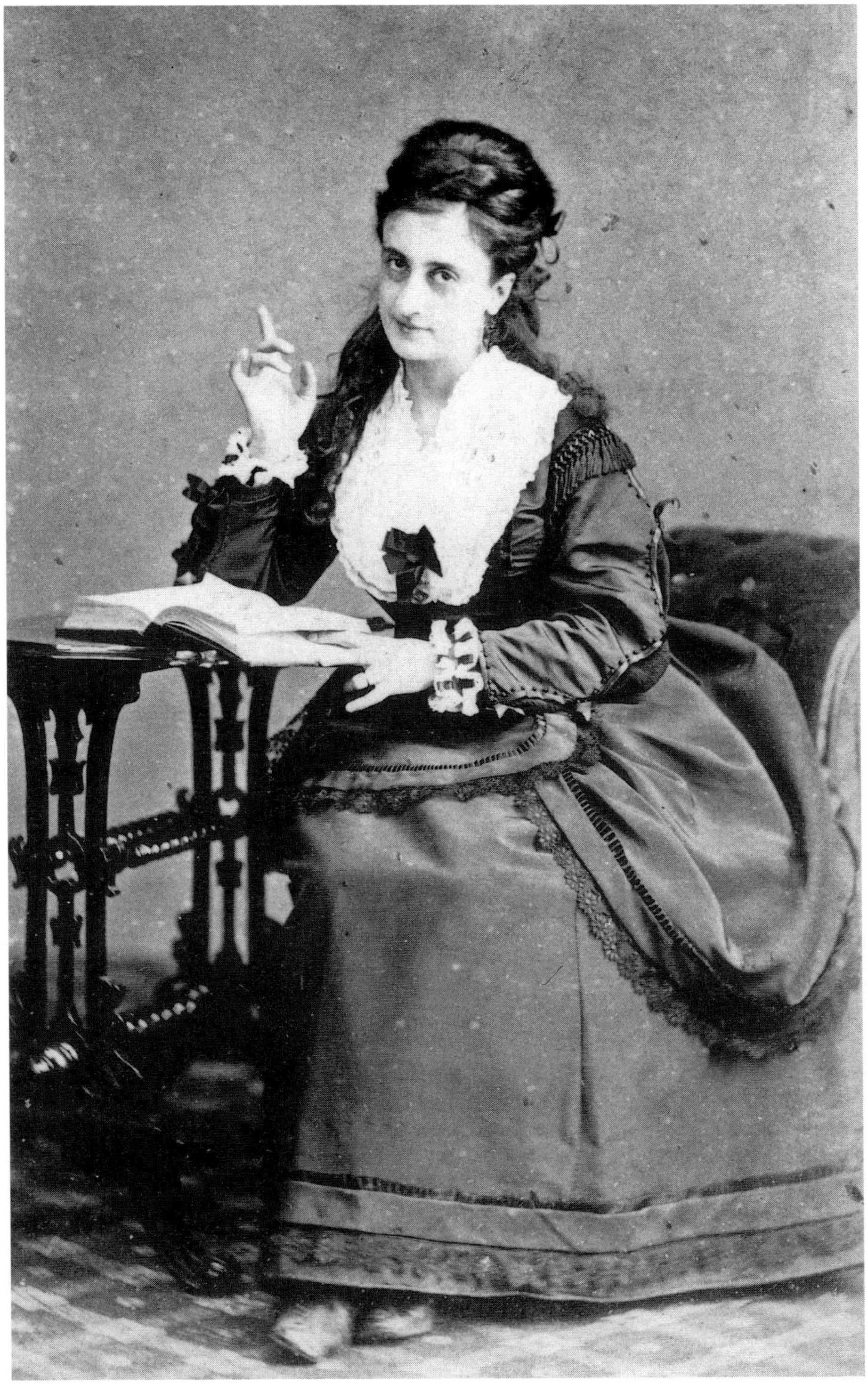

104. Mary Scott-Siddons
***c.* 1867**
Owen Angel (NPG x 22579)

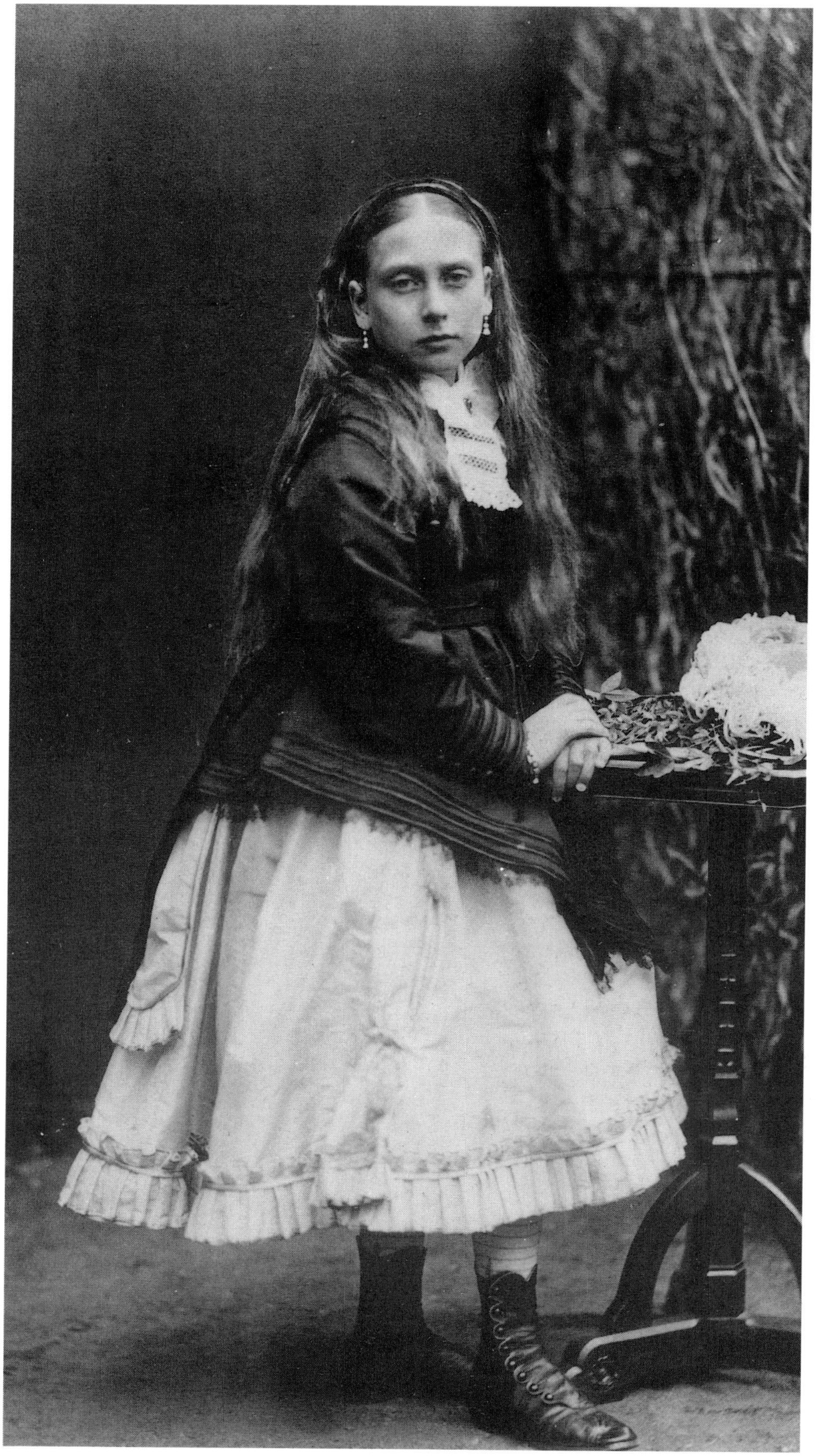

105. Princess Beatrice
1868
W. & D. Downey, Balmoral (Balmoral Album, P 22 (8))

105

Princess Beatrice was born in 1857, the youngest of Queen Victoria's children. Only four years old when her father died, she became the widowed Queen's great consolation and a close companion thereafter. After marrying Prince Henry of Battenburg, in 1885, she continued to reside with her mother at court.

Seen here aged 11, she is photographed at Balmoral in a walking outfit comprising belted cloth jacket or paletot, lighter-coloured knee-length skirt, striped-cotton stockings and ankle-length button boots.

By 1868 the Queen had established a routine of spending a month or so in Balmoral from the end of May. In this year, the Queen was accompanied by the Princesses Louise and Beatrice and by Prince Leopold, and they left Windsor at 6.30 in the evening by a special train consisting of 14 reserved saloon carriages, arriving at Balmoral at 2.30 the following afternoon.

The Queen spent the weeks at Balmoral walking and driving, attended by one or other of her dutiful daughters together with other appointed ladies such as the Duchess of Atholl or Miss Macgregor. Princess Beatrice would therefore have had many opportunities to wear her outdoor walking outfits when braving the often unreliable and inhospitable Scottish climate.

106

In 1868 Princess Louise accompanied her mother Queen Victoria to Balmoral with her younger sister Beatrice.

Shown here in a full-length profile portrait, the Princess is aged 20, and wears a dark-silk trained afternoon dress trimmed with contrasting white braid. Dark braids on plain light cottons and wools, or vice versa, were universally employed by the middle 1860s, particularly for walking outfits, to enliven an otherwise unremarkable fabric.

1868 saw the disappearance of the crinoline petticoat after a reign of ten years, during which skirt widths had reached vast proportions. *The World Of Fashion* (March 1868) declared: 'The reign of Crinoline may be said to be now completely at an end; the skeleton skirt is a thing of the past; small jupons of puffed horsehair or of merino is all that is required . . .'. Princess Louise clearly wears no crinoline, and her skirt falls in a long train behind her, in a style impossible to achieve with a crinoline. Impractical and awkward to manoeuvre, trained skirts nonetheless caught on for walking wear: 'The long trained skirts . . . most fashionable for the afternoon promenade; they are made plain at the front and sides and with a good deal of fullness at the back. (*The World Of Fashion*, September 1868.)

Posed in a rustic setting, Princess Louise holds her white lace shawl over the back of a folding garden chair against which leans her dark-silk parasol.

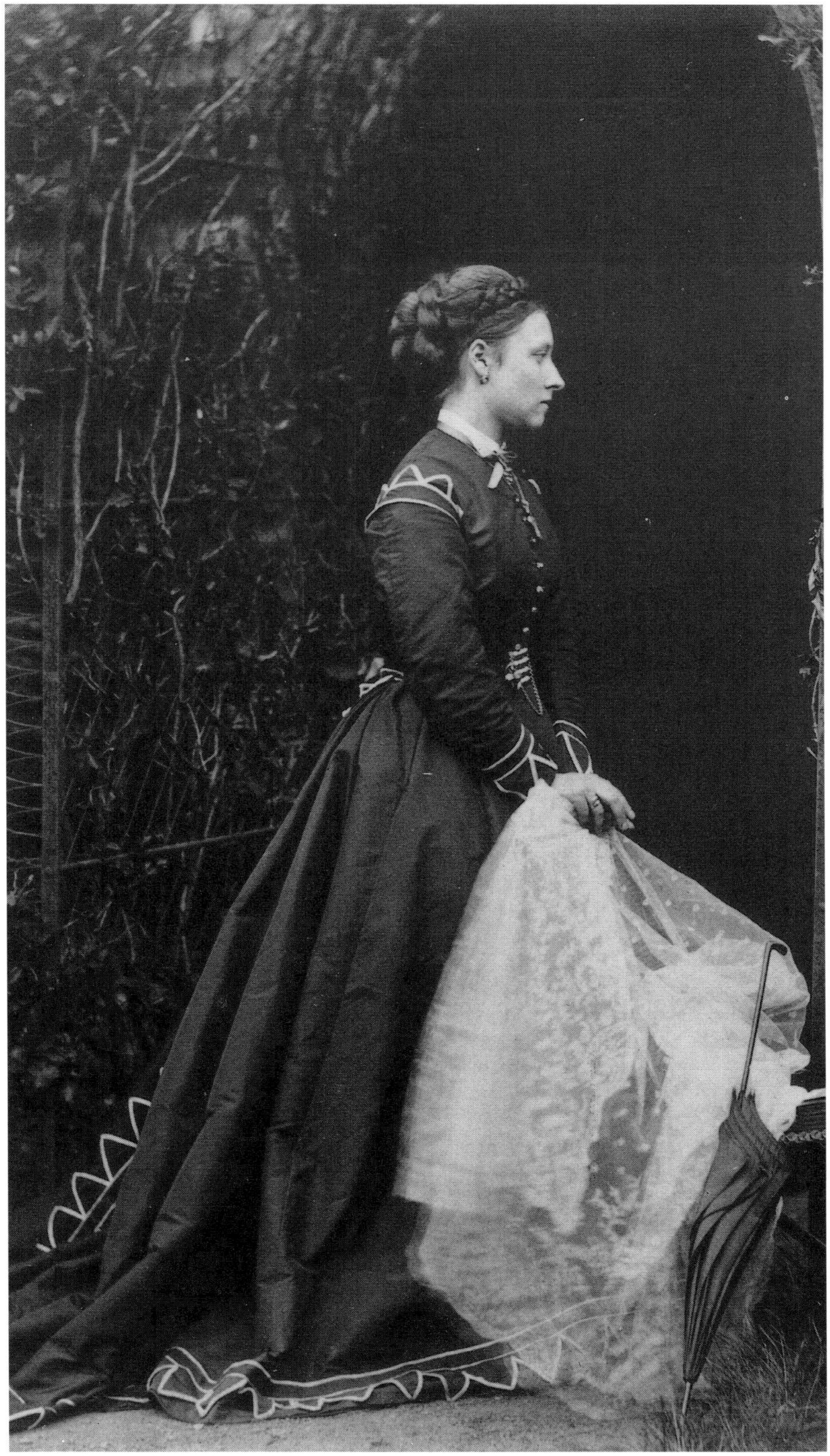

106. Princess Louise
1868
W. & D. Downey, Balmoral (Balmoral Album, P 22, (6))

107

This high-quality head-and-shoulders portrait is of a girl in her late teens. The close-up nature of the photograph reveals fine details of dress construction, such as the very narrow piping set in at the shoulder seam and collar; or the creasing at the back-sleeve seam where the stitching puckers the silk. The image is intended very much as a facial portrait with attention concentrated on the coiffure and neck. Miss Duncombe's long hair is drawn back over a false pad and plaited into a full chignon at the back.

Many women who aimed at a similar hairstyle required artificial locks and tresses to assist nature, and the trade in human hair from the Continent assumed vast proportions by the 1860s giving rise to rather lurid rumours:

> Ladies who wear chignons will be glad to know that it is not true that the hair for chignons is procured from corpses of people who die in hospitals . . . when death ensues, the hair becomes brittle and cannot be curled and twisted into form. Marseilles is the great entrepôt for the trade in human hair, more than 40,000lbs weight of this commodity being imported there annually, chiefly from Italy . . .[21]

England seemed unable to provide for her false-hair industry from her native resources, and had an insatiable appetite for this foreign supply:

> The number of chignons exported from France to England during the past year was 11,954, in addition to which there was exported a sufficient quantity of hair for 7,000 chignons to be made up in England. The total value of hair and chignons exported from France during 1865 amounted to . . . £45,000 sterling.[22] (Supplement to *The Queen*, 12 January 1867.)

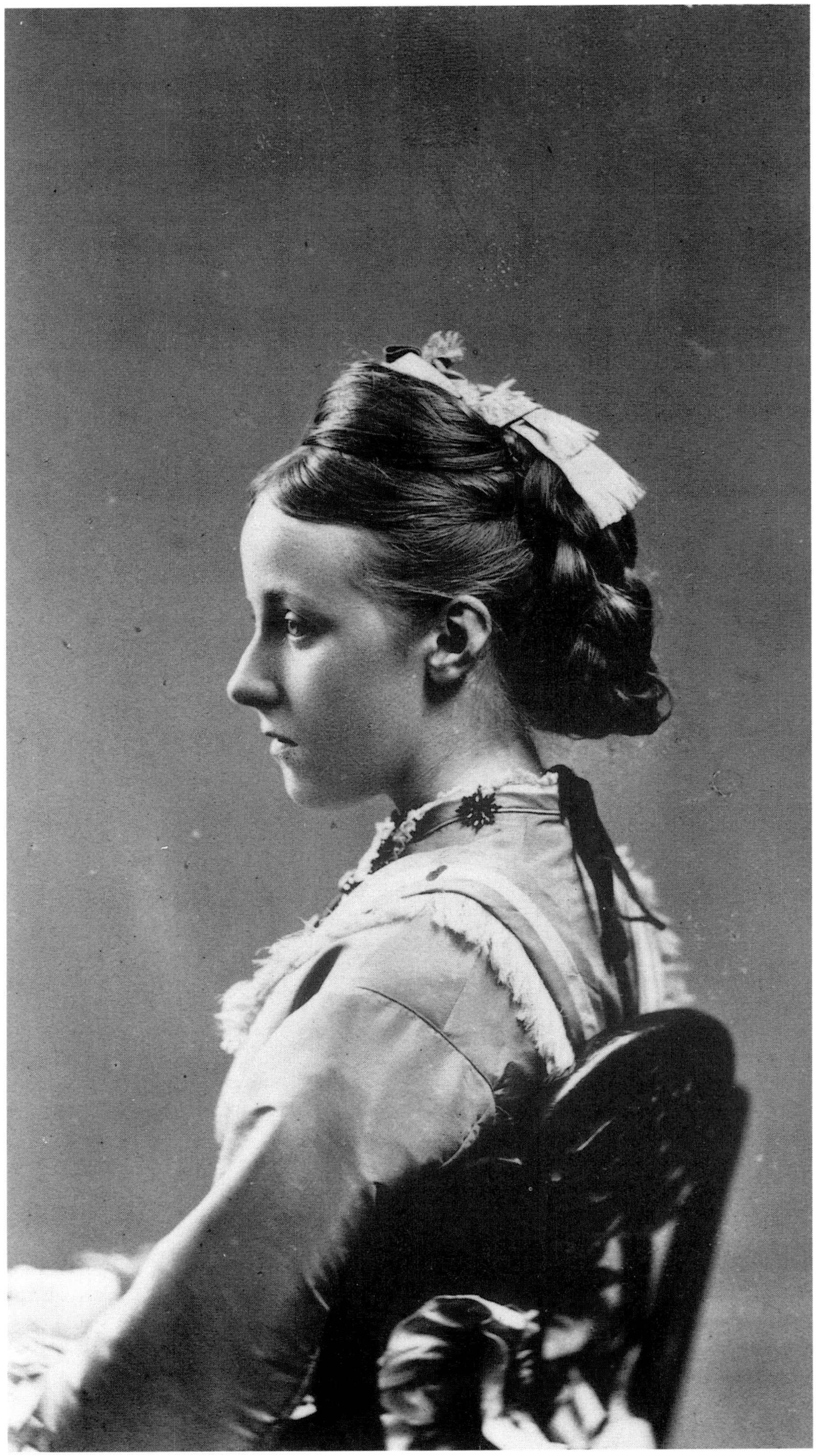

107. Isabel Duncombe
Late 1860s
Elliott & Fry, London (Eykyn Album (42) p. 43) (NPG Ax 33509)

GROUP

108

Although intimate in nature, this is a published portrait of Charles Dickens reading to his daughters in his garden at Gads Hill.

Born in 1812, Dickens achieved early fame and fortune with the publication in 1836 of *The Pickwick Papers*, and with a spate of subsequent celebrated novels in the 1840s and 1850s. He married in 1836 and had a total of ten children before separating from his wife, Catherine in 1856, some nine years before this photograph.

Dickens, here aged 53, wears a light-cloth lounge suit or 'suit of dittos'. His appearance, with the turn-down shirt collar and tie-cravat in the modern four-in-hand manner, seems very familiar. His Bohemian stance, sitting reverseways on a Gothick-style wrought-iron garden seat, is in studied keeping with his literary lifestyle.

Both his daughters are here aged about 20: Kate, standing, wears a lightweight cloth dress, the bodice fastening centre-front with five, circular, metal buttons. She wears a Swiss belt, a popular accessory in the mid 1860s to complete and enliven a plain 'promenade' or 'home' costume, or to finish an outfit of separate skirt and contrasting bodice.

The seated sister, Minnie, wears a striped-silk dress with bishop sleeves, fastening with long, three-button cuffs. Her outfit has a narrow belt with a large rectangular metal buckle, and in her lap, she holds her flat, straw, boater-shaped hat over her black-silk apron, which is trimmed with horizontal rows of lighter ribbon.

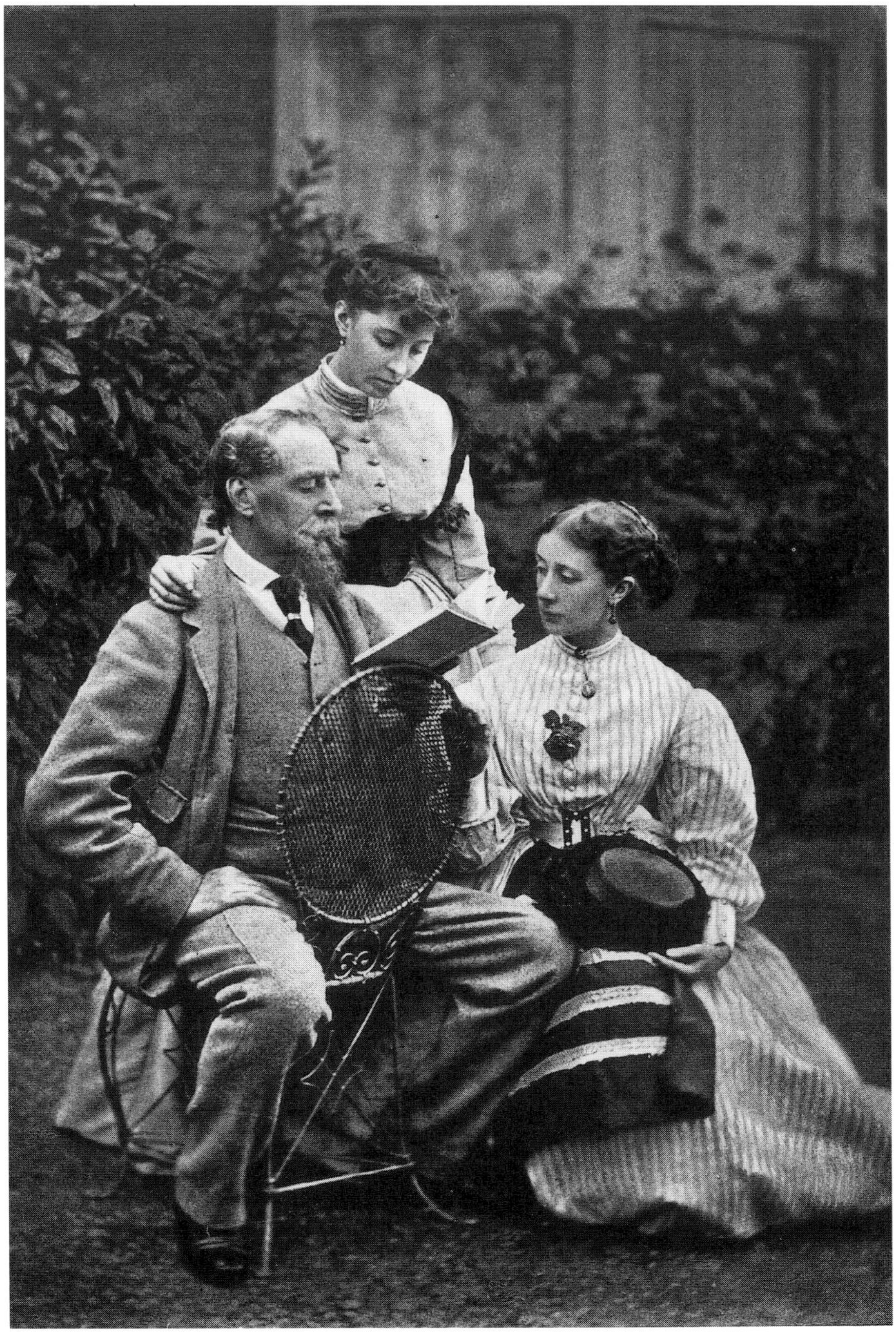

108. Charles Dickens with his daughters Kate and Minnie 1865
Mason, Rochester (NPG x 24930)

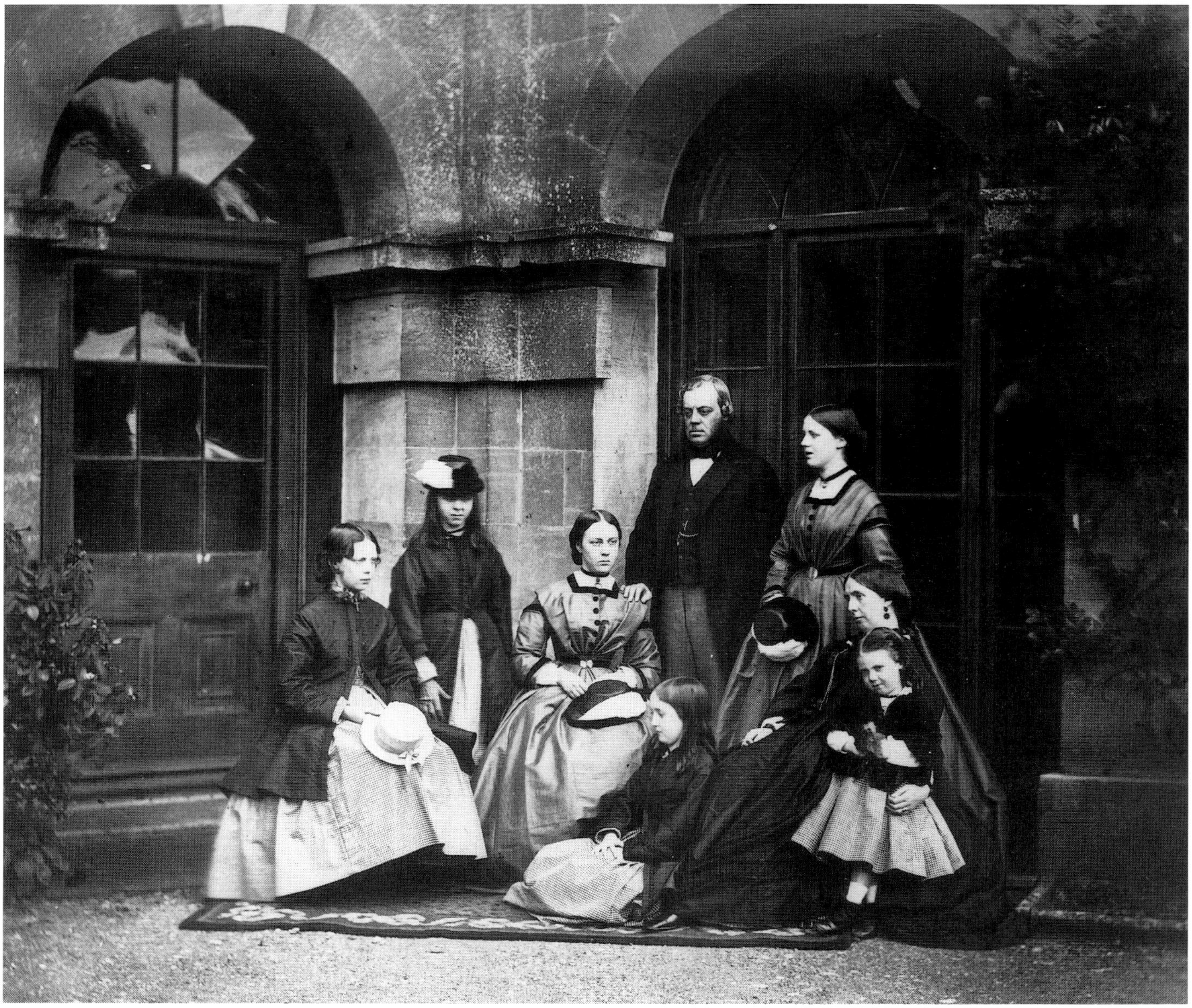

109. The Duke and Duchess of Marlborough with their six daughters
Mid 1860s
Hills and Saunders, London (Album 47, p. 19) (NPG Ax 33523)

109

John Winston, 7th Duke of Marlborough, married Lady Frances Vane, daughter of the Marquess of Londonderry in 1843, aged 21. They had a total of eight children; six daughters, shown here, and two sons: George Charles, the heir and future 8th Duke, and Randolph, father of the future Winston Churchill.

The six daughters, Cornelia, Fanny, Anne, Georgina, Rosamond, and Sarah pose, wearing walking dress, in front of an elevation of Blenheim Palace. The younger four girls, with loose hair, all have matching checked-cotton dresses and dark-silk paletots; the elder two, with their hair dressed into chignons, wear matching silk daydresses. Between the six of them, in the later 1860s and 1870s, these girls were to marry one Duke, one Earl, three Barons, and one Lieutenant-Colonel.

Pictured here in the mid 1860s, the 7th Duke had inherited the title from his father in 1857, having hitherto served as Conservative MP for Woodstock. In the House of Lords, he was to become Viceroy of Ireland (1876–1880) before his death in 1883. He also began a series of notorious sales from his family collections, beginning with 'The Marlborough Gems' in 1875, which fetched £10,000 in a single lot at Christie's.

The Duchess of Marlborough, seated to the right, was also born in 1822 and in later life devoted herself to the political interests of her second son, Lord Randolph Churchill, who became Leader of the House of Commons in 1886.

110, 111

Henry, 6th Duke of Newcastle (1834–79), stands, gloriously bearded, beside his young wife Henrietta Adela (1843–1915). Sitting in attendance are their companions: Lady Susan Vane-Tempest, the Duke's sister, who had married the son of the 3rd Marquess of Londonderry in 1860; and Charles, 20th Baron Clinton.

The 6th Duke had succeeded his father in 1864, slightly pre-dating this photograph. He had married his 17-year-old bride in 1861, in seemingly hurried circumstances, at the British Embassy in Paris. Henrietta, the future, illustrious Duchess, was the illegitimate daughter of Henry Hope of Deepdene, Surrey and a certain Anne Bichet, whom Henry Hope married in 1851.

When widowed in 1879, Henrietta immediately turned Roman Catholic and remarried. In 1895 Lady Paget described her as 'Still very pretty and smart looking, though given up to good works in the East End . . . She loves the worst cases . . .'.[1]

All four sitters wear outdoor walking dress and pose in the conservatory at the Duke's principal residence at Clumber Park near Ollerton, Nottingham. Lady Susan Vane-Tempest wears a dropped-bun, or chignon, in both portraits.

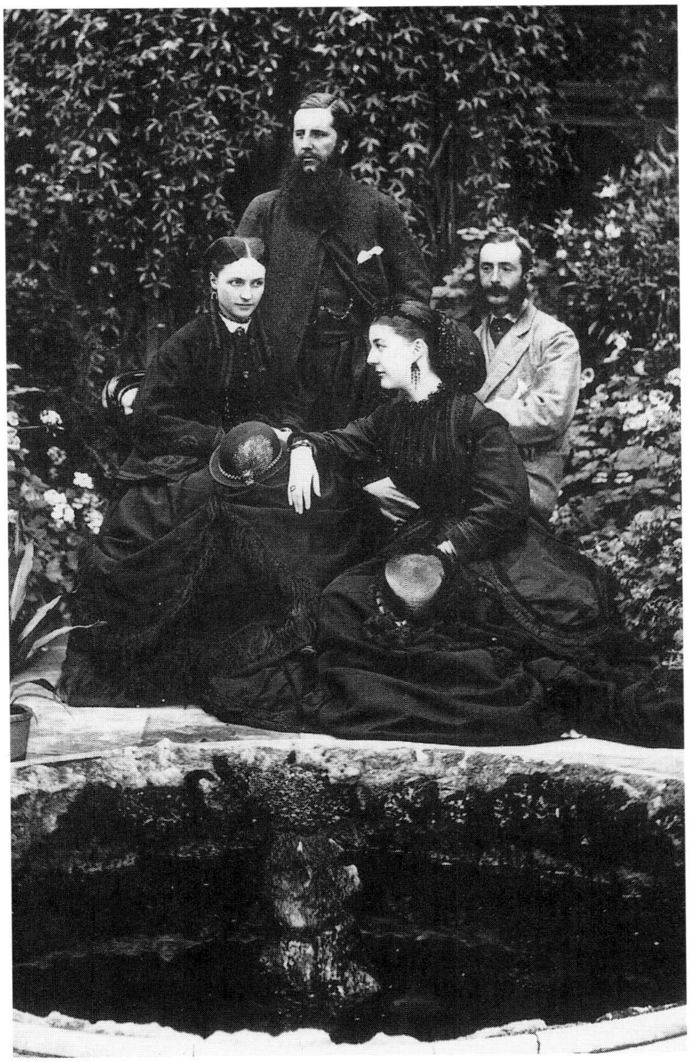

110. The Duke and Duchess of Newcastle, Baron Clinton, and Lady Susan Vane-Tempest *c.*1865

Theophilus Smith, Nottingham (Wilberforce Album, vol. 2, p. 12) (NPG Ax 33521)

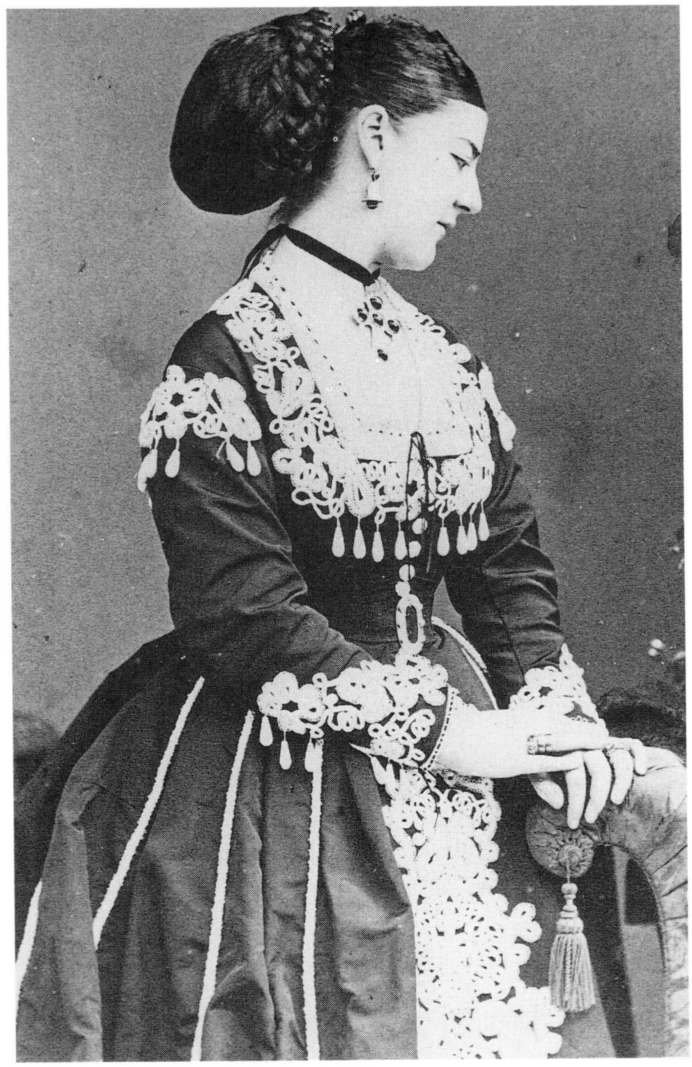

111. Lady Susan Vane-Tempest 1867

Disderi, London (Platt Hall)

112,113

These large-scale companion portraits are of Josslyn Francis Pennington, 5th Baron Muncaster, and his wife Constance Anne, whom he had married in 1863.

They pose separately amidst the potted plants and luxuriant vegetation on the verandah at Muncaster Castle, Ravenglass, Cumberland. Lord Muncaster sits somewhat stiffly at a makeshift desk, perhaps musing about his army career.

His morning coat has very wide, round-cut lapels, partly faced in satin, and is worn over lighter-cloth trousers and a double-breasted waistcoat. His spotted, dark-silk cravat completely covers his shirt-front, whilst his full, untrimmed whiskers and beard obscure his collar.

Lady Muncaster, in a rather more convincing outdoor pose, wears a dark-silk paletot or jacket with a piped border decoration and a silk fringed edging. The lighter silk of her dress contrasts with the silk of her jacket and with that of her dark parasol shade. Her straw hat is tipped forward over the eyes and trimmed with a white feather.

The fullness of the skirt is now concentrated at the back, from where it is soon to blossom forth into the full-blown bustle.

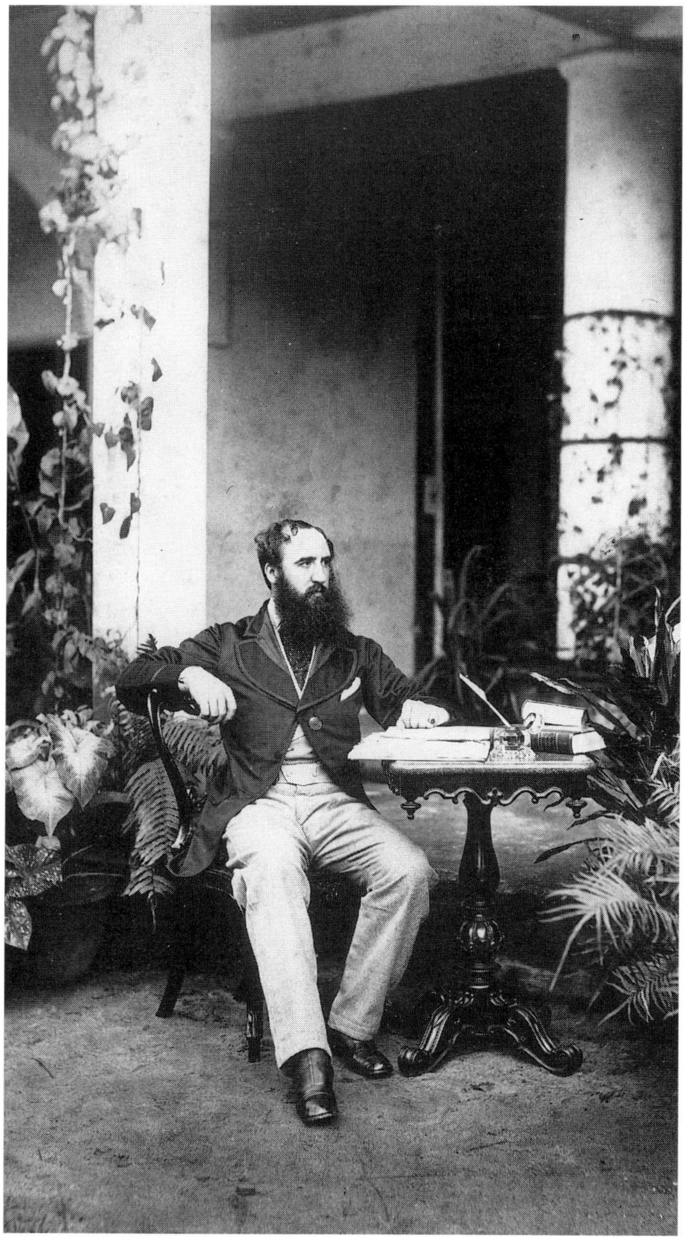

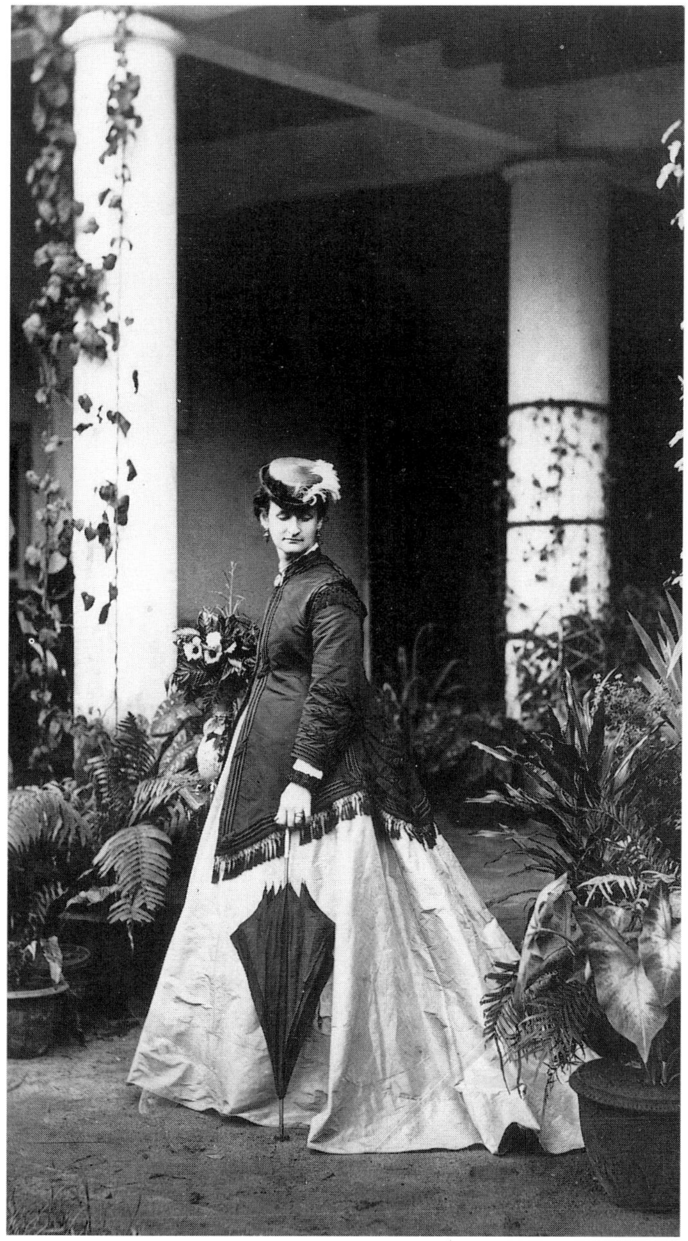

112 & 113. Lord and Lady Muncaster
Late 1860s
Photographer unknown, Ravenglass (NPG x 33714)

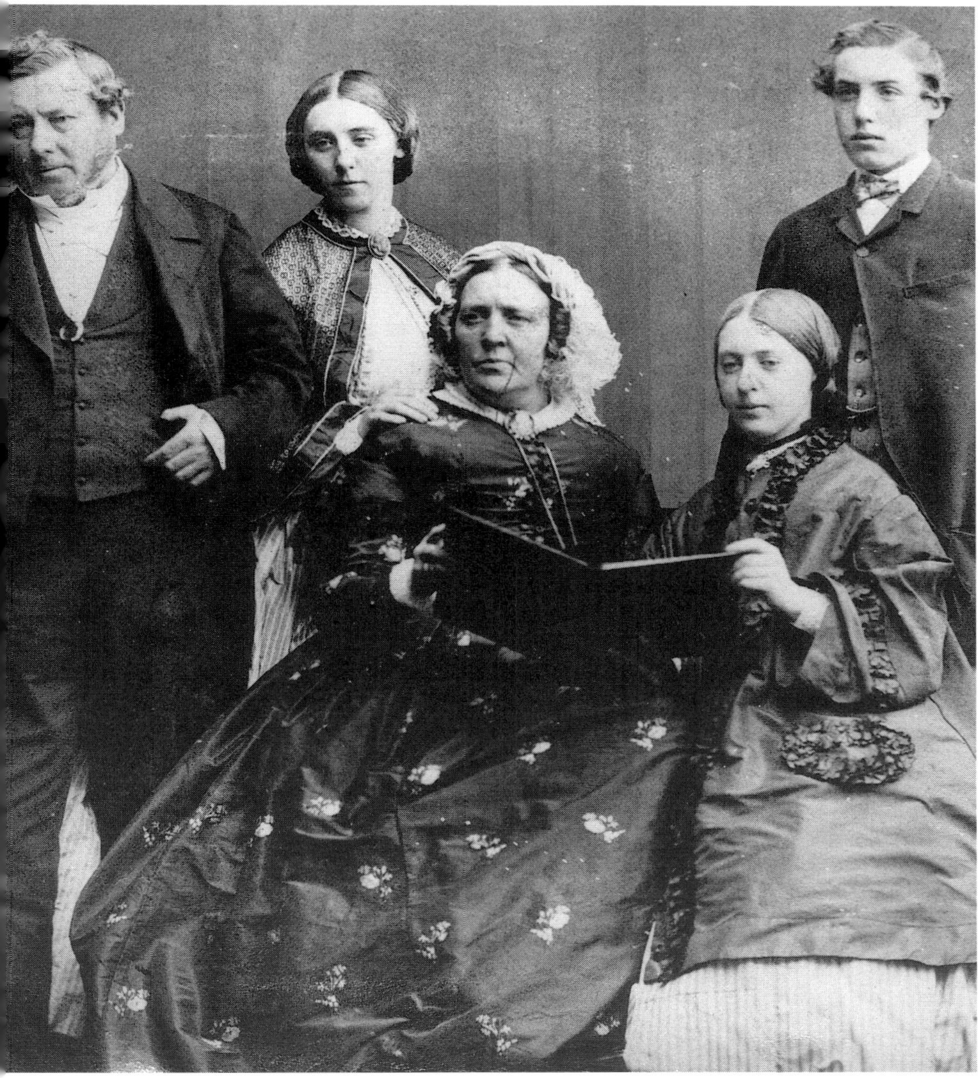

114. **Mr and Mrs R. C. Gardner with their three children**
1867
Camille Silvy, London (Daybook 8, no. 10786)

114

Posed in a domestic musical setting, eyes uniformly to the right, the Gardners represent a comfortable, rather conservative, middle-class family; typical of portrait sitters, if not of Silvy's studio.

Mr Gardner senior – short, stocky, and fairly portly, like his seated wife – wears a formal tailcoat, with cutaway, horizontal fronts over a waistcoat with a wide shawl-collar. He carries his black-silk top hat in his right hand.

His wife wears a dark-silk dress, woven with lighter, widely spaced, scattered floral motifs. She wears a white indoor cap, trimmed with a drooping ostrich feather.

The daughters have matching hairstyles and striped skirts; the standing sister wears a patterned jacket fastening at the top only and bordered with silk ribbon. Her sister wears a dark-cloth paletot reaching to her knees and trimmed with matching bands at the collar, fronts, cuffs, and pockets. As can be seen, where the standing daughter's skirt projects beyond her father's legs, the girls wear full crinoline petticoats, shortly to be abandoned by the fashionable world.

Their brother wears a morning coat, fastened at the top button and worn over paler waistcoat and trousers.

115

Caroline, daughter of William Keppel, 6th Viscount Barrington, married James, Viscount Somerton in 1856. Her eldest child Charles was born in 1858 (*see* Plate 20) and there then followed the four children shown here: Mary Beatrice (b. 1859); Margaret (b. 1863); Sidney James, future Earl Normanton, (b. 1865); and Augustus (b. 1868). Lady Normanton's husband succeeded as 3rd Earl in 1868, the date of this portrait.

The two elder daughters seem to be wearing velvet jackets and silk skirts which match their mother's, as do their porkpie hats. Little Sidney wears a sailor suit with straw boater, a style rivalling the ubiquitous knickerbocker and Highland suits in popularity by the later 1860s. A 'sailor costume for a boy between four and six' in *The Queen* (14 November 1868) is described as comprising 'a grey poplin blouse, with large collar; the sash is blue likewise the stockings and necktie. Grey felt cap with blue ribbon . . .'.[2] The boater was more usually worn than the cap, and sometimes covered with decorative fabric: 'a small sailor hat of straw, covered with black wax cloth and trimmed with blue ribbon . . .' (*The Queen*, 18 August 1866).[3]

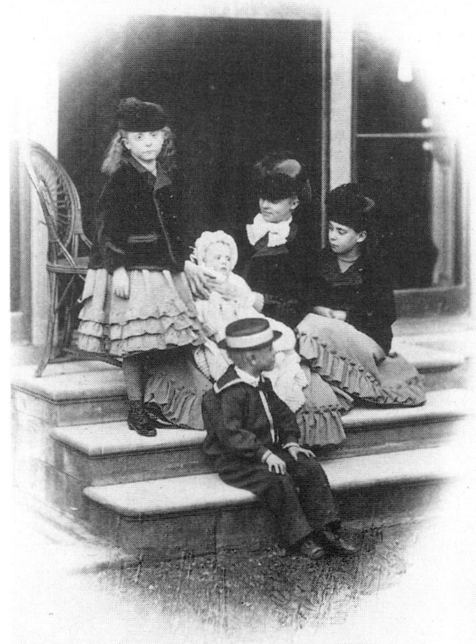

115. **Caroline, Countess of Normanton, with four of her children**
1868
Photographer unknown (Barrington Album, p. 67)

PART THREE: 1870-80

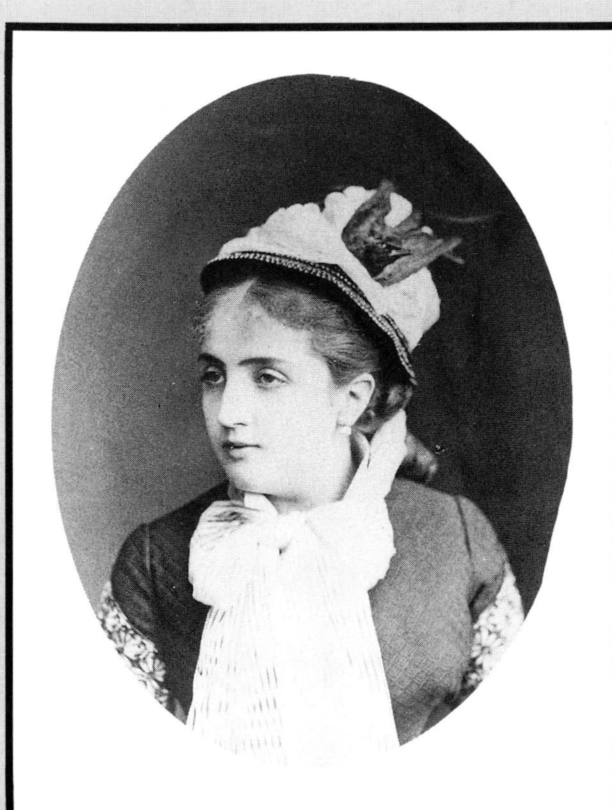

MALE

116

Rudolphe Francis Charles Joseph, heir to the Imperial House of Hapsburg, was born in August 1858 and is here aged 11 or 12.

In this portrait, Rudolphe wears a matching, three-piece cloth suit for riding, complete with spotted silk cravat, leather riding boots and round, bowler riding hat. He had begun to learn riding at the age of ten, and rapidly achieved the confidence and skill on horseback possessed by both his parents.

The only heir to a troubled and disjointed Empire, foreboding about his future was expressed even at this early age: *The Queen* (11 June 1870), in a short article about the prince, ended

> after considering the many occupations and studies consequent upon the high position Prince Rudolphe occupies, we must acknowledge that the burden laid upon the great ones of the earth is far from small and that it begins to be felt in very tender years . . .[1]

Indeed, the Prince's 'frank and cheerful' disposition was not equal to the many burdens of his lonely position, and he was to commit suicide at Mayerling in January 1889 aged only 30.

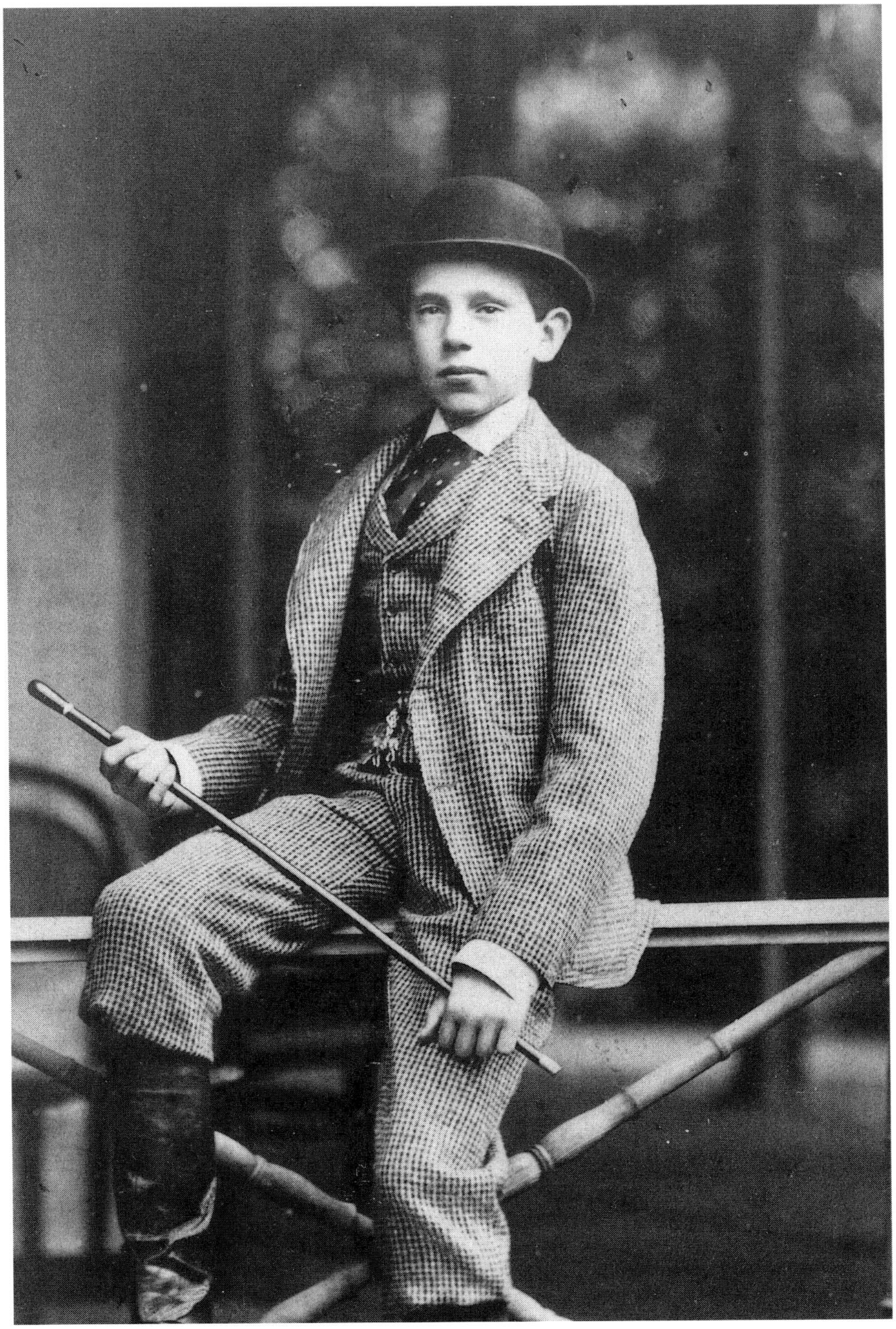

116. Crown Prince Rudolphe of Austria
***c.* 1870**
Emil Rabending, Vienna (NPG x 5825)

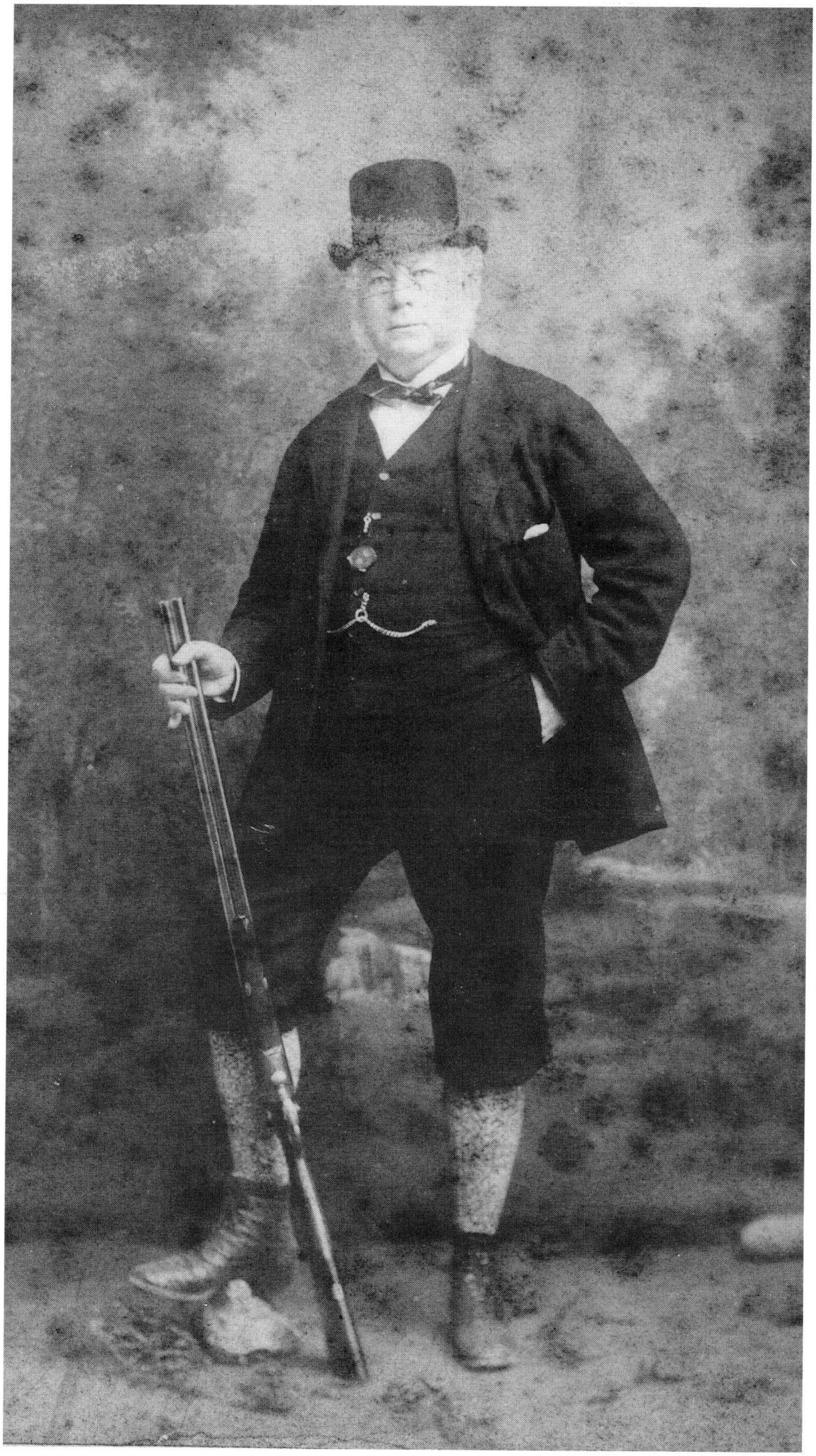

117. Henry Shaw
***c.* 1871**
A. F. MacKenzie, Birnam (NPG x 12409)

117

Dating from the very early 1870s, this portrait shows Henry Shaw in a shooting outfit. An architectural draughtsman and engraver by profession, Shaw wrote a series of antiquarian works from the 1830s including the influential *Illuminated Ornaments of the Middle Ages* (1832). By the date of this portrait, he was the Treasurer to the Middle Temple.

For shooting, breeches or knickerbockers were invariably worn. Mr Shaw wears dark-cloth breeches with matching short jacket and waistcoat. *The Tailor and Cutter* for August 1871, roughly the date of this photograph, shows a fashion drawing of Prince Arthur in a shooting outfit and in a similar pose to Henry Shaw. The Prince wears a more tailored and stylish 'short sac' coat with a belt fastened across the waist. The report relates that:

> knickerbockers, or what we may more correctly describe as wide breeches, are the universal favourites: they are cut about three inches wider in the leg and about two inches longer than in ordinary breeches, the extra width being allowed in the leg seam . . . short leggings of the same material as the breeches are pleasant to wear but not so serviceable in protecting the legs as those made of stout leather . . .[2]

Henry Shaw appears to wear thick woollen stockings instead of leather gaiters, but his ankle boots match those worn in the fashion plate, as does his hard, crowned hat.

The fabrics recommended for the illustrated 'shooting costume' are 'heather mixtures and soft pliable six-quarter fancy coatings'. For 'the old style of shooting coat', more akin to Mr Shaw's outfit, 'light Tweeds, Angolas, and Shetland tweed' are advised.

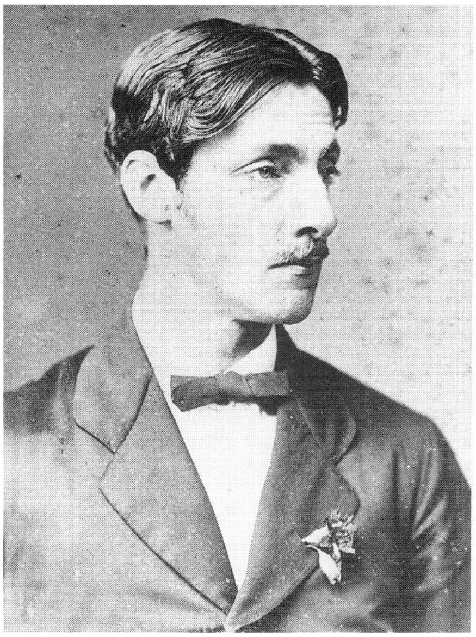

118. A. S. Herschel Esq.
1872
Thomas Annan, Glasgow (Platt Hall)

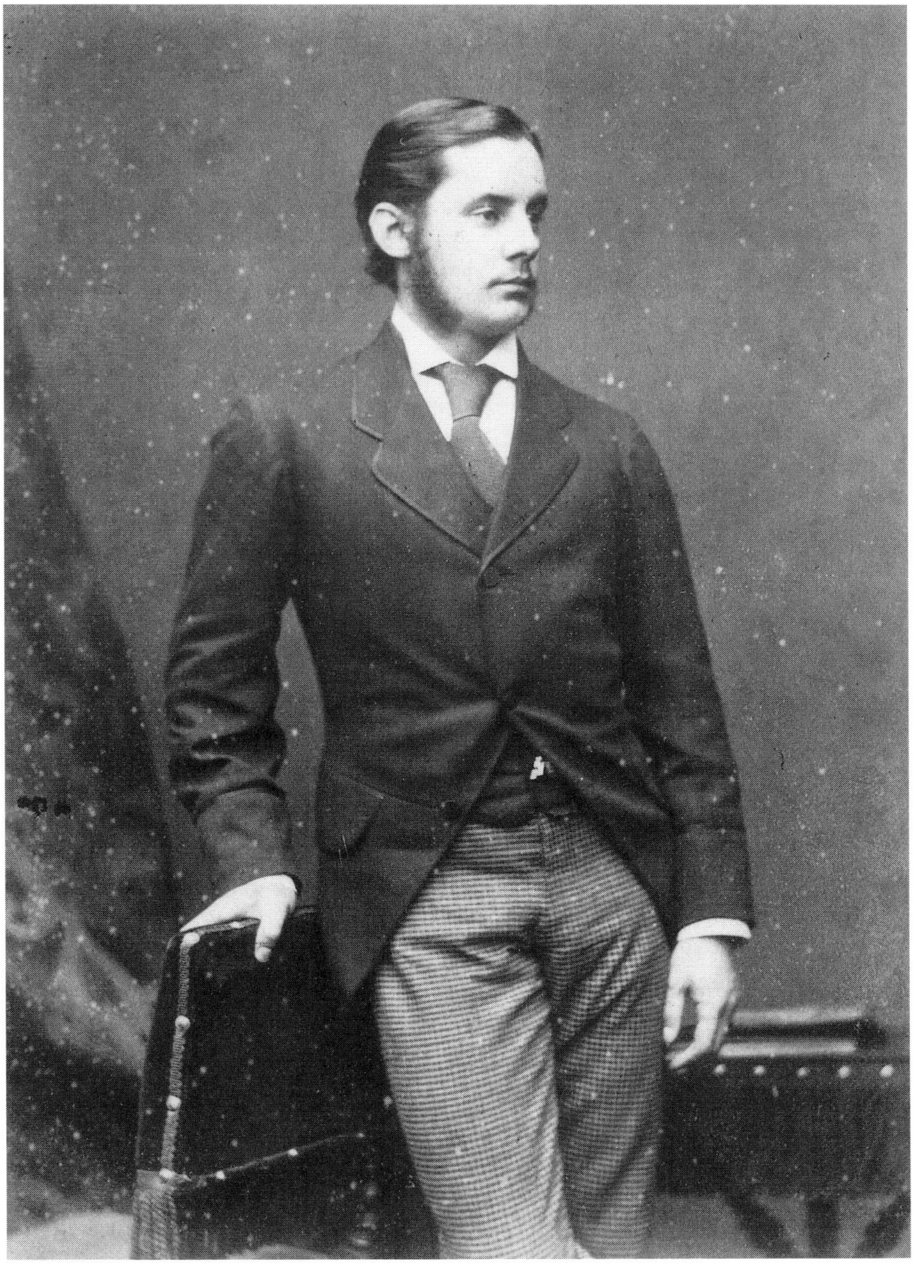

119. Willis Compton
1874
Alexander Bassano, London (NPG x 6343)

118

Mr Herschel exemplifies the understated, restrained, masculine style of the 1870s: 'Gentlemen dress as quietly as it is possible to do, and there are no remarkable extremes in dress'. (*Tailor and Cutter*, 1871.)[3]

Herschel's black morning coat with the sheen of superfine or face cloth, has a moderate collar and revers; his narrow tie is also black and fastened in a neat bow; his hair is cut fairly close with a centre parting and smoothed back with hair oil. Neat moustaches would now be worn without side-whiskers or beards, paving the way for the exuberant late-Victorian and Edwardian moustaches.

Mr Herschel wears a rather limp buttonhole, perhaps signifying that he is a wedding guest.

119

Willis Compton wears the ubiquitous morning coat of the 1870s, with matching waistcoat and contrasting check trousers. This three-button morning coat, with the revers cut quite high, was known as a 'University', and sometimes appears in a four-button variety.

The Tailor and Cutter (Spring 1876) shows a very similar coat which is described as 'essentially that of a business gentleman. The same coat . . . has been worn by this class for some years back . . .'. A contrasting morning coat is also illustrated with only two buttons, and cut lower at the revers: 'a style more suitable for fashionable promenade'.[4]

Willis Compton wears a starched collar with turn-down wings and a tie-cravat in the modern four-in-hand manner.

By the middle 1870s, the formal frock coat and the tall, black-silk top hat, were worn only by older men or else those conservative by nature. Commentators such as *The Graphic* noted the change:

> The great institution of British respectability, the tall black hat, along with its equally respectable adjuncts, the frock coat and all the attributes of what is called 'morning dress' totters to its fall . . .[5]

The morning coat, as worn by Willis Compton, and the lounge jacket, were the two coats which replaced the frock coat.

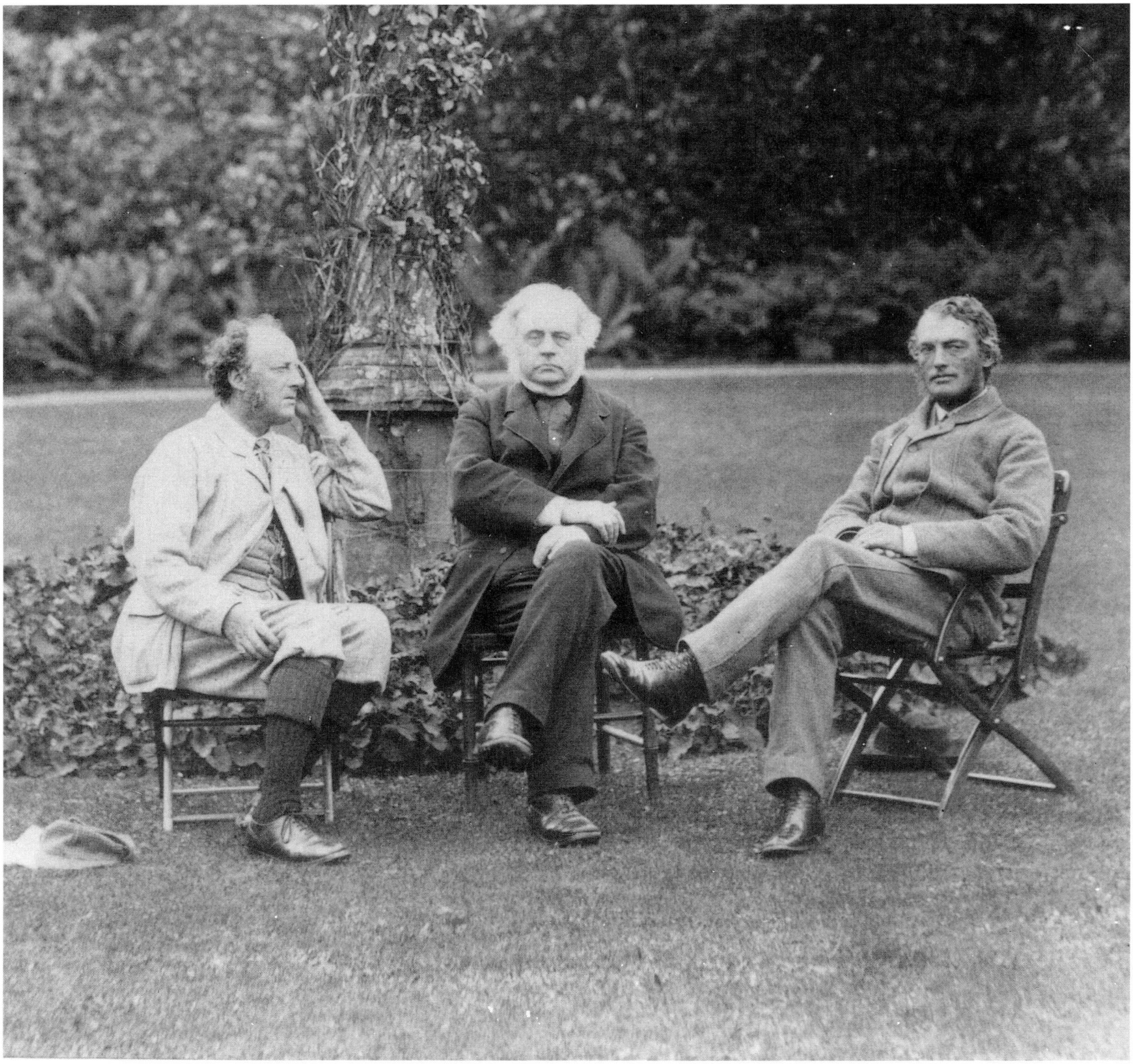

120. John Bright, John Everett Millais, and Henry James, 1st Baron James 1875
Rupert Potter, Dalguize (NPG ref. neg. no. 26134)

120

A trio comprising celebrated politician, artist, and MP and lawyer: John Bright is flanked by his friends Millais and James; and the three pose in Millais' garden at Dalguize, Perthshire.

John Bright, an austere Quaker and reformer, is dressed most formally in a dark frock coat. He was MP for Durham, Manchester, and Birmingham respectively (from 1857) and a notable orator, both in the House of Commons and at public meetings. President of the Board of Trade in Gladstone's Cabinet from 1868 to 1870, he returned to the Cabinet from 1873 to 1874, and from 1880 to 1882.

His younger companion and host, John Everett Millais, one of the founder members of the Pre-Raphaelite Brotherhood (1848), sits on Bright's right. Painting furiously in the 1850s and 1860s, he turned increasingly to landscapes and portraits in the 1870s, inspired by his retreat in Perthshire. Here he wears a cloth knickerbocker suit with thick woollen stockings.

James wears a figure-hugging, cloth country suit, double breasted, with decorative vertical flaps either side of the centre-front.

121

'So much promise nipped in the bud! Such manliness, modesty, gentleness and highly trained intelligence snatched from this life by the hand of a few barbarians'. Such was the rhetoric of *The London Illustrated News* when it reported the death of the Prince Imperial on 28 June 1879.[6]

The only child of Emperor Napoleon III and the Empress Eugénie, the prince was born in 1856 after a difficult and dangerous childbirth. The heir to the throne was raised carefully in France until the sudden collapse of the French Empire after the battle of Sedan in September 1870. The prince and his mother fled to England, and were later joined by the Emperor, who was soon to die in exile.

The prince became a military cadet at the Royal Military Academy at Woolwich from November 1872. He proved himself an exceptionally able student, finishing first in his year in horsemanship. In 1879, he visited South Africa with the British Zulu campaign where he met a sudden death in an ambush.

Reputedly the possessor of a blameless reputation, the prince emerges as scarcely more than an ethereal figure in the eulogies published after his death: Dean Stanley in Westminster Abbey declared that 'he left a stainless name behind him, honoured and respected even by his adversaries'.[7]

For this studio portrait, the prince presents a very dapper figure in an immaculately cut and styled double-breasted frock coat, carrying his cane and black-silk top hat. He wears a silk Ascot cravat pinned in place and completely obscuring his shirt front, leaving only the stiff, upstanding collar visible.

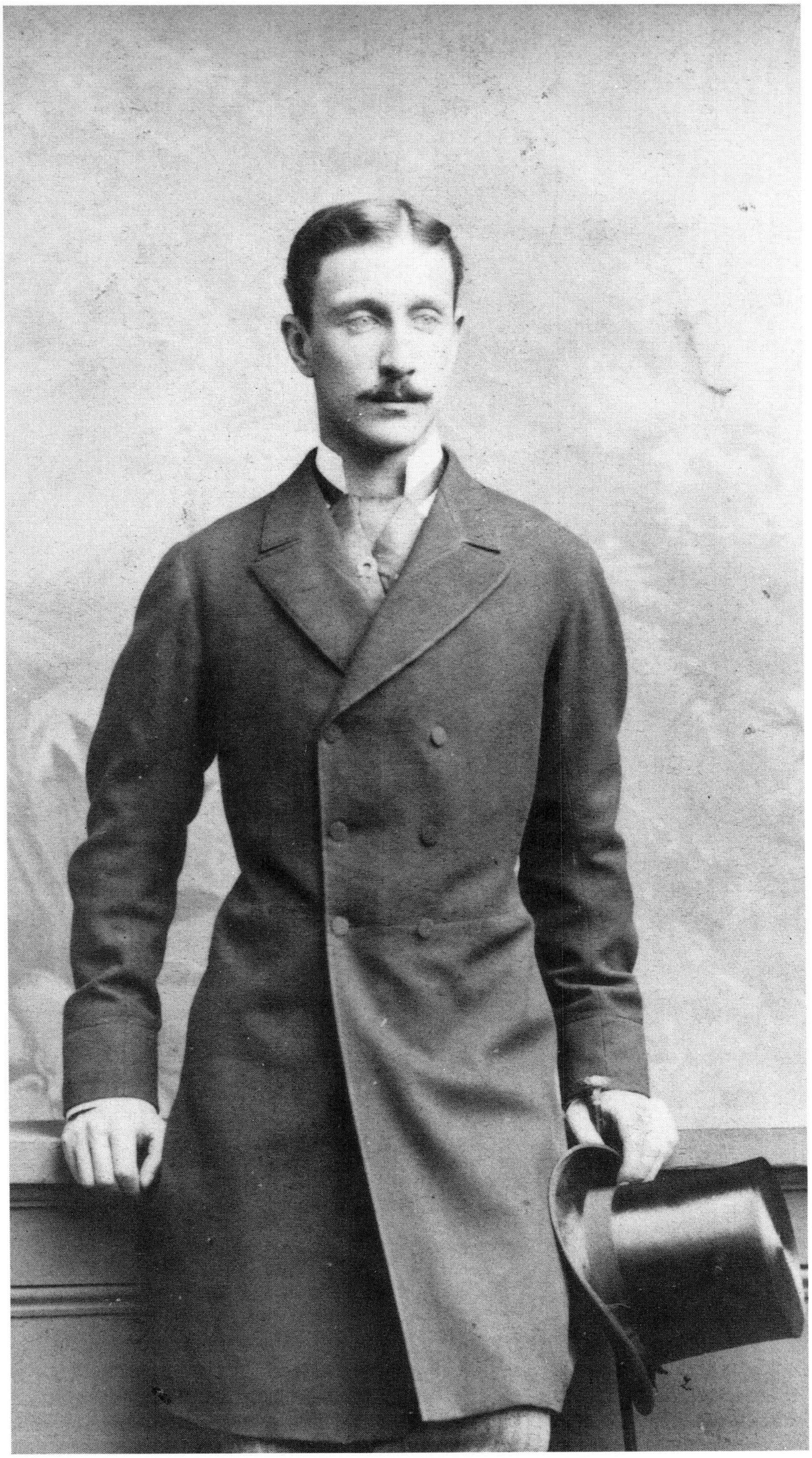

121. Prince Louis Napoleon, the Prince Imperial
1878
Elliott and Fry, London (NPG x 32944)

122

Born in 1804, Redgrave was a respected mid-Victorian landscape and genre painter, elected a Royal Academician in 1851, and the painter of such narrative-title works as *Flight to Egypt* and *The Outcast*.

In his seventies in this portrait, Redgrave poses in a velvet smoking cap which is rather worn, and reflects his artistic leanings. His coat, probably a frock coat, has wide lapels cut with buttonholes. *The Tailor and Cutter* (February 1878) includes an article on making a frock coat which, like Redgrave's, has the edges bound in narrow silk braid, and has five holes in each lapel, two or three that would actually button.[8] This example has three not intended to button. Redgrave also wears a single-breasted dark-cloth waistcoat, white shirt and small black tie.

He sports a full beard without moustaches, sometimes called the 'Nokomis' beard.[9] Throughout the 1860s beards and moustaches became increasingly popular, in spite of being pilloried in the columns of *Punch* magazine. By 1870, the question for most men was usually not whether to wear facial hair, but in what style the facial hair should be worn. Even so, etiquette books preferred the clean-shaven look, perpetuating the age-old prejudice against 'unclean' and 'boorish' facial hair:

> A smooth shaven beard is a mark of cleanliness, and evidence of attention to the duties of the toilette never absent from the person of a gentleman; want of time, the only available apology, scarsely forms an excuse for a mechanic to appear careless in this respect . . . (*c.* 1880)[10]

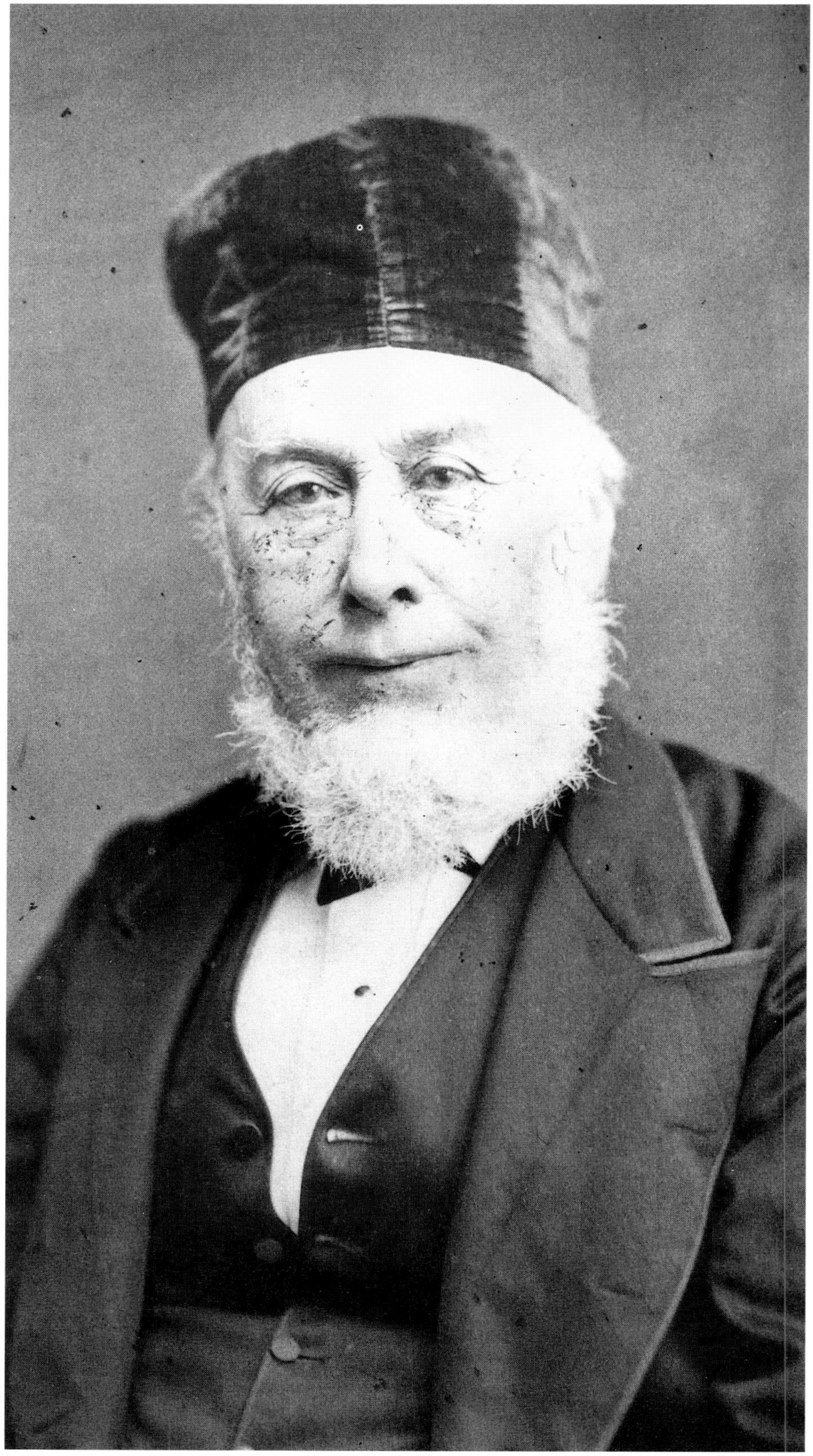

122. Richard Redgrave
1879
Boning and Small, London (NPG x 14716)

FEMALE

123

After her triumphant London début in 1861, Adelina Patti's career became wearisome in its monotony of unvarying success; a contemporary put it somewhat quaintly: 'Space would fail to tell of a tithe of her great triumphs . . .'.[1] Berlin, Brussels, Madrid, Vienna, Paris, Moscow: all experienced her mastery of all the established operatic roles.

This portrait was taken around 1870, shortly after her first marriage to a French soldier and courtier: Henri, Marquis de Caux. This marriage, at the Roman Catholic chapel on Clapham Common, was widely reported: 'The bride wore a white satin dress half hidden in clouds of lace and had a wreath of orange blossom in her hair. Her four bridesmaids wore white with sashes of blue . . .'.[2]

In this photograph, Miss Patti wears a light-silk daydress woven with dark-satin stripes alternating with patterned stripes. The hem is decorated with three self-fabric, ruched rouleaux and three rows of muslin frilling. The sleeves, in sham eighteenth-century style with ruffles, are trimmed with dark-silk ribbon matching that on the bustle. Her tall, coiled coiffure with long, back ringlets serves to accent the lengthening silhouette as the crinoline disappears and skirts become tight and straight.

Miss Patti was later to separate from her first husband, divorcing him in 1885, and then marrying the singer Ernesto Nicolini. On Nicolini's death, she married the Baron Cederström.

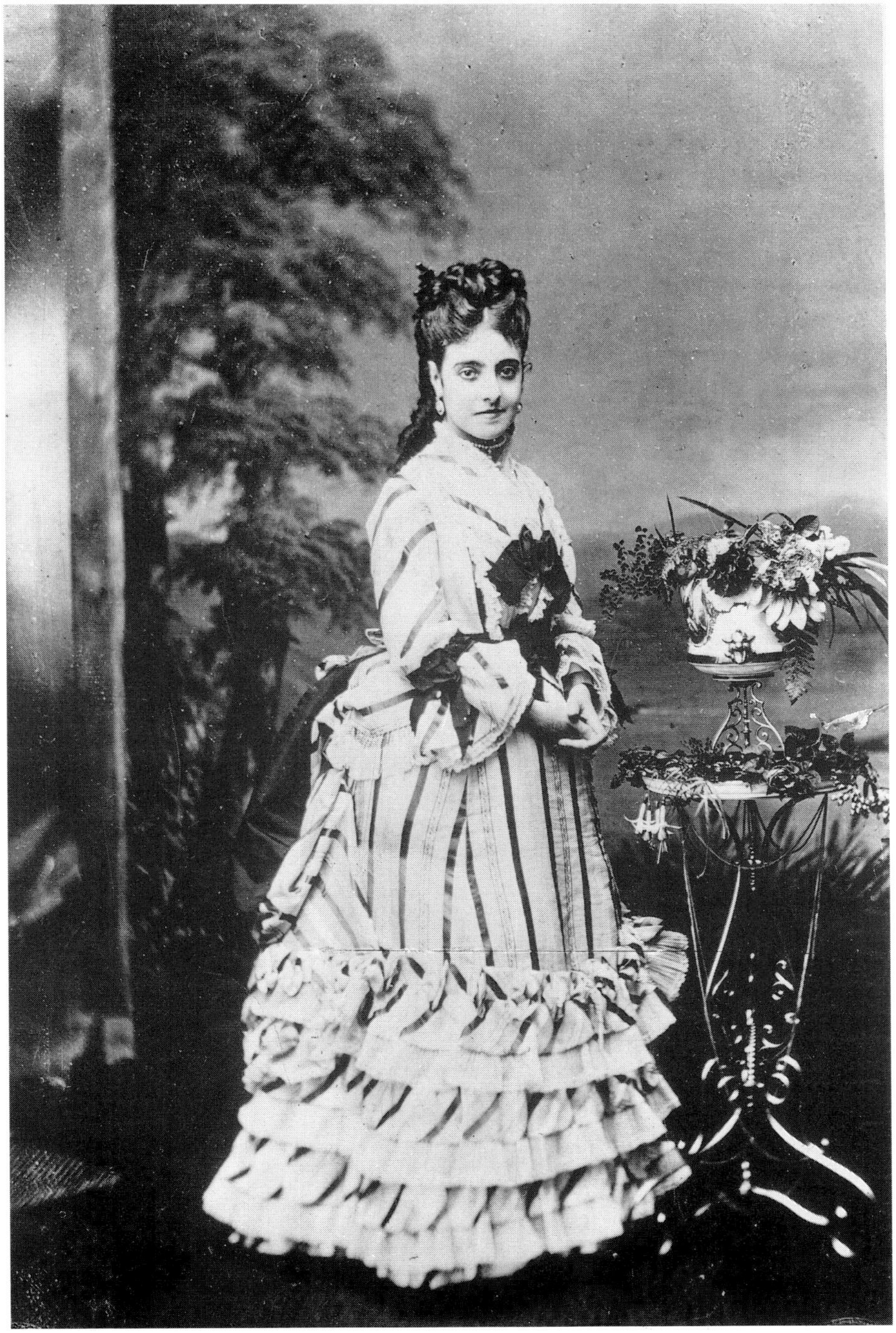

123. Adelina Patti
***c.* 1870**
W. & D. Downey (NPG x 32979)

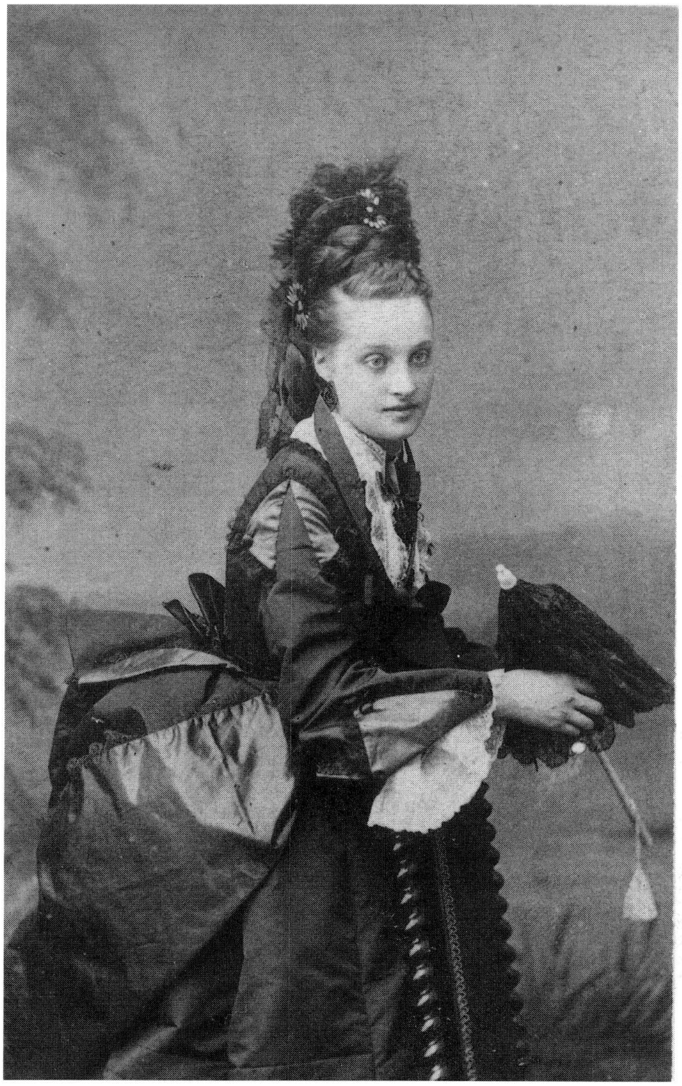

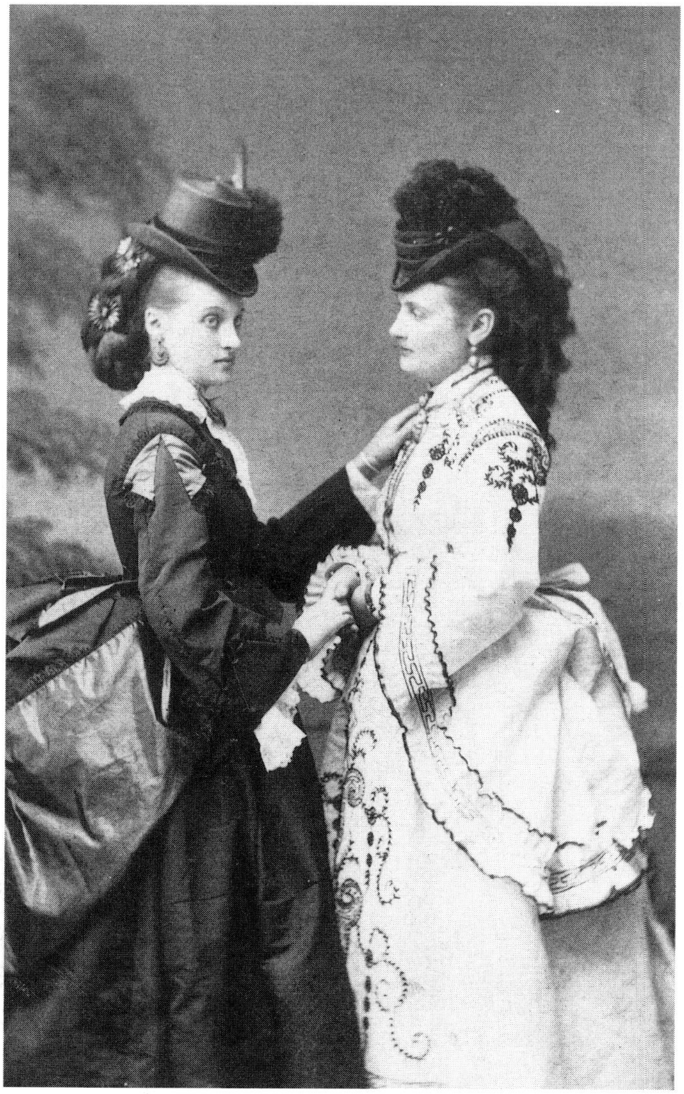

124 & 125. Fannie, Lady Wentworth 1870
W. & D. Downey, Newcastle (NPG x 32959)

124, 125

The daughter of the Reverend George Heriot of Newcastle, Fannie married Ralph, 13th Baron Wentworth, in 1869 aged only 16. Here aged 17, Lady Wentworth poses with an unknown friend, possibly the 'Sophie' inscribed on the reverse of the carte. Lady Wentworth's marriage was short-lived, as *Burke's Peerage* somewhat baldly relates: 'Within two years, Wentworth found it necessary to separate himself from his wife. He never saw her again . . .'.[3] Lord Wentworth secured custody of their only child, Ada, and Fannie was to die, aged only 25, in 1878.

In these two views, Fannie wears a dark-silk polonaise-style dress, with the over-drapery pulled up high at the back to form an immense bustle. The silk lining is revealed as a contrasting fabric at the back, and on the turned-back cuffs and shoulder epaulettes. Horizontal creasing can be seen across the skirt-front, suggesting that this is a brand new outfit. Fannie sports voluminous lace ruffles and, in the single portrait, carries a black lace parasol.

Her hair is dressed very high with false plaits and rouleaux, and is drawn into a huge chignon at the back. The addition of false hair pads and chignons, so essential in towering coiffures such as Fannie's, was commonplace from the mid 1860s to the mid 1870s. Dr Andrew Wynter wrote in 1874:

> The fashion of wearing false hair has become so universal that the exception of the few persons content with the crop Nature has supplied, simply serves to prove the rule. Those who do not adopt a whole chignon will wear part of one or bring a simple plait into requisition. Even ladies who profess to scorn such additions, insert a few surreptitious 'frisettes' to shape their head-tire . . .[4]

Critics railed ceaselessly against the follies of false hair, even asserting (falsely) that the imported hair was cut from the corpses of poor Latin peasants (*see* Plate 107).

Lady Wentworth's friend wears a white piqué polonaise-style dress embroidered with scrolling black braid.

Both women wear 'postillion' hats, pushed forward over their foreheads to accommodate the huge chignons.

126, 127

These two portraits of Lady Douglas, from the same sitting, show a full-length and three-quarter-length view, one in profile, the other full on, enabling us to see the front and back of her dress.

Eleanor Louisa Douglas, née Liffleton, married Sir Robert Mackenzie, 3rd Baron Douglas of Glenbervie in 1866.

For her portrait, she wears a lightweight evening dress with a fashionable, square-cut neckline, and a high waist tied with a black-silk sash. The skirt is gored to provide a straight front and fullness at the back, where it trails to a train. Two, deep, appliqué bands of dark net surmount flounces of white muslin, whilst a back apron panel is attached at the waist and falls from an inverted 'V' at the front.

Mrs Douglas's jewellery of black jet possibly denotes secondary mourning, and forms a matching parure of pendant earrings, necklace, bracelet, front brooch, and head ornament. She carries a fan, although she does not wear the obligatory gloves to complete the evening ensemble.[5]

Her hair is parted in the middle with a front portion formed into a waved bandeau and the rest drawn back to a curled chignon at the back. This coiffure is very similar to one illustrated from three angles in *The Young Englishwoman* (August 1870), which also has a decorative, carved comb resting as a crescent on the bandeau centre-front.[6]

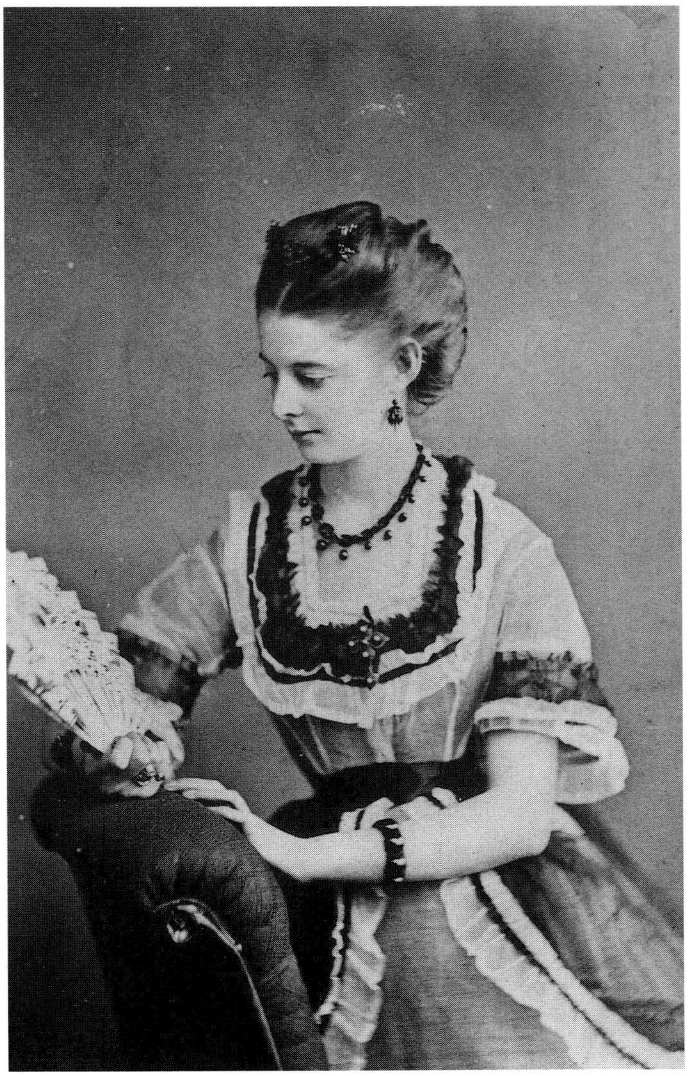

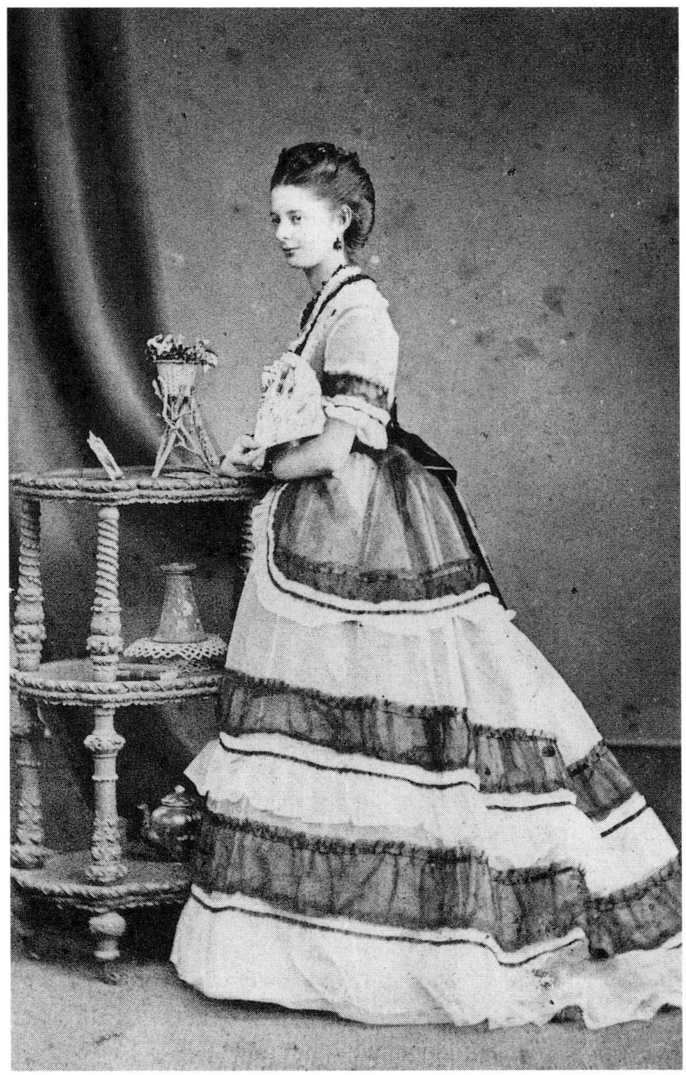

126 & 127. Lady Louisa 'Louie' Douglas
1870
R. Boning, St Leonards on Sea, (Wilberforce Album, vol. 1 p. 6) (NPG Ax 33524

128

Mrs Gollan wears her wedding dress, which has been suitably adapted for presentation at court after her marriage.

The Queen (12 March 1870) relates in its report of the first Drawing Room of the Season that:

> there were a great many brides presented, an unusual number it seemed, by the many handsome white costumes covered with costly lace to be seen . . . forming a very pretty contrast to the simpler white tulle, tarlatane and silk dresses of the débutantes.[7]

The report continued with a theme consistent in *The Queen's* critiques of Drawing Rooms: 'It required no little courage to don a low dress at 2 o'clock in the afternoon, on a cold afternoon in March'. Certainly, Mrs Gollan wears a low *décolletage* with the very short sleeves and long, white gloves required for a presentation gown. She also has the regulation train, gathered into the back waist seam. Her fashionable wedding dress has been altered by the lowering of the neckline and the removal of the sleeves, which in essence creates an evening bodice.

Mrs Gollan also wears the ostrich-feather plumes, which were an essential part of court costume, and which, by 1870, as *The Queen* report continues: 'are worn smaller and stand up more over the face, not dropping onto the neck quite so much as of yore.'

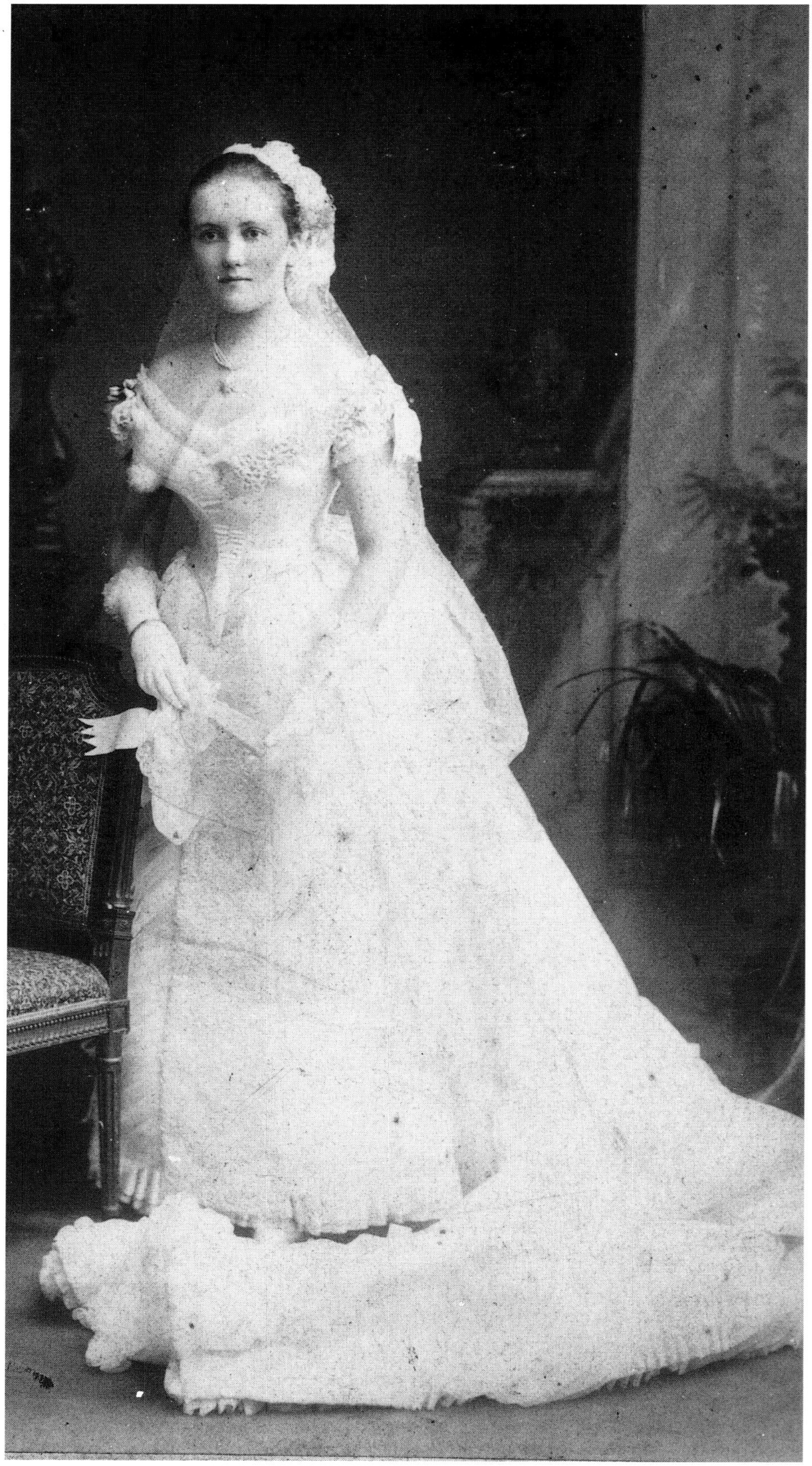

128. Mrs Spencer Gollan
1870
John Edwards, London (NPG x 33715)

129

Having been presented at Court as a married woman, not as a recent bride or as a débutante, Mrs Falmer wears court dress consisting of a dark-velvet bodice, pointed to the centre-front with matching train from the waist, over a pale-silk skirt with over-drapery looped up at the sides. The bodice neckline and hem are cut in pointed tabs and the front of the bodice is decorated with a panel of Honiton lace. Mrs Falmer also wears a long, white, net veil descending from the back of her head-dress, three-quarter-length white kid gloves, and matching plain gold bangles. Her bouquet posy is prominently displayed on the adjacent table.

The Queen (12 March 1870), commenting on the Drawing Room of 9 March, which may be the one Mrs Falmer attended, relates that 'bright colours of all kinds seemed to be in favour; especially bright red and cerise, and several of the new deep plum coloured shade . . .' It also describes dresses similar to Mrs Falmer's, with side drapery and tunic-style fronts.[8]

The Presentation itself was a daunting affair as *The Queen* (6 April 1867) relates, in the form of a letter from a certain 'Kitty', entitled 'What we saw and did at Court':

> I thought it dreadfully nervous work, the actual Presentation; and as I entered the Presence Chamber and my train was removed from my arm, I would have given anything to have foregone the ordeal – but that was useless . . . I had soon made the requisite number of courtseys and the royal pages were placing my train on my arm and desiring me to pass on . . .

In spite of her nerves, Kitty 'ignored as long as possible' these pages, 'for it was a sight well worth the looking at'. Later, the only thing she regretted is 'that it was so soon over'.[99]

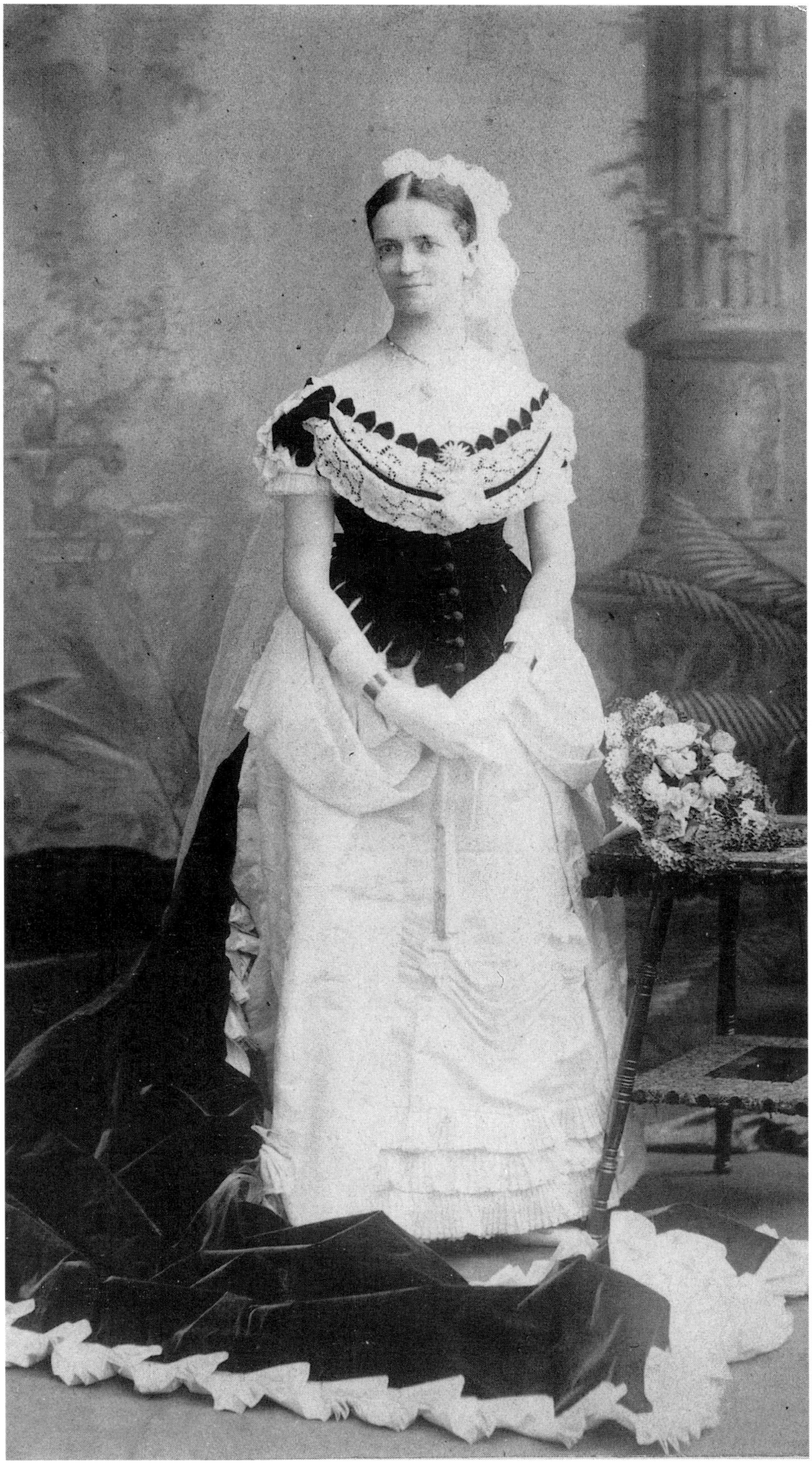

129. Mrs Falmer
1870
John Edwards, London (NPG x 33716)

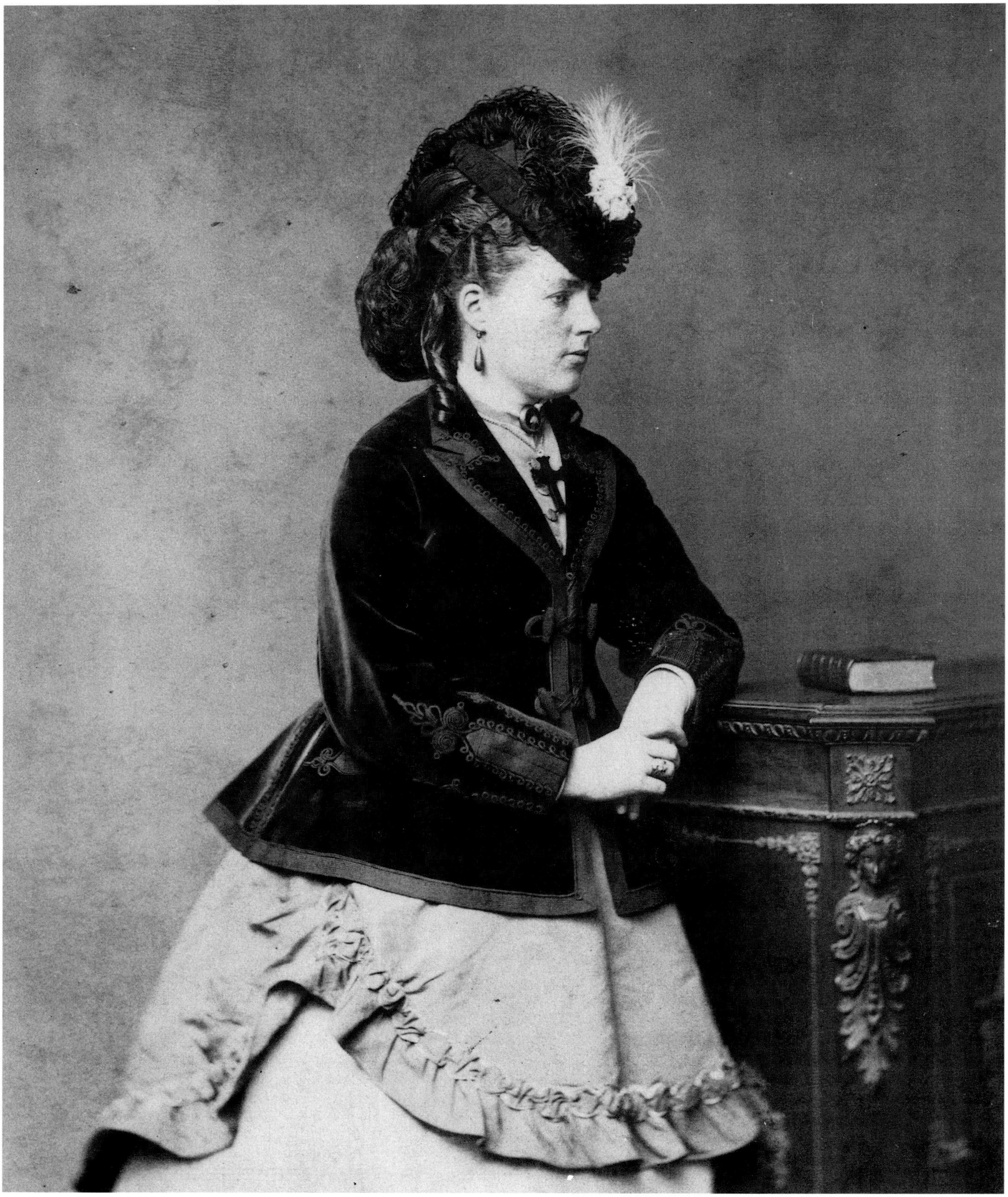

130. Mrs Beaumont Fetherston Dilke
***c.* 1870**
Netterville Briggs, Leamington (NPG x 28090)

130

This three-quarter-length portrait, although by a provincial Leamington photographer, nonetheless shows a very fashionable sitter from about 1870.

Mrs Dilke wears a dark-velvet jacket-bodice trimmed with wound braid and cord at the cuffs, pockets, revers, and fronts, and with all the edges bound. There are decorative toggles and frogging at the centre-front. *The Young Ladies Journal* (1 October 1870) relates that 'Jacket-bodices are decidedly fashionable this autumn. The flounced skirt and jacket-bodice, neither of them very new, have come into favour again as they always must . . .'[10] Below, Mrs Dilke wears a pale-silk daydress with a looped apron-front with a ruched self-fabric edging.

For jewellery, she wears pendant earrings, a collar brooch, a ring and a heavy jet cross. Her 'postillion' hat, trimmed with black ostrich feathers and a white aigrette plume, tips as far forward as possible over her eyes, revealing the huge chignon at the back. These wound and plaited *coiffures* had reached vast proportions by the late 1860s and were much ridiculed in the contemporary press. *The Young Ladies' Journal* (1 December 1870) assured its readers that it 'never saw chignons half so big as those that are *still* worn in London.' Chignons of this size required quantities of false hair and as late as 1879, Mrs Haweis, in *The Art Of Dress*, warns:

> I have no prejudice against false hair . . . but the enormous masses of hair which load fair heads now are purely ugly and ridiculous. Where a plait is palpably bigger than one human head can supply, it ceases to be an ornament and becomes a burden and annoyance.[11]

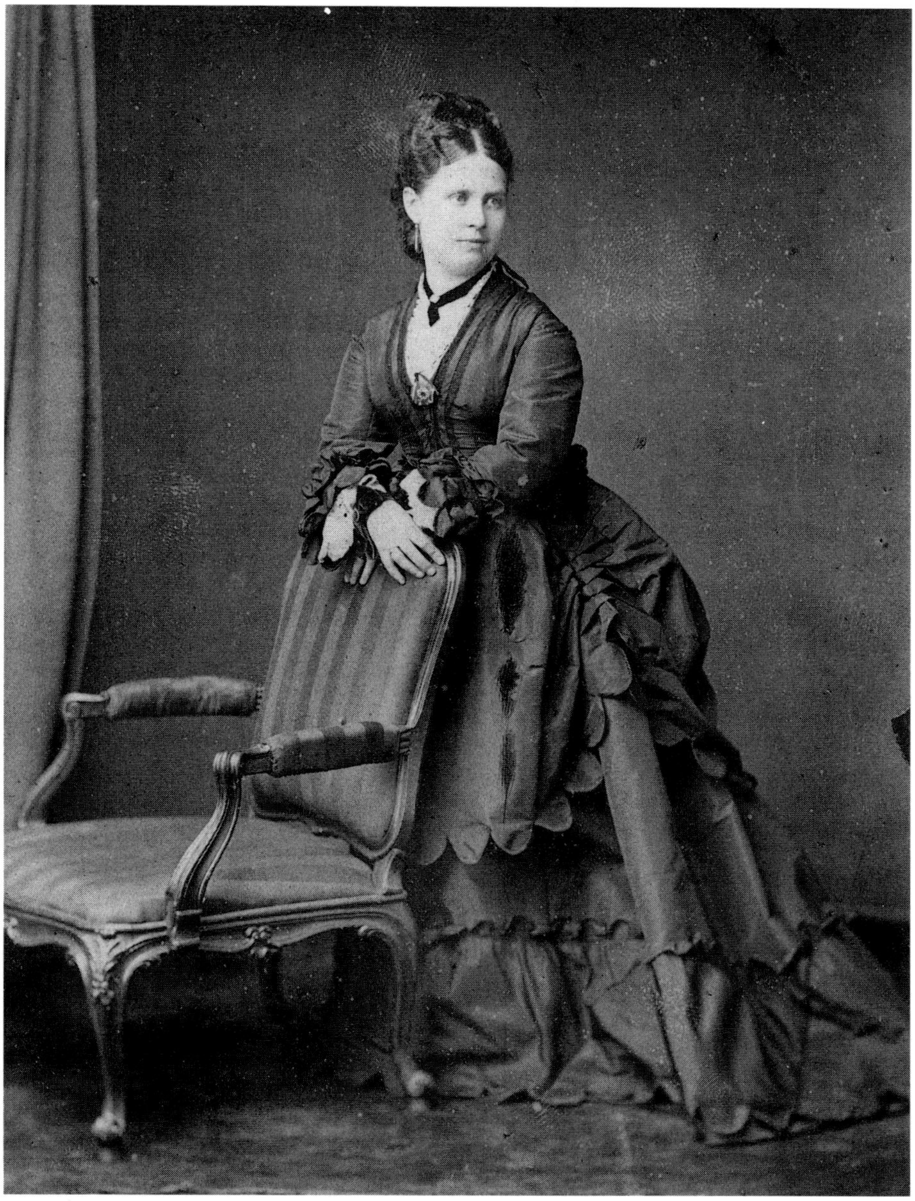

131. Marie Alexandrovna, later Duchess of Edinburgh 1872
Caldesi & Co., London (NPG x 6860)

131

The Archduchess Marie Alexandrovna is here aged 19, and yet to become the bride of Alfred, Duke of Edinburgh. She was to be a popular figure in England, as *The Ladies' Treasury* wrote, on 2 March 1874: 'The Grand Duchess speaks English better than most English girls; she has a most pleasing and easy manner, and a presence singularly ladylike and distinguished . . .'[12]

The Duchess poses in the Pall Mall studios of Caldesi & Co, leaning forward over a chair back to emphasize the fashionable forward-tipped stance, also made pronounced by the bustle and the trained skirt. Her daydress of dark silk has a scalloped overskirt looped up and fastened with pleats at the side, in a style typical of the first years of the 1870s: 'It is easy to talk of giving up the double skirt, which loops up so gracefully; but far less so to find any equivalent . . .' (*Englishwoman's Domestic Magazine*:, May 1872).[13] However, by December 1872, it was related that 'the double skirt, looped up at the side is quite depassé'.[14]

Dress skirts were invariably cut with substantial trains in 1872, as indeed is the Duchess's. The impracticality of this was a cause for complaint in fashion periodicals: 'undoubtedly, all skirts except those kept purposely for walking dresses are made with trains . . . for the street they are simply ridiculous and uncleanly [sic] . . .' (*The Ladies' Treasury*, February 1872).

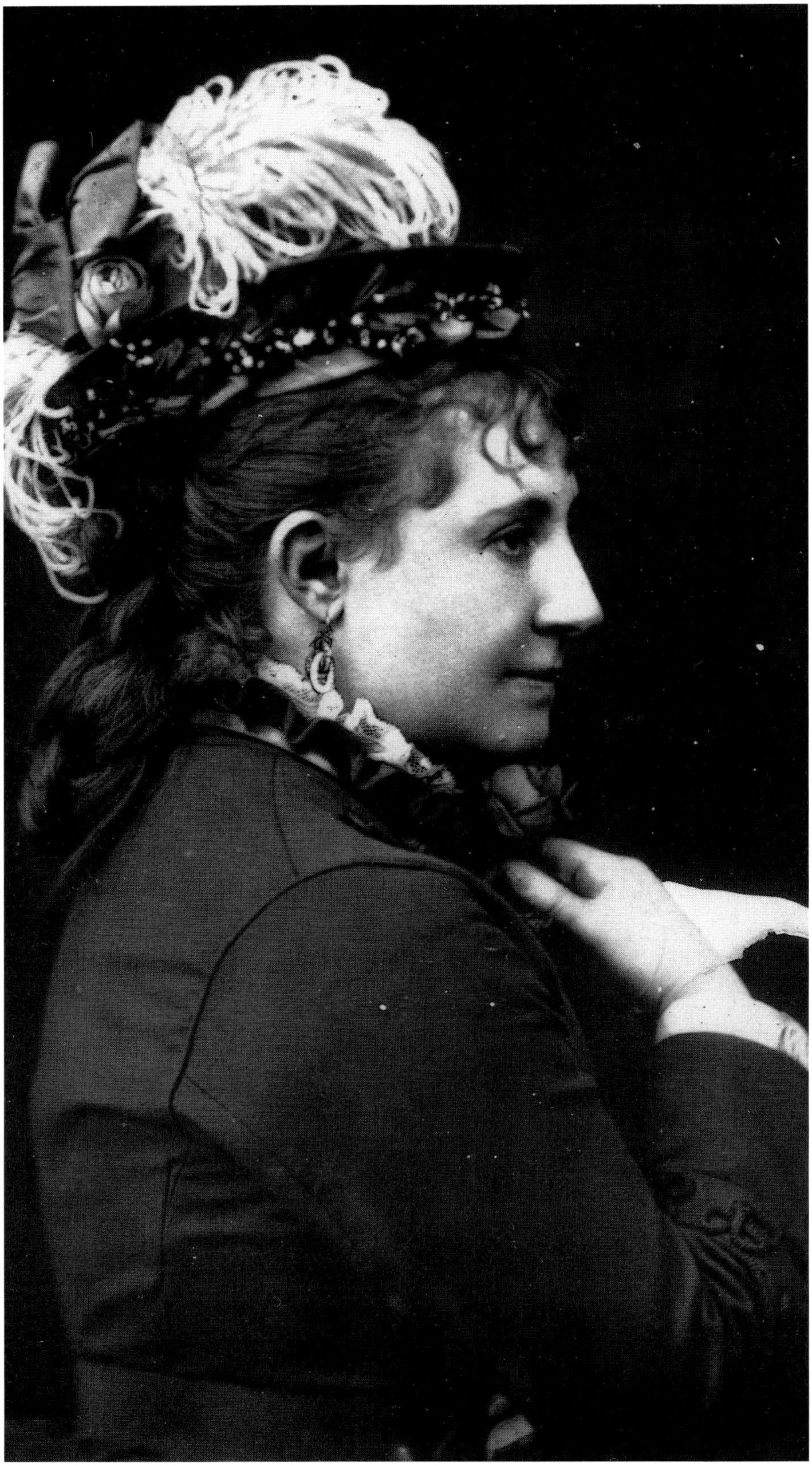

132. Lydia Thompson (Mrs Alexander Henderson)
1873
Lock & Whitfield, London (NPG x 26863)

132

Born in 1838, Miss Thompson was launched onto the stage as a child dancer and actress, with a début at the age of 15 in *Little Silverhair* at the Haymarket Theatre. She later specialized in comedy-burlesque and married the Manager of the Folly Theatre in London. According to *The Dramatic List* of 1879, her triumphs in 'this department of the histrionic art' included productions of *Blue Beard* and *The Field of the Cloth of Gold*.[16]

In this half-length portrait, Miss Thompson wears a dark-cloth daydress with a frill of lace and ruched satin at the neck. Her hat, which sits squarely on her head and is not tipped forward as it would have been a few years previously, has a loosely plaited, voluminous chignon behind. The hat closely resembles examples pictured in *The Queen* for 26 April 1873: 'New Spring Bonnets'. The 'Senora hat' has an identical silhouette, with similar ostrich feathers in front and 'falling at the back' and the same *coiffure*. The other hats, also given romantic yet meaningless names like 'D'Egmont', 'Fleurette' and 'Condé', all preserve the same basic shape, and the model drawn wearing the 'Condé' has a similar neck frill to Miss Thompson's.[17]

Clearly, Miss Thompson is fully up to date with fashion, as were most successful actresses, and she may even have purchased her hat from the same French milliner as illustrated in *The Queen*: 'Madame Moreau-Didsbury, 23 Boulevard des Capucines, Paris'.

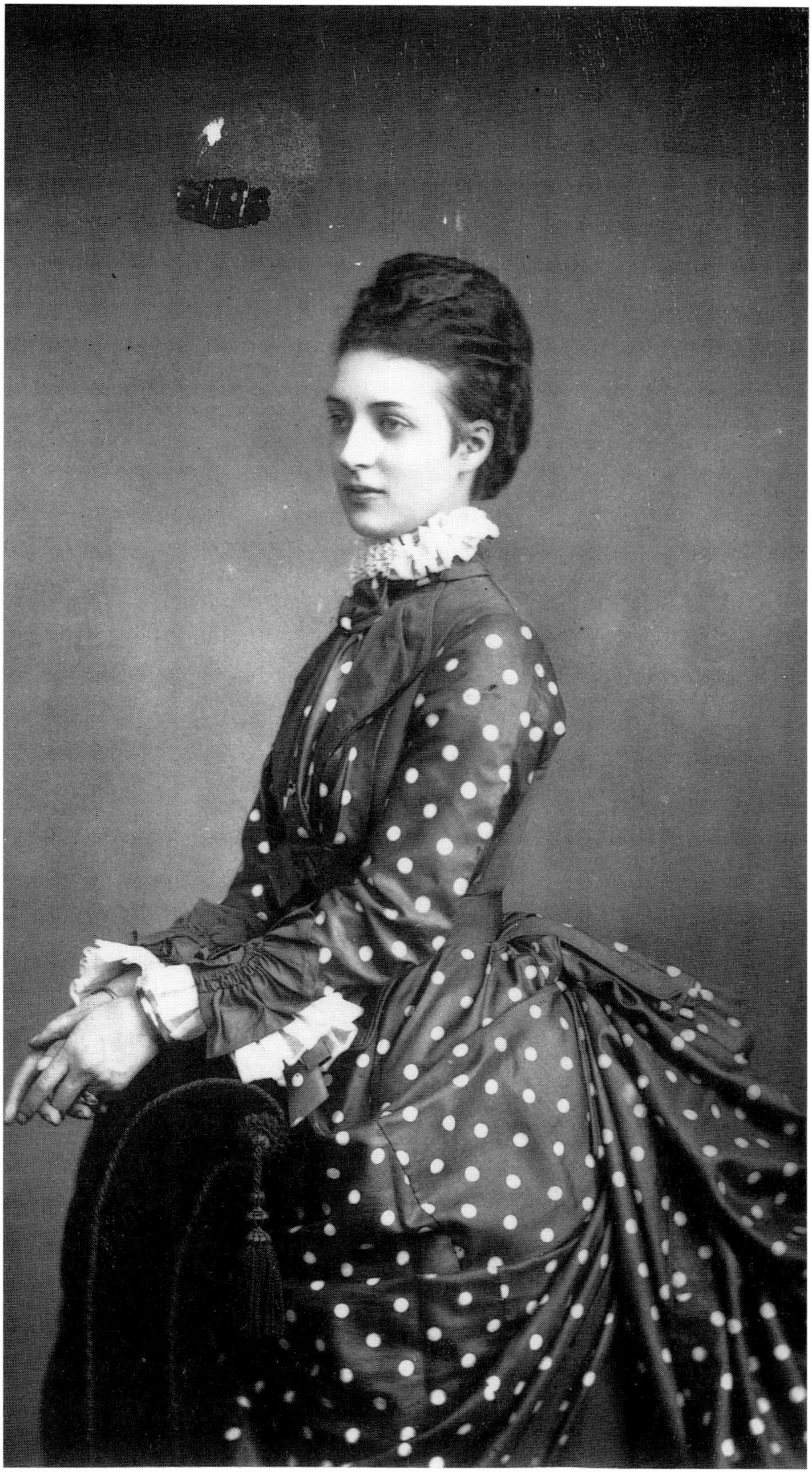

133. Alexandra, Princess of Wales
1873
Maull & Co., London (NPG x 33252)

133

The Princess wears a daydress of contrasting plain and white-spotted dark silk. Appropriately enough, the dress is in the princess style, with an overskirt cut in one with the bodice, and worn over a separate, plain skirt.

The spotted overskirt is caught up at the sides and gathered into a bustle at the back. The revers, dress cuffs and sash-belt are also of contrasting plain silk, like the underskirt. The pleated, white cotton cuffs and neck frill were detachable for frequent laundering.[18]

The Princess wears her hair slightly parted in the centre, over her forehead and then waved and frizzed back over a pad. The hair at the sides is drawn in over the ears to join the chignon at the back. The height of her *coiffure* emphasizes the rather statuesque appearance of the Princess, always a celebrated beauty, in contrast with the diminutive and demure looks of the Queen and her daughters.

By 1873, Alexandra had borne her husband five children, whilst her last pregnancy in 1871, two years before this portrait, had ended tragically when the son lived for only a day. All her children were born prematurely; Albert Victor, the eldest, was two months premature in 1864 and caused consternation when no preparations had been made.

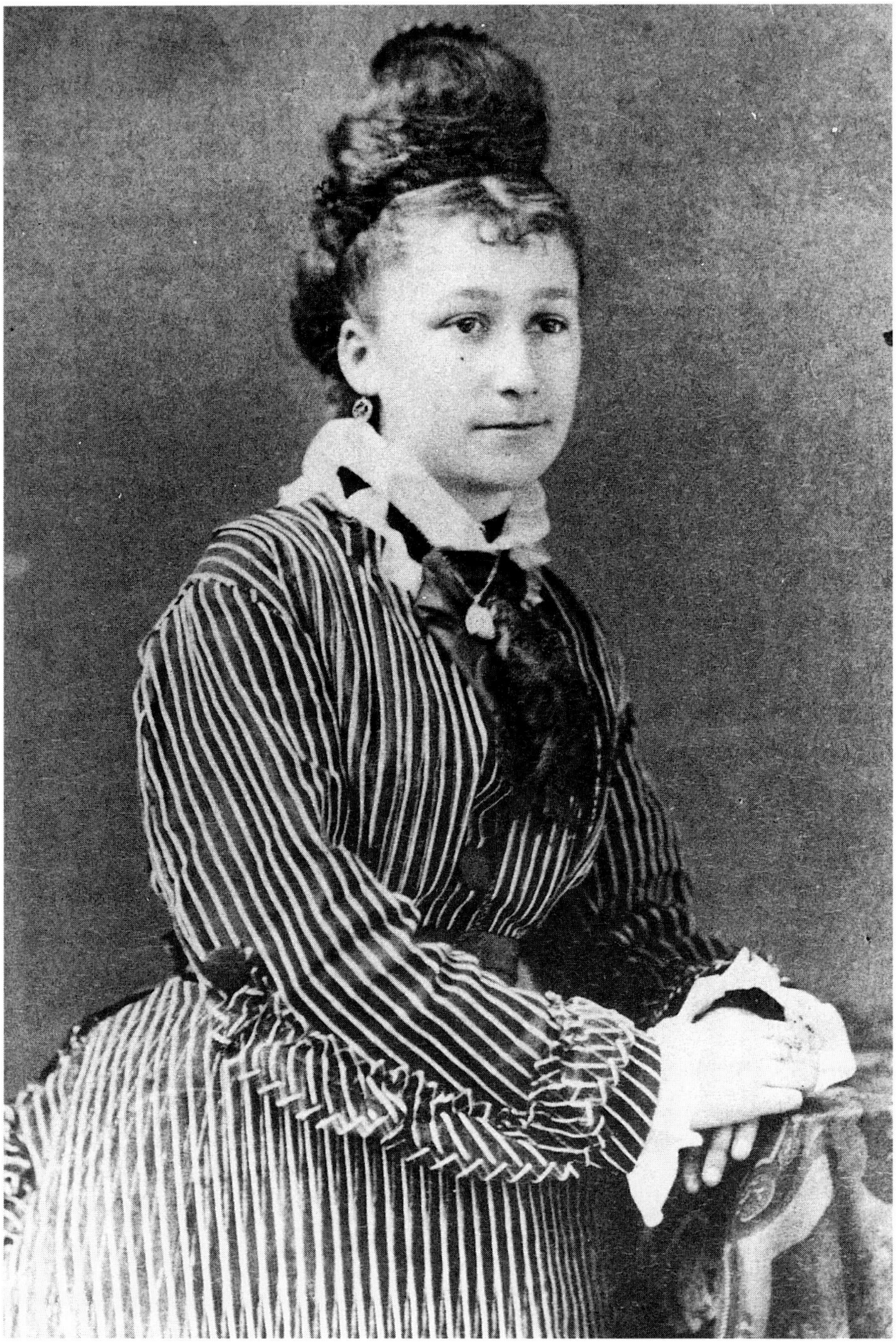

134. Miss Elizabeth Shaw
1874
Spencer, Victoria (Canada), (Platt Hall)

134

Aged only 17 and, according to the family history, dying the same year, Miss Shaw is shown here in a Canadian portrait.

Her narrowly striped daydress is perhaps made of one of the two popular 'washing' fabrics: 'percale', a lightweight cotton, or 'foulard', a similar material but of silk. Many of the 'robes de chambre' and 'walking costumes' as distinct from evening toilettes are composed of striped fabrics in the mid 1870s. 'Percale', 'foulard', 'moulinée', poplin, and cashmere were most popular.

With her striped outfit, Miss Shaw wears a white lawn collar and cuffs, and plain dark belt, jabot and decorative buttons. Her hair is dressed fashionably high in a tightly coiled bun.

135, 136

Alice Mary Maud, third child and second daughter of Queen Victoria, married Prince Louis of Hesse-Darmstadt in 1862. They were to have five children before Princess Alice's premature death in 1878, aged only 35. The most famous of these children was the ill-fated Alix, who married Nicholas II, the last Czar of Russia.

For these studio shots, the Princess wears a silk daydress, woven with a lighter, trailing scrollwork design. The skirt is profusely trimmed with silk tassel fringing, a new type of which had just been introduced. *The Young Englishwoman* in its Paris fashions for August 1875 relates:

> In passementerie, we were shown this week some pretty new articles. Fringes with tassels placed one above the other, fastened to a network foundation, to be had in all colours to match the dress.[19]

Fringing was indeed a conspicuous feature of fashions in 1875; *The Ladies' Treasury* in its 'Paris Letter' (1 December 1875) declares, again in breathless first person narrative:

> there is a continuously growing tendency towards fringes. I have seen tunics almost entirely composed of wide

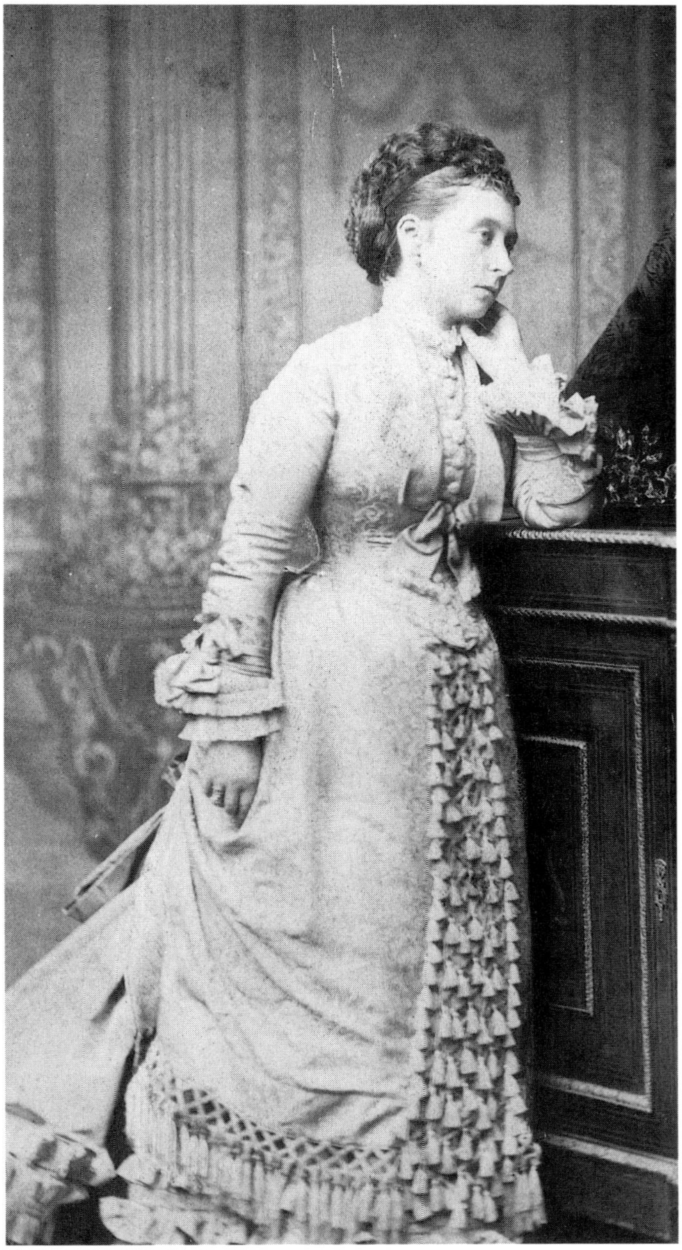

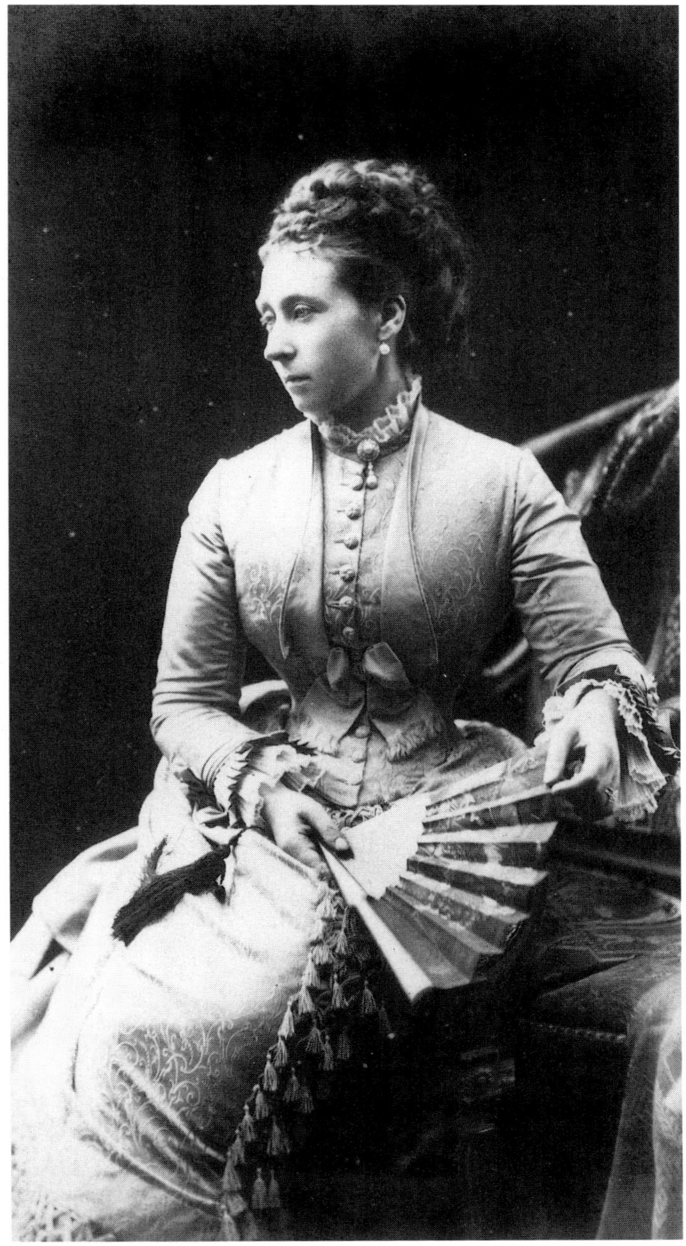

135 & 136. Princess Alice, Grand Duchess of Hesse 1875
Alexander Bassano, London (NPG x 20130, 26108)

fringes and very little indeed of the tunic itself was seen . . .

Princess Alice's hair is a coiled edifice sitting squarely on the back of her head and arranged in plaits and rouleaux over the ubiquitous false hair pads. By the middle 1870s, hairstyles were less high than earlier in the decade although still complex; as *The Young Englishwoman* for January 1875 relates: 'Coiffures are much less high than they were, though still arranged in coques and rouleaux all over the head . . .[20]

137

This striking portrait, so modern in its composition and spontaneity, shows the ever youthful Princess carrying her umbrella against the rain at the Cowes Regatta in 1876.

Dressed eminently suitably for an outdoor walking expedition, she wears a tailored cloth jacket-bodice, drawn in tight to the waist with a matching belt, and worn with a matching skirt.

The bodice, with an upstanding round collar and simple, vertical, seamed decoration centre-front, fastens with 12 circular metal buttons. A small handkerchief is visible, protruding from a concealed pocket. Her plain sleeves end in four button-cuffs resembling a man's jacket sleeve cuffs.

The cut of the outfit demonstrates the expertise of the London tailoring world, renowned the world over by the mid nineteenth century.

Alexandra's ensemble is completed by a matching, functional, round cloth hat with narrow brim, reminiscent of a man's bowler.

The Princess was obviously fond of this jacket, as there is another photograph of her wearing it, dated August 1880, this time with a different hat, but again for the Cowes Regatta at Osborne.[21] Alternatively, Alexandra might wear a knitted jersey bodice for the Regatta; in 1878 she wore 'St Margaret' jerseys made by Corahs of Leicester and supplied by Morgans of Cowes on the Royal Yacht.

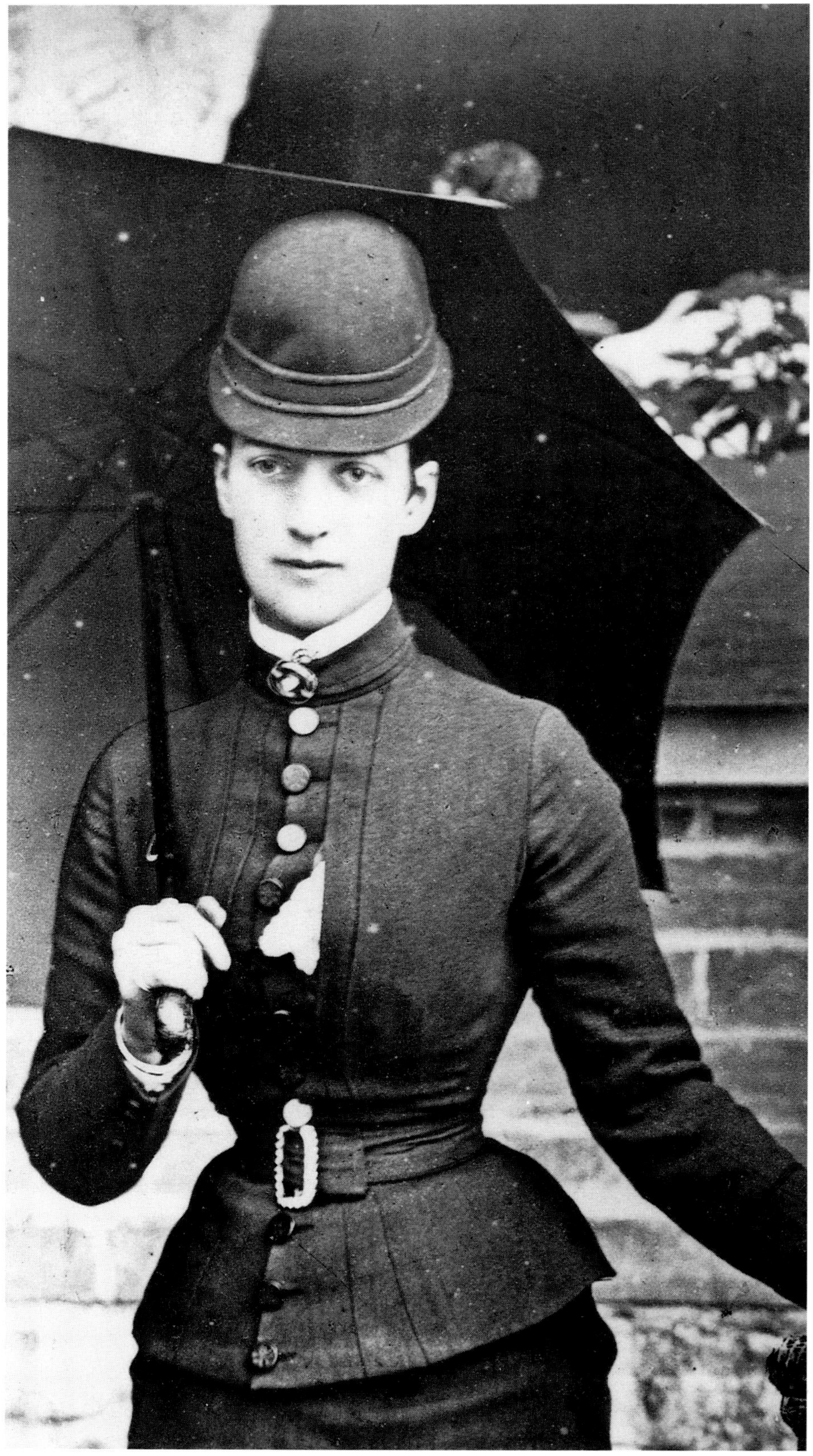

137. Alexandra, Princess of Wales
1876
James Russell, Chichester (NPG x 29180)

138

After marrying the Crown Prince of Prussia in 1858 the Princess Royal, oldest child of Queen Victoria and the Prince Consort, spent the rest of her life in Germany.

Here aged 36, she is dressed in black silk, trimmed with black lace and jet, almost certainly mourning wear. When she first lived in Prussia, her mother had written to her expressing her dislike for mourning dress, even though she herself was to remain in black for 40 years after the death of the Prince Consort in 1861:

> To wear black woollen and high-up gowns always and long veils is dreadful. But I suppose you wear barège, for that is as neat and I wore it for poor Grandpapa with crepe . . . (Queen Victoria, June 1859).[22]

Otherwise, the Crown Princess wears a fashionable, trained, bustle daydress with an apron-fronted overskirt caught at two points at the side-back. A similar dress is described in *The Young Englishwoman* (April 1876):

> For a black silk dress, suitable either for home receptions, demi-toilette evening parties, or walking costume . . . all the front part of the skirt is trimmed across with plissés, alternately wide and narrow. . . . The skirt is cut very long but can be taken up by an ingenious system of loops and buttons. Plain cuirasse bodice; two scarves commencing from under the plain basque are loosely tied rather low down at the back . . .[23]

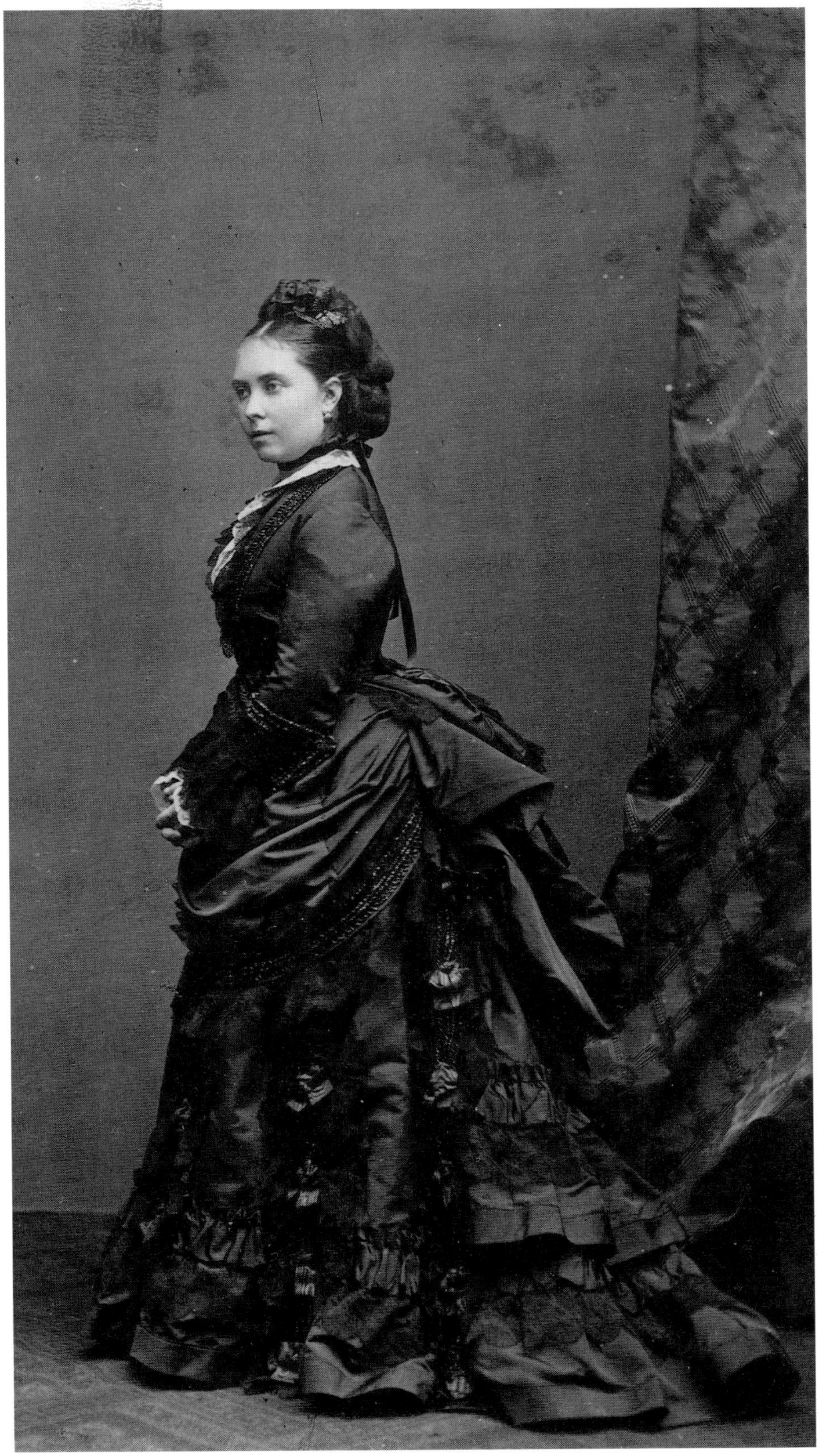

138. Victoria, Crown Princess of Germany
1876
Mondel & Jacob, Wiesbaden (NPG x 5583)

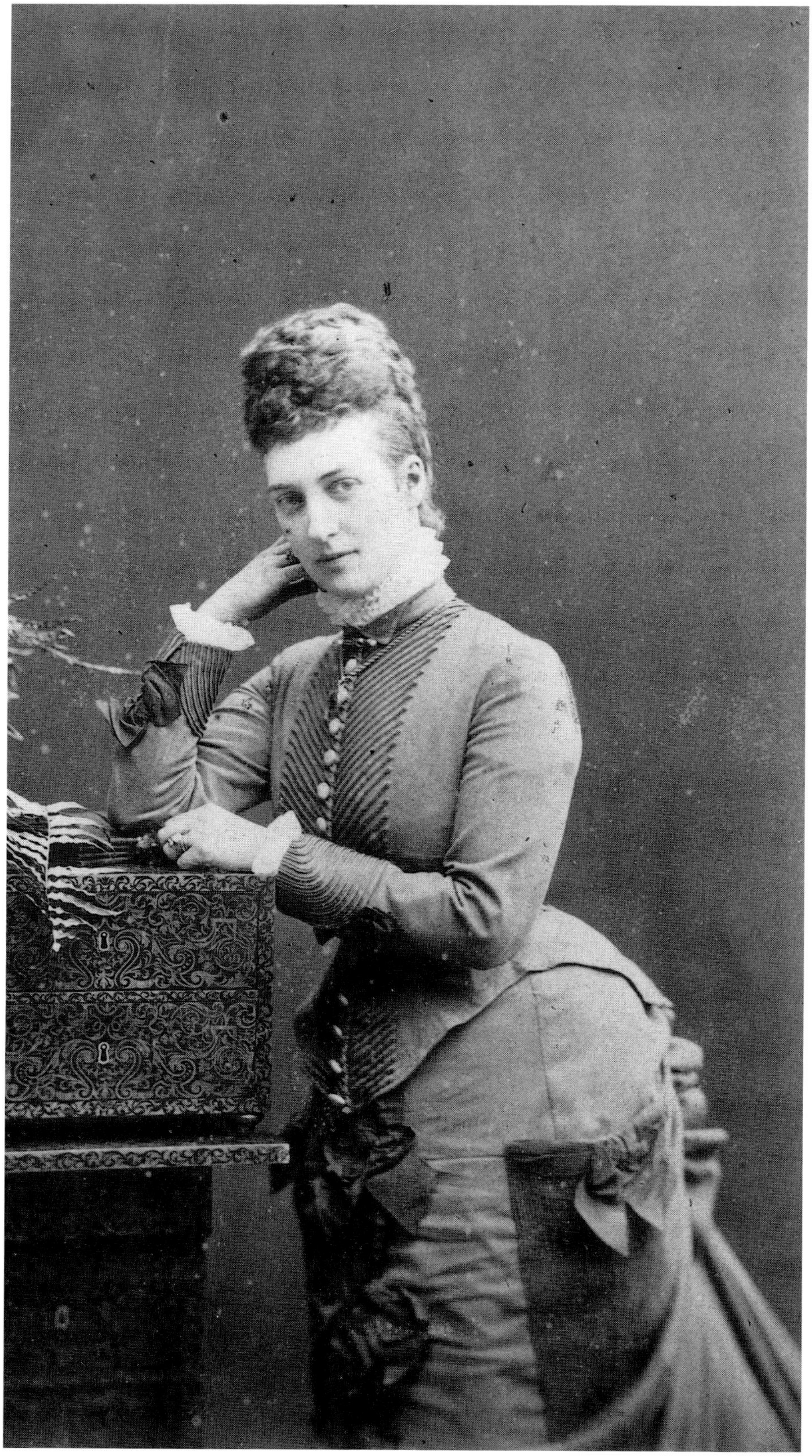

139. Alexandra, Princess of Wales
***c* 1876**
W. & D. Downey (NPG x 12854)

139

The Princess wears a daydress with *cuirasse* bodice and matching skirt, probably constructed from a silk-and-wool-mix fabric.

Dated to around 1876, the bodice dips to a point centre-front and centre-back and curves up typically over the hips. The front of the bodice fastens with 15 circular buttons and is decorated with dozens of parallel diagonal bands of dark braiding. Curved turn-back cuffs are similarly trimmed, and finished with neat, white-lace ruffles, as at the collar which is pinned with a horizontal tie-pin brooch. Other jewellery includes a locket and chain, and a large ring worn on the wedding finger.

The skirt, straight in front, is gathered in from the sides to a low bustle and train at the back. A contrasting darker panel has been applied from the front side-seams and trimmed with a ribbon bow which matches similar bows down the front of the skirt.

Alexandra's hair is tightly curled, and frizzed up over a pad at the front, giving considerable height to the style. She leans on an elaborately painted wooden desk, one of the photographer's many studio props.

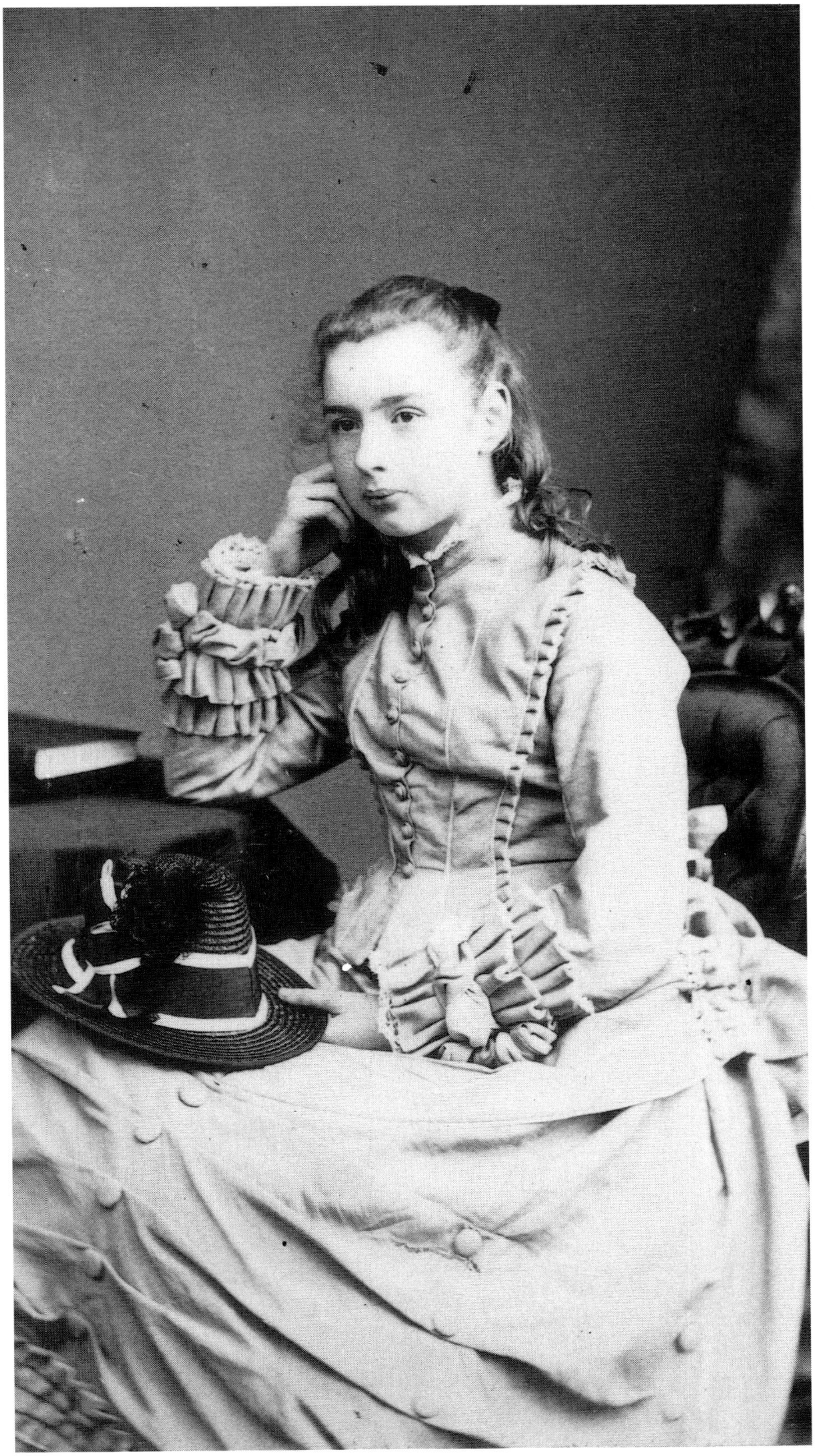

140. Peggy Stanton
***c.* 1876**
Maull and Co., London (NPG x 26555)

140

At the age 17, young girls usually had their hair dressed and put up as a visible sign of their entry into adulthood. Miss Stanton therefore is aged about 16, not yet a young lady but nonetheless very fashionably dressed. Her light-coloured cloth daydress is cut with a separate bodice and skirt, the former buttoning centre-front with pleated trimming either side, and large bouffant cuffs which were known as 'mousequetaires', and were a feature of 1876, approximately the date of this photograph. *The Young Englishwoman* (May 1876) shows an illustration of a sleeve of brown serge with; 'at the wrist, pleating of the same material bound with brown velvet . . . and . . . finished off with bows of cashmere with velvet centres.'[24] Cuffs arranged in narrow pleats are common on most sleeves cut in the coat style.

Miss Stanton's skirt is drawn into horizontal pleats swathed across the front and trimmed with vertical rows of self-fabric covered buttons.

The dark straw hat which she holds in her lap has a wide brim and a high conical crown; it is bound with a wide ribbon and trimmed with a dark feather cockade. This was a popular style for girls aged 13 to 17 according to *The Queen* (27 May 1876) and the style was known as the 'Marion': 'a straw hat . . . of black [with] trimmings consisting of black grosgrain ribbon of a rich quality and a straw coloured feather.'[25]

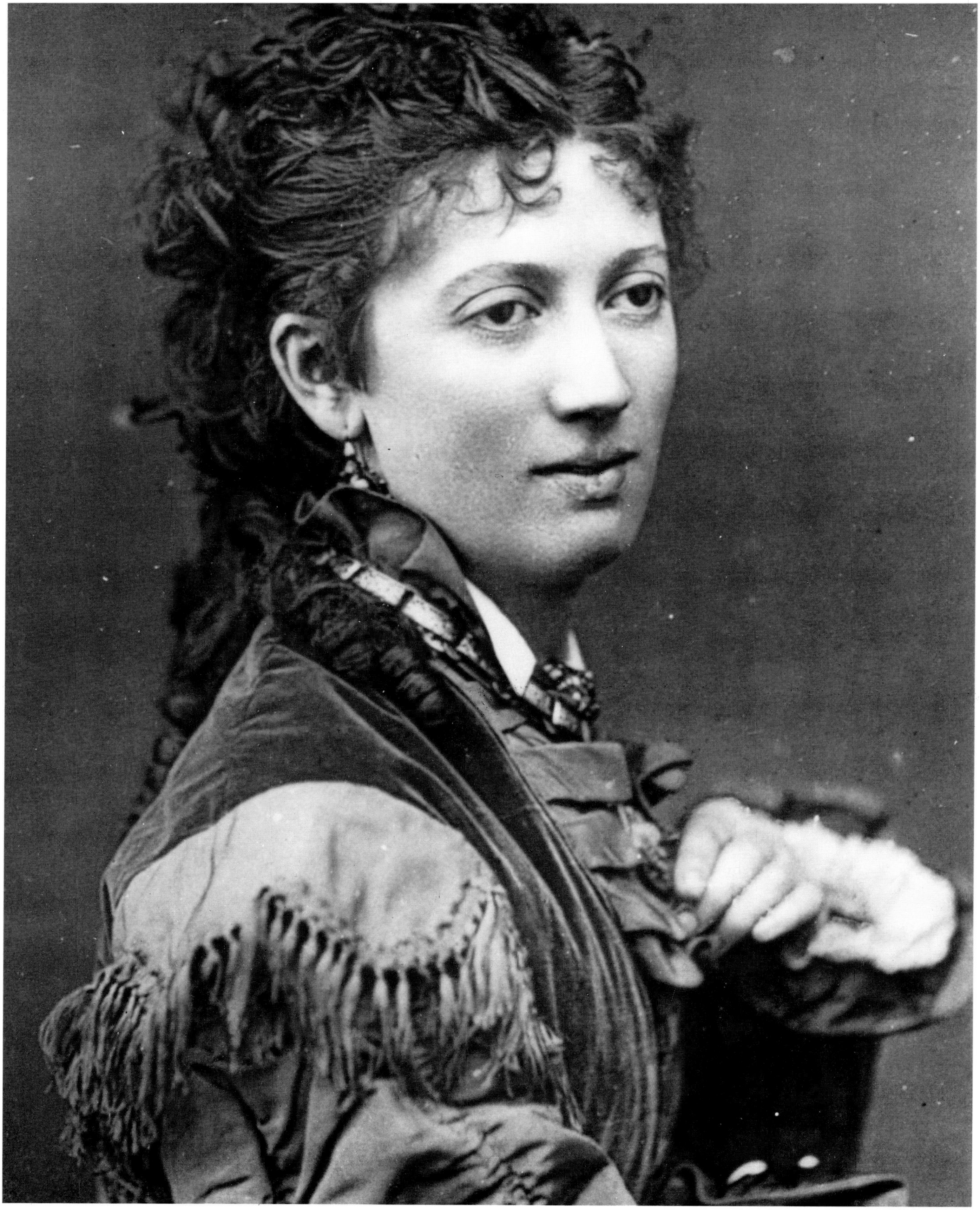

141. Jessie Vokes, 1876, *Lock and Whitfield, London (Platt Hall)*

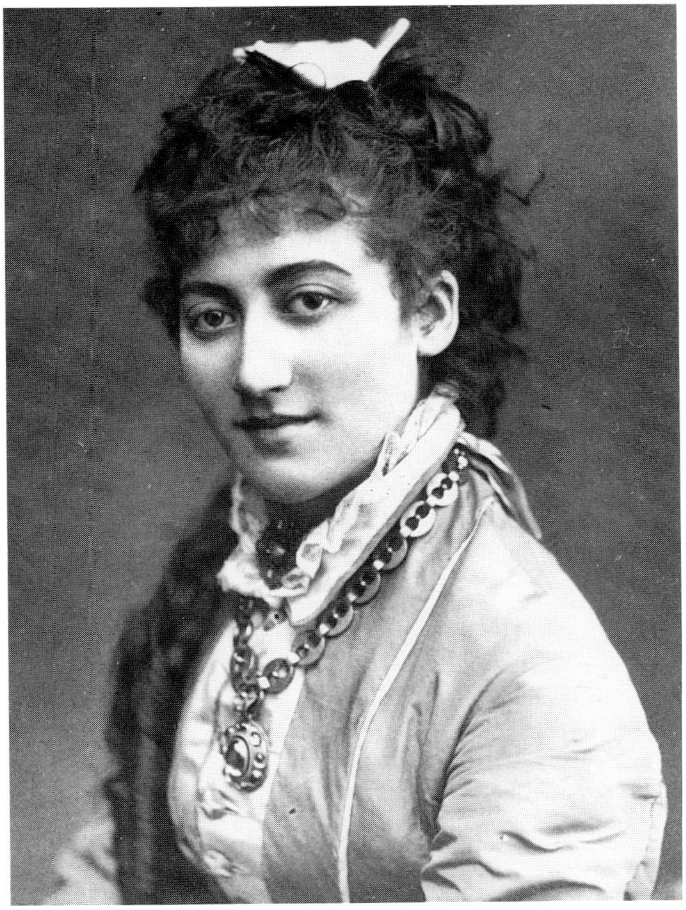

142. Victoria Vokes
1876
Lock and Whitfield, London (Platt Hall)

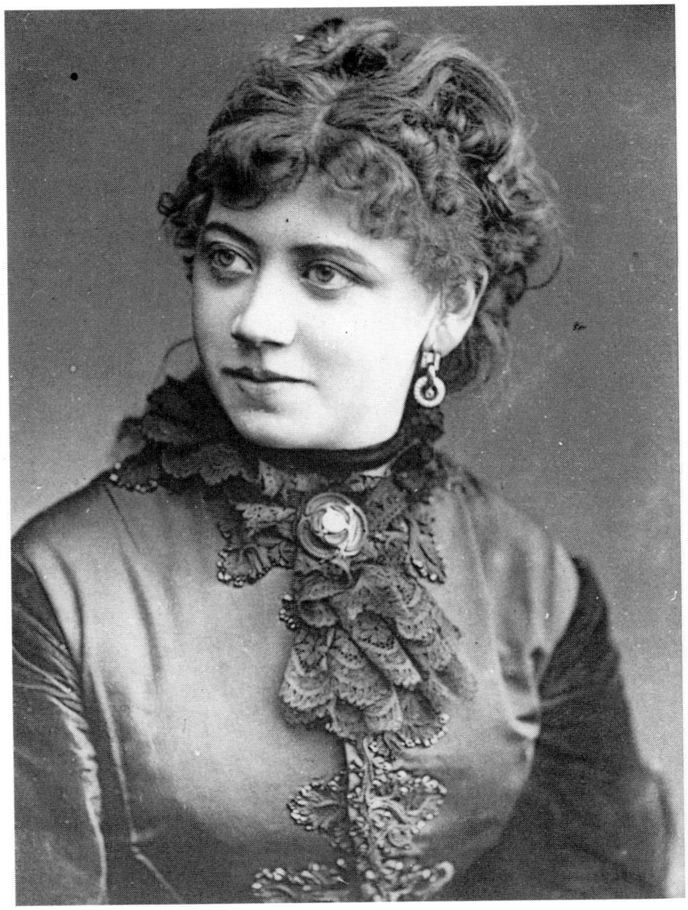

143. Rosina Vokes
1876
Lock and Whitfield, London (Platt Hall)

141, 142, 143

Born in the 1850s, the Vokes sisters, with their brother Frederick, toured music halls and theatres during the later 1860s and 1870s, becoming celebrated for their performances of light comedy, burlesque, and pantomime. They achieved great success in 1875 with the revival of *Belles of the Kitchen* at the Adelphi in London, followed by Blanchard's *Bunch of Berries* in 1876. They were also renowned for their regular London pantomime appearances, often at Drury Lane: 'It can certainly be said that the Vokes family *is* the pantomime, and that pantomime *is* the Vokes family'. (*Englishwoman's Domestic Magazine*.)[26]

Rosina, the youngest sister, married in 1879, precipitating the break-up of the family act. All three sisters, and their brother, died prematurely, predeceasing their mother.

These three head-and-shoulders portraits, published at the height of the family's popularity, show each sister electing to sit for her portrait with a full, long *coiffure*, curled and frizzed and worn loosely over the shoulders. Undressed, loose hair worn in this manner serves to emphasize the sisters' theatrical lifestyle.

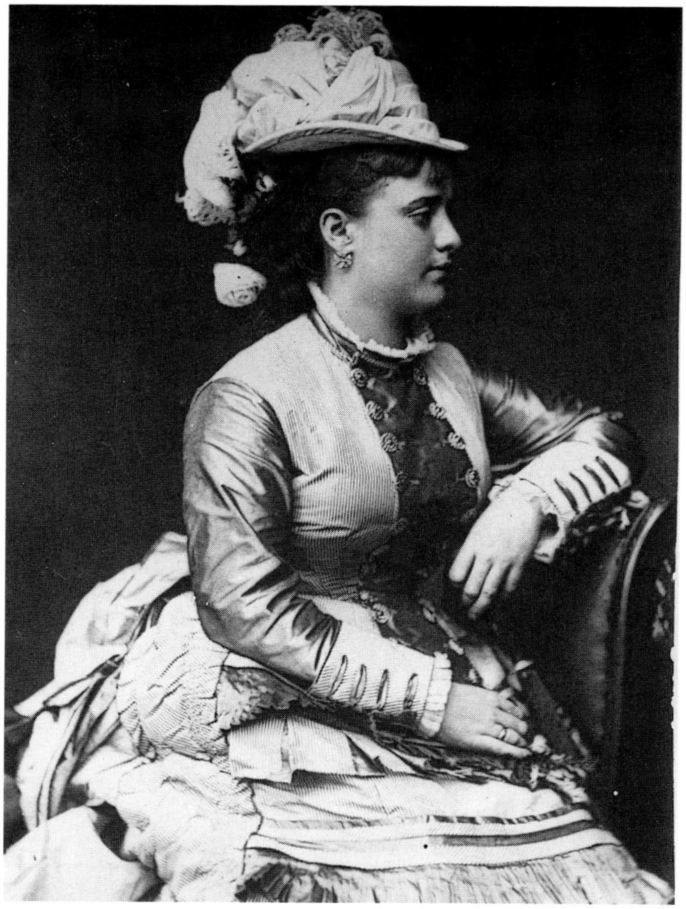

144. Minnie Walton
1876
Lock and Whitfield, London (Platt Hall)

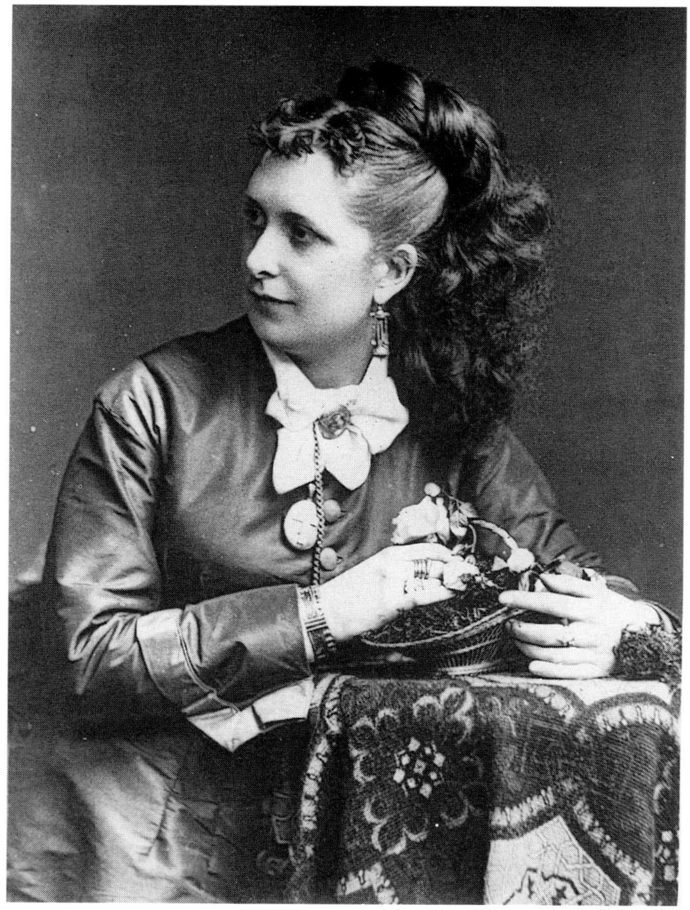

145. Blanche Cole
1876
Elliott and Fry, London (Platt Hall)

144, 145

Posing for seated, half-length studio portraits, both these music-hall artistes wear fashionable silk daydresses. If never considered entirely respectable, actresses were frequently admired for their flair and panache in dress, and for the money which they were able to lavish upon it:

> Actresses give 'ton' to modern modes, their toilets are copied because they are dressed by the couturiers most in vogue, who invent expressly for these marvels of elegance and good taste. (*The Young Englishwoman.*)[27]

Miss Walton's dress, in two-tone plain dark and lighter-striped silk, shows the fussy construction and overloaded trimming that burdened fashionable dresses of this date: the sleeves contrast with both the side-bodice and with the cuffs, which themselves contrast with a central bodice panel. Pleated and tucked flounces decorate the front of the skirt whilst ruched bias-cut bands snake across the bunched and looped back-draperies. Her hat, also elaborately trimmed, sits squarely on her dressed *coiffure*.

Miss Cole, dressed in a plain-silk dress, is distinguished by an extremely full, curled hairstyle, almost certainly incorporating a false-hair plaited circlet.

146

It was the charm of her personality quite as much as the glory of her wonderful voice that won her a position in public estimation which no other singer has attained. (*Dictionary of National Biography.*)[28]

Born in Stockholm in 1820, Jenny Lind trained at the singing school attached to the Swedish Royal Theatre, and was launched on her meteoric operatic career in 1838. She travelled throughout Europe, first appearing in England in April 1847, when 'Jenny Lind fever' and great public acclaim swept the country. She retired from the stage as early as 1849 to concentrate on concert tours, notably for charitable causes. Marrying the German conductor Otto Goldschmidt in 1852, she and her husband were naturalized as British subjects in 1859. Settling in England, she helped to found the Bach Choir in London in 1876, shortly before this portrait-sitting.

For this portrait, Miss Lind wears a dark-silk daydress, trimmed with vertical bands of dark velvet, and with beaded net epaulettes at the shoulders. Her hair is parted centrally in the simple style of the early 1860s. Miss Lind was not unusual, as a mature woman, in eschewing the elaborate hairstyles of the 1870s. At the same date, Mrs Hayes, wife of the President of the USA, was described as being

courageous enough during all these days of frizzes and puffs and headedness, into which ninety-nine hundredths of the woman have run, to maintain the simple style which she adopted years ago for dressing her jet black hair. It is placed smoothly and neatly, well down on the sides of her face, then passed over the ears where a 'finger-puff' is the only adornment. (*The Englishwoman's Domestic Magazine.*)[29]

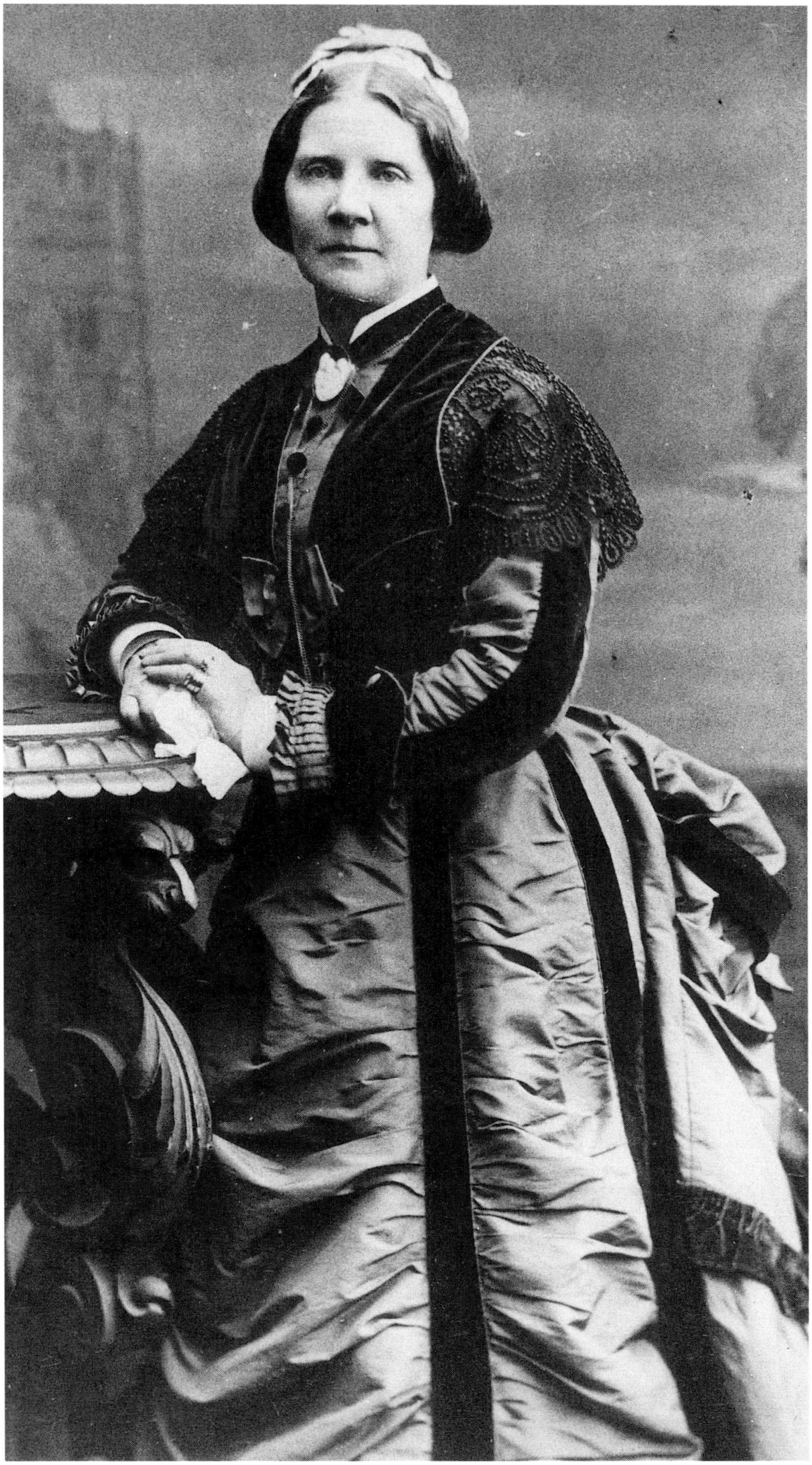

146. Johanna (Jenny) Lind
1877
W. & D. Downey, London (Platt Hall)

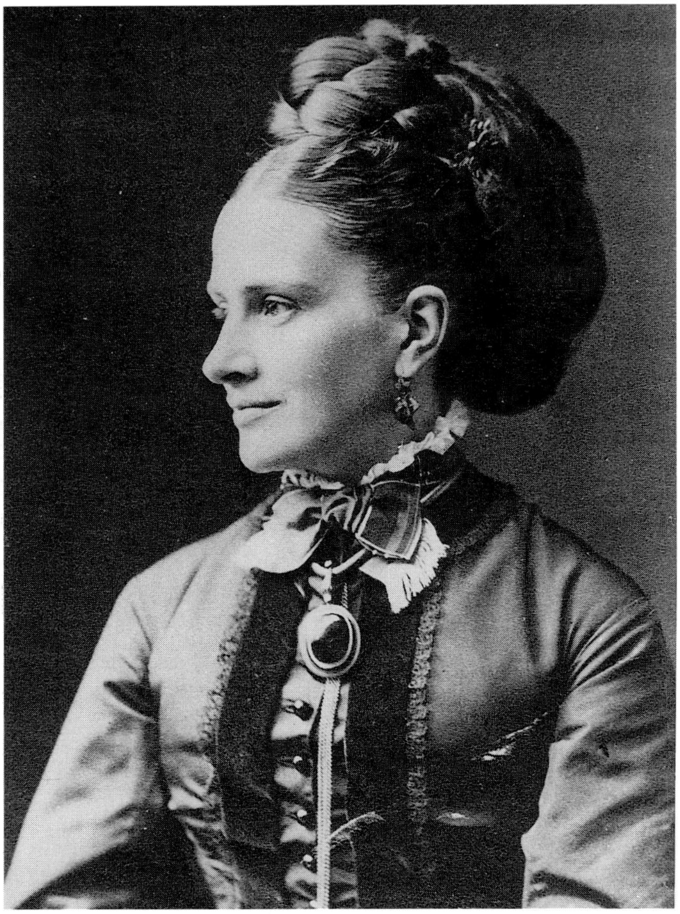

147. Emma Bathurst
1877
Sawyer & Bird, Norwich (Platt Hall)

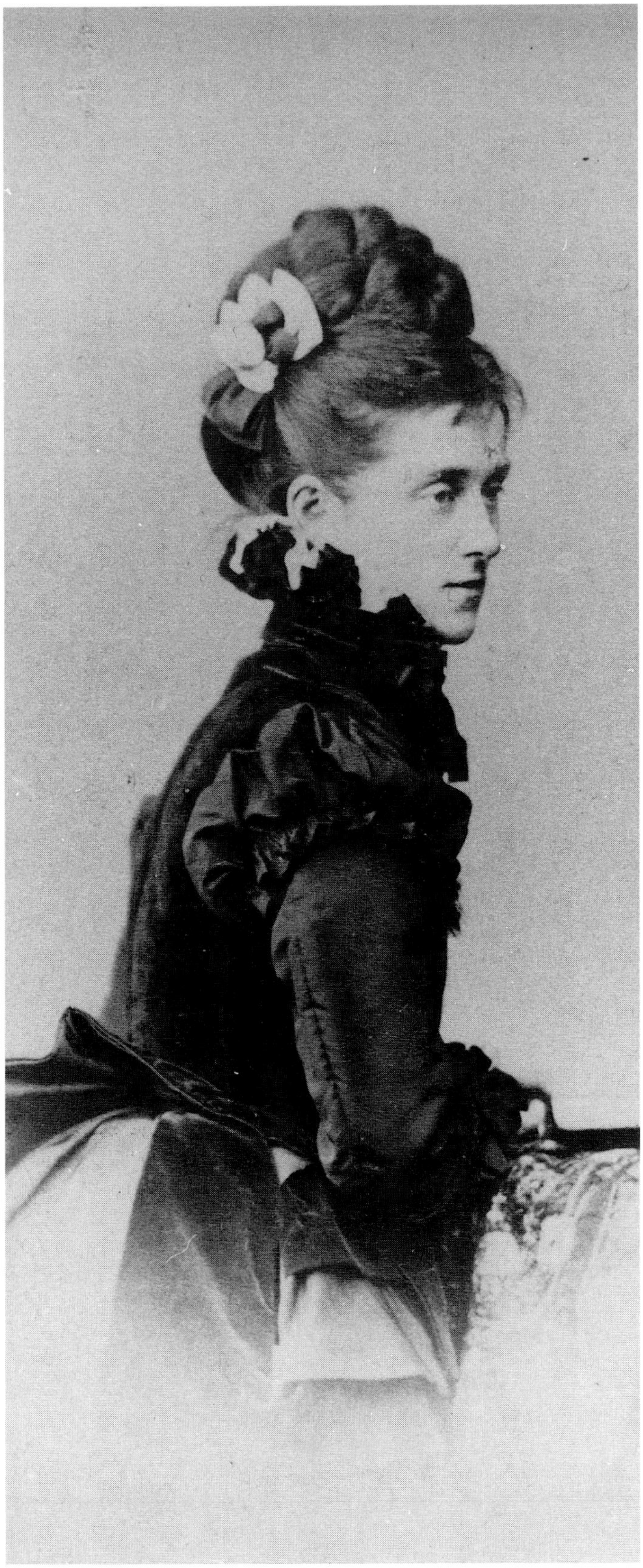

148. Mrs Brereton Brighton
1877/8
Mayall, Brighton (Platt Hall)

147, 148

Hairstyles of the later 1870s developed into full and complex, coiled and plaited arrangements, placed high and apparently precariously, on the back of the head. Both women demonstrate this vast style of *coiffure*, worn with dark-silk daydresses. Both subjects also have high, upstanding, ruffled collars that meet the back of their dressed hair. Mrs Bathurst wears a striped silk ribbon bow as a necktie, whilst Mrs Brereton Brighton has a similar black ribbon bow beneath her elaborate 'Medici' collar.

149, 150

Both sitters wear the princess-line, sleek, sheath-like dresses of the later 1870s, cut with long over-tunics and contrasting skirts.

Miss Horniman, seated, wears a strikingly contrasted woollen dress with wide, dark side-panels and a broader, pale central panel. The skirt, showing at the hem, has narrower, vertical stripes. Small metal buttons trim both the cuffs, in five pairs, and the centre-front in a long line of 60.

The second half of the 1870s saw colour contrasts and brighter colours as popular as in the early 1860s. *The Ladies' Treasury* (August 1877) relates:

> As to colour, all miserable tints of drab, brown, black, making their wearers look like lichened boles [*sic*] of trees, are now discarded. All the hues of the rainbow in full splendour are the fashion, whether appearing in stripes or in ribbons . . .[30]

Miss Ottighole wears a plainer, dark dress, trimmed with a black-lace collar, cuffs, and flounces, and with triple cords of frogging centre-front. Hooked on to the right-hand side of her waist, she has a metal chatelaine from which hangs the useful domestic paraphernalia required by a housewife.

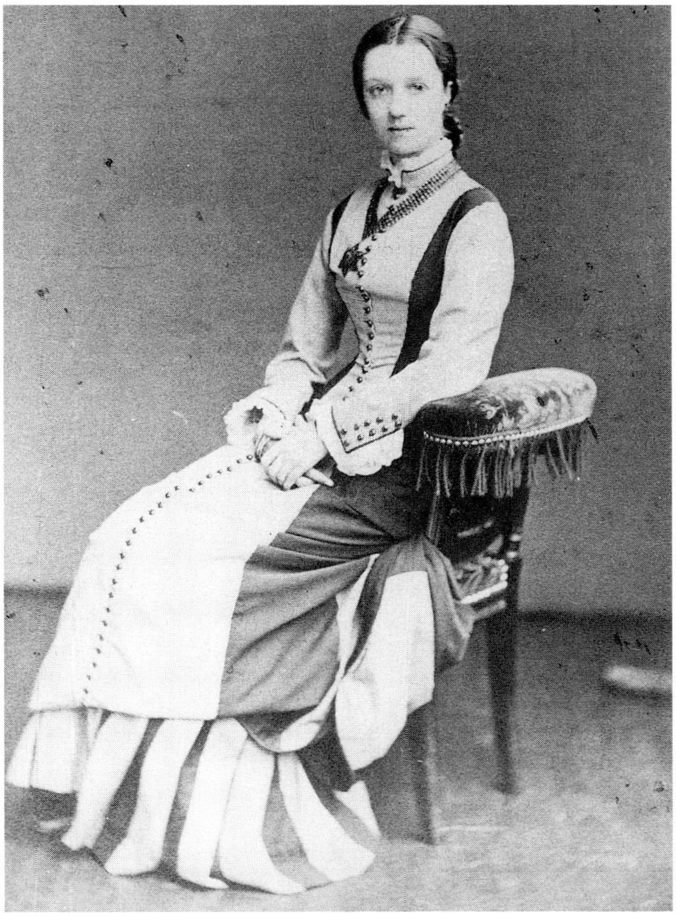

149. Miss Horniman
1877
Chambray, Paris (Platt Hall)

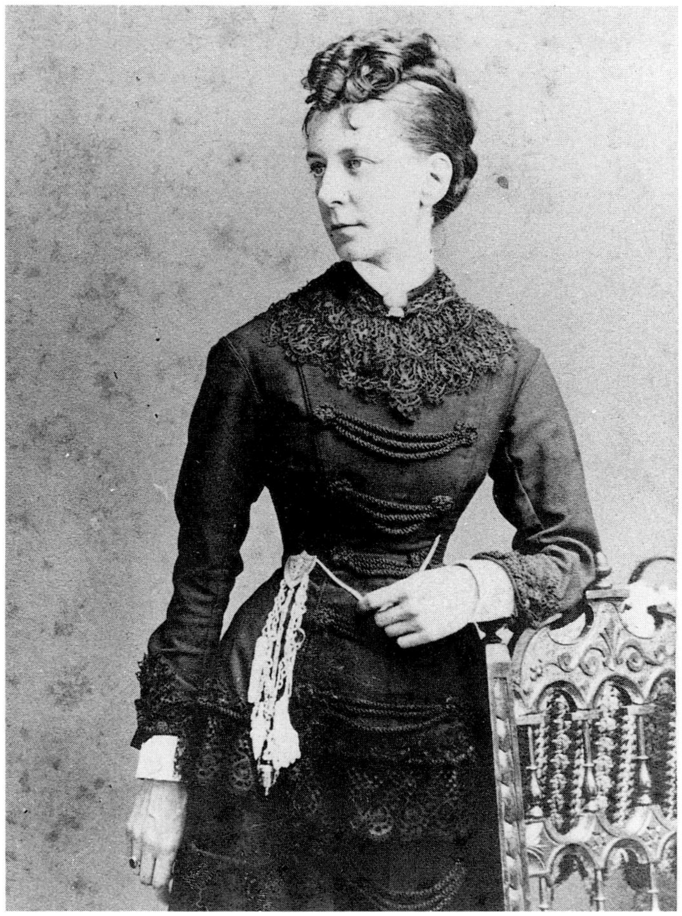

150. Miss Emily Ottighole
1878
Locke, Margate (Platt Hall)

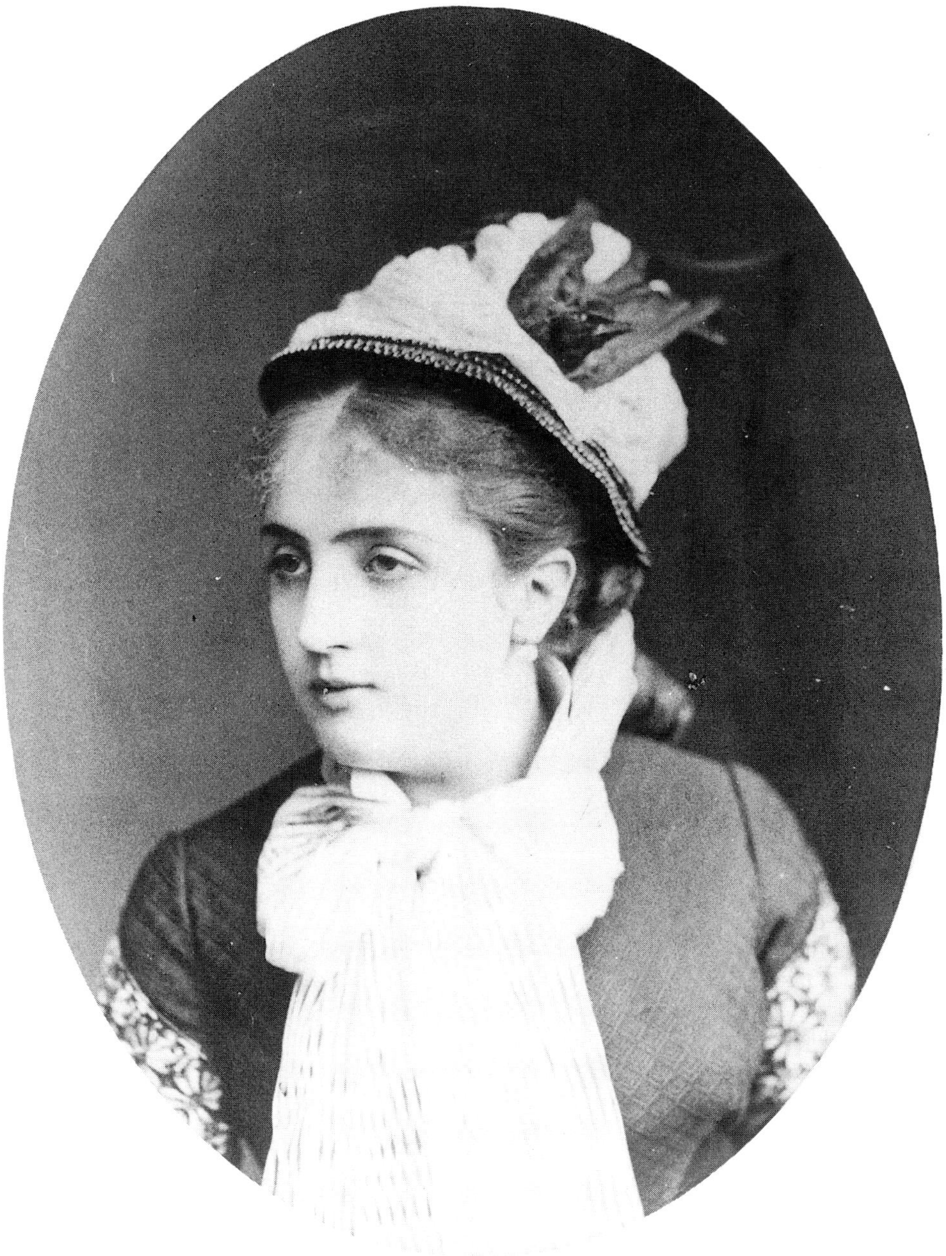

151. Marie Benardarup
1878
C. H. Bergamasco, St Petersburg (Platt Hall)

151

Russian Miss Benardarup wears a dark wool jacket-bodice, printed with diamonds to resemble quilting. Her voluminous, striped silk scarf is loosely tied and conceals most of her front bodice. Her dark-straw hat is trimmed with a folded silk scarf and, more noticeably, with the full body of a bird, poised as if to take off in flight.

Full and part bird trimming was popular in millinery through to the 1890s, although opposition and distaste were increasingly expressed. The fashion writer of *The Englishwoman's Domestic Magazine* illustrated a hat in January 1876 and commented: 'Here is a pretty felt hat, but I am sorry to see that there is a bird on it. After reading the dreadful accounts of wholesale bird slaughter . . . one would scarcely wear a bird with comfort . . .'. The same month's 'Conversazione' in this journal included a letter from 'Flora R.' relating how fashion was promoting the slaughter of English and French songbirds. *The Queen* (4 December 1875) related how 'Whole birds and heads, wings and tails of birds are necessary adjuncts to every hat and bonnet. The consequent destruction of feathered songsters is sad to think of . . .'. 'Flora R.' concluded hopefully that she felt 'perfectly certain that no Englishwoman would wear a bird's wing or feathers, if she were aware how the bird had been killed with no other object than to supply the requirements of fashion'.[31] Unfortunately, the unprecedented popularity of feathers in millinery in the next decade only disproves her assertion.

152

Laden with heavy jewellery, fussy lace, and fringed and pleated trimming, Mrs Forbes-Gibbon demonstrates the fondness for extreme decoration in women's dress prevalent in the 1870s:

> Never was there so much jewellery worn as at the present moment, and never were dresses longer and fuller than they are now at the back. It takes thirty five metres or more if they be yards, of silk to make a dress according to present fashion . . .'

So declared the writer of 'Parisian Gossip' for *The Ladies' Treasury* (April 1877), a year before this portrait was taken.

Mrs Forbes-Gibbon's daydress of black silk and velvet is decorated with triple-pleated sleeve ruffles; deep, beaded fringing on the hem of the jacket-bodice and across the tunic front; scalloped, lace edging to the neckline and cuffs; and puffings and tucks to the skirt hem.

Her dress is clearly brand new, the fold marks visible across the tunic-skirt front, and proudly exhibited, as was the fashion.

Angelina Forbes-Gibbon, née Bowle, was born in 1844 and married in 1870. She is seen here aged 34. Another portrait survives, from the year of her marriage, and shows her with a very similar hairstyle and the same love of lace edging, multitudinous trimmings and heavy jewellery.

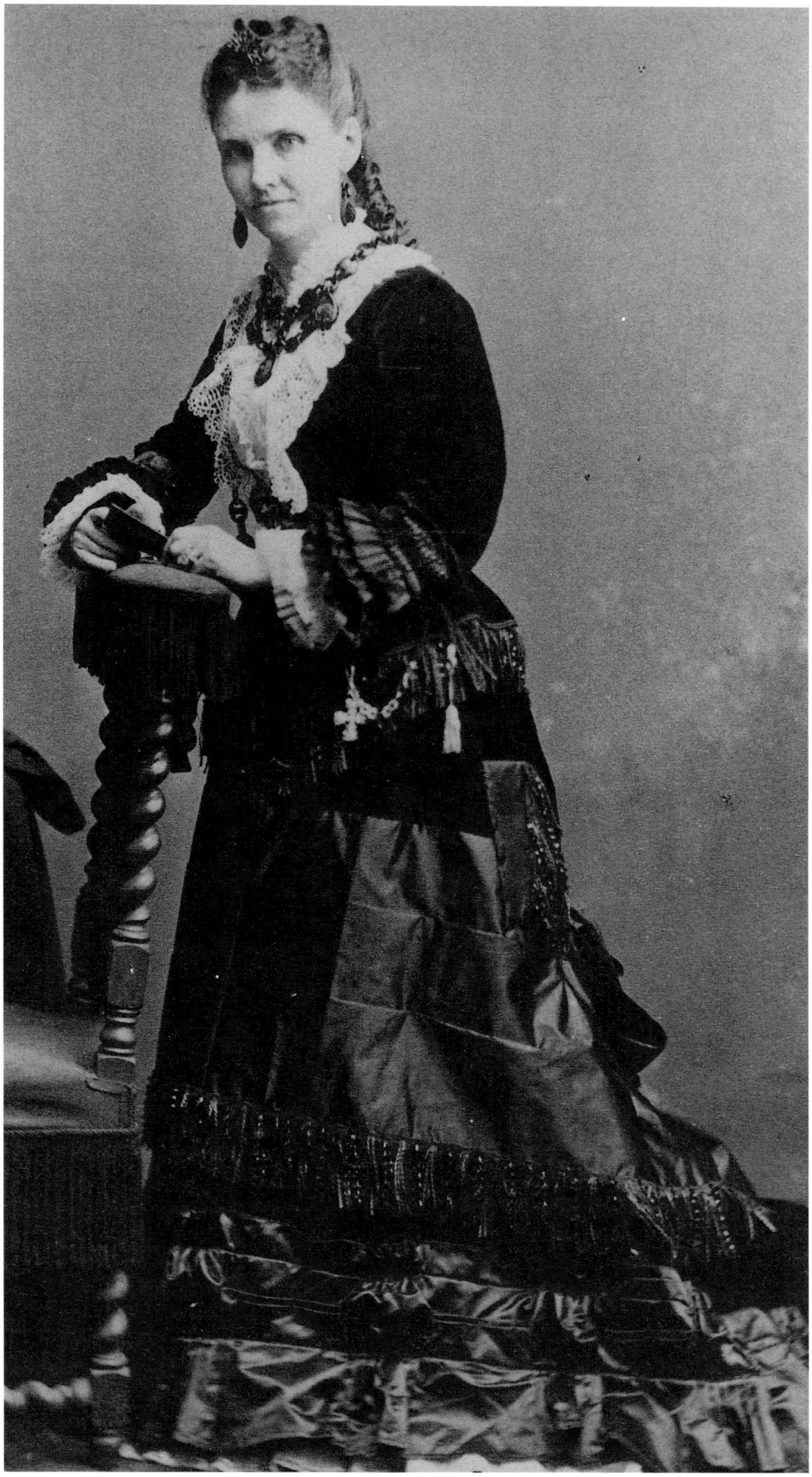

152. Mrs Angelina Forbes-Gibbon
1878
Bourne and Shepherd, India (Platt Hall)

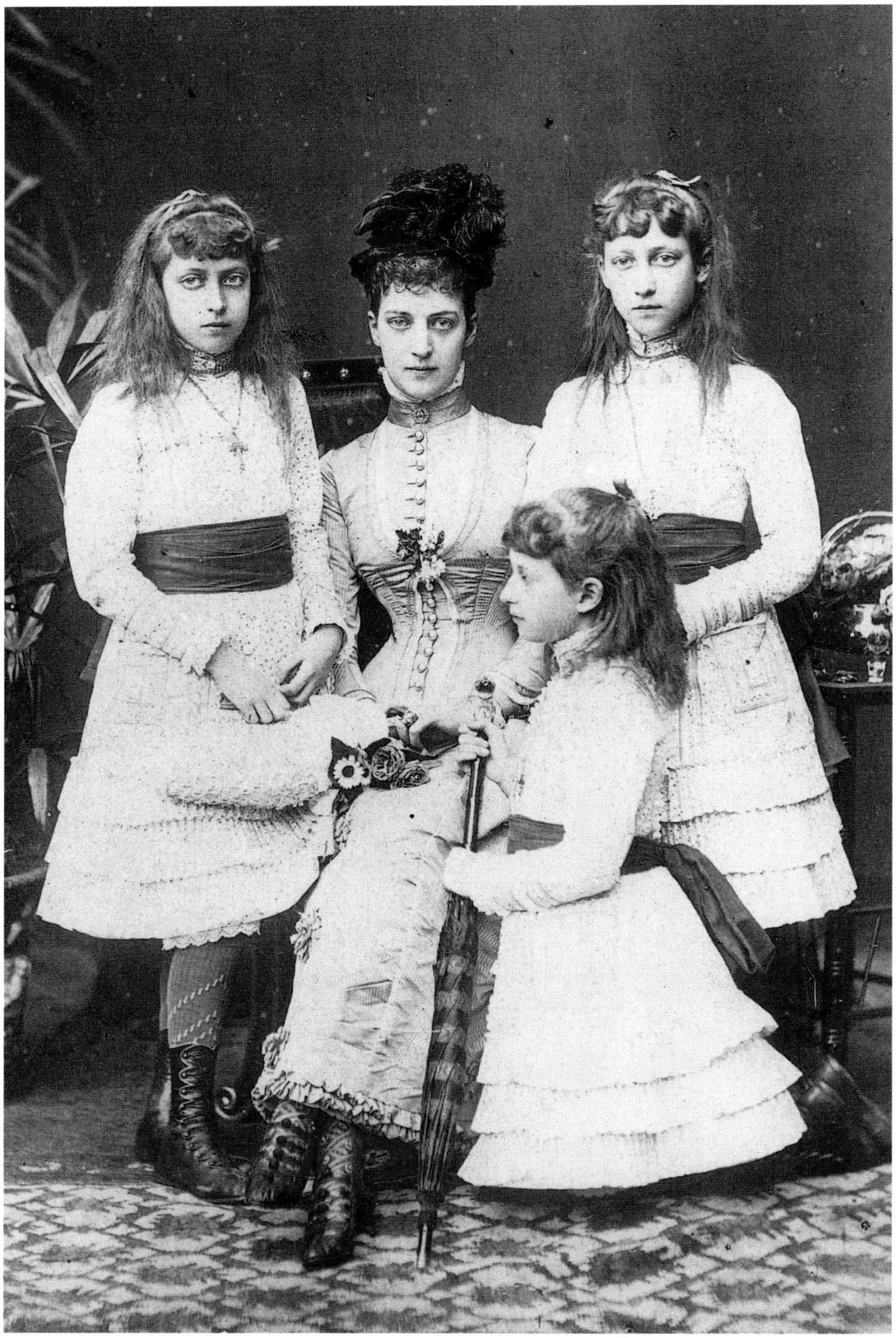

153. The Princess of Wales with her three daughters: Louise, Victoria, and Maud 1879
W. & D. Downey (NPG x 33253)

153

The Prince and Princess of Wales married in 1863 and within six years were the proud parents of two sons: Eddie and Georgie, and three daughters: Louise, Princess Royal (b. 1867); Victoria (b. 1868); and Maud, (b. 1869). Louise (far right) later married the Duke of Fife; Maud (kneeling) married the King of Norway; and Victoria remained unmarried.

The Waleses provided a happy, close-knit family life for their children, based around their house at Sandringham in Norfolk. The girls were renowned for their boisterous behaviour, not, of course, apparent in this portrait.

Alexandra wears a sheath dress of corded silk. Her *cuirasse* bodice moulds itself over her hips, and fastens centre-front with over 20 buttons. The bodice fits tightly over her stays, emphasizing the Princess's trim waist; her figure having recovered remarkably after her pregnancies. The high neckline and collar, trimmed with ribbon, is decorated with a circular brooch. The centre-front of the skirt is trimmed with rosettes of pleated silk, matching the double frill at the hem. She also wears button-boots and a high, black-velvet hat trimmed with ostrich feathers.[32]

Her daughters wear matching dresses of spotted white-cotton voile, pleated, and worn with wide satin sashes. Victoria (left) reveals the broderie anglaise embroidery on the hem of her drawers and also her dark-wool knitted stockings.

All three girls have fashionable front curls, like their mother, but the rest of their hair falls free, as befits young girls.

GROUP

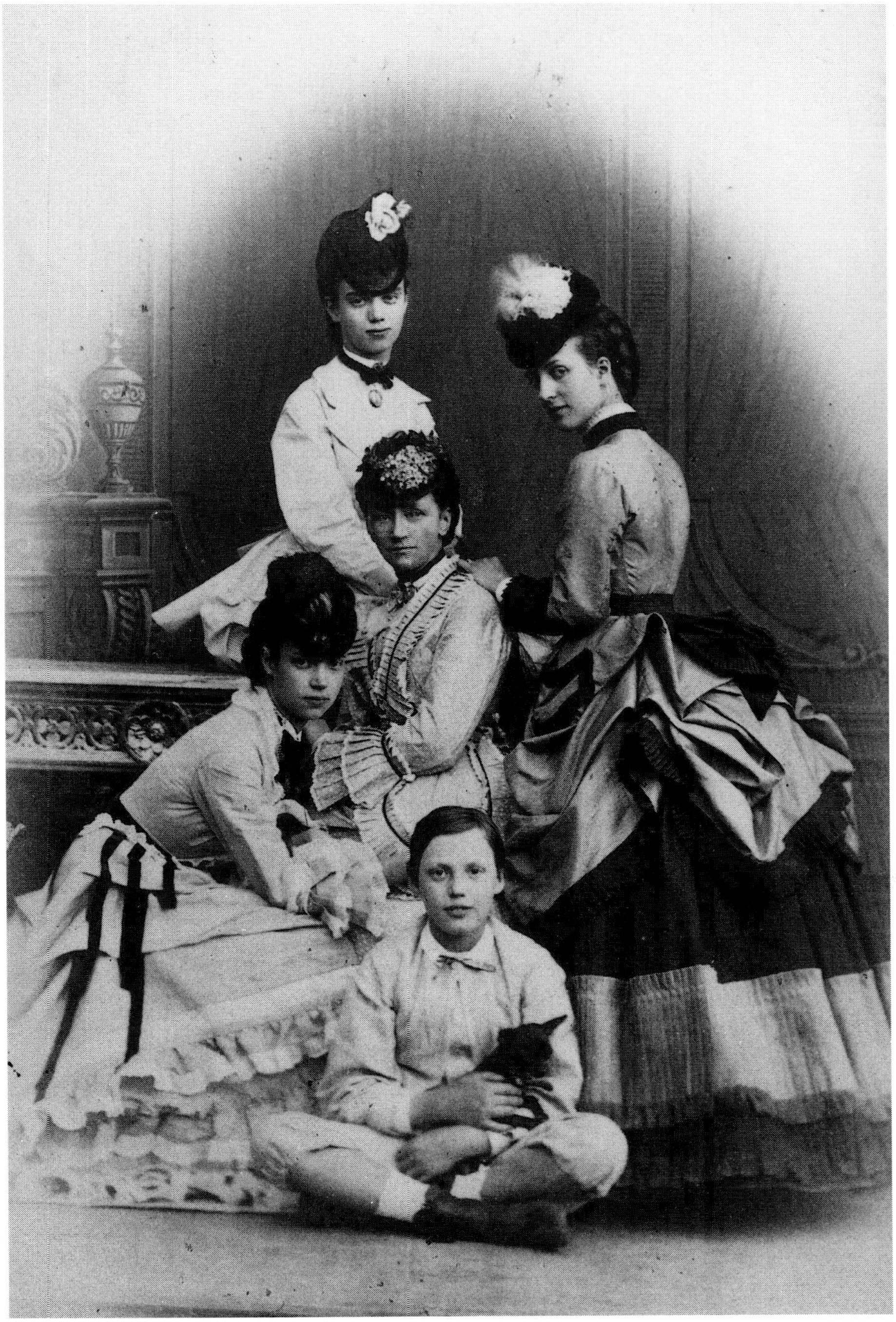

154. Queen Louise of Denmark with her children
***c*. 1870**
Georg Hansen, Copenhagen (NPG x 33510)

154

Queen Louise (1817–98) is here surrounded by her children: Alexandra, Dagmar, Thyra, and Waldemar. The portrait shows all four women wearing casquette-style hats tipped forward over the forehead to expose full chignons at the back. Alexandra, on the far right, wears a bustle dress with a polonaise overskirt, trimmed with contrasting silk frilling at all edges. Bustles by this date were extremely full, padded out with wire and horsehair pads. Some enterprising women used more imaginative padding as an under support: M. Vivian Hughes relates in *A London Child of the Seventies* that her mother had once

> asked a visitor how she managed to have such an effective bustle. The astonishing answer was: 'The Times; I find its paper so good; far more satisfactory than the Daily News'; and putting her hand under her skirt, she tore off a piece to show us.[1]

If Alexandra had any such sartorial secrets, they died with her; and indeed, it seems likely that she wore the conventional wire bustle constructions, more robust and dependable.

In spite of the fact that only Alexandra, of all the sisters, was celebrated as a beauty, all three went on to secure illustrious matches: Alexandra was to become Queen of England; Dagmar, Empress of Russia; and Thyra, Duchess of Cumberland.

Prince Waldemar wears a youthful knickerbocker suit with his bare shins clearly visible over his short white socks.

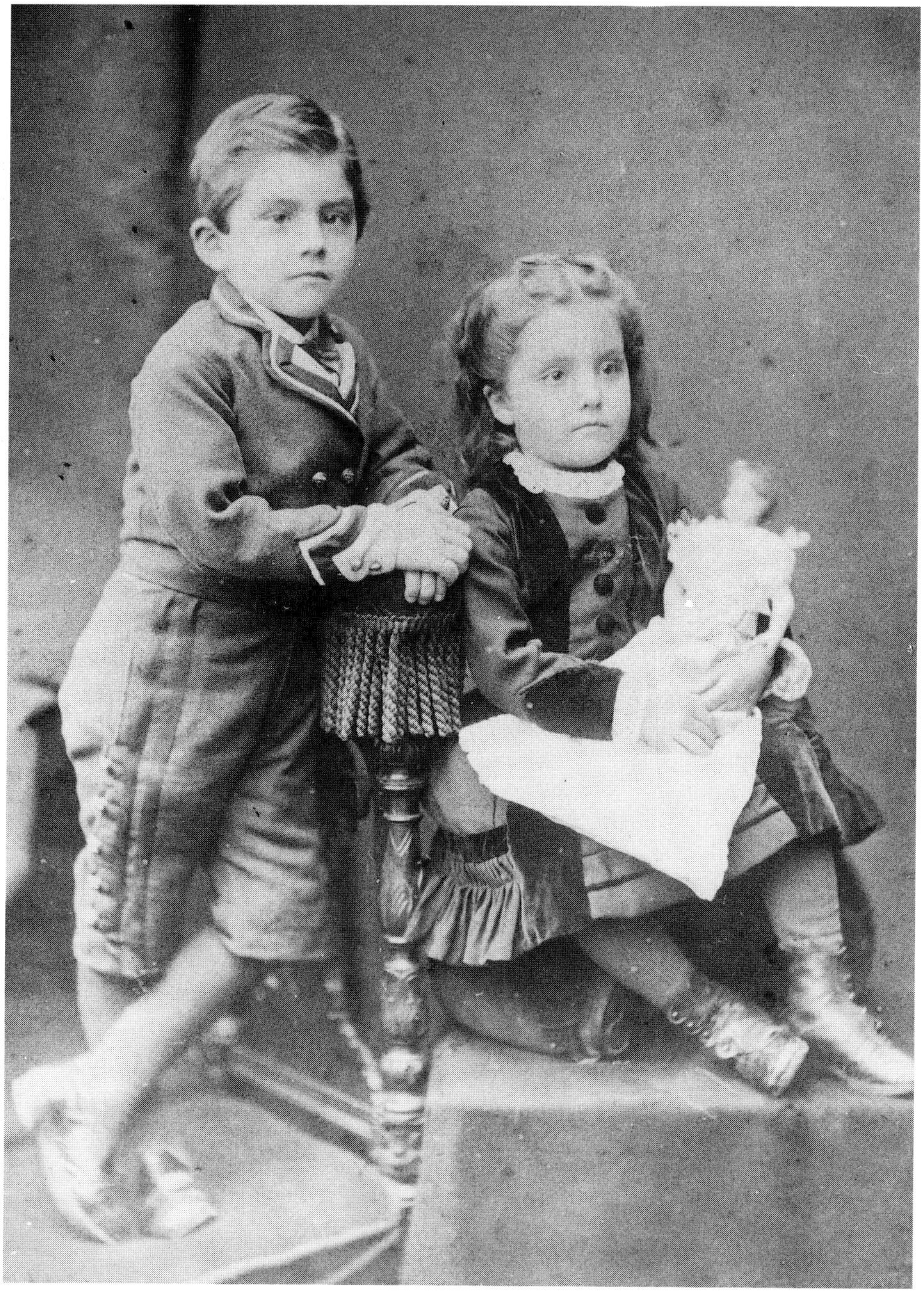

155. Hugh and Maud Aldis
1875
William Heath, Plymouth (Platt Hall)

156

Alfred Duke of Edinburgh married the Grand Duchess Marie Alexandrovna, only daughter of Tsar Alexander II of Russia, in February 1874. He was aged nearly 30; she was only 20.

The festivities in England were virtually as elaborate as those for the Prince of Wales 10 years earlier, even though the marriage itself was solemnized in St Petersburg. The bride was splendidly dressed in

> a wedding costume in accordance with the style of the Russian National costume. It consisted of a white satin petticoat trained, and so richly embroidered with silver that it looked like silver itself. Over this was a train of the most exquisite lace ever made at the Imperial Lace factory at Moscow.

So related *The Ladies' Treasury*. The Duke wore the uniform of a 'post-captain' of the British Navy with the collar of the Russian order of St Andrew.[2]

The alliance was to produce five children in rapid succession: Alfred (1874), Marie (1875), Victoria (1876), Alexandra (1878), and Beatrice (1884). The baby pictured here, in his broderie anglaise dress, is probably Prince Alfred.

The Duchess wears a military-inspired jacket with frogging and astrakhan trim to the collar and cuffs. The Duke wears an informal, checked-wool lounge jacket, and sports a considerable array of jewellery, flouting the Englishman's usual restraint, and including a gold chain bracelet, two rings, and a large tie-pin.

155

Brother and sister Hugh Lancelot and Maud Emily were born in 1870 and 1871 respectively. Hugh, just four years old, wears a short, woollen, double-breasted jacket, with knee-length trousers or open breeches. According to the *Tailor and Cutter* (Summer 1876) these were known as 'trousers of the Grecian type' and were 'cut with a view to combine elegance with freedom'.[3]

His jacket revers and cuffs are faced in white and trimmed with bands of dark velvet or silk.

Maud, a year younger, wears a princess-line cloth dress, trimmed with contrasting bands, cuffs, and buttons of dark velvet. Her ankle-length boots fasten securely with four buttons, and she sits clutching her baby doll in its snowy-white cotton robe.

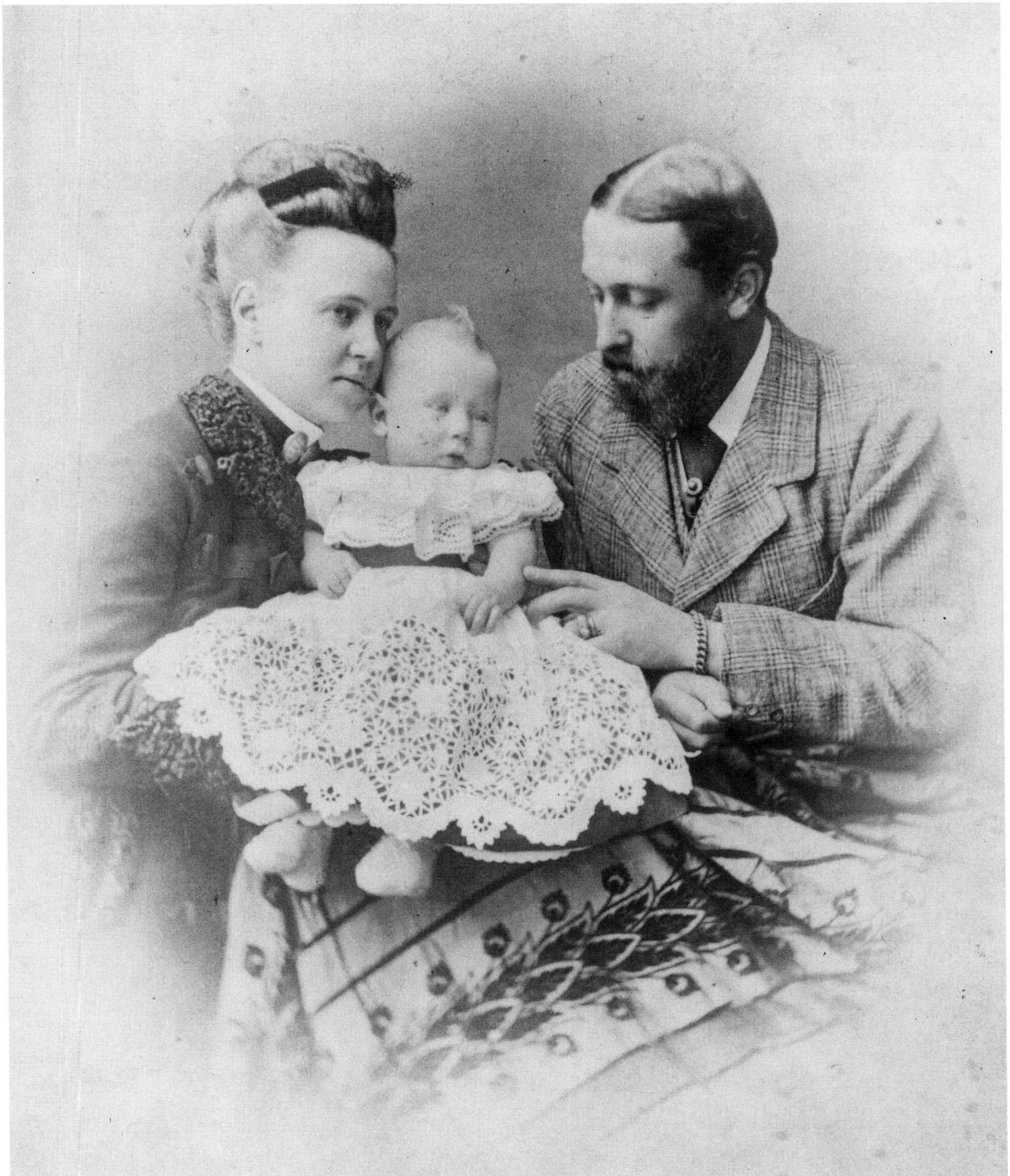

156. The Duke and Duchess of Edinburgh, with Prince Alfred
1875
Hills & Saunders, London (NPG x 33254)

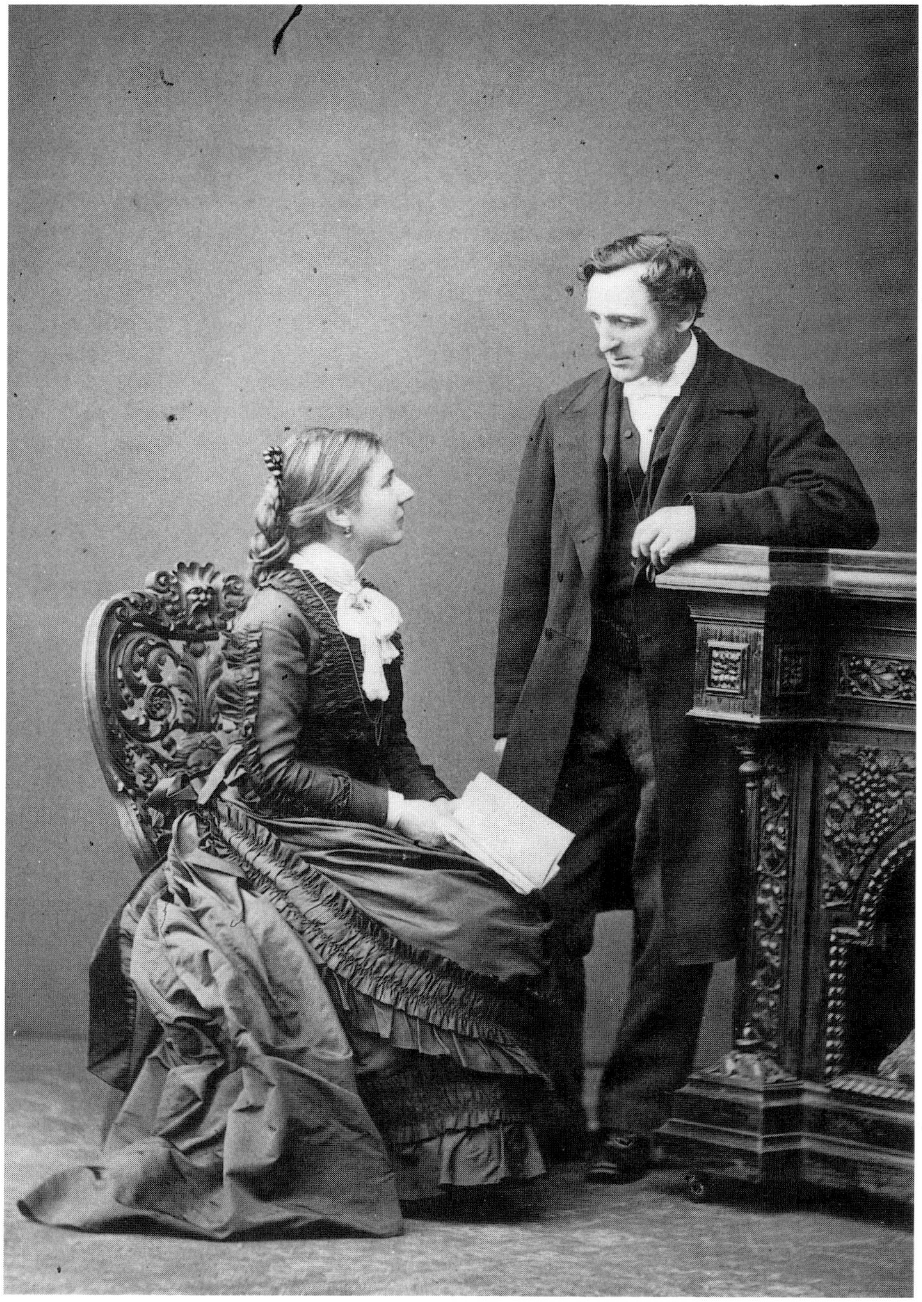

157. Dr George and Lady Laura Ridding 1876
Schemboche, Turin (NPG x 4975)

157

Dr George Ridding, Headmaster of Winchester School, married his second wife Laura on 26 October 1876, and this portrait, taken in Turin, is from their honeymoon tour. Ridding was born in 1828 and after an education at Winchester and Oxford, became second master at Winchester in 1863, and Headmaster three years later. His first wife had died in 1859, only a year after their marriage. An ordained Anglican minister, he went on to become Bishop of the new diocese of Southwell in 1884.

Lady Laura was the daughter of Roundell Palmer, 1st Earl Selborne, who had enjoyed a meteoric ascent up the legal hierarchy whilst also being a Member of Parliament. A QC in 1849 at the age of only 37; by 1863 he was Attorney General, and in 1872 Lord Chancellor. He was created a baron in 1872, and a viscount and earl in 1882.

Dr Ridding wears a black 'top-frock coat' over another coat, probably a morning coat, and a dark waistcoat. Lady Laura, gazing intently at her new husband, wears a dark-silk trained daydress with an apron-fronted overskirt. Trimming of broad bands of ruched self-fabric runs as borders along the hem, apron and neckline, and along the outer sleeve seams. She wears a loosely knotted light-coloured silk scarf as a cravat or jabot.

This photograph was donated to the Gallery as part of the Ouless bequest, and was apparently sent to the painter as a study for the portrait, which he completed in 1879.

The Italian studio shows a completely plain background with Dr Ridding leaning somewhat precariously on an elaborately carved heavy 'mobile' fireplace on casters.

158

Victorian architectural restoration is a feature of many local parish churches, and here are two amateurs in action. Colonel and Mrs Miles stand at either end of a wooden platform, trowel and chisel in hand, beside an arched doorway at Malmesbury Church in Wiltshire. Built around the surviving nave of a Benedictine abbey, the church is largely Anglo-Norman.

Mrs Miles wears a broad-brimmed straw hat.and a short cape, whilst her husband sports a Norfolk-style jacket and breeches. Their companions seem less dressed for work than for conversation and encouragement. Three young men in lounge jackets and bowler hats drape themselves around a pair of high stepladders. An older gentleman, similarly attired, leans on his walking cane. Both lounge jackets and bowler hats achieved popular fashionability for smart, casual outdoor wear in the 1870s.

The young lady observer poses more stiffly in a plain, princess-line, woollen dress with a typical long over-tunic forming an apron front. She has a watch and chain pinned to the left-hand side of her chest, and wears a round, felt hat with turned-up brim.

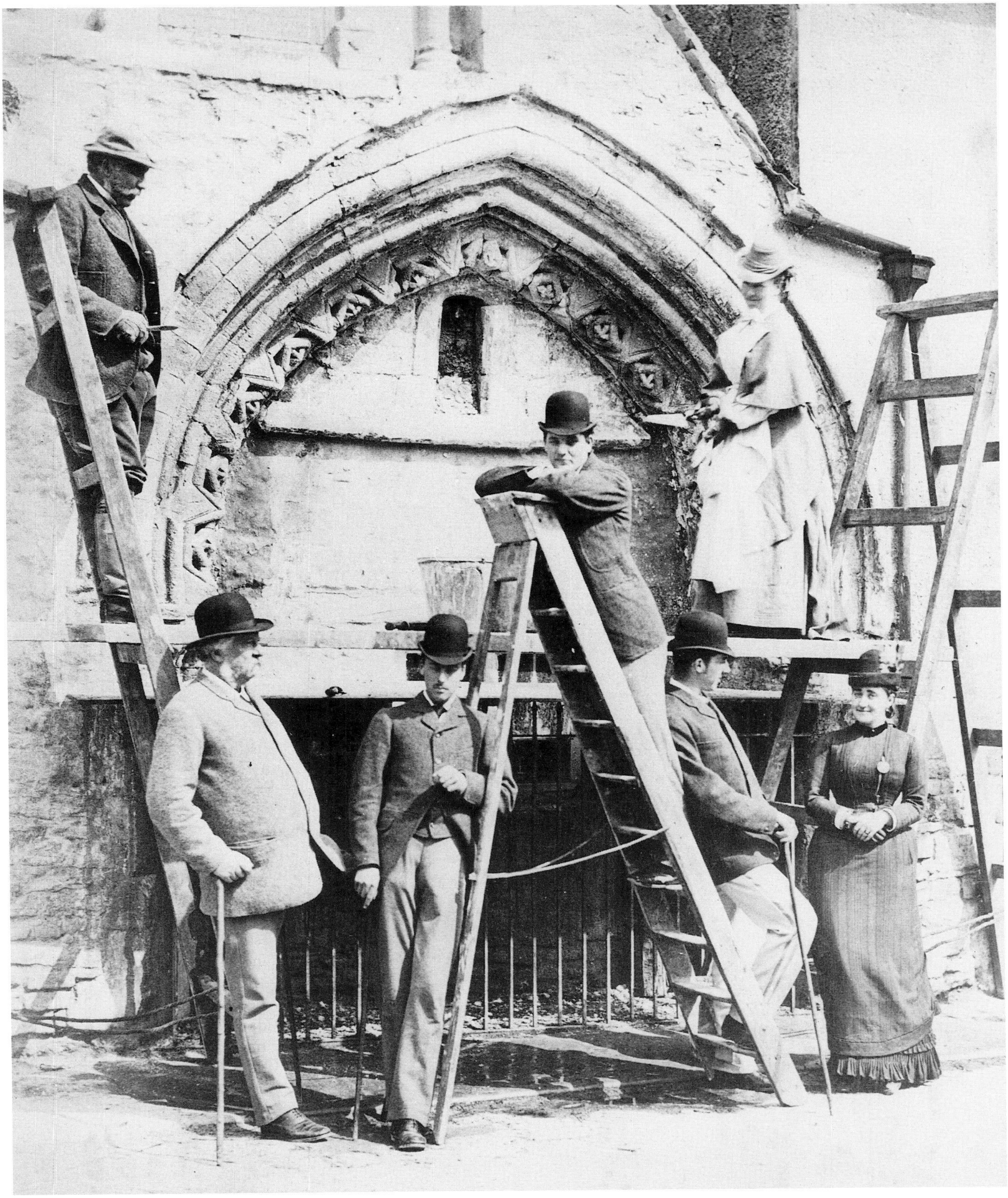

158. Colonel and Mrs Miles, and five friends
1877
Photographer unknown, Malmesbury (Platt Hall)

NOTES

INTRODUCTION

1. Ginsburg, Madeleine, *Victorian Dress in Photographs*, Batsford, 1982, p. 11.
2. Gernsheim, Helmut, *The Rise of Photography* (*History of Photography*, Vol. 2) Thames & Hudson, 1988, p. 19.
3. Ginsburg, op. cit., p. 13.
4. Gernsheim, op. cit., p. 190.
5. Linkman, Audrey E., 'The Itinerant Photographer in Britain, 1850–80', Taylor and Francis, (*History of Photography* Vol. 14, no. 1) 1990, p. 50.
6. Gernsheim, op. cit., p. 23.
7. *The Illustrated London News*, 27 May 1865. An advertisement from the London Stereoscopic Company includes a '£3 set of photographic apparatus, replete with every appliance for taking positives or negatives'.
8. Gernsheim, op. cit., p. 199.
9. *The Queen*, 12 July 1862, p. 372.
10. Carlyle, Jane, *Letters and Memorials*, Vol. 3, October 1864.
11. *British Journal of Photography*, 'The Victorian studio', Henry Greenwood & Co., 7, 14 February 1986, p. 190.
12. *The Queen*, 5 March 1864, p. 181.
13. *Godey's Lady's Book and Magazine*, May 1865, p. 469.
14. Gernsheim, op. cit., p. 25.
15. A lecture by Audrey Linkman at the Documentary Photography Archive in Manchester, 1989.
16. Disderi, André A., 'Essai sur l'art de la photographie', Part 3, 1863, pp. 263–95.
17. *The Graphic*, 18 March 1864, p. 181.
18. *The Illustrated London News*, 4 January 1862, p. 14.
19. Ibid., 'Rodrigues, 42 Piccadilly'.
20. Gernsheim, op. cit., p. 196,.
21. *The Queen*, 9, 16 February 1867, Exchange columns.
22. *Godey's Lady's Book and Magazine*, July 1865, p. 93.
23. Example in Platt Hall library and archive.
24. The Queen, 14 April 1866, p. 294.
25. *The Young Ladies' Journal*, 1 June 1867, p. 319.
26. *The Young Ladies' Journal*, 1 August 1867, p. 431.
27. *The London Journal*, 1 October 1869, p. 176.
28. *The London Journal*, 1 October 1870, p. 176.

PART 1: 1860–64

Male – Plates 1–22

1. Cunnington, C. W. & P., *Handbook of English Costume in the Nineteenth Century*, Faber & Faber, 1959, p. 206.
2. *The Queen*, 19 April 1862, p. 139.
3. *Tailor and Cutter*, July 1874.
5. Wilson, Robert, *Life and Times of Queen Victoria*, Cassell & Co., 1889 vol. iii, p. 23.
4. Courtney, Nicholas, *Royal Children*, Dent & Sons, 1982, p. 72.
6. *Tailor and Cutter*, 1 January 1870, pp. 121–2.
7. Gernsheim, Helmut, *The Rise of Photography* (1850–1880, Vol. 4), Thames & Hudson, 1988, p. 194.
8. Courtney, Nicholas, op. cit., pp. 71–2.
9. Hartnell, Phyllis (ed.), *Oxford Companion to the Theatre*, OUP, 1983.
10. Gernsheim, Helmut, op. cit., p. 194.
11. *Tailor and Cutter*, December 1877.
12. Strachey, Lytton, *Queen Victoria*, Bloomsbury, 1921, p. 198.
13. *Tailor and Cutter*, 18 June 1870. Gladstone is pictured wearing a single-breasted morning coat; the following month, Disraeli wears a Cambridge lounge jacket.
14. Ibid., 24 April 1869.
15. Ibid., 26 February 1870, p. 204.
16. Cunningtons, op. cit. p. 229.
17. Ibid., p. 253.
18. *The Englishwoman's Domestic Magazine*, November 1862, p. 45.
19. Ibid., March 1863, p. 237.
20. *The Englishwoman's Domestic Magazine* (September 1860) relates that: 'The most elegant riding hats for ladies are made of Tuscan, of a rather oval form with turned up brims, ornamented with herons' or pheasants' feathers. Brown straws with a long white feather on one side, or falling behind, are not as yet discarded . . .'

Female – Plates 23–56

1. Ibid., p. 237.
2. *The Young Lady's Equestrian Manual*, David Bogue, *c.* 1830, p. 31.
3. *The Englishwoman's Domestic Magazine*, August 1860, p. 190.
4. 'Sylvia': *How to dress well on a shilling a day*, Ward Lock & Co., 3rd edn, 1876.
5. *The Englishwoman's Domestic Magazine*, September 1860, p. 238.
6. Ibid., December 1860, p. 93.
7. *The Ladies' Treasury*, March 1860, p. 88.
8. *La Belle Assemblée*, August 1860, p. 111.
9. Monsarrat, Ann, *And the Bride wore . . .*, Gentry Books, 1973, p. 118.
10. *The Ladies' Treasury*, October 1860, p. 322.
11. Ibid., May 1860, p. 154.
12. *The Englishwoman's Domestic Magazine*, October 1860, p. 258.
13. *The Ladies' Treasury*, September 1863, p. 266.
14. Burnham, Dorothy, *Warp and Weft*, Royal Ontario Museum, 1980, p. 178.
15. *Illustrated London News*, 16 November 1861, p. 501 (reference to King & Co.)
16. *The Englishwoman's Domestic Magazine*, December 1860, p. 93.
17. *The Ladies' Treasury*, February 1860, p. 56.
18. Ibid., May 1861, p. 152.
19. *The Englishwoman's Domestic Magazine*, June 1862, p. 93.
20. Ibid., July 1862, p. 142.
21. Ibid., May 1860, p. 47.
22. Ibid., April 1860, p. 333.
23. *The Ladies' Treasury*, January 1861, p. 26.
24. *The Englishwoman's Domestic Magazine*, May 1861, p. 69.
25. Ibid., July 1861, p. 165.
26. *The Young Englishwoman*, March 1875, p. 149.
27. Canning, John, *100 Great Nineteenth-Century Lives*, Methuen, 1983.
28. Ginsburg, Madeleine, *Victorian Dress in Photographs*, Batsford, 1982, p. 171.
29. *La Belle Assemblée*, October 1859, p. 22.
30. *The Ladies' Treasury*, March 1863, p. 6.
31. Ibid., August 1863, p. 234.
32. Taylor, Lou, *Mourning Dress*, George Allen & Unwin, 1983, pp. 234–6.
33. *The Queen*, 7 March 1863, p. 12.
34. Wilson, Robert, op. cit., vol. iii, p.

158.
35. Ibid., p. 157.
36. Monsarrat, Ann, op. cit., p. 164.
37. Ibid., p. 165.
38. Ewing, Elizabeth, *History of Children's Costume*, Batsford, 1977, p. 78.
39. *La Belle Assemblée*, September 1863, p. 167.
40. *The Englishwoman's Domestic Magazine*, September 1861, p. 261.
41. *The Young Englishwoman*, February 1865, p. 134.
42. Ormond, Richard & Blackett-Ord, Carol (eds), *Franz Xaver Winterhalter and the Courts of Europe 1830–70*, NPG, 1987, p. 217.
43. *The Queen*, 4 June 1864, p. 438.
44. Blom (ed.), *Grove's Dictionary of Music and Musicians*, 5th edn, 1954, p. 1025.
45. Cunnington, P. & Mansfield, A., *English Costume for Sports*, A. & C. Black, 1969, p. 118.
46. *The Young Ladies Equestrian Manual*, op. cit., pp. 31–2.

Group – Plates 57–69

1. *The Ladies' Treasury*, March 1860, p. 90.
2. Pritchard, H. Baden, *Photographic Studios in England and on the Continent*, 1880, pp. 19–20.
3. *Tailor and Cutter*, March 1869.
4. Monsarrat, Ann, op. cit., p. 166.
5. Corson, Richard, *Fashions in Eyeglasses*, Peter Owen, 1980, p. 135.
6. Anon., *Etiquette for Ladies*, Warne's Bijou Books, *c.* 1870, pp. 89–90.
7. *World of Fashion*, January 1858.
8. *The Englishwoman's Domestic Magazine*, December 1864, p. 382.
9. Ibid., August 1864, p. 142.

PART 2: 1865–69

Male – Plates 70–84

1. *Complete Etiquette For Gentlemen*, Ward Lock & Co., *c.* 1880, p. 24.
2. *The Englishwoman's Domestic Magazine*, September 1861, p. 261.
3. Cunningtons, op. cit., p. 252.
4. Armstrong, Rev. B. J., *Further passages from the Norfolk Diary*, Hodder & Stoughton '22 February 1864', 1963.
5. *The Queen*, 6 October 1866, p. 236.
6. *The Englishwoman's Domestic Magazine*, May 1867, pp. 256–60.
7. *The Queen*, 18 August 1866, p. 117.
8. *Tailor and Cutter*, 21 November 1868.
9. *Illustrated London News*, 17 July 1869, p. 71.
10. *The Queen*, 22 July 1876, p. 60.

Female – Plates 85–107

1. *Etiquette for Ladies*, Warne's Bijou Books, *c.* 1870, p. 93.
2. Wilson, Robert, op. cit., vol. iv, p. 717.
3. *The Ladies' Treasury*, 1 April 1864, pp. 126–7.
4. Cunnington, C. W. & P. & Beard, Charles, *A Dictionary of English Costume*, A. & C. Black, 1960, p. 239.
5. *The Ladies' Treasury*, March 1860, pp. 88–9.
6. *The Englishwoman's Domestic Magazine*, April 1867, p. 213.
7. *The Queen*, 21 September 1867, pp. 228–9.
8. *Etiquette for Ladies*, op. cit., p. 89.
9. *Illustrated London News*, supplement, 12 August 1865.
10. *The Queen*, 12 January 1867, p. 29.
11. *The Young Englishwoman*, July 1875, pp. 375–9.
12. Gosling, Nigel, *Nadar*, Secker & Warburg, 1976.
13. *The Queen*, 23 March 1867, p. 237.
14. *Etiquette for Ladies*, op. cit., p. 94.
15. *The Queen*, June 1867, pp. 436 & 498.
16. *The Englishwoman's Domestic Magazine*, December 1866, p. 382.
17. *The Young Englishwoman*, March 1867, p. 121.
18. *The Queen*, 19 October 1867, p. 298.
19. Ibid., 2 May 1863, pp. 178–9.
20. Ibid., 14 September 1867, p. 211.
21. *The Queen*, supplement, 12 January 1867, p. 29.
22. Ibid.

Group – Plates 108–115

1. *Burke's Peerage*, 'Newcastle', p. 536.
2. *The Queen*, 14 November 1868, p. 279.
3. Ibid., 18 August 1866, p. 117.

PART 3: 1870–80

Male – Plates 116–122

1. *The Queen*, 11 June 1870, pp. 364–5.
2. *Tailor and Cutter*, August 1871, pp. 448–50.
3. Ibid., 1871. Quoted in Cunnington's *Handbook of Costume in the Nineteenth Century*.
4. Ibid., Spring 1876, pp. 107–8.
5. *The Graphic*, 20 February 1875, p. 170.
6. *Illustrated London News*, 28 June 1879, pp. 614–15.
7. Ibid., p. 615.
8. *Tailor and Cutter*, February 1878, p. 108.
9. Corson, R., *Fashions in Hair*, Peter Owen, London, 1965, p. 417.
10. *Complete Etiquette for Gentlemen*, Ward Lock & Co., p. 95.

Female – Plates 85–107

1. *The Young Englishwoman*, March 1875, p. 149.
2. Ibid., p. 151.
3. *Burke's Peerage*, vol. XII, p. 515.
4. Gernsheim, Alison, *Fashion and Reality, 1840–1914*, Faber, 1963, p. 61.
5. Lady Douglas wears a 'demi-toilette' evening dress, described in *The Englishwoman's Domestic Magazine* (1 January 1870): 'the kind of toilet which is "la mieux comprise" [*sic*] is that suitable for demi-toilette evening dress . . . the half-low silk dress open either in the shape of a heart or in a square and showing delicate frillings of white lace about the throat and bosom, and the Marie Antoinette sleeves finished off at the elbows with engageantes are perhaps more becoming that the altogether low bodice and invisible sleeves of the ball toilet'.
6. *The Young Englishwoman*, August 1870, p. 442.
7. *The Queen*, 12 March 1870, p. 171.
8. Ibid.
9. Ibid., 6 April 1867, p. 276.
10. *The Young Ladies' Journal*, 1 October 1870, p. 610.
11. Haweis, Mrs, *The Art of Dress*, Chatto & Windus, 1879, p. 123.
12. *The Ladies' Treasury*, 2 March 1874, pp. 153–8.
13. *The Englishwoman's Domestic Magazine*, May 1872, p. 291.
14. Ibid., December 1872, p. 322.
15. *The Ladies' Treasury*, February 1872, p. 107.
16. Pascoe, C. E. (ed.), *The Dramatic List*, Hardwicke and Bogue, 1879, pp. 318–19.
17. *The Queen*, 26 April 1873, p. 335.
18. Gernsheim, A. & H., *Edward VII and Queen Alexandra*, Frederick Muller, 1962, Plate 64 (another pose from the same sitting; including Alexandra's sister, Dagmar).
19. *The Young Englishwoman*, August 1875, p. 454.
20. Ibid., January 1875, p. 34.
21. Gernsheim, A. & H., op. cit., Plates 84 and 85.
22. Fulford, R. (ed.), *Dearest Child, Letters between Queen Victoria and the Princess Royal, 1858–61*, ('June 1859'), Evans Bros, 1964.
23. *The Young Englishwoman*, April 1876, p. 215.
24. Ibid., May 1876, no. 255, p. 286.
25. *The Queen*, 27 May 1876, pp. 366–7.
26. *The Englishwoman's Domestic Magazine*, February 1876, p. 107.
27. *The Young Englishwoman*, February 1876, p. 92.
28. *Dictionary of National Biography*, vol. XI, p. 1154.
29. *The Englishwoman's Domestic Magazine*, October 1877, p. 278.
30. *The Ladies' Treasury*, p. 475.

31. *The Englishwoman's Domestic Magazine*, January 1876, pp. 54–5.
32. Gernsheim, A. & H., op. cit., Plate 79 (another pose from the same sitting, with her two sons).

Group – Plates 154–158

1. Comberlege, Geoffrey (ed.), M. Vivian Hughes, *A London Family 1870–1900*, OUP, 1946, p. 84.
2. *The Ladies' Treasury*, 2 March 1874, vol. i, pp. 153–5.
3. *Tailor and Cutter*, Summer 1876, p. 198.

BIBLIOGRAPHY

Photography 1860–80

'The Victorian Studio,' 3 articles, *British Journal of Photography*, February 1986.

COE, BRIAN, *The Birth of Photography: the story of the formative years 1880–1900*, Ash & Grant, 1976.

DARRAH, WILLIAM C., *Cartes de Visite in Nineteenth-Century Photography*, W. C. Darrah Publications, 1981.

GERNSHEIM, H., *The Rise of Photography 1850–1880*, Thames & Hudson, 1988.

GERNSHEIM, H. & A., *A History of Photography*, Thames & Hudson, 1955.

HILLIER, BEVIS, *Victorian Studio Photographs* (from the collections of Studio Bassano & Elliott & Fry), Ash & Grant, 1975.

LINKMAN, A. E., *The Itinerant Photographer in Britain 1850–1880*, in *History of Photography*, vol. XIV, no. 1, 1990.

MATHEWS, OLIVER, *The Album of Cartes de Visite and Cabinet Portrait Photographs 1854–1914*, Reedminster Publications Ltd, 1974.

Early Photographs and Early Photographers: A Survey in Dictionary Form, Reedminster Publications Ltd, 1973.

Costume 1860–80

CUNNINGTON, C. W. & P., *Handbook of English Costume in the Nineteenth Century*, Faber & Faber, 3rd edn, 1970.

GERNSHEIM, A., *Fashion and Reality: 1840–1914*, Faber and Faber, 1970.

GINSBURG, MADELEINE, *Victorian Dress in Photographs*, B. T. Batsford, 1982.

LANSDELL, AVRIL, *Fashion A La Carte*, Shire Publications, 1985.

INDEX

(by plate number)

General

Photographers